A·N·N·U·A·L ED·

Drugs, Society, and Behavior

Seventeenth Edition

02/03

EDITOR

Hugh T. Wilson

California State University, Sacramento

Hugh Wilson received his Bachelor of Arts degree from California State University, Sacramento, and a Master of Arts degree in Justice Administration and a Doctorate in Public Administration from Golden Gate University in San Francisco. Dr. Wilson is currently a professor of criminal justice at California State University, Sacramento. He has taught drug abuse recognition, enforcement, and policy to police officers and students of criminal justice for more than 20 years.

McGraw-Hill/Dushkin

530 Old Whitfield Street, Guilford, Connecticut 06437

Visit us on the Internet
http://www.dushkin.com

Credits

1. **Living With Drugs**
   Unit photo—© 2002 by PhotoDisc, Inc.
2. **Understanding How Drugs Work—Use, Dependency, and Addiction**
   Unit photo—United Nations photo by John Isaac.
3. **The Major Drugs of Use and Abuse**
   Unit photo—United Nations photo by John Robaton.
4. **Other Trends in Drug Use**
   Unit photo—© 2002 by Cleo Freelance Photography.
5. **Drugs and Crime**
   Unit photo—© 2002 by PhotoDisc, Inc.
6. **Measuring the Social Cost of Drugs**
   Unit photo—© 2002 by Cleo Freelance Photography.
7. **Creating & Sustaining Effective Drug Control Policy**
   Unit photo—Courtesy of U.S. Drug Enforcement Agency.
8. **Prevention and Treatment**
   Unit photo—© 2002 by Cleo Freelance Photography.

Copyright

Cataloging in Publication Data
Main entry under title: Annual Editions: Drugs, Society, and Behavior. 2002/2003.
1. Drugs—Periodicals. 2. Drug abuse—United States—Periodicals. 3. Alcohol—Periodicals.
4. Drunk driving—Periodicals. I. Wilson, Hugh, *comp.* II. Title: Drugs, society, and behavior.
ISBN 0–07–250674–1   658'.05   ISSN 1091–9945

Seventeenth Edition

Cover image © 2002 PhotoDisc, Inc.
Printed in the United States of America   1234567890BAHBAH5432   Printed on Recycled Paper

Editors/Advisory Board

Members of the Advisory Board are instrumental in the final selection of articles for each edition of ANNUAL EDITIONS. Their review of articles for content, level, currentness, and appropriateness provides critical direction to the editor and staff. We think that you will find their careful consideration well reflected in this volume.

To the Reader

In publishing ANNUAL EDITIONS we recognize the enormous role played by the magazines, newspapers, and journals of the public pre ss in providing current, first-rate educational information in a broad spectrum of interest areas. Many of these articles are appropriate for students, researchers, and professionals seeking accurate, current material to help bridge the gap between principles and theories and the real world. These articles, however, become more useful for study when those of lasting value are carefully collected, organized, indexed, and reproduced in a low-cost format, which provides easy and permanent access when the material is needed. That is the role played by ANNUAL ED ITIONS.

It is difficult to define the framework by which Americans make decisions and develop perspectives on the use of drugs. There is no predictable expression of ideology. A wide range of individual and collective experience defines our national attitude toward drugs.

One in three Americans has someone close to them who has been negatively affected by drugs. There are an estimated 30 to 40 million chemically dependent people in this country. Social costs from drugs are measured in the billions. Drugs impact almost every aspect of public and private life. Drugs are the subjects of presidential elections, congressional appointments, and military interventions. Correlations between drug use and the deadly attacks on the World Trade Center are emerging—one important source of funding for Osama bin Laden's terrorist network was the Southwest Asian heroin trade. There are always linkages between drug use and war. Drugs also impact schools, health care systems, and families in more ways than many believe imaginable.

Although it is easy to despair and lament the past and present consequences of pervasive, harmful drug use within American society, we must realize the potential for progress as we begin this new millennium. This new year brought with it discoveries, knowledge, understanding, and resolve that may propel us away from the darkness of so many drug-related ills. Scientific discoveries of how the brain transforms as it enters and leaves an addicted state are providing hope never before realized. Hope, literacy, and understanding have always been some of the most powerful tools of progress.

The articles contained in *Annual Editions: Drugs, Society, and Behavior 02/03* are a collection of facts, issues, and perspectives designed to provide the reader with a framework for examining current drug-related issues. The book is designed to offer students something to think about and something with which to think. It is a unique collection of materials of interest to the casual as well as the serious student of drug-related social phenomena. Unit 1 addresses the historical significance that drugs have played in American history. It emphasizes the often overlooked reality that drugs, legal and illegal, have remained a pervasive dimension of past as well as present American history. Unit 2 examines the ways that drugs affect the mind and body that result in dependence and addiction. Unit 3 examines the major drugs of use and abuse, along with issues relative to understanding the individual im-

pacts of these drugs on society. This unit also illustrates the necessity to perceive the differences and similarities of legal and illegal drugs. Unit 4 reviews the dynamic nature of drugs as it relates to changing patterns and trends of use. Unit 5 analyzes the link between drugs and crime. Implications of individual criminal behavior as well as organized, syndicated trafficking are discussed. Unit 6 focuses on the social costs of drug abuse and why the costs overwhelm many American institutions. Unit 7 illustrates the complexity and controversy in creating and implementing drug policy. Unit 8 concludes the book with discussions of current strategies for preventing and treating drug abuse. Can we deter people from harming themselves with drugs, and can we cure people addicted to drugs? What does work and what does not?

We encourage your comments and criticisms on the articles provided and kindly ask for your review on the postage-paid *article rating form* at the end of the book.

Hugh T. Wilson

Hugh T. Wilson
Editor

Contents

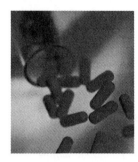

UNIT 1
Living With Drugs

Five articles in this unit examine the past and present historical evolution of drugs in the United States.

UNIT 2
Understanding How Drugs Work—Use, Dependency, and Addiction

Eight articles in this section examine the ways that drugs affect the mind and body. The relationship of pharmacology with dependence and addiction is described.

The concepts in bold italics are developed in the article. For further expansion, please refer to the Topic Guide and the Index.

UNIT 3
The Major Drugs of Use and Abuse

This unit addresses some major drugs of use and abuse. Cocaine, heroin, marijuana, alcohol, and methamphetamine are discussed.

The concepts in bold italics are developed in the article. For further expansion, please refer to the Topic Guide and the Index.

UNIT 4
Other Trends in Drug Use

The eight articles in the unit discuss some developing patterns of drug use along with their subsequent implications for society.

The concepts in bold italics are developed in the article. For further expansion, please refer to the Topic Guide and the Index.

UNIT 5
Drugs and Crime

Four articles review the numbing social malady caused by criminal behavior that is created, sustained, and perpetuated by the use of drugs.

The concepts in bold italics are developed in the article. For further expansion, please refer to the Topic Guide and the Index.

UNIT 6
Measuring the Social Cost of Drugs

Five articles speak to the diverse way in which the impacts of drugs affect and overwhelm numerous public and private American institutions.

UNIT 7
Creating & Sustaining Effective Drug Control Policy

The seven essays in this unit illustrate the complexity of creating effective drug-related policy.

The concepts in bold italics are developed in the article. For further expansion, please refer to the Topic Guide and the Index.

UNIT 8
Prevention and Treatment

Addressing some tough questions concerning previously accepted ideas about drug treatment, the eight unit articles review effectiveness, financial costs, education, and controversial new treatments.

The concepts in bold italics are developed in the article. For further expansion, please refer to the Topic Guide and the Index.

The concepts in bold italics are developed in the article. For further expansion, please refer to the Topic Guide and the Index.

Topic Guide

This topic guide suggests how the selections in this book relate to the subjects covered in your course. You may want to use the topics listed on these pages to search the Web more easily.

On the following pages a number of Web sites have been gathered specifically for this book. They are arranged to reflect the units of this *Annual Edition.* You can link to these sites by going to the DUSHKIN ONLINE support site at *http://www.dushkin.com/online/.*

ALL THE ARTICLES THAT RELATE TO EACH TOPIC ARE LISTED BELOW THE BOLD-FACED TERM.

World Wide Web Sites

The following World Wide Web sites have been carefully researched and selected to support the articles found in this reader. The easiest way to access these selected sites is to go to our DUSHKIN ONLINE support site at *http://www.dushkin.com/online/*.

AE: Drugs, Society, and Behavior 02/03

The following sites were available at the time of publication. Visit our Web site—we update DUSHKIN ONLINE regularly to reflect any changes.

General Sources

Alcohol and Drug Links
http://www.realsolutions.org/druglink.htm

This set of Internet links provides information on Alcohol and Drug Use and Abuse. These links have been gathered by Real Solutions, a nonprofit organization dedicated to the needs of family and community.

Higher Education Center for Alcohol and Other Drug Prevention
http://www.edc.org/hec/

The U.S. Department of Education established the Higher Education Center for Alcohol and Other Drug Prevention to provide nationwide support for campus alcohol and other drug prevention efforts. The Center is working with colleges, universities, and preparatory schools throughout the country to develop strategies for changing campus culture, to foster environments that promote healthy lifestyles, and to prevent illegal alcohol and other drug use among students.

National Clearinghouse for Alcohol and Drug Information
http://www.health.org

This site provides information to teens about the problems and ramifications of drug use and abuse. There are numerous links to drug-related informational sites.

UNIT 1: Living With Drugs

National Council on Alcoholism and Drug Dependence, Inc.
http://www.ncadd.org

According to its Web site, The National Council on Alcoholism and Drug Dependence provides education, information, help, and hope in the fight against the chronic, and sometimes fatal, disease of alcoholism and other drug addictions.

UNIT 2: Understanding How Drugs Work—Use, Dependency, and Addiction

AMERSA
http://center.butler.brown.edu

AMERSA is an association of multidisciplinary health care professionals in the field of substance abuse. They are dedicated to improving education about alcohol, tobacco, and other drugs.

Centre for Addiction and Mental Health (CAMH)
http://www.camh.net

One of the largest addictions facilities in Canada, CAMH advances an understanding of addiction and translates this knowledge into resources that can be used to prevent problems and to provide effective treatments.

The National Center on Addiction and Substance Abuse at Columbia University
http://www.casacolumbia.org

The National Center on Addiction and Substance Abuse at Columbia University is a unique think/action tank that brings together all of the professional disciplines (health policy, medicine and nursing, communications, economics, sociology and anthropology, law and law enforcement, business, religion, and education) needed to study and combat all forms of substance abuse—illegal drugs, pills, alcohol, and tobacco—as they affect all aspects of society.

National Institute on Drug Abuse (NIDA)
http://www.nida.nih.gov

NIDA's mission is to lead the nation in bringing the power of science to bear on drug abuse and addiction.

UNIT 3: The Major Drugs of Use and Abuse

Drugs, Solvents and Intoxicants
http://www.termisoc.org/~harl/

This United Kingdom Web site presents the history, effects, dangers, and legal issues surrounding most legal and illegal drugs.

QuitNet
http://www.quitnet.org

The QuitNet helps smokers control their nicotine addiction. This site operates in association with the Boston University School of Public Health.

UNIT 4: Other Trends in Drug Use

Marijuana as a Medicine
http://mojo.calyx.net/~olsen/

This site promotes the concept of marijuana as medicine. This is a controversial issue that has been in the news quite a bit over the past few years. At this site, you will find numerous links to other sites that support this idea, as well as information developed specifically for this site.

UNIT 5: Drugs and Crime

Drug Enforcement Administration
http://www.usdoj.gov/dea/

The mission of the Drug Enforcement Administration is to enforce the controlled substances laws and regulations of the United States.

The November Coalition
http://www.november.org

The November Coalition is a growing body of citizens whose lives have been gravely affected by the present drug policy. This group represents convicted prisoners, their loved ones, and others who believe that the U.S. drug policies are unfair and unjust.

TRAC DEA Site
http://trac.syr.edu/tracdea/index.html

The Transactional Records Access Clearinghouse (TRAC) is a data gathering, data research, and data distribution organization

www.dushkin.com/online/

associated with Syracuse University. According to its Web site, the purpose of TRAC is to provide the American people—and institutions of oversight such as Congress, news organizations, public interest groups, businesses, scholars, and lawyers—with comprehensive information about the activities of federal enforcement and regulatory agencies and the communities in which they take place.

UNIT 6: Measuring the Social Cost of Drugs

DrugText
http://www.drugtext.org

The DrugText library consists of individual drug-related libraries with independent search capabilities.

The National Organization on Fetal Alcohol Syndrome (NOFAS)
http://www.nofas.org

NOFAS is a nonprofit organization founded in 1990 dedicated to eliminating birth defects caused by alcohol consumption during pregnancy and improving the quality of life for those individuals and families affected. NOFAS is the only national organization focusing solely on fetal alcohol syndrome (FAS), the leading known cause of mental retardation.

National NORML Homepage
http://www.natlnorml.org

This is the home page for the National Organization for the Reform of Marijuana Laws.

UNIT 7: Creating & Sustaining Effective Drug Control Policy

The Drug Reform Coordination Network (DRC)
http://www.drcnet.org

According to its home page, the DRC Network is committed to reforming current drug laws in the United States.

DrugWatch International
http://www.drugwatch.org

Drug Watch International is a volunteer nonprofit information network and advocacy organization that promotes the creation of healthy drug-free cultures in the world and opposes the legalization of drugs. The organization upholds a comprehensive approach to drug issues involving prevention, education, intervention/treatment, and law enforcement/interdiction.

United Nations International Drug Control Program (UNDCP)
http://www.undcp.org

The mission of UNDCP is to work with the nations and the people of the world to tackle the global drug problem and its consequences.

Marijuana Policy Project
http://www.mpp.org

The purpose of the Marijuana Policy Project is to develop and promote policies to minimize the harm associated with marijuana.

Office of National Drug Control Policy (ONDCP)
http://www.whitehousedrugpolicy.gov

The principal purpose of ONDCP is to establish policies, priorities, and objectives for the nation's drug control program, the goals of which are to reduce illicit drug use, manufacturing, and trafficking; drug-related crime and violence; and drug-related health consequences.

UNIT 8: Prevention and Treatment

Creative Partnerships for Prevention
http://arts.endow.gov/partner/Creative.html

The goal of this national initiative is to provide current information, ideas, and resources on how to use the arts and humanities to enhance drug and violence prevention programming, foster resiliency in youth, and implement collaborations within communities to strengthen prevention programs for youth. The materials developed for this initiative have been designed with the guidance of educators, prevention specialists, youth workers, and professionals from cultural institutions (arts and humanities organizations, museums, libraries, etc.).

D.A.R.E.
http://www.dare-america.com

This year 33 million schoolchildren around the world—25 million in the United States—will benefit from D.A.R.E. (Drug Abuse Resistance Education), the highly acclaimed program that gives kids the skills they need to avoid involvement in drugs, gangs, or violence. D.A.R.E. was founded in 1983 in Los Angeles.

Hazelden
http://www.hazelden.org

Hazelden is a nonprofit organization providing high quality, affordable rehabilitation, education, prevention, and professional services and publications in chemical dependency and related disorders.

Indiana Prevention Resource Center
http://www.drugs.indiana.edu/home.html

The Indiana Prevention Resource Center at Indiana University is a statewide clearinghouse for prevention, technical assistance, and information about alcohol, tobacco, and other drugs.

We highly recommend that you review our Web site for expanded information and our other product lines. We are continually updating and adding links to our Web site in order to offer you the most usable and useful information that will support and expand the value of your Annual Editions. You can reach us at: *http://www.dushkin.com/annualeditions/*.

xv

UNIT 1
Living With Drugs

Unit Selections

1. **The Perils of Pills**, Nancy Shute, Toni Locy, and Douglas Pasternak
2. **E-commerce**, Ethan Brown
3. **American Banks and the War on Drugs**, Stephen Bender
4. **America's War on Drugs**, Jann S. Wenner
5. **Stumbling in the Dark**, *The Economist*

Key Points to Consider

- Why is history important when attempting to understand contemporary drug-related events?

- What historical trends are expressed by the use of legal drugs versus illegal drugs?

- What are the historical drug-related landmarks of drug prohibition and control?

- How is the evolution of drug-related influence on American society like and unlike that occurring in other countries?

- What can we learn from these comparisons?

 Links: www.dushkin.com/online/
These sites are annotated in the World Wide Web pages.

National Council on Alcoholism and Drug Dependence, Inc.
http://www.ncadd.org

When attempting to define the American drug experience, one must examine the past as well as the present. Too often drug use and its associated phenomena are viewed through a contemporary looking glass relative to our personal views, biases, and perspectives. Although today's drug scene is definitely a product of the counterculture of the 1960s and 1970s, the crack trade of the 1980s, and the sophisticated, criminally syndicated, technologically efficient influence of the late 1980s and early 1990s, it is also a product of the past. This past and the lessons it has generated, although largely unknown, forgotten, or ignored, provide one important perspective from which to assess our current status and to guide our future in terms of optimizing our efforts to manage the benefits and control the harm from drugs.

The American drug experience is often defined in terms of a million individual realities, all meaningful and all different. In fact, these realities often originated as pieces of our national, cultural, racial, religious, and personal past that combine to influence significantly present-day drug-related phenomena.

The contemporary American drug experience is the product of centuries of human attempts to alter or sustain consciousness through the use of mind-altering drugs. Early American history is replete with accounts of the exorbitant use of alcohol, opium, morphine, and cocaine.

Heroin and cocaine "epidemics" of the twentieth century are analogous to opiate and cocaine epidemics of the eighteenth and nineteenth centuries. A review of early American history clearly suggests the precedents for our continuing pursuit of stimulant and depressant drugs such as cocaine and heroin. In terms of social costs produced by our historical use of legal and illegal drugs, it is no wonder that some describe us as a nation of addicts. On what grounds do we justify 10 percent of the American population as alcoholic and over 1,000 tobacco-related deaths each day? On one hand, we recoil from the consequences of drug use while, on the other, we profess our helplessness to change.

Drug use and its concomitant influences are pervasive. We will all be affected and forced to confront a personally, professionally, or socially troublesome or even tragic event instigated by someone's use of drugs. Drugs are in our homes, our schools, and our workplaces. The most recent surveys of drug abuse in the United States indicate that an estimated 8 to 12 percent of Americans suffer from some form of drug abuse. These numbers do, however, reflect a continued leveling off of illicit drug use by adults. The largest number of adult users was believed to be in 1979 when survey results reported 25 million users. This leveling off is also now reflected, for the first time since 1992, in drug use by those 12 to 17 years of age. The usage rate for youths was highest in 1979 at 16.3 percent and lowest in 1992 at 5.3 percent. Since 1992, drug use by youth climbed steadily. Most survey research suggests the need to continue targeting drug abuse by young persons. Most experts believe parents to be the most important factor in protecting children from drugs. More than two-thirds of teens and two-thirds of their parents believe that American culture glamorizes smoking cigarettes and drinking alcohol. Currently, about 10.4 million young people ages 12 to 20 drink alcohol. Of these, about 2.3 million are reported to be binge drinkers. The use of cigarettes and alcohol by youth is a significant variable in predicting further drug use in almost all drug-related research.

Drugs impact our most powerful public institutions on many fronts. Drugs are *the* business of our criminal justice system, and drugs compete with terrorism, war, and other major national security concerns as demanding military issues. Many argue eloquently that drugs pose a "clear and present danger." Additional millions to fight drugs were pledged to South American countries this past year. Only terrorism and war distract the continuing military emphasis on drug fighting. As you read through the pages of this book, the pervasive nature of drug-related influence will become more apparent. Unfortunately, one of the most salient observations one can make is that drug use in our society is a topic about which many Americans have too little knowledge. History suggests that we have continually struggled to respond and react to the influence of drug use in our society. The lessons of our drug legacy are harsh, whether they are the subjects of public health or public policy. Turning an uninformed mind toward a social condition of such importance will only further our inability to address the dynamics of changing drug-related issues and problems.

The articles and graphics contained in this unit illustrate the multitude of issues influenced by the historical evolution of drug use in America. The development of drug-related phenomena is reflected within the character of all issues and controversies addressed by this book. Drug-related events of yesterday provide important meaning for understanding and addressing drug-related events of today and the future. Creating public policy and controlling crime surface immediately as examples with long-standing historical influences. As you read this and other literature on drug-related events, the dynamics of drug-related historical linkages will become apparent. As you read further, try to identify these historical linkages as they help define the focus at hand. For example, what are the implications for public health resulting from a historical lack of drug-related educational emphasis? What will history reflect 20 years from now? Is there a historical pattern of drug-related educational shortcomings that we should change?

The Perils Of Pills

The psychiatric medication of children is dangerously haphazard

BY NANCY SHUTE, TONI LOCY, AND DOUGLAS PASTERNAK

Before Joshua Andrews turned 1 year old, he was leaping out of his crib and tearing through the house. By 2, he was darting out the front door and bolting straight into traffic. By 3, he was endangering the life of the family hamster with well-aimed pencil pokes through the cage wires. He'd kick his friends, say he was sorry, then kick them again. He'd cuddle in his mother's arms for a moment, then elbow her aside to dart around wildly. By the age of 4, he had been asked to leave his Norwood, Mass., preschool, told never to return to summer camp, and sent to a special residential school three times—each time for about a month—for impulsive, aggressive behavior. "That was my little son," Joshua's mother, Susan, recalls. "Dr. Jekyll and Mr. Hyde."

About nine months ago, Susan and Joshua's psychiatrist decided to treat the boy with Wellbutrin, an anti-depressant, to calm him down and help him focus. "At first I was afraid. I didn't want to medicate him," Susan recalls. "But I was at my wit's end."

Although most people picture the toddler years as a time of peekaboo and *Pat the Bunny*, more and more preschoolers like Joshua are being treated with powerful psychiatric drugs. Last week, researchers reported in the *Journal of the American Medical Association* that the number of 2-to-4-year-old children on Ritalin, antidepressants, and other psychoactive drugs increased dramatically from 1991 through 1995. Startling as it is, the news about toddlers merely underscores the rise in the use of powerful psychiatric drugs in kids of all ages—despite the fact that these drugs are largely untested for use in the young. According to the surgeon general, almost 21 percent of children age 9 and up have a mental disorder, including depression, attention deficit hyperactivity disorder, and bipolar disorder.

A little knowledge. But the treatment children get is often dangerously haphazard. Some are heedlessly medicated, with no follow-up; other children don't get the treatment they desperately need to be able to play and learn and grow. The problem is exacerbated by the fact that the majority of psychiatric prescriptions written for children and adolescents are handled by general practitioners and pediatricians who lack mental health training. Of nearly 600 family physicians and pediatricians who responded to a 1999 University of North Carolina survey, 72 percent said they had prescribed antidepressants to children under 18. But only 16 percent of the doctors said they felt "comfortable" doing so, and just 8 percent said they have adequate training to treat childhood depression. Peter Jensen, a professor of child psychiatry at Columbia University, says bluntly: "Pediatricians and family practitioners should not be prescribing these drugs for children under 18. They don't have the time or the skills. This is a complicated area of medicine."

Kathy Hale of Lexington, Ky., knows this scenario all too well. When her daughter Katie saw the pediatrician at age 7, the doctor quickly diagnosed ADHD and prescribed Ritalin. But Katie's temper and aggression only intensified. The grade schooler pulled a butcher knife on her older sister and gave her stepfather a black eye. Kathy called the pediatrician several times and begged to have her daughter sent to a hospital, but he refused. Last October, Kathy decided to take Katie, now 13, to a psychiatrist at the University of Kentucky, who diagnosed bipolar disorder. Katie is now on lithium and Risperdal, and her mother says she's on the right track.

Psychiatric drugs can help youngsters, but they have not been tested even in older children, and most are not approved by the Food and Drug Administration for pediatric use. Almost nothing is known about how antidepressants and other psychoactive drugs affect a child's developing brain.

Behavior in a pill

These are some of the most common psychiatric medications

NAME OF DRUG	USED TO TREAT	TOTAL PRESCRIP-TIONS IN 1999 (ALL AGES)	INTENDED EFFECT	SIDE EFFECTS
Methylphenidate, (Ritalin)	Attention deficit hyperactivity disorder	11.4 million	Mildly stimulate the central nervous system	Addiction, nervous-ness, insomnia, loss of appetite
Amphetamines (Dexedrine, Biphetamine, Desoxyn)	Hyperactivity in children, narcolepsy, obesity	6.5 million	Stimulate the central nervous system	Addiction, nervous-ness, insomnia, loss of appetite
Tricyclic antidepressants (Tofranil, Norpramin, Aventyl)	Major depression. In children, Tofranil is used to treat bed-wetting	31.5 million	Restore the brain's normal level of neurotransmitters	Dry mouth, constipa-tion, blurry vision, difficulty urinating
SSRI antidepressants (Prozac, Zoloft, Paxil)	All types of depression and several anxiety disorders	84.0 million	Influence the brain chemical serotonin	Insomnia, nausea, diarrhea, headache, nervousness

The increased use of psychiatric drugs in children also raises larger questions on how our society deals with difficult behavior. Last week, a United Nations panel lambasted the United States for overprescribing psychiatric drugs, particularly stimulants; according to the panel, the United States consumes 80 percent of the world's methylphenidate (the generic name for Ritalin). Are American youngsters indeed suffering more behavioral illnesses, or have we as a society become less tolerant of disruptive behavior? Mental health officials say they don't know. Much of the official psychiatric diagnostic manual's entry on ADHD reads like a catalog of a typical young child's behavior: "squirms in seat"; "is often 'on the go'"; "interrupts or intrudes on others." Child psychiatrists uniformly report that diagnosing mental disorders in children is a difficult, delicate task–and the younger the child, the tougher the call. "How are these children qualifying for the use of these medications?" asks Julie Magno Zito, an associate professor of pharmacy and medicine at the University of Maryland–Baltimore and lead author of the *JAMA* study. "The fact that there are such dramatic increases means that something's changing. Why?"

Raising questions. Zito's report is the first large-scale look at psychiatric drug use among the very young. The data show that the use of Ritalin and other stimulants, which are used to treat attention disorders, increased almost threefold in the early 1990s. By 1995, 12 of every 1,000 children in the Midwestern Medicaid group were on a stimulant. The children's use of antide-

pressants doubled, to 3 out of every 1,000 at Midwestern Medicaid. In other research, Zito has found increased medication use among older children, too.

Given that 3 percent to 5 percent of school-age children are affected by ADHD and 2.5 percent by depression (the number rises to 8 percent in teens), psychiatrists say it's not surprising to see 1.2 percent of children being treated for ADHD and 0.3 percent for depression. What does upset the doctors is the paucity of research on how the drugs work in children and how the drugs affect future growth and development.

WHAT TO ASK

Queries for a doctor or a therapist:

• **How will you make a diagnosis?** At a minimum, the provider should interview you for at least an hour about the child's medical and family history, observe the child for a similar amount of time, and talk to teachers or baby sitters.
• **If medication is called for, how long should my child take it to know if it works?** Since psychotropic medications are untested on children, it will be a process of trial and error. If a drug causes any troubling side effect, talk to your doctor immediately about stopping it.

Until very recently, the FDA didn't require drug companies to test the safety and effectiveness of drugs on children, because of ethical and safety concerns. Prozac is not FDA approved for children under 18; Ritalin, which has been much more extensively studied in children than the antidepressants, is not approved for children under 6. But doctors can still legally prescribe those drugs to children, and frequently do, for whatever therapeutic use they decide is appropriate. The situation is changing; the FDA has made testing of drugs intended for children mandatory starting in December. But for now, doctors have almost no data to turn to in deciding how to use psychiatric drugs on kids.

Children are not miniature adults. Their bodies metabolize medications differently. Their brains are in the midst of rapid development. Animal studies suggest that the brain's developing neurotransmitter system can be exquisitely sensitive to drugs, leading to permanent changes in adult life. Thus doctors who prescribe psychiatric drugs to children, even with the best intentions, are experimenting on their patients. Says Robert Johnson, director of adolescent medicine for the University of Medicine and Dentistry of New Jersey: "We know more about the effects of marijuana on kids than Prozac."

For their part, practitioners say that they're often pressured by managed-care companies and insurers to avoid referring their patients to mental health specialists and to reduce the time they spend with families. Time is money in health care today, and it takes a lot of time to properly assess a child's behavior, emotions, and family situation. "You need at least four 45-minute sessions, observing the child, with the family, taking a family history," says Stanley Greenspan, a child psychiatrist in Bethesda, Md., and author of *Building Healthy Minds*. "But in many situations a child is being prescribed and diagnosed in one half-hour meeting. Insurance coverage doesn't support the kind of assessment you need."

Two wrongs. The push to diagnose quickly and simply creates a paradoxical result: Children are both undermedicated and overmedicated. "Twenty percent or less of kids with major depression get treatment," says Neal Ryan, a professor of child psychiatry at the University of Pittsburgh. Many of the children who are diagnosed are massively undertreated, Ryan says, in part because of parents' fears of stigmatizing their children.

Martin Teicher, an associate professor of psychiatry at Harvard Medical School, estimates that as many as half of the children diagnosed with depression actually have bipolar disorder and that many are mistakenly placed on antidepressants or stimulants. "That is a bad cocktail," he says.

Kelly Bagwell of Silver Creek, Miss., saw her 2-year-old daughter, Tori, flail and thrash for hours, uncontrollably, after her pediatrician put her on Ritalin. After Tori tried to jump out a second-story window, the Bagwells took her off the medication. It took four more years before Tori was diagnosed with bipolar disorder. Tori is now doing well on Zyprexa, an antipsychotic, and Topamax and Depakote, mood stabilizers. "Without this diagnosis, she'd be in an institution," her mother says.

Because there are no treatment guidelines and dosage standards, the prevalence of psychotropic drugs for children varies wildly, from doctor to doctor, school to school, and county to county. Ritalin use, for instance, ranges from 7 percent among children in inner-city Baltimore to 1 percent in Salt Lake City. Psychiatrists were particularly alarmed at the evidence in last week's *JAMA* study that doctors are increasingly prescribing tricyclic antidepressants for children, as well as more clonidine. Tricyclics such as Elavil have never been proven to work in children, and they can cause fatal overdoses, unlike newer antidepressants such as Prozac and Paxil. Clonidine, a blood-pressure medication prescribed for children as a tranquilizer, also has dangerous side effects. "There's all risk and very little benefit for

these two drugs," says Steven Hyman, director of the National Institute of Mental Health.

A PARENT'S GUIDE

Tools to treat a troubled child

When a child under age 5 is constantly fighting, flitting, running, biting, bouncing off the walls, and otherwise annoying grown-ups, he or she could have a serious behavioral problem. Or maybe the kid's just a typical toddler. Prescribing drugs for these children is the final treatment tool, child psychiatrists stress, and should come only after child and family have been evaluated and other approaches have been tried.

Behavioral therapy can help when a child, even a preschooler, has attention deficit hyperactivity disorder, says Enrico Mezzacappa, child psychiatrist at Children's Hospital in Boston. The therapy is a consistent system of rewards and consequences. "You catch them being good, you praise them and give lots of rewards," said Bruce Black, a child psychiatrist in Wellesley, Mass. If they're bad, a parent gives them a timeout or takes away a toy.

Children with obsessive-compulsive disorder can benefit from behavioral therapy as well as exposure therapy. If a girl feels a need to constantly wash after touching a toy that she fears is dirty, or just plain yucky, she might be led to touch the toy and taught relaxation techniques to ease anxiety.

When such therapies fail to provide relief, they may begin to work with medication. Parents should be advised that little is known about immediate or long-term effects of psychotropic drugs; virtually all are untested on children younger than 6.

Severe depression in a very young child is almost always caused by a major upheaval. "In kids under 5, it's marital discord, divorce, witnessing violence," says Glen Elliott, director of child and adolescent psychiatry at the University of California–San Francisco. A pill won't help. The daunting solution is to change family life or move from a dangerous neighborhood.

—Susan Brink

All too often, children get drugs with none of the behavior modification, counseling, and long-term follow-up that mental health experts say are essential. "The quickest and easiest thing is to write a pre-

scription," says Paul Lipkin, a pediatrician and head of clinical programs at the Kennedy Krieger Institute in Baltimore. "It's harder to convince parents to go in for weeks of psychotherapy." A cost-conscious health care environment encourages the use of medication—about $20 a week for selective serotonin reuptake inhibitor (SSRI) antidepressants like Prozac—over therapy, which runs $150 for a 45-minute session. But even the pharmaceutical companies say it is inappropriate to prescribe antidepressants for children without exploring other methods of treatment, particularly behavioral therapy. Rajinder Judge, director of neuroscience at Eli Lilly, the maker of Prozac, says these antidepressants should not be used as "the first line of treatment."

Judy Coburn has seen a system where psychotropic medications were handed out to children indiscriminately. Three years ago, a few months after Judy's husband committed suicide, her 13-year-old daughter, Amy, was admitted to a hospital near their Perry, Utah, home. She was contemplating suicide. When her mother picked her up a week later, the discharge nurse said that Amy had been placed on 20 mg a day of Paxil, an SSRI antidepressant—the same drug her father had been taking when he killed himself. He had been taking just 10 mg a day. "I remember I asked the counselor at the hospital, 'Am I supposed to bring her back for a follow-up?'" recalls Judy. "And he said, 'No, the medication will keep her calmed down.' And he did not say anything about any side effects at all." The drug insert for Paxil lists paranoid reactions, antisocial behavior, trouble concentrating, and hostility as some of the rare, but serious, behavioral side effects of the drug. Amy experienced all of these reactions. She stopped taking Paxil because of the side effects, and counseling helped her deal with the grief over her father's death. Today Amy, 16, is a girl with a broad smile who enjoys acting in school plays.

Many parents say that without medication, their children would not have been able to learn in school, play with friends, and do all the little things that are essential to the business of growing up. Eydie Alguadich will never forget the day her 5-year-old daughter, Danielle, started to say, "Mommy, I wish I was dead." It went on for two years. "I had a major, major prejudice against using drugs on children," says Alguadich, an interior designer and stay-at-home mom in Herndon, Va. When a pediatrician recommended that her older

CAUSE AND EFFECT

Can drugs spark acts of violence?

By any measure, Jarred Viktor was a troubled kid. The 16-year-old was experimenting with illegal drugs, drinking heavily, and talking about suicide. In 1995, Brenda Viktor brought her son to their family physician, David Borecky, near the Viktors' Escondido, Calif., home. After a brief visit, Borecky handed Jarred a three-week supply of the antidepressant Paxil. He said the drug would take time to kick in and told Jarred that he wouldn't need to see him for two to three weeks. Ten days later, Jarred stabbed his grandmother 61 times. He was convicted of first-degree murder and is doing life without parole.

No one will ever know what role Paxil played in Jarred's actions. Borecky believes it played none and that his treatment of Jarred was appropriate. In 1991 the Food and Drug Administration found no link between Prozac, a cousin to Paxil, and suicide or violence in adults. But the FDA has not examined the drug's effect on kids. And none of this class of drugs is approved for use in kids with depression.

Doctors are divided on the issue of antidepressants and violence. Many experts say it's impossible to know whether violent acts are linked to the drug or to the disease itself. But others find the anecdotal evidence convincing. "What jumped out at me," says psychiatrist Alan Abrams, who testified for the defense at Jarred's trial, "was this very withdrawn kid who started acting as though he was primed to explode" days after he started taking Paxil. Abrams believes the drug caused Jarred to become violent.

Known risks. SmithKline Beecham, the maker of Paxil, and other drug companies say their medications play no role in violent behavior or suicide. Still, the companies do warn in package inserts that a small number of patients, fewer than 1 percent, may experience side effects, including abnormal dreams, agitation, hostility, suicidal thoughts, and delusions. But with an estimated 1.5 million youngsters receiving these antidepressants in 1996 alone, that's about 15,000 who could be vulnerable.

Matt Miller's parents believe their child was among the vulnerable. Miller, a 13-year-old from Overland Park, Kan., was given free samples of Zoloft in 1997 by his psychiatrist. There was no printed information; the Millers say they were told Matt might get a bellyache and have trouble sleeping. "We were ecstatic that there was a pill that we were told could fix Matt," his father says. Seven days later, Matt's mother went to collect laundry from her son's room and found him hanging inside his closet. The Millers have filed suit against Pfizer, the manufacturer of Zoloft. The company believes the drug is not linked to violence.

Even experts who believe these drugs can cause violent behavior blame not the drugs themselves but the way in which physicians diagnose and monitor their patients. Psychiatrist Frederick Goodwin, a former head of the National Institute of Mental Health, contends that kids who get violent may have been misdiagnosed and placed on the wrong drug in the first place. That is why it is critical to see a doctor with expertise in mental health care, experts say. Unless things change, says Goodwin, "then the likelihood of these negative events happening goes way up."

—D.P. and T.L.

daughter, Samanthe, take Ritalin at age 2, Alguadich enrolled her in a gym class instead. But as she watched Danielle founder despite intensive tutoring from her mother, she decided it was time to seek help and brought her in for an assessment by psychologists and pediatricians. Danielle, 8, now takes Ritalin, as do her two older sisters. Their mother says they're no longer struggling in school, and the drug appears to have no side effects. "Kids know when there's something wrong," Alguadich says. "It's the parents who are the last to know."

National experiment. The vast pharmacological experiment on America's children raises larger questions of whether behavior is a medical or social issue. Two hundred years ago, the mentally ill were considered cursed or evil. Only in this century have doctors come to understand that depression, schizophrenia, and other disorders arise from the genes and cells, not from the Devil. Even 20 years ago, children were thought to be incapable of becoming depressed, a holdover from the Freudian belief that it took an adult superego to suffer angst. By recognizing the biological basis of mental disorders, medicine has offered millions of people the possibility of a real life. But in elevating the biological causes of mental disorders, society risks ignoring other key factors: family, environment, culture. If a child behaves badly because the parents' marriage is in turmoil, is the problem with the child or with the family? Are today's parents too busy to give difficult children the one-on-one attention and patience they need? Do teachers demand that children be drugged rather than accept a rambunctious classroom?

Lawrence Diller, a behavioral pediatrician in Walnut Creek, Calif., and author of *Running on Ritalin*, says that society's increased demands on children make it harder for them to cope and force teachers and parents to consider drugs for troubled children. "The expectations of children are going down in age and up in standards. More and more is asked of kids, with less and less support."

With Susan Brink, Mary Lord, John S. MacNeil, Mark E. Madden, Stacey Schultz, and Rachel Sobel

E-commerce

Once just for raves, **ecstasy is now all the rage**—the favorite party pill of Wall Streeters, prep-school kids, and mall rats alike. Smugglers (JFK is their favorite route) may be the most ecstatic of all—but the government is definitely not amused.

By Ethan Brown

AT AROUND 3 A.M. ON A WARM FRIDAY night, Paul, a stockbroker in his late twenties, is waiting for his ecstasy dealer in front of the Gramercy Tavern, where he's just had a few drinks with friends. John, a club kid who delivers the drug to clients who beep him or call on his cell phone, is running 45 minutes late, and Paul, who took a hit of ecstasy half an hour ago, is furious. "My girl is already rolling"—tripping on ecstasy—he says. "She's just waiting to get f----d."

Paul starts dialing his dealer's cell phone and launches into a tirade. "I don't need this shit," he says. "I've got another delivery service that's way better—a team of three hot girls who deliver ecstasy to your apartment." Besides, he continues, "I've been telling John that if he gets his shit together, he could make some real bucks. The older guys on the Street are into coke, but there are traders on the floor who would order hundreds of pills a day from him. They don't know shit about ecstasy, either. They'd probably pay $50 a pill—money doesn't mean a thing to them."

Moments later, John stops short by the curb and swings open the front passenger door of his Jeep Cherokee. "Sorry, Paul,"

he says, wiping sweat from a pale forehead partly covered with boyish brown bangs. "I've been mad busy tonight." Paul snaps his cell phone shut and hops in. "Here's 90 percent of your order," John says, handing Paul two large Ziploc bags filled with 200 white pills between them. "I've gotta run back downtown to get the rest." Paul glances at his purchase—about $5,000 worth of ecstasy that should last him and his stockbroker buddies through the weekend—and says, "You'd better be back fast. I'm not waiting on the street for drugs. This isn't 1974, man."

Certainly not. A big guy with short hair, black jeans, and a frat-boy swagger, Paul couldn't have less in common with the club kids who popularized ecstasy in the early nineties. After all, he has to keep track of trades in the morning. But although he's been using the drug for just a year, he's doing so with a similar abandon—he says he goes through 20 or 30 pills a weekend. "This," says Paul, holding up a bag, "is for my best buddy's going-away party tomorrow night. We're gonna hire a bunch of strippers and give them as much ecstasy as they want." A crooked smile crosses his face, the first effect of the

pill he just took. "This"—he holds up the other—"is for tonight with my girl and the Hamptons tomorrow."

ONCE FOUND ALMOST EXCLUSIVELY at raves or in college dorms, ecstasy is nearing the cultural ubiquity marijuana reached at the beginning of the seventies and cocaine achieved in the mid-eighties. "It's sweeping through our society faster than crack," says Gary Murray, East Coast representative of the U.S. Customs Ecstasy Task Force, a division formed four months ago in response to the drug's growing popularity. Except that "with crack you could say, 'These people over here are doing it, and these people aren't.' You can't do that with ecstasy now. Everyone's doing it."

Patented by the German pharmaceutical company E. Merck in 1914 (under its chemical name MDMA, or 3,4 methylenedioxymethamphetamine), ecstasy was first widely used during the seventies to help patients open up to psychiatrists during therapy. By the end of the decade, the drug had crossed over from the couch to the dance floor at gay discos in New York, Chicago, and especially Dallas. In 1985, then-Texas senator Lloyd Bentsen successfully lobbied to have the DEA make MDMA a "Schedule 1" drug, subject to criminal penalties similar to those for cocaine and heroin.

Now, like pot in the seventies and coke in the eighties, ecstasy—also called X, E, or rolls—is seen as fairly harmless, hangover-free fun. Unlike cocaine, which leads to obvious trips to the bathroom, accusations of being stuck in the Greed Decade, and often addiction, ecstasy is inconspicuous and physically nonaddictive. Usually taken as a pill that has a small, stamped logo "borrowed" from pop or corporate culture—Nike, Calvin Klein, Mitsubishi, Motorola, and Tweety Bird are among the popular "brands"—ecstasy induces waves of euphoria and heightened physical sensations (especially tactile ones). But it's not disorienting enough in moderate doses to prevent users from remaining aware and outgoing. Aside from occasional cautionary tales about dehydration and overdoses, the word-of-mouth on ecstasy is overwhelmingly positive. "There's this perception of harmlessness surrounding ecstasy that other drugs simply don't have," says Bridget Brennan, the DEA's special narcotics prosecutor for New York City. At $20 to $30 for a pill that lasts four to six hours, it's also a bargain in the age of the $9 Cosmopolitan. "You could spend that kind of money in fifteen minutes at any bar in the city," notes a thirtysomething A&R executive who often takes the drug with friends at his country house in Sag Harbor.

Though ecstasy is still nowhere near as mainstream in the U.S. as it is in England, much of its jump in popularity can be explained by older ecstasy users whose clubgoing days are long behind them—if they ever happened at all. "It's such a cool drug because you can mold it into whatever you want to do," says Steve, an artist in his late twenties who sheepishly admits, "I missed the whole rave thing." Instead of hitting nightspots like Twilo, Steve takes ecstasy when he hangs out with friends at bars. "When you do ecstasy, you realize how paranoid you've been around people," he says. "Ecstasy breaks down those barriers."

Plenty of other users began taking the drug in college and simply never stopped. A thirtysomething architect named Mark remembers using it with his fraternity brothers and their "groupies" at a California college in the late eighties. "We'd have this little lovefest where everybody was making out with everybody—not crazy sex games or anything but just the whole ecstasy thing of wanting to wrap your

tongue around somebody," he says. He's grown up now, with a high-paying job and a nice loft downtown, but he still uses ecstasy as a social lubricant. His architect girlfriend "was one of those people who wanted to rebel but came from a very conservative household," he says. "It made her relax and cut loose and not be so self-conscious. She absolutely loved it."

Nor is ecstasy confined to party-prone young people. Tom, a 44-year-old movie executive, takes ecstasy with the intensity of a club kid ("If it's good, I'll take like six in one evening"), but only in his downtown loft. "Usually when we do ecstasy, it's a very quiet, intimate thing," he says. "I've never understood the whole concept of doing ecstasy out in public. One time we did E and went to Vinyl. I just ended up sitting there for about ten minutes and leaving."

> **"Everybody is into ecstasy,"** says Suave, who deals to professionals, "straight, gay, black, yellow, red, white, brown, whatever."

Just how widespread is ecstasy in New York? "It's everywhere," a suburban Long Island teenager now enrolled at Daytop Village's Huntington, Long Island, adolescent drug-rehab facility told *New York*. "It's easier to get an E pill than a pack of cigarettes. You need I.D. for that, you know." Another teenage patient there agreed. "We'd talk about it during social studies: 'You gonna do E this weekend?'" One dealer even said his aunt asked him about it: "A friend of hers read about it and was interested in trying it."

"Everybody is into ecstasy," says Suave, another dealer, "straight, gay, black, yellow, red, white, brown, whatever."

WELL PAST 2 A.M. ON A Wednesday night, Suave is kicking back on a tan leather couch in the VIP room of Float, a multilevel midtown nightspot known for hosting dot-com launch parties and boasting Prince as a regular. Discreetly holding a cigarette-size joint by his side, he's regaling a dozen or so fellow partyers—editors, stylists, Web designers—with stories about his week of club-hopping. "Yo, the VIP room at NV is the illest," he says, pausing to look down at the cell phone on

his hip that vibrates with an incoming call every few minutes. "There were so many models up in there I thought I was in a fashion shoot." The Gucci-and-Fendi-clad group, here for promoter Derek Corley's weekly upscale hip-hop party, laughs in unison. "Have y'all been to Joe's Pub on Tuesday nights?" Suave asks. "The girls are so fine."

But Suave isn't there for the women. Like so many of the beautiful people around him, he goes clubbing to network. He's a new kind of ecstasy dealer, one who sells from a cell phone instead of a crinkled plastic Baggie full of pills. "I would never sell in a club," he says. "The security sweats you like mad. Plus, you have no idea who you're selling to. It could easily be an undercover cop."

At first glance, Suave seems like just another sociable single guy on the make—albeit one who hits several high-end hot spots like Ohm, Cheetah, and Justin's in a single night. "I'll see a pretty girl or maybe a guy that looks cool and strike up a conversation," he explains, adjusting the brim of the Ralph Lauren baseball cap that hides a shock of kinky hair. "I'll ask, 'Do you smoke weed?' or 'Do you do ecstasy?' If they seem cool, they get my number, and we'll get a relationship going from there."

Suave's casual networking style suits his clientele perfectly: His regular customers include editors from at least one national magazine, brokers at major investment banks, and Website designers at dot-com start-ups. In fact, he only deals to professionals, because "they treat me right," he says. "These aren't the kind of people who'll be begging me for free pills." He won't sell to ravers, because they always ask to meet him in nightclubs and "they're terrible with money," he says. "They can't hang on to it for a minute."

Like Suave, Greg, who has dealt ketamine, cocaine, marijuana, and mushrooms at one time or another, conducts business far from the limelight. He sells only out of his Chelsea apartment and only to friends of friends who have one of the yellow business cards with his pager number. "You don't have to go to a club to get E anyway," he says. "You can just make a few calls and have it before you go out for the night." To keep his neighbors from getting suspicious, he maintains well-known "office hours"—by 10 P.M. most nights, he's in bed or watching a movie on his DVD player. Some of his customers keep similar hours. "I've sold to couples in their sixties and people in their forties who have families," he says. "Just last month, a friend of mine who's in his mid-thirties finally tried ecstasy for the first time," he continues. "He bought a couple of pills from me and took his girlfriend out on a rowboat in Central Park."

Because of increasing demand and his high profit margin, he says, "selling ecstasy is a ridiculously easy way to make money." Greg sells pills for $30 that most dealers buy for $8 to $11. Suave buys pills for $11 from a distributor in Brooklyn, then sells them for $20 to $30 to customers who beep or call him. "If they're buying a bunch of pills," Suave says, "I'll throw in two or three to make them feel good about working with me." For purchases of 100 or more, he charges $20 per pill. "Quantity calls are what keep me in business," he says. "Keep those orders for 100 and more coming, and I'm a very happy man."

"Once you do the first pill, **your whole perspective on life changes**," says Kristin, 14. "I would look at clean people and be like, 'They don't know what they're missing.'"

A typical day for Suave begins in the late afternoon, when he's awakened by a phone call or beeper message from a customer at a law firm, publishing house, or Internet start-up. "My music-industry customers are my favorites," he says, "because they hook me up with concert tickets and free CDs." (Another regular client is helping him put together a portfolio so he can pursue a career as a model.) He delivers ecstasy on foot or by taxi until around midnight, then heads out to clubs to meet more potential customers. "On a bad week, when I'm not getting many calls or I'm too lazy to really work it, I'll make $1,000," he says. "On an average week, where things are business as usual, I'll make about $3,000 to $4,000. A great week, where there's a holiday or a big party, I'll make $5,000."

THOUGH THE FRENZY FOR ECSTASY is national—legislators in both the House and the Senate are working on bills to increase penalties—the two most popular U.S. points of entry for the drug are JFK and Newark airports, according to law-en-

forcement sources. So far this year, New York accounts for more than 2 million of the nearly 7 million hits of ecstasy seized by Customs. "Because of our airports and the presence of organized crime, New York is a critical port for the importation of ecstasy," says Brennan. Even given these conditions, Brennan struggles to account for the ecstasy explosion. "The numbers are staggering," she says.

ACCORDING TO INFORMATION compiled by U.S. Customs, many distributors pay Dutch or Israeli smuggling rings $100,000 for bringing them 200,000 pills from the Netherlands or Belgium. They then sell those pills to dealers for $8 to $11 apiece, earning a profit of $1.5 million. That might seem like an awful lot of ecstasy to unload, but demand is so high, most dealers purchase by the thousand. "Ecstasy is a much neater business [than cocaine or heroin]," says Customs commissioner Raymond W. Kelly. "You can invest $100,000 as a distributor and get $5 million back."

Before it was busted in February, the Israeli ecstasy ring that supplied Greg out of an apartment in Forest Hills sold dealers as many as 100,000 pills a week, according to the Queens district attorney's office. One member was observed by the DEA saying he needed 10,000 ecstasy tablets immediately and 25,000 more within the hour.

Both the reach and the organization of the Forest Hills ring were impressive. "They were very, very smart—even if you were buying a few thousand pills, you'd always deal with the guy lowest on the totem pole," says Greg. "And their reach was amazing. I would buy pills from them, and the next week I'd talk to friends out in San Francisco and Dallas who had the exact same pills."

An even bigger Israeli ring, allegedly run by 29-year-old Amsterdam resident Sean Erez, recruited Hasidic Jews from Williamsburg, Brooklyn, and Monsey, New York, to smuggle ecstasy from Amsterdam through Paris. Although Erez and his girlfriend remain in Dutch custody fighting extradition, the other people named in the indictment all pleaded guilty, including Shimon Levita, an Orthodox Jew from Brooklyn who helped Erez recruit Hasidim, who were given $1,500 for each trip. When the ring was busted, Erez had almost $475,000 in a Luxembourg bank account, and law-enforcement officials estimated it had smuggled more than a million tablets of ecstasy into the U.S.

Even those operations pale in comparison with the Los Angeles-based ecstasy ring allegedly run by a 44-year-old Israeli national named Jacob "Koki" (pronounced "Cookie") Orgad that was busted by Customs in June. During the past two years, the group allegedly brought at least 9 million pills into the U.S. "We've only identified 30 couriers so far, and there could have been many more," says a source at Customs. "So 9 million pills is actually our low estimate, because we know that each courier brought in at least 30,000 pills."

Beyond sheer numbers, the group was run with a "level of sophistication that until now has only been associated with heroin and cocaine smugglers," according to the Customs source. Orgad's group recruited poor families from Texas and Arkansas who would then be taken by lower-level associates to "local malls where they would be outfitted in conservative clothing like plaid shirts and penny loafers. They would then be coached on how to act when going through Customs at the airport."

The group also employed decoys. "They would send a pair of girls in their twenties who wore tie-dyed shirts and looked as though they had just taken a vacation in Amsterdam," according to the Customs source. A Texas couple working for Orgad brought a mentally handicapped teenager with them, but the ruse didn't work—the pair were caught with more than 200,000 ecstasy pills in their luggage. Sometimes the decoys also served as monitors to make sure the smugglers didn't make off with the drugs. To give their couriers a better chance, Orgad's organization even booked them on flights scheduled to land during an airport's busiest hours, says the source. "They wanted to send their guys through when our inspectors were overwhelmed. That proves their level of sophistication."

Orgad allegedly maintained the kind of high life usually associated with cocaine and heroin kingpins. He had a fleet of luxury cars and, according to the Customs source, "was often accompanied by two women, usually exotic dancers." It has also been reported that in the early nineties, he was an associate of Heidi Fleiss who helped her recruit prostitutes.

As Orgad awaits trial, Customs continues to bust his associates. On Thursday, four of his Texas-based smugglers were arrested, one for allegedly facilitating the transport of pills from Europe to Houston. A week before, a more important Orgad associate, Ilan Zarger, was busted for running what Customs officials allege was the largest ecstasy-distribution network in New York City. Customs estimates that Zarger's organization distributed more than 700,000 ecstasy pills in the New York area over the past six months alone. The organization, which also included another alleged Orgad associate named Assaf "Assi" Shetrit, supplied ecstasy to a violent Brooklyn-based street gang called BTS ("Born to Scheme" or "Brooklyn Terror Squad"), who sold the drug at raves in New York, Connecticut, New Jersey, and Washington, D.C. Zarger also arranged for 40,000 ecstasy pills to be delivered to the Hamptons in April, according to Customs. Zarger allegedly charged his associates an extra 2 percent if they brought him anything smaller than a $100 bill, thought nothing of lending $100,000 to friends (as long as they paid him back in hundreds), and socked away $1.5 million of drug profits in a safe.

The organization, which Zarger himself claimed on wiretap was protected by the Russian Mafia, was unusually well run, according to Customs. "It would appear that he controlled all ends of the ecstasy business, from importation to retail," says Customs special agent Joe Webber. The group's reach extended beyond the New York area, too: Zarger allegedly threatened to have Sammy "the Bull" Gravano "whacked" during a price dispute.

As demand rises, ecstasy smugglers are becoming as diverse as those who use the drug. "We used to be able to break down the trade fairly easily," says Murray. "We could put the Israelis at about 50 percent, the Netherlands at 15 percent, and the rest everybody else. But that 'everybody else' is getting larger every day. Our math no longer works." Kelly agrees. "We're seeing smugglers from incredibly diverse backgrounds," he says. "Older people, younger people, black, white—it's an across-the-board demographic."

Thanks to sky-high profits, fairly light federal penalties, and the relative ease of smuggling ecstasy as opposed to cocaine or heroin (U.S. Customs finished training the first group of dogs to sniff out the drug only this March), many of those would-be smugglers aren't exactly practiced criminals. In March, Joseph Colgan, the 33-year-old owner of the Minetta Tavern, was charged with masterminding a ring to import more than 80,000 pills to the U.S. from Amsterdam via Paris over five months. (He pleaded guilty last week.) His courier? Scott E. Rusczyk, a lawyer with the New York firm Kronish, Lieb, Weiner & Hellman.

Most couriers are less upscale. The Amsterdam-based writer Hendrikus Van-Zyp, 54, and his wife, Maria Van-Zyp Landa, 47, agreed to bring a package they were told contained a few thousand ecstasy pills to the U.S. in exchange for a trip to Aruba and $10,000 that Hendrikus told *New York* he needed for his wife's bone-cancer treatments. "They had a good feeling about us," Van-Zyp says now, speaking from the visitors' room at the Otisville Federal Correctional Penitentiary, where he's serving a five-year sentence for ecstasy smuggling, "because we were an older couple." But when he and his wife were bumped from their original Amsterdam-Newark flight on October 22, their luggage remained aboard the plane. During a routine check of unclaimed baggage, ecstasy was found in their suitcases, and the couple were arrested by Customs officials posing as airline workers.

"E was around every weekend," says Charlie, 16. "My brother played on a soccer team with my dealer, so I knew him well."

The Van-Zyps were carrying what was then a record seizure of ecstasy at a U.S. airport, but their loss probably put barely a dent in the organization that recruited them. "I think they put ten people on the airplane, so when they catch two, then they're not out much money," Van-Zyp says.

"I knew we were in trouble," he says with a throaty, nicotine-scarred laugh, "when they brought the suitcase and I tried to tip the guy and he said, 'Keep it.'"

A GOOD PORTION OF ALL THE ecstasy coming into New York ends up in the hands of high-school students, and not just young ravers, according to Caroline Sullivan, director of Daytop Village's Huntington, Long Island, adolescent drug-rehab facility. "We're not talking about kids in the club or bar scene—we're talking about kids with ten o'clock curfews," Sullivan says. "Their first experience is usually at a party or friend's house. The feeling they get from the pill is incredible, and they want to replicate that experience over and over again, until they build up a tolerance

for the drug. Then they start to take several doses at a time." Sullivan says 85 percent of the teenagers admitted to Daytop have used ecstasy, an increase from just 20 to 30 percent one year ago (though none have been admitted solely because of ecstasy).

At one elite private school on the Upper West Side, the drug "has become more popular than weed," according to Laura, a 17-year-old who has done ecstasy several times and has a regular dealer. "Most of the kids at school do it. They do it at house parties or when they're just hanging out, not really at clubs."

The ecstasy scene at Bronx High School of Science "ranged from preppy kids to this kid who was in my Hebrew-school class," according to Shari, a recent graduate. A few of her fellow students sometimes sold pills, she says, and when they were out, "we all knew this guy on 46th Street in the theater district who literally had boxes full." Often, they took ecstasy at home: "I hosted my share of ecstasy parties where someone would walk in the room with 100 pills and they'd be gone within twenty minutes."

Neither Manhattan teens nor several young Daytop Village patients from suburban Long Island interviewed by *New York* say they had much trouble finding the drug. "E was around every weekend—my brother played on a soccer team with my dealer, so I knew him well," says Charlie, 16. "I've never been to a club. I was like, 'Why waste money on the club when I could just save it for drugs?'"

Leah, a 16-year-old who lives on the Upper East Side, says most of her friends do ecstasy and doesn't think her occasional use of the drug will do her any harm. "I've had some of the best times of my life on ecstasy, and I'm not an addict, so what's the problem?" she says. "For the Fourth, me and my friends took some pills really early in the night and then we went to Exit," she explains. "When we got out of the club in the morning, the weather was so nice we decided to take a few more rolls. It was just amazing." The club might have enhanced her high, but she's not interested in becoming part of that scene. "It's way too druggy," she says, without irony.

"Kids who are going to birthday parties or hanging out at friends' houses are doing it," says Carrie, a Trinity graduate who says she was one of the few students at her high school who didn't try ecstasy. "It's the drug of our generation," she says. "I know friends who are scared to do coke, but they've done E more than a few times."

"Ecstasy has enormous appeal, but **people crash** afterward," says Dr. Robert Klitzman. "If they're doing ecstasy on a Saturday night, there's 'Suicide Tuesday.'"

That attitude persists because "the jury is still out" about ecstasy's addictiveness, according to A. Jonathan Porteus, a doctor of psychology at Daytop Village. "It's definitely habit-forming, though. It becomes associated with certain things, like sex or dancing, and becomes a habit. You'll hear people say, 'To have sex, you need X.'" He pauses and laughs. "And some people can't listen to Orbital without it."

Whether or not the drug is addictive, says Porteus, "ecstasy is going to affect your ability to concentrate, you're going to have more trouble feeling happy, there's going to be a bit of spaciness there." Because MDMA alters the brain's serotonin levels, which control mood, Porteus also believes the comedown ecstasy users experience after a weekend of partying could last longer than they think. "There's going to be a lot of people taking anti-depressants in the future."

"Ecstasy has enormous appeal, but people crash afterward," says Dr. Robert Klitzman, a clinical psychiatrist at Columbia University. "If they're doing ecstasy on a Saturday night, there's 'Suicide Tuesday,'" a brief but deep depression. Still, teenagers are particularly vulnerable, Klitzman says, because "high school is an awkward time for everyone, and this is sort of the anti-rejection drug."

Kristin, a shy, blonde 14-year-old with braces who hugs herself nervously while talking, began drinking and smoking marijuana at age 12, but neither drug had the pull of ecstasy, which she first tried in the spring of 1999. "I didn't think it was gonna be that good, but once I tried it, it was like my life," she says. "I couldn't wait until the next time I did it, so I did it the next day."

Like the club kids who proselytized about ecstasy ("Everything begins with an E" was a raver mantra), Kristin found herself E-vangelizing about the drug the way Timothy Leary's followers extolled the virtues of LSD. "Once you do the first pill, your whole perspective on life changes," she says. "Your whole view on the world around you, the way you look at people. I

would look at clean people and be like, 'What is wrong with them? They don't even know what they're missing.' And I wanted to show people ecstasy."

Though ecstasy is relatively expensive for cash-poor teenagers, Kristin says she rarely had to pay for it. "Most girls I know who don't pay for their drugs had sex with the dealer and he'd give it to them for free, but it wasn't like that for me," she says. She got the drug by hosting afternoon ecstasy parties at her parents' home.

On the drug, "if someone says something just a little nice, like 'Hi, how are you?,' you'll be like, 'Oh, my God, that's so nice of you,' and you'll fall in love with them on the spot," she says. But the bonds created by the drug vanish just as quickly. "I remember this kid who I was so in love with when I was on ecstasy," she continues. "Then the next day I called him and told him to come over and he said no, and I was like, 'Whatever, I don't really care about you anyway.' He wasn't important to me at all—we just had that connection when we did E together. I call it 'E love,' 'cause that's what it is, really."

After she began to miss more school, her mother read her diary and "saw a completely different person 'cause every page was filled with 'Oh, my God, I can't wait till the next time I can do E,'" she says. She's been enrolled with Daytop since the fall, but it's still difficult for her to imagine life without ecstasy. "I give myself pats on the shoulder every day, like, 'Today I'm clean another day,'" she says, "but it's still constantly in the back of my head, because nothing can make me feel like that."

IN THE EARLY NINETIES, WHEN ECSTASY was prevalent only in European rave culture and the few underground American clubs that identified with it, two outer-borough teens named Frankie Bones and Michael Caruso went to England to check out London nightlife. They were fateful trips: Bones was inspired to begin throwing raves in Brooklyn, and Caruso started Manhattan's first techno party at the Limelight. Eventually, Bones's "Storm Raves" planted the seed for the U.S. rave scene; the drug-distribution network Caruso allegedly ran at the Limelight gave the city its first bona fide ecstasy bust.

"We weren't really even aware of ecstasy until the Limelight case in 1995," says Brennan. Indeed, the DEA-NYPD joint investigation into the Limelight began only after police were contacted by the parents of an 18-year-old New Jersey man

who had died from an overdose of ecstasy he had allegedly bought there. Until 1997, ecstasy wasn't even a controlled substance in New York State.

By then, the drug was already old news in clubland—it had started spreading to the mainstream. "Law enforcement is always playing catch-up," Brennan admits. Because it got such a late start monitoring the ecstasy trade, Brennan says, the NYPD's lab doesn't "have a baseline to start with in terms of assessing the purity of ecstasy pills" the way it does with cocaine or heroin. Lately, however, Brennan has been surprised to find supposed ecstasy pills that actually contain antihistamine laced with insecticide. "We're seeing all kinds of adulterated substances," she says. "You honestly don't know what you're putting in your mouth when you're taking ecstasy."

The current ecstasy explosion has made the market for fakes even hotter. "People don't have qualms about what they sell as ecstasy," according to Murray, "as long as people pay for it." Indeed, when the NYPD used the nuisance-abatement law to shut down the Tunnel last year after a raid targeting ecstasy dealers there, only four of the pills that were seized tested positive for MDMA. (Tunnel has since reopened.) And as user demand builds for "brands" like Mitsubishi—a particularly potent pill illicitly stamped with the car manufacturer's three-diamond logo—drugmakers are putting the same insignia on impure pills, much the way knockoff-makers sew Prada labels onto cheap backpacks.

"We're at the point right now with ecstasy that we were with cocaine in the seventies," says New York State Senator Roy Goodman. **"It's being passed out like mints** by people who have no idea of its negative effects."

But adulterated or weakened pills are the least of law enforcement's problems: Smugglers are getting more sophisticated, and other organized-crime rings are competing with the Israelis. Several men have been nabbed at JFK wearing skintight bodysuits that held more than 7,000 ecstasy pills each; Customs officials have also found pills hidden in software packaging, stuffed animals, and secret compartments in carry-on luggage. In March, Customs scored its first internal seizure when it arrested a passenger flying into JFK from Amsterdam who had swallowed 2,800 pills in 70 condoms.

"It's worse in the cities, " says Dr. Mike Nelson, a physician at the St. Vincents emergency room. **"But it's also in middle America,** because they don't have anything else to do."

At the same time, "organized-crime groups are putting their feelers out" to the ecstasy trade, according to Murray. "There's so much money to be made that these groups are saying, 'Let's get this going on,'" Murray says. "We're going to see a stronger Mexican connection, a much stronger Dominican connection. We're going to see bikers who were running methamphetamine labs in the Midwest convert those labs into ecstasy labs. We've already seen it in Vancouver. The only difference is you start with a different chemical."

To combat the spread of the drug locally, New York state senator Roy Goodman issued a recommendation that a defendant be charged with ecstasy possession based on the weight of his or her stash rather than its purity. "We're at the point right now with ecstasy that we were with cocaine in the seventies," Goodman says.

"It's being passed out like mints by people who have no idea of its negative effects." On July 3, New Jersey governor Christine Whitman signed into law a bill that would put ecstasy in the same legal class as heroin and cocaine.

"It's worse in the cities," says Dr. Mike Nelson, a physician at the St. Vincents emergency room. "But it's also in middle America, because they don't have anything else to do." Congresswoman Judy Biggert, who represents the suburban Thirteenth District of Illinois, is sponsoring a bill to double the minimum jail time for ecstasy traffickers. "Ecstasy has been around for 20 or 30 years now, but we're finally seeing it in the suburbs," she says. "So we're trying to send a message to dealers and traffickers—right now, the penalties they receive are a joke." Similar legislation, the Ecstasy Anti-Proliferation Act, has been introduced by Senator Bob Graham of Florida.

Harm-reduction advocates argue that under such laws, the least powerful people in the ecstasy-distribution business, the "mules" who carry the drugs, would receive some of the harshest penalties. "They'll always arrest people like me—poor people and idiot people," argues Van-Zyp. "The people higher up will make a lot of money but they won't get arrested." Indeed, ecstasy couriers are hardly an upscale bunch. The Customs source notes with some amusement that many of the mules recruited by the Orgad network used their $10,000 fee as a down payment on a trailer home.

CUSTOMS AND THE DEA HAVE LABELED ecstasy "agony" in order to raise awareness about the dangers of the drug, but unlike crack or cocaine before it, ecstasy seems to have negligible social effects. "Crack is categorically an addictive sub-

stance, so the crack epidemic was much easier for people to understand," says Daytop Village's Porteus. "Unlike crack or cocaine, ecstasy is the sort of drug people use to compensate for something rather than to fulfill a craving."

While nearly every week brings the arrest of a newer, more powerful ecstasy baron who seems to have been plucked right out of the cocaine era, there hasn't been the kind of gang violence seen in the late eighties and early nineties. "Ecstasy itself might not cause violent crime," acknowledges Brennan of the DEA. But she predicts that "there will be a rise in violence associated with organized crime as a result of the ecstasy trade." Some cities, like Chicago, aren't taking any chances. In response to a series of ecstasy-related overdoses in the city (most of which were due to pills laced with a deadly drug called PMA, or paramethoxyamphetamine), the City Council there passed an "anti-rave" ordinance, which makes holding such a party punishable by a $10,000 fine. One Chicago police officer even vowed to the Chicago *Tribune* that "if D.J.'s know it's dangerous to come to Chicago… they may think twice about coming here."

But to those who use the drug, such moral panic is hard to understand, much less agree with. "I really don't understand what the big deal is. Yeah, you might get a little too happy, a little too emotional; you might even say some really stupid, cheesy things you regret later. And yeah, there can be a pretty harsh comedown if you overdo it," argues one user. "But compared to crack or coke? Please! When was the last time you saw two crackheads hugging?"

Note: *Names of ecstasy users and dealers have been changed in this story.*

Laundering

American Banks and the War on Drugs

U.S. banks are the largest financial beneficiaries of the drug trade

By Stephen Bender

When discussing the war on drugs, the political class and hence the mainstream media focus their collective heft on military intervention in the South and mass incarceration in the North. The targets, almost invariably, are the poor and brown. Yet, an understanding of the drug trade's machinations is incomplete without an analysis of the crucial role transnational banks play in the laundering of drug proceeds. Indeed, Washington is proclaiming its readiness to take the "drug war" to the jungles of Colombia in an El Salvador-style intervention, while the real beneficiaries of the drug trade repose much closer to home.

That was the finding by none other than a minority report written by House Democrats on the Permanent Subcommittee on Investigations last year. "Despite increasing international attention and stronger anti-money laundering controls, some current estimates are that $500 billion to $1 trillion in criminal proceeds are laundered through banks worldwide each year, with about half of that amount moved through United States banks."

A large proportion of the conservatively estimated $250 billion in ill-gotten funds is derived from the drug trade, predominantly cocaine. That enormous sum, the Subcommittee determined, makes Uncle Sam's banks collectively the world's largest financial beneficiaries of the drug trade.

James F. Sloan, Director of the Financial Crimes Enforcement Network, (FinCEN) a subdivision of the Department of the Treasury, was also less than sanguine, when commenting on the current state of affairs. Testifying before the Congressional Subcommittee on Criminal Justice, Drug Policy and Human Resources in June of 2000, Sloan stated, "money laundering is the lifeblood of narcotics trafficking and other financial crimes.

These criminal organizations now dwarf some of the world's largest legitimate business enterprises, laundering enormous sums of money throughout the international financial system."

Raymond Baker, a career international businessperson and analyst associated with the Center for International Policy and the Brookings Institution, testified before the same Subcommittee. Noting "An absolute explosion in the volume of dirty money during this, the first decade of the globalizing world," Baker quoted U.S. Treasury Department estimates that "99.9 percent of the laundered criminal money that is presented for deposit in the United States gets comfortably into secure accounts."

So, we find testimony before Congress exploding the pious rhetoric about the drug war. If Uncle Sam is capable of interdicting only 0.1 percent of the dreaded drug kingpin's "life blood," then what exactly are we getting for our nearly $20 billion in drug war largesse?

The key institution in the enabling of money laundering is the "private bank," a subdivision of every major U.S. financial institution. Private banks exclusively seek out a wealthy clientele, the threshold often being an annual income in excess of $1 million. With the prerogatives of wealth comes a certain regulatory deference.

The General Accounting Office, (GAO), the research arm of Congress, reported in late 1999 on the difficulties surrounding the regulation of private banks. "It is difficult to measure," the report comments, "precisely how extensive private banking is in the United States, partly because the area has not been clearly defined and partly because financial institutions do not consistently capture or publicly report information on their private banking activities." As a result, estimates at the cumulative value of "private banking" assets are difficult to estimate, but the total undoubtedly reaches well into the trillions of dollars.

That U.S.-based private banks operate in a regulatory twilight zone enabling the laundering of drug profits is confirmed by the GAO. Private banks are "not subject to the Bank Secrecy Act," thus exempting banks from complying with "specific anti-money-laundering provisions… such as the one requiring that suspicious transactions be reported to U.S. authorities."

Instead of monitoring formal compliance, U.S. banking regulators "try to identify what efforts the branches are making to combat money laundering." In determining whether the off-shore branches are doing an adequate job in screening for money laundering, regulators "must rely primarily on the banks' internal audit functions to verify that the procedures are actually being implemented in offshore branches where U.S. regulators may be precluded from conducting on-site examinations.

Not only is government oversight lax, but banks are willfully ignorant about their own client's account holdings, an outgrowth of the cult of secrecy surrounding private banking. The Subcommittee on Investigations report continued: "The reality right now is that private banks allow clients to have multiple accounts in multiple locations under multiple names and do not aggregate the information. This approach creates vulnerabilities to money laundering by making it difficult for banks to have a comprehensive understanding of their own client's accounts." Some banks go so far as to forbid their employees to keep information linking clients to their accounts and shell corporations. One private banker told the Subcommittee that he "had 30–40 clients, each of which had up to fifteen shell corporations and, to keep track, he and other colleagues in the private bank used to create private lists of their clients' shell companies. He said that he and his colleagues had to hide these 'cheat sheets' from bank compliance personnel who, on occasion, conducted surprise inspections to eliminate this information from bank files. When asked why the bank would destroy information he needed to do his job effectively, the former private banker simply said that it was bank policy not to keep this information in the United States."

The report then quoted the Federal Reserve's 1998 "system wide study," which analyzed the practices of seven private banks. The study concluded, "That internal controls and oversight practices over private banking activities were generally strong at banks that focused on high-end domestic clients, while similar controls and oversight practices were seriously weak at banks that focused on higher risk Latin American and Caribbean clients."

The reasons for the disparity are not complicated, the Subcommittee concluded. "Federal Reserve officials told the Subcommittee staff that private banking has become a 'profit driver' for many banks, offering returns twice as high as many other banking areas. Private banks interviewed by the Subcommittee staff have confirmed rates of return in excess of 20 percent."

In such a profitable business, competition is fierce, which leads to a whole host of other problems as outlined in a 1997 Federal Reserve report on private banking. "As the target

market for private banking is growing, so is the level of competition among institutions that provide private banking services. Private banks interviewed by the Subcommittee staff confirm that the market remains highly competitive; most also reported plans to expand operations. The dual pressures of competition and expansion are disincentives for private banks to impose tough anti-money laundering controls that may discourage new business or cause existing clients to move to other institutions." In short, a rising tide of coca funds lifts all banks.

Apart from the institutional competitive forces at work, the Subcommittee found that private bankers and their clientele operate under a symbiotic relationship in which the banker identifies more closely with the client than with the duty to uphold the law.

The textbook case of this shady entente came in 1995 in a massive money laundering scandal involving the former president of Mexico's brother, Raul Salinas de Gotari, and Citibank. The case only came to light after Salinas was implicated in the assassination of Ruiz Massieu, a prominent member of Mexico's corrupt and now largely discredited Institutional Revolutionary Party (PRI). Subsequent investigations linked Salinas to the cocaine cartels that paid staggering bribes in the hundreds of millions to the political class in the early 1990s.

Citibank's private banker catering to Salinas was Amy Elliot. As the most senior private banker in New York dealing with Mexican clients, Elliot took the word of Carlos Hank Rohn (an oligarch recently linked by the Mexican press to the drug trade) in setting up the Salinas accounts. Salina's only known source of income was his annual government salary of $190,000 in addition to funds derived from his work in the "construction business" and his proximity to the president. In testimony before the Subcommittee, Elliot recounted that she estimated in June 1992 that the Salinas accounts had "[p]otential in the $15–$20M range." After multiple appeals, Salinas now sits in a Mexican prison.

In a June 29, 1993 email, shortly after the account passed the $40 million mark, Elliott wrote to a colleague in Switzerland: "This account is turning into an exciting profitable one for us all. [M]any thanks for making me look good." Salinas eventually deposited "in excess of $87 million" by way of Citibank's New York headquarters.

Although the case of Citibank and Raul Salinas generated some media interest and nudged banks to revise their internal regs, the Subcommittee found that banks had "set up systems to ensure that private banker activities are reviewed by third parties, such as supervisors, compliance personnel or auditors. The Subcommittee staff investigation has found, however, that while strong oversight procedures exist on paper, in practice private bank oversight is often absent, weak or ignored."

Another bark worse than bite facet of the drug war lies in the punishment meted out by our "zero tolerance" drug warriors to high level money laundering bankers, such as Amy Elliot and her superiors. This was a point not neglected by Kenneth Rijock, testifying before the aforementioned Government Reform Subcommittee. Rijock spoke before Congress with a background as a former "career money launderer" whose operations were based in Florida. Now a government consultant on dirty money matters, Rijock obliquely touched on the drug war's hypocrisy. "No federally chartered commercial bank has ever lost its charter for money laundering violations, no matter how serious the crime. Senior bank officers themselves are rarely indicted for money laundering; the institution simply pays a multi-million dollar fine.… Only now are we going to name and ostracize the most blatant offshore tax haven banks; we still don't indict their presidents and directors for violations of the Money Laundering Control Act." That, likely is a manifestation of the standard practice in the American justice system that "suite crime" is punished much less harshly than "street crime."

In recent years, government efforts to more effectively intercept laundered funds have been rebuffed. In 1998, the Clinton administration proposed new rules governing the reporting of banks to the government on suspicious financial transactions. The government correctly insisted that more invasive regulations were necessary to make headway against money launderers. Opponents, across the political spectrum, from the ACLU to the Cato Institute (cheered on by the banks who played a low-key role) created a firestorm of public opposition. John J. Byrne, senior council for the American Bankers Association, responded tersely to the proposed preliminary reporting to the government on suspicion of illegal activity. "We don't support the notion that we need to investigate, profile, and monitor account activity."

A subsequent attempt by the Clinton administration in January 2001 to monitor the accounts of foreign leaders laundering funds in American banks fell flat. As the *New York Times* put it: "Citigroup was among a consortium of leading New York banks that led an effort in late December to water down the new guidelines. The banks, members of the New York Clearing House, complained that the guidelines were too 'sweeping' and were based on 'unrealistic' expectations.…" Although law enforcement authorities considered the proposed regulation "too weak," Justice Department officials "signed off on the voluntary guidelines." At issue was the monitoring of accounts held by foreign leaders and their families, based on the experiences of the Salinas case and others.

The point is not to apply the level of 4th Amendment protection currently enjoyed by street dealers and casual users to bankers. Rather, it is to recognize the struggle facing governments attempting to meaningfully deter drug-related money laundering. From there, consideration of decriminalization is crucial.

The problem goes deeper than one government's futile struggle. The drug trade has successfully learned to mimic the tricks of international banking and commerce, copying the methods of "legitimate" business. The favored tool in this endeavor is the use of tax havens—often used to disguise sundry forms of financial swindling. As Raymond Baker commented: "In fact, the easiest thing for criminals to do is to make their criminal money look like it is merely corrupt or preferably commercial tax-evading money, and when they do it passes readily into foreign accounts. With American and European banks and corporations aggressively competing to service gains from cor-

ruption and illegal flight capital, money laundering is almost universally successful."

The State Department admits as much when they annually categorize the world's nations based on their adherence to Washington's ground rules for drug war probity. Unsurprisingly then, Foggy Bottom finds among its "high priority" money laundering countries, the leading "free market" states: the U.S., UK, Germany, Italy, the Netherlands, Canada, and Switzerland.

While decrying the undermining of "democratic market economics" by the hemorrhaging of capital from the South, Baker conceded that the wealthy countries ultimately benefit. "The costs and benefits of the components of dirty money which we facilitate, i.e., yields from corruption and commercial tax evasion, merit clear analysis. The benefit is that it spreads several hundred billion dollars annually across North America and Europe, in bank accounts, markets and properties. The cost can be seen in the impact on both our domestic and foreign interests." Baker, the former international businessperson, then very succinctly elucidates the issue, sounding rather like a leftist. "The foreign cost of our pursuit of corrupt riches and illegal flight capital is that it erodes our strategic objectives in transitional economies and impairs economic progress in developing countries, draining hard currency reserves, heightening inflation, reducing tax collection, worsening income gaps, canceling investment, and hurting competition, all contributing to political instability."

The essential issue is neither the lack of adequate government oversight, nor the malfeasance of banks individually or collectively, although they are symptoms of the problem. Rather, the problem lies in the triumph of market forces over government and civil society.

As the late British academic Susan Strange pointed out in her 1998 book *Mad Money,* there are three distinct market forces driving the drug trade. The first is the "market for banking services" which has exploded in this era of intensified globalization of capital and integration of world markets. The second relates to the "market for hallucinatory or mood altering drugs," which has remained consistently strong for some 30 years. The final component, Stange comments, "is often overlooked in transnational organized crime… the market for [licit] tropical crops." To an impoverished peasant attempting to feed his family, it is economically irrational to grow coffee, cocoa or bananas (whose values fluctuate at meager levels) at a subsistence level when cocoa growing enables a substantially better livelihood. Moreover, it is hypocritical for the leaders of the rich countries to expect them to do so.

A further dodge lies in placing the blame on "offshore" banks. The Cayman Islands for instance, according to Ken Silverstein writing in *Mother Jones,* "with 570 banks holding $670 billion is now the 6th largest financial center in the world after London, Tokyo, New York, Berlin, and Zurich." Then again, what other options do these otherwise economically stagnant countries have? Lacking land and labor, the ability to attract capital is their "comparative advantage," and its pursuit is conducted with the otherwise much lauded "entrepreneurial spirit." It is further worth noting another facet of what *Le Monde Dip-*

lomatique last year called the "dirty money archipelago." Namely, that money launderers among others "take advantage of the existence of 250 free [trade] zones and tax havens, 95 percent of which are former British, French, Spanish, Dutch or U.S. colonies or concessions that remain dependent on the former colonial powers."

Analyzed in the broadest sense, the drug war has unleashed horrendous destruction on the very people it is supposedly designed to save. The wages of this war are eroded civil liberties, incarceration as a preferred social policy, a steady stream of violence as various gangs compete for a share in an illicit market, and the further corruption of many Latin American governments. Note however, that the powerful uniformly benefit from it. Banks reap massive profits, the military is given a further rationale for its ballast, the corporate sector obtains new invest-ment opportunities (prisons) and markets (para-military gear and counterinsurgency weaponry), and the state obtains a post-Cold War justification for foreign intervention. In short, a class war by other means.

The drug war, understood as a campaign to ameliorate the scourge of drug addiction, is a fraud. The greatest scandal, beyond even the connivance of the great banks in a drug trade, is that this fraud is today being deployed as a justification for war. The United States is sending $1.3 billion to Colombia to fight the "narcoterrorists," Americans are told. It was not a coincidence that Clinton accompanied 30 CEOs when he visited Cartagena to inaugurate "Plan Colombia." Unless enough Americans can see through this audacious propaganda, a lie fortified by a fraud, our government may well carry out the bloodiest pacification program since Vietnam.

Stephen Bender has written on topics of interest for the *San Francisco Bay Guardian* and Salon.com.

America's War on Drugs

Lawmakers, CEOs, police chiefs, academics and artists talk about one of the most controversial issues of our time

Since 1968, the United States has spent increasing amounts of taxpayers' money—more than $40 billion last year—trying to stop drug use through the criminal-justice system. Three-fourths of federal anti-drug money goes to police, prisons, border patrol and interdiction efforts in countries like Colombia. Only one-fourth goes to prevention and treatment. Thirty years after war was declared, there are no fewer drug addicts but more people in prison for drug crimes than ever before. Half a million of America's 2 million prisoners are locked away for drugs, and 700,000 people are arrested each year for marijuana possession alone. In 2001, a record seventy-four percent of Americans say they believe the Drug War is failing. The majority say drug addiction should be approached as a disease, not a crime. In these pages, we asked lawmakers, scientists, police and law-enforcement officials, prominent journalists, musicians, academics, business leaders and authors to contribute to a newly energized debate about the future of American drug policy. Even President Bush's nominee to head the Drug Enforcement Administration, Republican congressman Asa Hutchinson, admits that the public is frustrated and that change is necessary. "We need to show that we're not simply trying to put nonviolent users in jail," he tells *Rolling Stone*. The War on Drugs has become a war against the nation's citizens. The time for drug-law reform is now.

Jann S. Wenner

Dan Rather
Anchor and Managing Editor,
The CBS Evening News

There's a general sense that what we have been doing in the so-called Drug War simply doesn't work. And the situation, in many important ways, has gotten worse, not better. There's a sense that we're in a losing game, and you don't stay in a losing game. So what should we do now? I agreed with [Clinton drug czar] Barry McCaffrey when he said it's been a mistake to do it as a war. He thought a better comparison is cancer. We've been in the fight against cancer with the real and certain knowledge that it's going to be long, and there's no

magic bullet. You have to keep experimenting. You have to keep researching. You have to go one small step at a time.

Things have gotten better in recent years. And I don't think journalism has led the public; I think it's the other way around. Honest people can differ about this, but this business of the press turning people against the Vietnam War... people didn't question the war until Johnny down the street came back in a flag-draped casket. Until that happened in every neighborhood, it was easy to see the war as something happening "over there." Maybe the same thing is happening in the Drug War. As long as people could believe it was confined to the wrong side of the

tracks or the elite that had money to buy fancy drugs, it was easy to say, "Whatever the police and government say is all right with me." But when Drug War casualties began to mount in the suburbs, people's eyes began to open.

John Timoney
Police Commissioner of the City of Philadelphia

Right now, the extremes govern policy. For example, the crack epidemic in the late Eighties was a big concern, but politicians overreacted by creating this difference between crack cocaine and powder cocaine.

Without a doubt, you feel bad when you send people to prison who need treatment. But very few people in jail are there for first-time possession.

The ones who are particularly affected by drugs are the minority communities. We get a lot of pressure to clean up neighborhoods where there are four or five drug dealers on the block. But then we also hear another cry: You're incarcerating a whole generation, giving up on too many people. Some members of the minority community may see an effort toward drug legalization as whites trying to continue genocide through drugs in the black community. The important thing is that you need to make sure the minority community is involved in this discussion.

Orrin Hatch
U.S. Senator, Utah (Republican)

I don't think there's any law that can prevent a teenager from taking that first puff of a marijuana cigarette, that first sniff of cocaine. If I knew what it was, I would dedicate my career to passing it. But we need more education. When you have a young person who has experimented, you know how fast they can get in trouble on methamphetamine. We have to get some treatment for them. We haven't concentrated as we should on first-time offenders. They can get drugs in jails, but there's no real education in the jails, and no treatment.

Keep in mind, treatment alone won't do it. Enforcement alone won't do it. Education alone won't do it.

We have to reduce both the demand for and the supply of drugs. The movie *Traffic* drives home the point that law enforcement alone won't solve the problem. And a lot of people have had to face the fact that their own children have experienced drugs. First-time use of drugs has gone way up. If you look at Ecstasy alone, use by tenth- and twelfth-graders is up sharply. A huge portion of those who used heroin for the first time last year were under eighteen. Like anything else, back in the 1980s, we thought we were right. There were too many judges being too permissive. But I do think it's time to re-evaluate and look for the injustice. And where there's injustice, correct it. The sentencing laws have worked to a large degree because people aren't being treated with disparity now the way they were. So there was a need for uniform standards for judges. But we've seen some flaws and some intractability.

I think marijuana is a gateway drug; nobody can deny that. And I get furious when I hear people say it's harmless. This is not the same marijuana that was used in the Sixties and Seventies. Potency is way up. We know that if you stop a kid from even smoking before twenty-one, they'll probably never touch drugs. If they start on marijuana, there's a high propensity to go on to harder drugs.

Bernard C. Parks
Chief of Police, Los Angeles Police Department

It's a failed policy to call anything a war when you're addressing issues in the community—when you declare war on your own community. There are many sides to address—the supply-and-demand side, prevention, intervention, rehabilitation, enforcement.

The hardest thing for most people to do is hold themselves responsible and show strength of will and character. In order for addicts to change, there must be some reward that forces them to do what they need to do, a lever to hold them to accountability.

It's hard to take crime out of the drug equation. The Department of Justice has done forecasting figures—random drug tests on people arrested on non-narcotic charges. Seventy to eighty percent of them had drugs in their system. In the city of L.A., drugs are intertwined with many of our crimes.

Our financing goes to the most sexy part: arresting people. It's not as sexy to put money into prevention and education. We need more K–12 education, and when we see early uses of gateway drugs—alcohol, cigarettes, marijuana—we need to intervene and double our educational efforts. We need to make the penalties for using and selling unattractive to people. Right now, people are going into custody as addicts and coming out as addicts. People also get out of jail and have no supervision. We have to have rehabilitation. We need a broader strategy focusing on education and health. It's not just about capturing seventeen tons of drugs a year. We know that if there's no demand for drugs, there's no market. We're still trying to figure out what the impact of Proposition 36 will be.

Proposition 36 views drug use as a singular crime or event when, often, it is inter-related with other crimes—auto theft, for example. Many of our bank robbers are doing it to fulfill their drug needs. If people have the ability to beat their drug habit,

they do it. But without a hammer hanging over their head, they don't. We're going to give them one or two chances without the hammer.

If you look at the records, most people we arrest are not just into marijuana, but a myriad of things. That's common. Look at Al Capone. They got him not on murder but on taxes.

Asa Hutchinson
U.S. Representative, Arkansas (Republican) Nominee, Administrator of the Drug Enforcement Administration

The War on Drugs has been successful in terms of individual lives saved and the billions of young people who have declined to use drugs. We're sending the right message to kids: Drugs are very bad, they're illegal, and don't experiment or use them. That must be articulated in a way kids understand.

We have to concentrate on high-level dealers. We need to show that we're not simply trying to put nonviolent users in jail. One way to do this, for example, is drug courts. I'm a strong advocate of drug courts—the threat of prison with long-term rehabilitation.

As a member of Congress—and I will continue this if I get the opportunity to head the DEA—I've supported steps to prevent racial profiling. We also need to diminish sentencing guidelines between crack cocaine and powder cocaine.

Currently you get a five-year sentence for 500 grams of powder, but only five grams of crack lands you the same prison time.

Marijuana can be a used as a gateway drug, and I believe that has been shown anecdotally and statistically. The current move toward legalization of drugs such as marijuana is harmful and sends the wrong message to young people.

Barney Frank
U.S. Representative, Massachusetts (Democrat)

Getting high on marijuana means you're rebellious, while getting drunk on beer means you're a good old boy. But ask any cop whether he'd rather go into a house full of people high on marijuana or one full of people drunk on beer. They'll tell you they'd much rather deal with people on marijuana.

I introduced legislation in the Massachusetts legislature to legalize marijuana twenty-five years ago. I currently have two bills on the subject. One would change the penalties for people currently in prison on marijuana charges—we ought to be letting them out, except in the most egregious cases. The other would permit medical marijuana. Of course medical marijuana ought to be legal. A lot of my friends on the left think that the public is on our side and it's always the politicians who are blocking everything good. I don't happen to think that's true. I don't think the public is as far left as some of my friends do. But on drug policy, the public is ahead of the politicians. You see it in the referenda [on medical marijuana]. The public is actually more sensible. The politicians are all afraid of being tagged "soft on drugs."

We need to stop the prosecution of users and low-level dealing of a bag or two. I would certainly make the use of marijuana not a crime, but I wouldn't change the rules on large-scale distribution.

Gary Johnson
Governor of New Mexico

I am forty-eight. I smoked pot when I was younger. I didn't get screwed up on pot, and I didn't know anybody who did. The reason I talk about legalization is, somebody has to sell people their drugs. You ask a room of a thousand people if you think you should go to jail for smoking pot. Nobody's hand goes up. Ask how many think you should go to jail for selling a small amount; a few hands go up. Ask how many think someone selling a lot of pot should go to prison, and a lot of hands go up. And I always say, "That's hypocrisy."

The two major criticisms of legalizing marijuana are: You're sending the wrong message to kids, and, use will go up. My problem is, we're measuring success on use. We should toss that out. If you or I read tomorrow that alcohol use was up by three percent, we wouldn't care. We understand that use goes up or down. What we care about is, is DWI up or down? Is incidence of violence up or down? Are alcohol-related diseases up or down? Those same rules ought to apply to drugs. We ought to be concerned about violent crime, hepatitis C, HIV, turf warfare among drug gangs and nonviolent users behind bars. Those are all distinct harms caused by drugs under our current policy.

If I were the dictator—and I'm not—and I had to set up a distribution system for marijuana tomorrow, it would be similar to liquor. I'd allow sales at liquor establishments. People say, "There will be bootleg pot." And there probably would be for a little while. But then it would die out. Why would you buy bathtub gin when you can buy Tanqueray?

The idea of a drug pusher is a myth. Most drug transactions are buyers seeking sellers. When I talk about legalization of other drugs, I adopt the term "harm reduction." What we're really after is reduction of the harms that drugs—and drug policy—do. If we can move from a criminal model to a medical model, we'll be going a long way.

I was elected in 1994, and I have been re-elected but cannot run for a third term under our term-limits law. People talk about being courageous. I'm living evidence of why term limits should be in effect. Would I have brought this issue out if I thought I could be elected to a third term? I don't know. I raised the legalization issue after my re-election. In the first term, I talked about the failure of the Drug War and that arresting people isn't going to work. But it wasn't until the second term that I made a conscious decision to turn up the volume and search out some solutions.

Loretta Sanchez
U.S. Representative,
California (Democrat)

When I was growing up, my youngest uncle was a heroin addict. I saw directly for about ten years the effect of that addiction: It manifested itself in his inability to hold a job; he was sent over and over to the California state penitentiary system, sometimes for heroin use, most of the time for armed robbery or breaking and entering; he would commit crimes to get money; he would go for a stint to prison, get as clean as you can get in that situation. He would write me a letter every two weeks, he would get out, then the problem was how to get a job, so he would end up using again. When I was eighteen, my mother and grandmother had to go to San Francisco and ID his body—he was found in a hotel room with a bullet between his eyes.

For every person we're putting into a drug court who gets diverted into drug treatment, there's got to be thirty who go straight to prison. What are they learning there? They are co-habitating with people who are hardened criminals and drug users. It would be much better if we did more

of these drug courts, where you get a second chance.

Henry A. Waxman
U.S. Representative,
California (Democrat)

We've always put the emphasis on the supply side when we ought to put the emphasis on the demand side. We ought to be making treatment available to anyone who wants it, to get a handle on addiction. That's clear. If you look at the voters in California, they were pretty clear [on Proposition 36]. They'd rather have people go to treatment than to a jail cell. How much longer can we keep warehousing people? It's not doing any good, and you can argue it's doing considerable harm.

I'm not sure the debate is really opening up. I'm not sure "everybody" is saying the Drug War is a failure and we ought to be doing more treatment and education than enforcement. I've always been against mandatory minimums, for example. Judges should have the discretion to decide each individual case on its merits. But you have to look at the people in control of the committees in the Congress. Maybe Hatch is saying some new things right now about drug treatment over incarceration. But he's the chair of the Judiciary Committee in the Senate, and if he believes these things, he could do something about it.

Dave Matthews
Musician

If you look at the generations that came before, I don't think youth have become more wild. Maybe they're more armed now, but young people have always been adventurous. We say that our young people shouldn't be using drugs, so we give them a little speech about how they'll become worse people, we give them some sort of minimalist education, and then we punish them for experimenting. We don't fix the problem—all we do is increase the problem. It turns the slight, adventurous recklessness of youth into criminal behavior. It's like we're manufacturing criminals. Whoever came up with the idea of restricting financial aid for drug offenses? He needs to be in prison.

At this point—and I don't want to be too cynical—the financial gain from building prisons has become what keeps the Drug War going. It's the one thing in America right now that I just find offensive. And in this climate, there's no limit to how violated our rights to privacy can be. When you live in a country that has insane laws like America's drug laws, then it is hard to argue for our privacy rights and our civil rights, because with the laws the way they are, we don't have any rights. I mean, if I get caught with a bag of pot, then, "You're going downtown, baby"—what kind of madness is that? If we're in an environment where that sort of crazy behavior is tolerated, test the mailman and see if he's been smoking pot on the weekend, or make the kid who's walking your dog take a urine test to make sure he's not high while he's watching Bingo poop on the lawn.

If the Drug War was halted tomorrow morning, the drug use in this country would not change a bit. The only thing that would change is that people would stop getting their heads blown off in the street trying to get their smack on the corner. There are so many arguments for stopping the Drug War and very few for keeping it going. It's just a distraction from real problems in the world. You know, hunger and bad education fall to the wayside when you have to deal with this imaginary plague that's destroying our country.

Carl Hiaasen
Novelist and Columnist

One of the first novels I wrote was *Powder Burn*, about the Colombians moving into the cocaine trade in south Florida. The bloodshed in those days was quite spectacular. This is in '79, '80, '81, and the only change in all that time is they've become a lot more considered about where and when they kill each other. It's done less publicly now. But the basic elements of the drug trade haven't changed. Every day there's another freighter from Haiti busted and there are tons and tons of cocaine in the hold.

The irony is, the price of a kilo on the street isn't much different than it was ten years ago. That tells you there is plenty of supply and plenty of demand. Lots and lots of people in jail, and the only difference is they're different people than they were back then. Or maybe not, actually.

I live in the Keys, which has been a smuggler's paradise forever. Many of the people I know here who are legitimate fishing guides and businessmen now were in the smuggling business once. Quite a few spent time in jail. Did it stop the smuggling? No. When I moved to the Keys from Fort Lauderdale in 1993, they took down the en-

tire Coast Guard station at Isla Morada. The Coasties were seizing drugs and then selling them. They were running a cocaine operation out of the Coast Guard station.

In 1983 and '84, I spent some time riding around with DEA street agents when I was writing for the *Miami Herald*. They weren't cowboys. They were pretty smart guys. They had a pick of deals they could be doing. Cocaine one day, heroin the next, marijuana the day after that. Every day, they were throwing people in the can. And, to a person, every one thought he was on the right side but making no difference at all.

I remember once, up by Homestead, they had a deal for a tractor-trailer full of marijuana, and the deal is going on in a Holiday Inn somewhere, and I'm sitting in a car with a DEA guy. Drug dealers are the most hapless people. They're always late, always f--king up. And we're waiting for the call to go rushing in and bust everybody. Two kids ride by on their bikes. They don't see us because of our tinted windows. One pulls out a joint and lights it up, right in front of a DEA agent. The agent just laughs and says, "You see how we're not going to stop this?" Now we're fifteen years later, and it's just as easy to get whatever you want.

I've seen whole neighborhoods destroyed by crack cocaine, and it's terrible. The question is, Would it be better or worse if it wasn't illegal? Would there be less killing? It's something worth considering. The same conservative pinheads who trot out their actuarial tables on lives saved per dollar spent on environmental regulations ought to be doing the same calculations on what it costs to lock up thousands and thousands of people—locking up Dad and sending Mom to the welfare office.

Scott Weiland
Musician

Prison isn't appropriate for drug users, if you're nonviolent. If you're a junkie or a crackhead or whatever, and do an armed robbery and someone gets injured, it's not nonviolent anymore. You could've made the decision to go on Santa Monica Boulevard and suck c--k. That's what I would do rather than hold a bank up. You don't throw people in prison because they suffer from bipolar disorder, or a personality disorder, or any of those mental deficiencies. And there's no difference, really. If somebody

has narcolepsy and falls asleep at the wheel, they're not going to go to prison for it.

One of the worst problems with drug offenders going to prison is the mandatory minimums. That's really where you see how it's pointed toward people of color and people who don't have money. There are people doing longer prison sentences for drugs in some states than the people doing time for murder. I know there are some experimental programs in Europe where you are a government-sanctioned heroin addict, and you register as you do a person on methadone. I don't think legalizing drugs is going to create more addicts. It might inspire more people to try it out, but not everyone's geared for that. Alcohol is legal, and most people aren't alcoholics.

Norm Stamper
Chief of Police, Seattle, 1994–2000

I've been a lawman thirty-four years. I think our national drug strategy that has spanned both Democratic and Republican administrations has been a total failure. I have no problem with spending time, money and imagination in attempting to interdict drug trafficking and those making obscene amounts of money trading illicit drugs. Those people rank, in my estimation, pretty damn low on the scale of social legitimacy. But dealers are there for reasons that anyone in a capitalist society ought to understand. There is a huge demand for illegal drugs, and as individuals who are also armed want to expand their share of the market, we wind up with a whole lot of cops, dealers and innocent citizens finding themselves literally in the line of fire.

If I were king for a day and was going to learn from history, I would, in fact, decriminalize drug possession. Legalization is a different concept. Decriminalization acknowledges the fact that we set out to criminalize certain types of behavior, most notably during Prohibition, and we found that was an abysmal failure. We decriminalized the possession of booze. We criminalized other substances and demonized those who use them and, in the process, created an outlaw class that includes everybody from a senator's wife to the addict curled up in a storefront doorway.

I'd use regulation and taxation of these drugs, much as we do with alcohol and tobacco, to finance prevention, education and treatment programs. I can't think of a stronger indictment of our current system than that there are addicts who don't want to be addicts queuing up for treatment and can't get it because we're spending too much money on enforcement and interdiction. I would regulate, and I would tax, and I would stiffen penalties for those selling to minors or those who hurt another person while under the influence. And that includes driving under the influence.

We've pursued this terrible policy because we've attached huge moral import to this issue: that it's immoral to think about decriminalization. That it's immoral to think about the government regulating everything from production to distribution. Any politician or police official who speaks out for a sane course of action is seen as soft on crime, and demonized as well. It's not an easy sell to talk to an African-American mom who has three or four children, some of them teenagers, about decriminalization when she's doing all she can to keep her kids out of drugs.

I was careful when I was police chief, but I've been saying these things for years. I did suggest that our fear is keeping us from having a conversation. American businesses, perhaps more than anyone else in society, are among the first to raise the question. And I've heard it raised bluntly: Isn't this insane, this policy we're pursuing? The number of men and women in prison is truly staggering compared with twenty or twenty-five years ago. That ought to tell us something.

The biggest obstacle to a saner drug policy is that the current one has become so rigid and unassailable in the circles in which it must be discussed flexibly and intelligently and with open minds. It's a religion. We've accepted on faith that if what we're doing isn't working, let's do more of it. [Former LAPD chief] Daryl Gates addressed a police chiefs' conference in Washington some years ago, and he made a statement that "one thing we're not going to talk about is decriminalization." There's something wrong with talking about it. To start entertaining doubts is a scary thing.

Eric Sterling
President, The Criminal Justice Policy Foundation

In January I spoke at the Drug Policy Forum of Hawaii, a very successful group that got the state legislature to pass a medical-marijuana bill with the governor's support. I asked for shows of hands: "How many of you think the War on Drugs is wrong?" Everybody raised his hand. I asked, "How many of you came to this

opinion in the last year or two?" Nobody raised his hand. I asked, "How many of you think there is a coherent strategy for achieving drug-policy reform?" Almost nobody raised his hand. I asked, "Who are the critical people to reach?" and somebody said, "Young people." I said, "Young people don't vote." Someone else said, "Poor people." I pointed out that they have the least political power.

Instead of preaching to the choir, we need to arrange discussions before chambers of commerce and Wall Street interests—the people who have the Republican Party's car—and explain how this affects the national bottom line. You're not going to move the Republican Party until you move them. Then you have to reach out to labor and teachers and point out how the War on Drugs is inconsistent with the ideals of the labor movement—how it hurts working people, how it damages schools, how it undermines education. You're not going to move the Democratic Party until you move them.

That scene in *Traffic* on the airplane, where the drug czar asks for new ideas and there is an embarrassed silence, is mirrored by the unembarrassed silence from this White House, which, two months in, hadn't named a new drug czar or announced a new policy. This administration has nothing to say on the subject of drugs. The fact that the position went unfilled says something about the position's ultimate emptiness, and perhaps even about the problem's paper-tiger quality. We say "the great drug crisis," but perhaps drugs are just a part of other real crises, such as child abuse, poverty, despair.

Drugs are more available, cheaper and more pure than ever. We still fail to treat the majority of drug addicts. Drug use among eighth-graders went up in the 1990s. High school seniors say heroin and marijuana are more available than ever. And the death rate from drugs has nearly doubled in the Nineties, from 3.2 to 6.3 per hundred thousand. Seventeen thousand deaths last year, from 7,000 in 1990.

People look at Proposition 36 in California and say, "Aha, there's a whole treatment-instead-of-incarceration paradigm shift." I don't think that's very profound. Lip service about treatment has been around for decades. Treatment is being advanced in the context of drug courts, and that's nothing new. When I first started practicing law in 1976, what you'd do for your drug-addicted clients was get them into treatment.

What would be a paradigm shift is a police commissioner saying he's not going to arrest people for possession of drugs. A prosecutor announcing she wasn't going to take drug-possession cases to court. A president commuting the sentences of thousands of nonviolent drug offenders. A legislature willing to decriminalize marijuana, refusing to have arrested those possessing marijuana or growing it in their own home. A superintendent of schools who allows teachers to talk to their students about their own drug experiences in honest discussions about drug use to prevent drug abuse. It would be a shift to give incentives to drug users to turn in dealers who sell adulterated drugs, to help drug users test their drugs for safety. To treat drug users as our children and accept that making it safer to be a drug user is in the public interest. It would be a shift to include drug users, not just recovered addicts, in the making of drug policy. What we do now is like making policy toward Indians and only allowing into the process those Indians who were members of Christian churches and have renounced Native language and Native ways.

David Crosby
Musician

When I was in prison, probably eighty-five percent of the people were there for drugs in one way or another. Either they got caught with drugs, or they got caught selling drugs, or they got caught doing something while they were on drugs, or they got caught doing something terrible for the money to get drugs. So I don't think prison is a valid solution for any kind of drug use or addiction—either one. Addiction is a very tough thing; I've been addicted, and I know what it's like. It requires a lot of treatment—long-term treatment—a lot more treatment than the insurance providers are willing to offer.

I think they should just legalize marijuana. Put it this way—they sell liquor in every corner store in the United States. And booze is much worse for you than marijuana. Much worse. Drastically worse. Orders of magnitude worse. So it doesn't make any sense—they should just legalize it.

Personally, I think we should send some very serious lads from the Army down to the fields where coca is being grown. You've got to understand that we know where all the coca plants are in the Western Hemisphere because all plants have different infrared signatures, and our satellites can locate exactly where they are. We also know, in the four countries where these plants are, what soil and what altitude they're in. We know all that. So send somebody down, take it out of the ground and say, "Look: Plant coffee; we'll buy it directly from you, we'll pay you three times as much because we won't go through a middleman, and you'll be fine. Plant coca again, and we'll be back again next year and somebody will get hurt. This is not all right anymore. Game over. Too many lives ruined, too many families shredded, too much wreckage. We're going to take it seriously now."

Richard Branson
Chairman, The Virgin Group

As far as marijuana is concerned, it's ridiculous that people are given criminal records and have their lives ruined for something that's less dangerous than a cigarette. I definitely support marijuana legalization, but also decriminalization for all drugs if it helps to combat the problem. If taking heroin is an illness, then people need to be given help.

In Liverpool, we have a place where addicts can go to get clean needles for free. They can go there every night, and they know that they can be helped off drugs. Because of this, the prevalence of HIV among drug addicts in Liverpool is low. In Edinburgh, where they don't have this program, the amount of addicts with HIV is much higher.

I used to go to Boy George's home to try and persuade him to get help with his addiction. Two of his friends had already died from drugs. He went to Necker Island to get away from the press and try to get off drugs, but some newspaper called the police and said he should be arrested. So the police arrested him at the point that he was almost clean. They arrested him, and he got back on drugs. The experience made me think that it's not a police matter but a matter of someone who has a problem and needs to get help.

Bob Barr
U.S. Representative, Georgia (Republican)

We finally have, after eight years, an administration that intends to give high priority to the war against mind-altering drugs. Time's a-wasting; I'd like to see some action.

Clinton was AWOL. President Reagan got it right—both he and first lady Nancy Reagan consistently and repeatedly talked publicly about the war against mind-altering drugs, the damage done to our young people, particularly, and the need for society to fight. And it had an impact, making it much easier for law enforcement to operate, because the citizenry was supporting them.

The most disturbing trend I see is the notion that marijuana is a medicine. The drug legalizers, I give them credit—they've been very effective in shifting the focus from drug legalization to medical use of marijuana, which makes it seem very benign. Once they get people to start accepting the notion that marijuana is a positive medicine to help people, that makes it very easy to go to the next drug. It's the most serious policy problem we have out there.

There's a fundamental question: What do we stand for in a society—accountability and rationality and responsibility? Or are we going to become a society that has to be propped up by mind-altering drugs in order to do the things that we want to do as a society?

Paul Wellstone
U.S. Senator, Minnesota (Democrat)

The first time I went to Colombia, they wanted to show me their aerial spraying operation [to eradicate coca and poppy crops]. And they sprayed me, after claiming it was so accurate. Sprayed me good, in fact. So I'm the only person in the U.S. Senate with the authority to speak on that subject.

The leftist revolutionaries aren't Robin Hoods. But the paramilitaries really trouble me. They are too often connected to massacres, and the military is very closely connected to them.

I don't think Plan Colombia [the $1.3 billion U.S. anti-drug aid package] will work because we're not insisting that Colombia's government live up to human-rights conditions. Second, when we spray the coca, we don't provide economic assistance. Third, there is evidence of nausea, skin rashes and other medical problems associated with the spraying. And the fourth reason is, our head is stuck in the sand when it comes to the demand side. I had an amendment on the Plan Colombia bill that would have taken $100 million and put it into drug treatment, and it failed.

William E. Kirwan
President, Ohio State University

The Drug War shows no signs of becoming a deterrent for drug abuse in the U.S. Education is our best hope: Quality educational opportunities for youth in the inner city, where drug abuse is especially high, can provide direction for lives that too often have none. More generally, systematic, persistent and extensive education about the perils of drug use given to all young people in the schools—starting in preschool and continuing through to our colleges and universities—is the best hope for meaningful deterrence.

I have seen both alcohol and drugs destroy the lives of friends and family members. In every case, the abuse began in a social context where the eventual addicts thought they were in complete control of their recreational use of drugs or alcohol. In these personal examples, I've been struck by the fact that the signs of addiction were evident in their behavior before the addiction occurred. The university has many programs that try to educate our students about substance abuse, starting with an orientation for new students and their parents. It's a powerful introduction, which is followed by education programs in different settings throughout the year.

John Gilmore
Computer Entrepreneur and Co-Founder of the Electronic Frontier Foundation

I support the legalization of marijuana. I believe, like Governor Gary Johnson [R-N.M.], that you and I can disagree about whether marijuana is useful, but that's not a reason to lock others up.

We need to stop conflating use with abuse, the choice to use the drug with addiction. The idea that people who use recreational drugs need treatment is false. I've known hundreds of people over the years who've used recreational drugs—teachers, parents, scientists—and who function normally. They're not rolling around on the ground tearing up the yard, yet if they're caught, they'll be kicked out of their jobs and their lives will be ruined. That's a crime. I've contributed money to drug education and research. There's been a lot of misinformation about Ecstasy and club drugs. I've given a significant amount of money to DanceSafe [a club-drug information network]. The largest danger is from adulterated substances, not pure drugs. In a legal market, you'd be able to buy MDMA and know it's pure. DanceSafe checks for adulterants. The only way for adults or teens to make responsible choices is to understand the drugs' long-term effects and addictive qualities, and then make an educated choice.

As an entrepreneur, I'm more tolerant of risk than the average person. I try things people haven't done before and see if they work, things that require a leap of faith. People listening to thirty-five years of anti-drug propaganda aren't willing to take a leap of faith that people they know have been taking drugs, and most of them are doing OK. It's not the end of the world if someone smokes a joint.

Jerry A. Oliver
Chief of Police, Richmond, Virginia

I am not a legalizer. But if you're going to hit the duck, you have to move your gun. This idea that we're going to arrest our way out of the problem isn't going to happen. Even though the politics of the past two decades has been to get tougher and tougher on drug users and drug dealers, the problem has gotten worse.

We have an industrial-strength appetite for drugs in this country—illegal, legal or alcohol. And we have to deal with that. We can't keep drugs out of maximum-security prisons; how are we going to keep them out of the country?

In most of the communities where the sales are made, there isn't enough money to support drug hot spots. The only reason they exist there is young African-American males in particular are willing to put their lives on the line to make that drug transaction, and usually there's a white person coming from the suburbs with the dollar contributing to that trade. Our police nets are able to pull out more African-Americans because they're the easiest ones to catch. Then we play it as if African-Americans are more prone to use drugs and be involved in drug activity. But, really, they're just the ones in the middle. The ones running the big drug operations, and most of the ones buying the drugs to use, are white. But we catch the ones in the middle—the ones selling on the street—because they're easier to catch.

Most homicides are drug- or alcohol-related; most rapes, robberies, child abuse, are generated by some sort of drug nexus. If the drug issue were addressed in a different kind of way, police would be free to do more quality-of-life enforcement. I think

we're on the edge of a lot of Fourth Amendment problems. I'm a police officer, so I argue, "Let's use all the tools available to us and get right up against the line on searches and seizures," because of the pressure of cleaning up those hot spots. A lot of people don't care about the Fourth Amendment. And that concerns me, especially as a black man. It doesn't take a law scholar to go back and look at all the major cases that have come to the Supreme Court—Miranda, Gideon v. Wainwright, Escobedo—all cases that have come about because of police taking advantage of minority people. I want to make sure that policing is professional and people's rights are protected. When we snoop and sneak to nab somebody, it takes away from the luster of the profession's integrity. The pressure to produce gets us into a lot of trouble. That's at the bottom of the racial-profiling issue. I really believe, as an African-American police chief, that we need to not go overboard with violating any rights we have as citizens.

Bill O'Reilly
Anchor, Fox's *The O'Reilly Factor*

Five years ago, I got a midcareer master's degree at the Kennedy School of Government at Harvard. I did one of my theses on coerced drug rehab. In Alabama, they have coerced drug rehab, which means if you're arrested, you get tested—they take hair from your head—and if you're positive, the case goes to the judge, and if you're not violent, you go to drug treatment. If it coincides with a guilty plea, you go to a drug-rehab prison. It's not like the old federal hospital at Lexington, Kentucky; it's tougher. You have to do a certain amount of rehab, and you have to do life-skills training.

The difference between this and the drug-court model is that in Alabama you're held accountable for your performance, and in drug courts you're not. In Alabama, if you have to come back, it's more punitive. Alabama has been doing this for eight or ten years, but has only ramped up in the past five. And the recidivism rate in Alabama is much lower than in other states because they keep addicts on a very short leash.

If you want to solve the drug problem, you cut the demand by taking addicts off the street and putting them in therapeutic centers. It's involuntary—coerced. There would be due process, of course; addicts would have to be convicted of a crime. You

offer them: "Plea-bargain down and go to a therapeutic center." If you cut the demand, the price will drop. Four to six million hard-core drug addicts are a resource that can't be replaced by drug dealers.

I've suggested this idea many times. President Bush asked me to send him my thesis, which I did. The federal government could wipe the drug problem out totally.

Woody Harrelson
Actor

People do drugs to deal with their pain. So you take a person who is in pain, take away their drug and throw them into prison? I don't consider that a very compassionate way to deal with someone who has some kind of issue. But, also, it's hypocritical. It's odd to me; this so-called Drug War is really what I would call a war against noncorporate drugs. I'm not saying that pot cannot be a problem and that it's totally innocuous, because it's a medicine that you can abuse or not abuse. But they basically take away a drug that is at least more natural in dealing with pain, and they say it's OK to use these drugs that are the most addictive and really hard to kick, like pharmaceuticals.

I can remember my mom telling me, "Now, son, if you ever smoke marijuana, I'll be so disappointed," you know, and she's sitting there with her first morning coffee and a cigarette, which are two of the most potent drugs I've ever run into. Incidentally, if you want to make a whole room full of drug addicts violent, cut off the coffee at Starbucks.

Tommy Lee
Musician

God, I've seen it all. I've overdosed and woke up surrounded by guys in white suits going, "Hey, dude, you're lucky to be alive." It was heroin. My buddy was the professional heroin user—I would just f--k with it here and there—he was like, "I'll hook you up," and then all of a sudden, I'm in the hospital. That s--t's like the best high that there is out there, and that's why it's so scary. But I've had friends who are completely in its grasp and can't get out. Heroin's a dangerous one, kids. The guy who sent me to the hospital, about a year after that, he was driving around all f----d up in a convertible Cadillac, and he drove right underneath a semitrailer and got killed. It was early in the morning, he was going over to a buddy of mine's house to score some more dope, and blam! I guess he didn't see the truck coming or nodded out and went right underneath it—no one really knows, but he died.

Peter Singer
Philosopher and Professor of Bioethics, Princeton University

There are simple things we could do that many other countries are doing. In Australia, where I come from, they've implemented a program that provides safe injecting rooms for heroin addicts so they're under supervision in case anything happens. I also support needle exchanges. People can't seem to face the truth: "Just say no" doesn't work.

We should rethink strategies like decriminalization and drug legalization. We need to think about how we can minimize the harm drugs cause and not automatically assume that law enforcement will do that. Legalization may be the way to go, or decriminalization for the possession of a small amount. If we take the drugs out of the hands of the illegal market by letting people grow three or five marijuana plants and not make the possession of small quantities a criminal offense, perhaps the market will drop.

Scott Turow
Novelist

I came on the job [of assistant U.S. attorney] as a child of the Sixties in 1978, and my colleagues viewed drug prosecution with a jaundiced eye. So it was an eye-opener for me to find that drug dealers were genuinely unappetizing. They weren't the nice guy down the hall from whom I scored dope in college. It is a vicious, murky, unlettered world.

My experience as a defense lawyer in narcotics was in night drug court five years or so ago. And I dealt with an enlightened prosecutor who was a breath of fresh air. He said to me, "Most of the people who are here are here because they're poor." He was a hard-nosed career prosecutor, yet he certainly understood the difference between low-level offenders and major drug lords. But I've certainly found that rare.

Clinton took a relentless position on drugs. He stifled a lot of criticism in the liberal community. Once he took office, there were viewpoints that weren't allowed to be heard. I have the misfortune of having actually been informed about this by people in the Justice Department. According to the people I was in touch with, the upper precincts of the Justice Department regarded [criticism of the Drug War] as absolutely politically taboo.

I'm the parent of three adolescents. And everybody draws the line when it comes to their children. That's the problem with decriminalization or legalization: Nobody's going to propose that it be OK to sell drugs to minors. Where there's a market, there will be entrepreneurs, and legalization wouldn't put all drug dealers out of business, because they'd still be selling to people younger than twenty-one. So all high school and college campuses would still be places where illegal drug money is made. And somebody selling cocaine to a sixteen-year-old is going to get in trouble—and should.

Tobias Wolff
Writer

People like getting high, and always have. They've always found ways to get high. There's that constant in human nature. As part of religious ritual, people have found ways to alter their sense of the world from the usual into something else. What's happening now is the absence of ritual that used to surround the process of leaving the everyday. Instead, we punish. Cultures have found ways of creating that moment that is not only respectable but even sacred. But it has passed beyond what is natural to us into something else, and that's because of what is offered out there in contrast to the drug. The obvious thing is to look at schools with bathrooms overflowing, not enough textbooks, ceiling tiles falling. When children are treated like garbage, that's the idea they have of themselves. And the desire to escape that kind of life becomes desperate. You look at kids in the suburbs, who are equally prone to drugs—they're not subjected to the material deprivation, but they do suffer a cultural deprivation. They're not offered much of a place in life except on a conveyor belt.

I have two boys in college—twenty and twenty-two—and an eleven-year-old daughter. Neither boy got in trouble with drugs. Both became extremely interested in music when they were young, and it took up a lot of the slack in their lives that might have made them available to the kinds of influences that can lead to drugs. One kid is in the jazz program at NYU. My other boy was courted by the conservatory at Oberlin for the flute.

I teach at Stanford, and I've been beside myself trying to figure out how to present to my kids—both my own and those in the classroom—a vision of life that's different from what society presents them, which is going to leave them screaming, "This isn't enough!" The media are also at fault—not just for the drugs but for the sense of life they convey. The answer is not to make children feel like they're being corralled into a kind of stockyard. You can't offer young people such limited options and then punish them for trying to break out of that very constricting mind-set.

Jonathan P. Caulkins
Drug-Policy Analyst, Rand
and Carnegie Mellon University's
Heinz School

I started working on drug policy in 1988, at Rand and at Carnegie Mellon. A lot has changed about the drug problem, and not much has changed about the policy. The language is often of epidemics. For many different drugs they exist at a low level of use, then explode. Then use plateaus, and usually tapers off. Sometimes it is a sharp drop-off, sometimes it settles only slightly. My basic question is: How should drug-control policies change over the course of an epidemic?

There is discrimination in criminal justice just as there is in hiring at grocery stores and in media reporting. The racism in our policy manifests in the absence of action, not in the action, necessarily. For example, we passed a set of laws against crack, not because crack is associated with blacks but because crack was spreading like crazy. We were in the explosion phase of the epidemic. Now, fifteen years later, we tolerate those laws even while they fall so heavily on minorities. We failed to repeal those laws when the explosion phase passed and the plateau and decline phases began. I don't condemn the people who went so overboard in 1986. There was a true emergency then. What I criticize us for is not having gone back and changed things now that we're in the plateau stage.

I think it's wrong to even use the term "War on Drugs." It's a term that people who want to critique the drug policy use. It isn't a term the people making the policy use. However, it provides a handy way for critics to make the policymakers look like fools. Drug policy is made in a diffuse way, in many agencies. And the vast majority of people working on it really do care about reducing harm and about justice.

There may well be too many nonviolent offenders in prison, but the way the data are presented is grossly distorted. If you want to make it sound like there are a lot of nonviolent drug offenders in prison, you ask, "How many people are in prison because they were convicted of drug possession?" But you get a much smaller number if you ask, "How many people are in prison because they were arrested for drug possession but nothing else?" Many people are dealers, sometimes very violent ones, but who pleaded down to possession. There's also a big difference between prison and jail, so if you want to inflate the figures, you say "incarcerate." It's hard to get into prison as a person who uses only marijuana and has no other criminal behavior.

Nelly
Musician

I done seen cocaine or heroin straight bring people's lives down to a halt. I done seen people get murdered over it, to a point where, yeah, I think they should be illegal. And I think the law should be fair. I think if there's gonna be a cocaine law, there's gonna be a cocaine law. It shouldn't be a cocaine law and a crack law, 'cause crack is cocaine. Make it one law for everybody. Not for one substance 'cause it's powder. That's s----y. If you gonna make it illegal, make it illegal. That's when it gets segregated.

"Just say no"—I'm with that. We joked about it as kids, but we knew it, you know? Drugs in a lot of urban communities is deeper. It's in the household; it's in the surroundings. Your parents straight ought to let you know that drugs ain't it. My daddy would have beat my ass if it was like that. Flat-out. If you gotta beat a little ass, beat a little ass. Get that point across. Rather beat your ass now than go to your funeral later.

Bob Weir
Musician

The band I'm playing with right now, every now and again we'll take mushrooms. The idea is pretty much on a musical level—to see if we can't kind of blast our way out of the old habits we've fallen into.

I've lost so many friends to heroin and cocaine, I can't really very freely sing the praises of those drugs. But, on the other hand, you have to recognize that they're

there and they're going to be there, and that a certain kind of person's going to find their way into that trap. Whether it be for social reasons or personal psychological reasons, people will find a way into that trap. Society should have compassion to begin with and try to reclaim these lives, as I say. It's self-serving—it would be enlightened self-service for society to do this; it would make these people productive again. I think these drugs should be legal and regulated. There's too much money to be made if they're illegal. I think the only way to trump the cartels is to legalize the drugs, and the cartels will disappear overnight.

The crux of the effort to stop drug abuse shouldn't be in the punishment, because that patently doesn't work. The best plan is to make them available to people who would otherwise be robbing, stealing and killing to get the drugs; just make it available to them, and see if you can't reel them back. Make treatment available, and do research. The government could easily be funding research that could find chemical or other ways of reclaiming the lives that are being lost to these drugs.

Violent drug users should be sent to camp and reprogrammed. I don't think jail's the right place for them. We're talking about reclaiming lives here. One of the problems we're facing now is that there's a prison system that's been set up. For instance, in Texas they have private prisons, and they're trying to do that elsewhere. There's a whole industry now that's dependent on these drug laws to fill their stables full of slaves, basically.

Kay Redfield Jamison
Professor of Psychiatry,
Johns Hopkins University

There's a big group of people who use drugs and alcohol and have major psychiatric illnesses. Patients are often self-medicating or prolonging a mania by getting higher or blotting out the pain they feel. It makes the illness worse and increases the risk of suicide. Kids don't know about depression but have access to drugs. One problem is that by the time we get around to treating the mood disorder, we're also dealing with a substance-abuse problem.

No matter how many times people say addiction is a disease, I don't know how effective it is. People need to understand that addiction is located in the brain—it's biological.

A long time ago, I had a patient who had a severe problem with marijuana and alcohol and was also bipolar. The clinical lore at that time was: Treat the mood problem and the substance abuse will go away on its own. That was a given fifteen years ago, but it's totally untrue.

I feel very strongly that legalization of all kinds of drugs should be publicly debated. Politicians are condemned for even discussing it. I can't believe that on an issue as important as this, we're not talking about all the options. Needle exchange is a perfect example. Not providing needles is exceedingly punitive. Right now, we're sending some of these people to their deaths.

Joe Arpaio
Sheriff, Maricopa County, Arizona

I'm supposed to be the toughest sheriff in the universe. I spent thirty years with the DEA. I'm also president of the International Narcotics Enforcement Officers Association. I'm going into my third term here as sheriff. I'm the guy who puts people in pink underwear and stripes, and runs chain gangs. Sixty to seventy percent of my 7,500 jail inmates are in there for drugs or drug-related crime. I have a great drug-prevention program in jail. Only eight percent come back, and, usually, recidivism is sixty or seventy percent. I'm the guy who gives them green bologna, and I went from giving them three meals to two a day last month. I'm going to have a reunion of all those who I had in my jail and who never came back. We have 500 already signed up.

I was a young federal narcotics officer in Chicago for forty years. The three ways to fight drugs then were enforcement, education and treatment. Today it's the same thing: enforcement, education and treatment. Nothing's changed.

We seized 300 meth labs last year. We should stop complaining and blaming foreign countries. We ought to look at our hometowns. These labs are made right here in the United States.

What changed my attitude since I became sheriff is I now run jails instead of just putting people in jail. I've changed more toward prevention and treatment. We need to do more to get people off drugs while we have them locked up.

When I was an agent, there was a six-month federal hospital in Lexington, Kentucky, where they sent addicts. Maybe we ought to be putting those nonviolent druggies in jail, but instead of going to the regular jail, you're going to a jail that's like a hospital-type thing. I now have 2,000 in my tents. Maybe we ought to do something like that. A jail just for drug users. Send them there and give them a large dose of drug-prevention education and still be eating that green bologna that I feed them.

When I was starting out, we used to say we caught ten percent of the drugs at the border. I'll bet it's still ten percent that we catch at the border. When I was an agent, if you made a two-kilo heroin case it was a headline. Now it has to be tons. I never thought we'd see tons of cocaine.

Our biggest mistake was that we gave up the streets of America to the drug traffickers. Everybody in law enforcement now is going for the biggest case they can find. Everybody wants to make the big conspiracy case, which takes years. We should be out on the streets more, undercover, gathering intelligence. Not busting people for joints but catching the middlemen.

I'm strictly opposed to the military being involved in law enforcement. I've worked in too many countries where the military does law enforcement. I worked with [Nicaraguan Gen. Manuel] Noriega. If you're going to build up an apparatus, build it up with legitimate federal agents. And the FBI should go away. Two agencies shouldn't do the same thing. Drugs should be left to the DEA.

Peter Jennings
Anchor and Senior Editor,
ABC's World News Tonight

I was in Mexico a few weeks ago talking to [President Vicente] Fox, and I asked him if he didn't think it was hypocritical to place the burden on Mexico and not pay more attention to demand. He exploded. He acknowledges that what's already happened in Mexico is the corruption of the Mexican government and military, but he said that almost every political leader in Mexico has always seen the war as a U.S. consumption issue rather than a Latin American production issue. I did an hour in Bolivia back in the mid-1980s. I said, "We're going to show you why the Drug War has failed." It had to do with the Bolivian military operation, and here we are doing the same thing now in Colombia fifteen years later. There's a fairly longstanding notion in the nonminority communities that if those evil Peruvians, Colombians, Mexicans and those dreadful cartels didn't exist, that we'd have less of a dreadful problem in the United States.

The media have been mixed. I, on the air, always make a point of saying "the so-called Drug War." But there's a tendency to accept the line from the drug czar's office on both the nature of the drug problem and the application of resources used to fight it. At the same time, a lot of the critical reporting about the futility of government policy and the seeming reluctance of the political establishment has been done by the establishment press. Ten years ago, the press in some ways believed that if you ran a military campaign, you could really solve the drug problem. We wouldn't have been having this debate ten years ago.

Robert A. Iger
President and Chief Operating Officer, The Walt Disney Co.

Drugs aren't as scarce or as taboo as they ought to be. There are those in the media who are more irresponsible than others. ABC and Disney have behaved extremely responsibly, I think. When you run a company that can affect behavior in the extreme, there's a huge responsibility. I think it's fine for movies and television shows to include story lines about drugs and drug use, but they shouldn't be glorified. And drugs shouldn't be used in humor. There's nothing funny about drugs or people on drugs.

Traffic is an unbelievably important and powerful film. I'd encourage kids to see it. It shows drugs at their cruelest. I think the film's message about treating drugs as an illness instead of merely trying to legislate and regulate is pretty legitimate. I've been in debates with parents who think kids shouldn't see it because it's too rough. Having testified about how movies should be marketed to kids, that's one where I think the responsible thing is for kids to see it.

From *Rolling Stone Magazine*, August 2001. ©2001 by Warner Media LLC. Reprinted by permission.

Stumbling in the dark

**Moral outrage has proved a bad basis for policy on illegal drugs, says Frances Cairncross.
Time for governments to go back to first principles**

IF ONLY it were legitimate, there would be much to admire about the drugs industry. It is, to start with, highly profitable. It produces goods for a small fraction of the price its customers are willing to pay. It has skilfully taken advantage of globalisation, deftly responding to changing markets and transport routes. It is global but dispersed, built upon a high level of trust, and markets its wares to the young with no spending on conventional advertising. It brings rewards to some of the world's poorer countries, and employs many of the rich world's minorities and unskilled.

However, it is an odd business. Its products, simple agricultural extracts and chemical compounds, sell for astonishing prices. A kilo of heroin, 40% pure, sells (in units of less than 100 milligrams) for up to $290,000 on the streets of the United States—enough to buy a Rolls-Royce car. These prices directly reflect the ferocious efforts by the rich countries to suppress drugs. The effect is to drive a massive wedge between

import and retail prices. The import prices of both heroin and cocaine are about 10–15% of retail prices in rich countries. In poor countries, the ratio may be more like 25%. Add a little more for seizures, valued at import prices, and the grand total is probably about $20 billion. That would put the industry in the same league as Coca-Cola's world revenues.

Taken at retail prices, it is almost certainly the world's largest illicit market, although probably smaller than the widely quoted estimate by the United Nations Office of Drug Control and Crime Prevention of $400 billion, which would put it ahead of the global petroleum industry. Every number about the production, consumption and price of drugs involves much guesswork, a warning that applies all through this survey. But global retail sales are probably around $150 billion, about half the sales of the (legitimate) world pharmaceutical industry and in the same league as consumer spending on tobacco ($204 billion) and alcohol ($252 billion).

The estimate of world drug sales comes from Peter Reuter, an economist at the University of Maryland and co-author (with Robert Mac-Coun) of a comprehensive new study of illegal drugs on which this survey frequently draws. He notes that the official estimate of retail drug sales in the United States is $60 billion, making America easily the world's most valuable market. European sales are at most the same again, probably less. Pakistan, Thailand, Iran and China account for most of the world's heroin consumption, but prices are low, and so sales in total are probably worth no more than $10 billion. Add in Australia and Canada; add, too, Eastern Europe and Russia, where sales are growing fast, but probably still make up less than 10% of the world's total. Exclude European marijuana, much of which is domestically produced.

It may seem distasteful to think of drugs as a business, responding to normal economic signals. To do so, however, is not to deny the fact that the drugs trade rewards some of the

How did we get here?
History has a habit of repeating itself

Voters—and governments—change their minds about ways to deal with activities they disapprove of. Governments used to ban gambling; now many run their own lotteries. Prostitution, although still generally illegal, is rarely the target of police campaigns. Attitudes to alcohol have changed in the past century-and-half. So have attitudes to drugs.

In 19th-century America, campaigners talked of the demon drink in much the same way that they now talk of drugs. The temperance movement blamed booze for crime, "moral degeneracy", broken families and business failure. In America, this led to Prohibition, with its accompanying crime and bootlegging. In England, campaigners won restrictions on access, in the shape of the pub-closing hours that have puzzled foreign visitors ever since. It may have been a bore, but it was a less socially costly way of dealing with an undesirable habit than a ban.

Today's illegal drugs were patent medicines in the 19th century. Morphine and opium were freely available in both Europe and America. Victorian babies were quietened with Godfrey's Cordial, which contained opium. Cocaine was the basis of remedies for the common cold. When Atlanta prohibited alcohol, John Pemberton, producer of a health drink called French Wine Coca, developed a version that was non-alcoholic but still contained traces of coca, thereby creating the world's best-selling soft drink. As for marijuana, Queen Victoria reputedly used it to soothe the royal period pains.

Far from opposing the drugs trade, the British and the Americans notoriously promoted it in the 19th century. In 1800 China's imperial government forbade the import of opium, which had long been used to stop diarrhoea, but had latterly graduated to recreational use. British merchants smuggled opium into China to balance their purchases of tea for export to Britain. When the Chinese authorities confiscated a vast amount of the stuff, the British sent in gunboats, backed by France, Russia and America, and bullied China into legalising opium imports.

Initial efforts to stamp out drug use at home had little to do with concerns about health. One of America's first federal laws against opium-smoking, in 1887, was a response to agitation against Chinese "coolies", brought into California to build railways and dig mines. It banned opium imports by Chinese people, but allowed them by American citizens (the tax on opium imports was a useful source of federal revenue). The drafters of the Harrison Act of 1914, the first federal ban on non-medical narcotics, played on fears of "drug-crazed, sex-mad negroes". And the 1930s campaign against marijuana was coloured by the fact that Harry Anslinger, the first drug tsar, was appointed by Andrew Mellon, his wife's uncle. Mellon, the Treasury Secretary, was banker to DuPont, and sales of hemp threatened that firm's efforts to build a market for synthetic fibres. Spreading scare stories about cannabis was a way to give hemp a bad name. Moral outrage is always more effective if backed by a few vested interests.

world's nastiest people and most disagreeable countries. Nor is it to underestimate the harm that misuse of drugs can do to the health of individuals, or the moral fury that drug-taking can arouse. For many people, indeed, the debate is a moral one, akin to debates about allowing divorce, say, or abortion. But moral outrage has turned out to be a poor basis for policy.

Nowhere is that more evident than in the United States. Here is the world's most expensive drugs policy, absorbing $35 billion–40 billion a year of taxpayers' cash. It has eroded civil liberties, locked up unprecedented numbers of young blacks and Hispanics, and corroded foreign pol-

icy. It has proved a dismal rerun of America's attempt, in 1920–33, to prohibit the sale of alcohol. That experiment—not copied in any other big country—inflated alcohol prices, promoted bootleg suppliers, encouraged the spread of guns and crime, increased hard-liquor drinking and corrupted a quarter of the federal enforcement agents, all within a decade. Half a century from now, America's current drugs policy may seem just as perverse as Prohibition.

For the moment, though, even having an honest debate about the policy is extremely difficult there. Official publications are full of patently false claims. A recent report on the National Drug Control Strat-

egy announced: "National anti-drug policy is working." In evidence, it cited a further rise in the budget for drugs control; a decline in cocaine production in Peru and Bolivia (no mention of Colombia); and the fact that the proportion of 12th-grade youngsters who have used marijuana in the past month appears to have levelled off at around 25%. If these demonstrate success, what can failure be like?

Nearer the truth is the picture portrayed in "Traffic", a recent film that vividly demonstrated the futility of fighting supply and ignoring demand. In its most telling scene, the film's drugs tsar, played by Michael Douglas, asks his staff to think creatively about new ideas for tackling the problem. An embarrassed silence ensues.

This survey will concentrate largely (but not exclusively) on the American market, partly because it is the biggest. Americans probably consume more drugs per head, especially cocaine and amphetamines, than most other countries. In addition, the effects of America's misdirected policies spill across the world. Other rich countries that try to change their policies meet fierce American resistance; poor countries that ship drugs come (as Latin American experience shows) under huge pressure to prevent the trade, whatever the cost to civil liberties or the environment.

Moreover, America's experience demonstrates the awkward reality that there is little connection between the severity of a drugs policy on the one hand and prevalence of use on the other. Almost a third of Americans over 12 years old admit to having tried drugs at some point, almost one in ten (26.2m) in the past year. Drugs continue to pour into the country, prices have fallen and purity has risen. Cocaine costs half of what it did in the early 1980s and heroin sells for three-fifths of its price a decade ago. Greater purity means that heroin does not have to be injected to produce a high, but can be smoked or sniffed.

A matter of fashion

However, American experience also suggests that the pattern of drug consumption is altering, arguably for the better. Casual use seems to have fallen; heavy use has stabilised. More American teenagers are using cannabis (which, strictly speaking, includes not just the herb—marijuana—but the resin), but the number of youngsters experimenting with cocaine or heroin has stayed fairly steady. The American heroin epidemic peaked around 1973, since when the number of new addicts has dropped back to the levels of the mid-1960s. The average age of her-

oin addicts is rising in many countries—indeed, the Dutch have just opened the first home for elderly junkies in Rotterdam. America's hideous crack epidemic has also long passed, and cocaine use has retreated from its 1970s peak. And a recent study shows that the likelihood of proceeding from cannabis to harder drugs such as cocaine or heroin has fallen consistently for a decade. "We are largely dealing with history," says Mr Reuter. "The total population of drug users has been pretty stable since the late 1980s."

This is not an unmixed blessing: heavy users seem to be using more drugs, and to be injuring and killing themselves more often. As with cigarette-smoking, drug-taking is increasingly concentrated among the poor. And in some rich countries other than America, such as Britain, the number of both casual and heavy users of most drugs is still rising. In the poorer countries and in Central and Eastern Europe too, drugs markets are flourishing. India and China are probably the fastest-growing large markets for heroin.

But in the rich countries, the drugs that increasingly attract young users are those that are typically taken sporadically, not continuously: cannabis, ecstasy, amphetamines and cocaine. In that sense, they are more like alcohol than tobacco: users may binge one or two nights a week or indulge every so often with friends, but most do not crave a dose every day, year in, year out, as smokers generally do. That does not mean that these drugs are harmless, but it should raise questions about whether current policies are still appropriate.

Today's policies took shape mainly in the mid-1980s, when an epidemic of crack cocaine use proved a perfect issue around which President Ronald Reagan could rally "middle America". His vice-president, George Bush, called for a "real war on drugs", which caught the mood of the time: opinion polls showed that drugs were at the top of people's lists of worries. By the early

1990s the crack scare had faded, but a series of increasingly ferocious laws, passed in the second half of the 1980s, set the framework within which Mr Bush's war on drugs is still waged today.

This framework is not immutable, although formidable vested interests—including the police and prison officers—now back tough drugs laws. Attitudes to policy change over time (see box), and drugs policies in many countries are changing with them. Governments are gradually putting more emphasis on treatment rather than punishment. Last autumn, in a referendum, California voted to send first- and second-time drug offenders for treatment rather than to prison. And the law on possessing cannabis is being relaxed, even in parts of the United States, where several states now permit the possession of small amounts of it for medical use.

In Europe and Australia, governments have relaxed the enforcement of laws on possessing "soft" drugs. In Switzerland, farmers who grow cannabis for commercial sale within the country will be protected from prosecution if a new government proposal goes through. In Britain, Michael Portillo, a top opposition politician, advocates legalisation. But it is hard for an individual country to set its own course without becoming a net exporter, as the experience of Europe's more liberal countries shows. Ultimately, the policies of the world's biggest drugs importer will limit the freedom of others to act.

At the heart of the debate on drugs lies a moral question: what duty does the state have to protect individual citizens from harming themselves? *The Economist* has always taken a libertarian approach. It stands with John Stuart Mill, whose famous essay "On Liberty" argued that:

The only purpose for which power can be rightfully exercised over any member of a civilised community, against his will, is to prevent harm to others. His own good, either physical or moral, is not a sufficient warrant. He cannot rightfully be compelled to do or forbear because it will be better for him to do so, because it will make him happier, because, in the opinions of others, to do so would be wise, or even right. These are good reasons for remonstrating with him, or reasoning with him, or persuading him, or entreating him, but not for compelling him, or visiting him with any evil in case he do otherwise. Over himself, over his own body and mind, the individual is sovereign.

This survey broadly endorses that view. But it tempers liberalism with

pragmatism. Mill was not running for election. Attitudes towards drug-taking may be changing, but it will be a long time before most voters are comfortable with a policy that involves only remonstration and reason. People fret about protecting youngsters, a group that Mill himself accepted might need special protection. They fret, too, that drug-takers may not be truly "sovereign" if they become addicted. And some aspects of drug-taking do indeed harm others. So a first priority is to look for measures that reduce the harm drugs do, both to users and to society at large.

Sources and acknowledgements

Among the sources for this survey, "Drug War Heresies: Learning from Other Vices, Times, and Places", by Robert MacCoun and Peter Reuter (Cambridge University Press), was particularly helpful. Others are on *The Economist*'s website, at www. economist.com/ surveys/sources.cfm/ 20010728. William Saulsbury of the Police Foundation, Robert Keizer of the Dutch Ministry of Health, Eric Sterling of the Criminal Justice Policy Foundation, Mark Kleiman of UCLA, the staff of the Lindesmith Centre Drug Policy Foundation, John Carnevale, Simon Jenkins and Martin Wolf all gave more help than may be apparent from the text.

UNIT 2

Understanding How Drugs Work—Use, Dependency, and Addiction

Unit Selections

Key Points to Consider

- Why are some drugs so reinforcing?

- Why do some people become dependent upon certain drugs far sooner than other people?

- Is it possible to predict one's personal threshold for becoming drug dependent or addicted?

 **Links: www.dushkin.com/online/**
These sites are annotated in the World Wide Web pages.

AMERSA
http://center.butler.brown.edu

Centre for Addiction and Mental Health (CAMH)
http://www.camh.net

The National Center on Addiction and Substance Abuse at Columbia University
http://www.casacolumbia.org

National Institute on Drug Abuse (NIDA)
http://www.nida.nih.gov

Understanding how drugs act upon the human mind and body is a critical component to the resolution of issues concerning drug use and abuse. An understanding of basic pharmacology is requisite for informed discussion on practically every drug-related issue and controversy. One does not have to look far to find misinformed debate, much of which surrounds the basic lack of knowledge of how drugs work.

Different drugs produce different bodily effects and consequences. All psychoactive drugs influence the central nervous system, which, in turn, sits at the center of how we physiologically and psychologically interpret and react to the world around us. Some drugs, such as methamphetamine and LSD, have great influence on the nervous system, while others, such as tobacco and marijuana, elicit less pronounced reactions. Almost all psychoactive drugs have their effects on the body mitigated by the dosage level of the drug taken, the manner in which it is ingested, and the physiological and emotional state of the user. Cocaine smoked in the form of crack versus snorted as powder produces profoundly different physical and emotional effects on the user. However, even though illegal drugs often provide the most sensational perspective from which to view these relationships, the oral abuse of prescription drugs is being reported as an exploding new component of the addiction problem.

Molecular properties of certain drugs allow them to imitate and artificially reproduce certain naturally occurring brain chemicals that provide the basis for the drug's influence. The continued use of certain drugs and their repeated alteration of the body's biochemical structure provide one explanation for the physiological consequences of drug use. For example, heroin use replicates the natural brain chemical endorphin, which supports the body's biochemical defense to pain and stress. The continued use of heroin is believed to deplete natural endorphins, causing the nervous system to produce a painful physical and emotional reaction when heroin is withdrawn.

A word of caution is in order, however, when proceeding through the various explanations for what drugs do and why they do it. Many people, because of an emotional and/or political relationship to the world of drugs, assert a subjective predisposition when interpreting certain drugs' effects and consequences. One person's alcoholic is another's social drinker. People often argue, rationalize, and explain the perceived nature of drugs' effects based upon an extremely superficial understanding of diverse pharmacological properties of different drugs. If the 10 percent of the American population suspected of being genetically predisposed to alcoholism were aware of their susceptibility, perhaps rates of alcoholism would be lower. A detached and scientifically sophisticated awareness of drug pharmacology might provide one with a sound defense to the negative consequences of drug use.

Drug dependence and addiction is usually a continuum comprising experimentation, recreational use, regular use, and abuse. The process is influenced by a plethora of physiological, psychological, and environmental factors. It is difficult to predict whether or not a particular individual will become dependent on cocaine after initial experimentation with the drug. The promotion of cocaine as a candidate for a safe recreational drug on the basis that certain people do use it recreationally without undue harm is therefore a misleading statement.

Largely, drugs are described as more addictive or less addictive due to a process described as "reinforcement." Simply explained, reinforcement results from a drug's physiological and psychological influence on behavior that causes repeated introduction of the drug to the body. Cocaine and the amphetamines are known as drugs with high reinforcement potential. Persons addicted to drugs known to be strongly reinforcing typically report that they care more about getting the drug than about anything else.

Reinforcement does not, however, provide the basis for understanding addiction. Addiction is a cloudy term used to describe a multitude of pharmacological and environmental factors that produce a compulsive, nonnegotiable need for a drug. A thorough understanding of addiction requires an awareness of these many factors. Additionally, the recent mapping of the human genome is providing a new understanding of the genetic influence on the process of addiction. With each passing year, discoveries related to genetics influence thinking on almost all processes related to addiction.

The articles in unit 2 illustrate some of the current research and viewpoints on the ways that drugs act upon the human body. An understanding of these pharmacological processes is critical to understanding the assorted consequences of drug use and abuse. Science has taken us closer to understanding that acute drug use changes brain function profoundly, and that these changes may remain with the user long after the drug has left the system. Subsequently, many new issues have emerged for drug and health-related public policy. Increasingly, drug abuse and drug addiction reassert themselves as public enemy number one. Further, the need for a combined biological, behavioral, and social response to this problem becomes more self-evident. Many health care professionals and health care educators, in addition to those from other diverse backgrounds, argue that research dollars spent on drug abuse and addiction should approach that spent on heart disease, cancer, and AIDS.

Drugs that flip your switches: TOP TO TOE

Andrew Derrington explains the mechanisms in the brain that can create addiction

It used to be easy to define drug addiction and to explain its causes. Heroin was the paradigm case. It produces a pleasant effect by acting directly on the brain circuits that control our feelings. Repeated use of the drug causes the brain to adapt to its presence; a larger dose is required to produce the same pleasant effect and removal of the drug results in unpleasant physical side-effects known as withdrawal symptoms.

All these facts are true of heroin. But the conclusion that people used to draw from them—that the overwhelming compulsion to take the drug, which is the essential component of addiction, is caused by the desperate need to avoid the withdrawal symptoms—is false. Study of other drugs of abuse and addiction shows this clearly.

People abuse a huge range of substances, including alcohol, amphetamines, barbiturates, cannabis, cocaine, glue, solvents and tobacco. Withdrawal symptoms, which, in the case of heroin, are about as bad as an attack of flu, are a side-effect that does not always go with addiction. It depends on the drug. Cocaine is more addictive than heroin but produces no physical withdrawal symptoms. Alcohol is less addictive but produces withdrawal symptoms that can be fatal.

By studying the mechanisms of action of a wide range of drugs, scientists are now working out the essential components of addiction. It seems that the basic mechanism of addiction may be similar for drugs ranging from alcohol to heroin. Unfortunately, successful treatment requires management not just of the addiction but also of the side-effects. Paradoxically, this may be much easier for the "hard" drugs, heroin and cocaine, than for soft, socially acceptable drugs, such as alcohol.

Drugs act on the brain by altering the operation of the chemical messenger systems that transmit information from cell to cell in the brain. In normal operation, the cell that wants to send the message spits out a minute dose of the messenger at a specialised connection between cells. The molecules of the messenger work by attaching themselves to protein switches on the receiving cell. Each messenger molecule is designed to fit one particular switch and it turns the switch on by attaching to it. After it has flipped the switch the messenger is removed and recycled.

Everything your brain does—all your perceptions, memories, thoughts, feelings and actions—is caused by 100bn or so neurones sending each other messages using about 100 different chemicals. It seems amazing that taking a drug, which simply adds another chemical to the mix, could have a specific, selective effect, like making you feel good.

The reason is that each brain system uses a particular set of chemical messengers in particular ways. The brain system concerned with sensations of pleasure and reward uses a messenger called dopamine, in a part of the brain called the *nucleus accumbens*.

Drugs that have potential for addiction—which can be tested by measuring how much work rats will do in order to administer the drug to themselves—hit the dopamine switches in the *nucleus accumbens*. The faster a drug hits the switches, the more addictive it is. Addicts prefer heroin to morphine because, although the two drugs have the same effects, heroin gets into the brain faster.

One of the surprises of recent years is that alcohol, which used to be thought of as simply a solvent that attacks the fatty membranes of brain cells, also acts through the dopamine switches. However, two aspects of the way alcohol works are interesting. First, alcohol acts rather slowly. Moreover, many people (and rats) find alcohol rather unpalatable, and so they never drink enough to experience its rewarding effects.

However, as many readers will know, with practice a dedicated drinker can acquire a taste for alcohol. Rats, too, can develop a drink problem if they receive alcohol in a sweetened form as a sort of "alcopop".

The second interesting property of alcohol, according to David Nutt of Bristol University, is that it affects several messenger systems that have other specific effects. For example, it can reduce anxiety. This explains why parties—minefields of social anxiety—never take off unless they are generously fuelled by booze.

It also explains the popularity of alcohol wherever there is a scent of danger, such as on aircraft and ski slopes. By removing anxiety in such situations alcohol probably has a secondary effect on the dopamine switches.

Higher concentrations of alcohol affect other messenger systems to produce sedation and clumsiness, to block learning, and finally at very high doses to cause death by respiratory depression. It is the brain's attempt to compensate for these effects that causes dangerous withdrawal symptoms when drinking stops. Managing withdrawal symptoms is an important part of curing addiction.

The first stage in treating addiction is to stop the craving for the drug. A substantial part of the craving is learned by the same process that Pavlov used with his dogs: a bell that was rung at mealtimes becomes associated with food and triggers the dogs' hunger.

Similarly, an addict's craving for heroin is triggered by the sight of a syringe, a newly reformed smoker will be unable to resist the sight of a cigarette, and an alcoholic who goes into the pub for a glass of lemonade is unlikely to come out sober.

Relearning these associations, or learning how to stay away from their triggers, is an important component of many treatments for addiction.

Preventing relapse is an enormous problem, says John Roberts of Cantab Pharmaceuticals in Cambridge. "You can be doing really well, and a single relapse means you are back to square one," he says. Cantab has developed vaccines against cocaine and nicotine that it hopes will solve the relapse problem by inactivating the drug before it has its effect.

The cocaine vaccine seems to work in rats and is at present undergoing trials in humans, says Roberts, although it will still be some years before the vaccine is widely available. If the vaccine proves to be safe and effective, it could even be possible to use it as a prevention as well as a cure.

* The author is professor of psychology at the University of Nottingham.

First published in *Financial Times*, April 29, 2000, p. 2. © by Andrew Derrington. Reprinted by permission.

Learning about addiction from the genome

Drug addiction can be defined as the compulsive seeking and taking of a drug despite adverse consequences. Although addiction involves many psychological and social factors, it also represents a biological process: the effects of repeated drug exposure on a vulnerable brain. The sequencing of the human and other mammalian genomes will help us to understand the biology of addiction by enabling us to identify both genes that contribute to individual risk for addiction and those through which drugs cause addiction. We illustrate this potential impact by searching a draft sequence of the human genome for genes related to desensitization of receptors that mediate the actions of drugs of abuse on the nervous system.

Eric J. Nestler* & David Landsman†

To understand addiction, it is important to define the types of molecular and cellular adaptation at the levels of neurons and synapses that account for tolerance, sensitization and dependence, which are often used to define an addicted state. Tolerance describes diminishing sensitivity to a drug's effects after repeated exposure; sensitization describes the opposite. Dependence is an altered physiological state caused by repeated drug exposure, which leads to withdrawal when drug use is discontinued. Each is seen in human addicts and is believed to contribute to continued drug use during addiction.[1,2] Considerable progress has been made in identifying the molecular and cellular adaptations that mediate these processes.[3]

Challenges in addiction

A cardinal feature of addiction is its chronicity. Individuals can experience intense craving for drug and remain at increased risk for relapse even after years of abstinence, so addiction must involve very stable changes in the brain. But it has been difficult to identify such change at the molecular, cellular or circuit levels. The molecular and cellular adaptations related to tolerance, sensitization and dependence do not persist long enough to account for the more stable behavioural changes associated with addiction.

This challenge is analogous to that faced in the field of learning and memory where there has been increasing appreciation for the role of learning-related processes in addiction.[1,2] Many molecular and cellular models of learning have been discovered and some have been related to simple forms of learning behaviour.[4,5] But little information is available concerning the molecular and cellular basis of essentially life-long memories. Proposed changes in synaptic structure, or in chromatin organization, remain speculative.

Another challenge is to identify the variations in specific genes that make some individuals vulnerable to addiction and others relatively resistant.[6] Epidemiological studies indicate that 40—60% of an individual's risk for an addiction, whether it is to alcohol, opiates or cocaine, is genetic. This is consistent with the widely differing sensitivity to drugs of abuse, including preferences to self-administer drug, among inbred rodent strains and lines.[7] However, we have not identified the specific genes involved in humans or animal models; nor do we understand with any specificity how external factors (including stress or drugs themselves) interact with those genetic variations to produce addiction.

Drugs of abuse seem to cause addiction by acting on evolutionarily old brain circuits. These circuits, which comprise several areas of the limbic system (for example, nucleus accumbens, amygdala and prefrontal cortex), regulate an organism's responses to natural reinforcers, such as food, drink, sex and social interaction.[1,2] The loss of control that addicts show with respect to drug seeking and taking may relate to the ability of drugs of abuse to commandeer these natural reward circuits and disrupt an individual's motivation and drive for normal reinforcers. There is evidence that 'natural addictions,' such as overeating, pathological gambling, compulsive shopping and perhaps excessive exercise, may involve analogous mechanisms. A major focus of current research is to explore the neurobiology of these conditions and the influence of genetic factors in their development.

Impact of sequencing the human genome

We now know the initial targets for most drugs of abuse, as well as some of the molecular and cellular adaptations that occur in limbic brain circuits in response to repeated exposure. The draft sequence of the human genome indicates the diversity of the molecular components that have been implicated in addiction. For example, cocaine acts on the reuptake transporters for dopamine and other monoamine neurotransmitters; we will soon know how many subtypes of such transporters are expressed in humans.

Another example is provided by genes whose products regulate desensitization of G-protein-coupled receptors. Such receptors are the initial targets for several drugs of abuse: opiates are agonists at opioid receptors, cannabinoids are agonists at cannabinoid receptors, and hallucinogens are partial agonists at serotonin $5HT_{2A}$ receptors. Dopamine receptors, which are indirectly activated by cocaine and other stimulants through potentiation of dopaminergic transmission, are also G-protein-coupled. The sensitivity of G-protein-coupled receptor signalling is controlled by complex regulatory processes (Fig. 1). Given the importance of changes in sensitivity in addiction, it is not surprising that mechanisms governing receptor sensitivity have been implicated in regulating responses to drugs of abuse and in models of addiction.[3,8-10]

A critical step in exploring such mechanisms is to identify all of the potential gene products that could be involved. Table 1 shows the results of an analysis of the current human protein dataset for some of the genes that regulate receptor desensitization: G-protein-receptor kinases (GRKs), arrestins, phosducins and regulators of G-protein signalling (RGS proteins). GRKs phosphorylate ligand-bound receptors, enabling association of the receptors with arrestins.[8,9] This seems functionally to uncouple receptors form their G proteins, perhaps through receptor internalization. Phosducins also appear to alter receptor/G-protein interactions by regulating the availability of G-protein ßγ-subunits.[11] RGS proteins serve as GTPase activating proteins for G-protein α-subunits and thereby alter the kinetic of a receptor-mediated response.[12]

Our analysis of these gene families reveals new candidate members for each, and in several cases many,

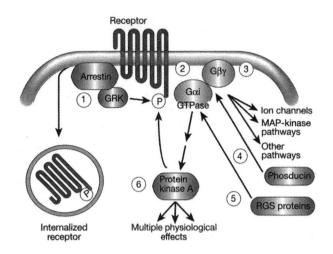

Figure 1 Possible mechanisms of drug-induced changes in the sensitivity of a G_i-coupled receptor (for example, opioid, cannabinoid and certain dopamine receptors). Drug-induced adaptations in the efficacy of receptor-G_i coupling could contribute to drug tolerance or sensitization. A possible mechanism is altered phosphorylation of the receptor by GRKs or its subsequent association with arrestins (1). Other possibilities include alterations in G-protein α– (2) or βγ-subunits (3) or in other proteins (for example, phosducin (4) or RGS proteins (5)) that modulate G protein function. Phosphorylation of the receptor by protein kinase A (6) or other kinases represents another potential mechanism. Also shown is agonist-induced receptor internalization, which may be mediated by receptor phosphorylation. From ref. 3.

which can be investigated for their roles in addiction. For example, the specificity of the GRK-arrestin system for various types of G-protein-coupled receptor is not yet known. Knowledge of the full complement of GRKs and arrestins in humans allows us to evaluate the role of each GRK and arrestin subtype in regulating the sensitivity of the opioid, cannabinoid, serotonergic and dopaminergic receptors implicated in addiction. Similarly, the identification of novel subtypes of phosducins and RGS proteins makes it possible to determine which are expressed in neurons that mediate responses to drugs of abuse and which are involved in longer-term adaptations to drug exposure. Analogous efforts aimed at the receptors and G-protein subunits, as well as the ion channels (for example, inwardly rectifying potassium channels) that are regulated by the G proteins,[3] will provide more complete understanding of how drugs of abuse alter receptor signalling to produce tolerance and sensitization.

Access to the complete human genome sequence will also help efforts to identify addiction vulnerability genes. One of the major obstacles to such efforts has been the technical difficulty of moving from genetic linkage analyses to identification of specific genes.[6] The mouse genome sequence will similarly improve the efficiency of identifying addiction vulnerability genes in quantitative trait locus analyses of animal models.[7]

Table 1 Diversity in genes that regulate desensitization of G-protein-coupled receptors

Gene	PSIBLAST[13] hits	SSEARCH[14,15] hits	New sequences PSIBLAST	New sequences SSEARCH	EST match
G protein-receptor kinases	576	361	91	57	48
Arrestins	5	5	1	1	1
RGS proteins	31	23	9	4	5
Phosducins	14	9	8	6	4

We queried the human protein dataset (42,227 sequences from the ENSEMBL dataset, http://www.ensembl.org/) with four human protein sequences: β-adrenergic receptor kinase-1 (SP:P25098; also called G protein-receptor kinase-2), β-arrestin (SP:P49407), regulator of G-protein signalling-5 (SP:O15539) and phosducin (gi:4505653). The columns labelled PSIBLAST and SSEARCH hits are the number of statistically significant hits obtained with each search method. To verify the expression of candidate gene products, each predicted human protein sequence in the `New sequences PSIBLAST' column was compared to the expressed sequence tag (EST) database using TBLASTN with default parameters. The total number of protein sequences that showed perfect matches to at least one human EST is shown in the column labelled `EST match.' (Some proteins gave perfect matches to ESTs in mouse or rat but not to human.) For details see Supplementary Information.

The power of genomics

Genomics (and the related proteomics) will provide powerful tools to identify the genes and gene products that are altered by repeated exposure to drugs of abuse and by external factors (for example, stress and drug-associated environmental stimuli) that influence the development of addiction. For example, DNA array technology makes it feasible to investigate thousands of gene products simultaneously after drug exposure. By combining genomic and proteomic tools with increasingly sophisticated models of addiction in animals, it will be possible to identify patterns of altered gene expression that are associated with particular features of the addicted state such as tolerance, sensitization, dependence, craving and relapse.

Detailed analysis of the genome will also reveal how genes are organized and transcribed, and indicate the regulatory elements that control their expression. In addition, such analysis will show the exonic and intronic sequences of individual genes and teach us how to predict their processing into splice variants. We will similarly better appreciate how individual translated proteins are processed into multiple polypeptide products. Knowledge of such rules will greatly facilitate research into addiction. For example, as we elucidate the rules of gene transcription, we may be able to compile a list of genes that are potentially regulated by a transcription factor implicated in addiction, on the basis of the presence of the appropriate response element within their regulatory regions.

Finally, animal models of addiction are well developed, in contrast to other psychiatric abnormalities (for example, depression, bipolar disorder and schizophrenia) for which animal models are less straightforward. As a result, genomic studies of addiction might lead the way in identifying the molecular and cellular basis of complex behavioural states. A better understanding of the biology of addiction should help us to understand the mechanisms underlying symptoms of depression, anxiety and other disorders that overlap with those of addiction. Such understanding might also lead to appreciation of the factors that regulate normal variations in motivation, reward and mood.

References

1. Koob, G. F., Sanna, P. P. & Bloom, F. E. Neuroscience of addiction, *Neuron* **21**, 467–476 (1998).
2. Wise, R. A., Drug-activation of brain reward pathways, *Drug Alcohol Depend.* **51**, 13–22 (1998).
3. Nestler, E. J. & Aghajanian, G. K. Molecular and cellular basis of addiction. Science **278**, 58–63 (1997).
4. Kandel, E. R. Genes, synapses, and long-term memory. J. Cell. Physiol. **173**, 124–125 (1997).
5. Malenka, R. C. & Nicoll, R. A. Long-term potentiation—a decade of progress? Science **285**, 1870–1874 (1999).
6. Nestler, E. J. Genes and addiction. Nature Genet. **26**, 277–281 (2000).
7. Crabbe, J. C., Phillips, T. J., Buck, K. J., Cunningham, C. L. & Belknap, J. K. Identifying genes for alcohol and drug sensitivity: recent progress and future directions. Trends Neurosci. **22**, 173–179 (1999).
8. Zhang, J. *et al.* Role for G protein-coupled receptor kinase in agoinit-specific regulation of mu-opioid receptor responsiveness. Proc. Natl. Acad. Sci. USA **95**, 7157–7162 (1998).
9. Bohn, L. M. *et al.* μ-opioid receptor desensitization by ß-arrestin-2 determines morphine tolerance but not dependence. Nature **408**, 720–723 (2000)
10. Potenza, M. N. & Nestler, E. J. Effects of RGS proteins on the functional response of the μ-opioid receptor in a melanophore-based assay. J. Pharmacol. Exp. Ther. **291**, 482–491 (1999).
11. Gaudet, R., Savage, J. R., McLaughlin, J. N., Willardson, B. M. & Sigler, P. B. A molecular mechanism for the phosphorylation-dependent regulation of heterotrimeric G proteins by phosducin. *Mol. Cell* **3**, 649–660 (1999).

12. Berman, D. M. & Gilman, A. G. Mammalian RGS proteins: barbarians at the gate. *J. Biol. Chem.* 273, 1269–1272 (1998).

13. Altschul, S. F. *et al.* Gapped BLAST and PSI-BLAST: a new generation of protein database search programs. *Nucleic Acids Res* **25**, 3389–3402 (1997).

14. Smith, T. F. & Waterman, M. S. Identification of common molecular subsequences. *J. Mol. Biol.* **147**, 195–197 (1981).

15. Pearson, W. R. Searching protein sequence libraries: comparison of the sensitivity and selectivity of the Smith-Waterman and FASTA algorithms. *Genomics* **11**, 635–650 (1991).

Supplementary information is available on *Nature's* World-Wide Web site (http://www.nature.com) or as paper copy form the London editorial office of *Nature.*

Acknowledgements

Preparation of this report was supported by the National Institute on Drug Abuse.

Correspondence and requests for materials should be addressed to E.J.N. (e-mail: eric.nestler@utsouthwestern.edu).

*Department of Psychiatry, The University of Texas Southwestern Medical Center, 5323 Harry Hines Boulevard, Dallas, Texas 75390-9070, USA

†National Center for Biotechnology Information, National Library of Medicine, Computational Biology Branch, Building 45, Room 6AN12J, 45 Center Drive, MSC 6510, Bethesda, Maryland 20892-6510, USA

Addiction and the Brain—Part II

In the first part [See *Harvard Mental Health Letter*, June 1998] we discussed the acute and chronic effects of addictive drugs on the brain's reward system and the internal processes of neurons. In this part we discuss genetic and social influences and the implications of brain studies for the treatment of addiction and an understanding of its nature.

Genetics of addiction

Individual differences in sensitivity to the addictive powers of drugs are almost certainly influenced strongly by genetics. Different strains of rats and mice prefer and avoid different drugs. Some animals have a congenital liking or dislike for alcohol, and some will not readily take even heroin or cocaine. At a given dose of alcohol, the sons of alcoholic parents feel less intoxicated than average, and their posture and gait are altered less. This apparent resistance, also found in susceptible rats, is an early sign of vulnerability to alcoholism. To put it another way, men (and rats) who can drink others under the table are the most likely future alcoholics. According to one theory, a high capacity for drink reflects a powerful counteracting response of the body and brain that is a sign of sensitivity rather than insensitivity to the effects of alcohol. Addiction may follow if the reward and motivation system is equally sensitive but less adaptable. Researchers have also speculated that some people genetically at risk for addiction have a congenitally high level of stress hormones or a deficit in dopamine function that is temporarily corrected by their drug of choice.

There are probably many genetic routes to addiction. For example, alcohol addicts are often divided into two classes. Type I alcoholics are usually male, vulnerable to drug addictions of all kinds, and inclined to crime and other antisocial behavior. Type II alcoholics, whose symptoms are usually less severe and develop at a later age, are more often female and rarely have antisocial tendencies. Studies of adopted children suggest that these types are genetically distinct. Depression, chronic anxiety, attention deficit disorder, and other mental disorders that are under genetic influence may also raise the risk of addiction by reducing the capacity for rewarding experiences. Researchers have looked for specific gene variants associated with addictions by examining DNA patterns (markers) that are transmitted in families along with an addictive propensity. Results so far have been disappointing, but variations in genes that direct the manufacture of dopamine receptors may turn out to be significant.

Social aspects of addiction

Social circumstances influence vulnerability and resistance to addiction in many ways. First, to state the obvious, a drug must be available in sufficient amounts to sustain an addiction. But it may be just as important that other sources of satisfaction are not available. Experimental animals are often confined under uniform, highly restrictive conditions—sometimes isolated in cages with catheters implanted in their veins. These arrangements promote addiction by cutting off other opportunities for rewarding experience. It is not surprising that isolated rats take more of an addictive drug than animals living in normal rat colonies (although both isolation and rat personality make less difference once an addiction is fully established). If human beings differ more than rats in individual susceptibility, it is not only because their brains are more complex but also because they live in more varied environments. People risk addiction most when they lack other capacities, interests, and choices, other ways to solve problems, other sources of attachment to something outside themselves. The brain's motivation system is more easily disturbed when varied sources of reward and expectation are not preserving its balance. In this way, the potential for addiction is affected by economic conditions, cultural traditions, formal and informal social controls, and the companionship and approval of other drug users.

Since the chemical stuff of addiction is already present in the brain, it does not even require an external substance. Injecting a drug is the quickest and often the most unhealthful and socially destructive way to disturb the motivation system. Certainly it is the easiest way to study the system in animals. But pathological gambling and other consuming habits that are sometimes called addictions might work on the brain indirectly with similar results. Money is the original stimulus for gamblers, but eventually they go on playing even when reason tells them they will lose. They are driven by emotional memories of past gains, and the thrill associated with the mere possibility of winning has become stronger than other pleasures.

Problems of treatment

Partly because addiction causes long-lasting changes in the brain, it is a chronic condition that sometimes requires long-term care and treatment. Repeated relapses should be expected (although, for reasons that are not clear but probably include loss of tolerance for the physical side effects, drug addictions often lose their strength with age). Sometimes the brain changes can be partially reversed, and often ways can be found to compensate for them.

Addiction will probably prove difficult to counteract by chemical means alone. Fairly effective drug treatments are available for some of its secondary symptoms, especially the acute withdrawal reactions produced by opiates and sedatives. Anticonvulsants prevent seizures, beta-blockers reduce anxiety and agitation, and clonidine alters the sensitivity of the locus ceruleus, the brain region where opiate withdrawal effects are concentrated. There are also drugs that neutralize the pleasurable effects of opiates and alcohol. Acamprosate discourages drinking, probably by altering the transmission of glutamate; disulfiram (Antabuse) prevents the digestive system from assimilating alcohol, making drinkers nauseated and sometimes seriously ill. Naltrexone and naloxone block receptors for the action of opiates and alcohol. Another common technique is the substitution of less harmful addictive substances, oral methadone and levo-alpha-acetyl-methadol (LAAM), for more harmful ones, intravenous heroin and morphine. A nicotine patch can be used to reduce craving for cigarettes while the smoker tries to quit.

Limits of treatment

But this kind of treatment has limited value. For example, there is no drug that will reliably prevent people from using cocaine or make them stop taking it. Drugs that lower the activity of dopamine have not proved effective, although more selective ones that act on particular kinds of DA receptors may turn out to be useful. Researchers have inoculated experimental rats with a vaccine that works by provoking the body to produce antibodies against cocaine. Methylphenidate

(Ritalin), an amphetamine-like stimulant, in some ways bears the same relation to cocaine that methadone bears to heroin. It is taken by mouth, enters and leaves the brain more slowly than cocaine, and evokes a less intense response both when it enters and when it leaves. Unfortunately, methylphenidate reduces the craving for cocaine only temporarily. But the main obstacle to chemical treatment of addiction is the difficulty of persuading addicts to participate. Heroin addicts usually refuse to take naltrexone, and alcoholics often discard their Antabus. Even if they do accept these treatments for a while, they are in danger of eventual relapse, because addiction is a disorder of motivation. They can easily arrange to prevent themselves from feeling pleasure when they use the drug. What they cannot do is prevent themselves from wanting it.

As the philosopher and psychologist William James pointed out, we can often renounce the immediate satisfaction of a desire for the sake of long-term health and happiness if we can group the desire with others in a general category and make a rule that applies to them all. Addiction often persists because the addict is unwilling or unable (the distinction becomes doubtful) to acknowledge the kind of problem it is, the category to which it belongs. The word often used today to describe this condition is "denial." For each of the many situations and moods in which they are impelled to take the drink or drug, addicts can supply a different justification, excuse, or rationalization. Often they are able to change only when they come to understand that all their many allegedly different reasons for drinking or taking drugs belong under the heading of addiction. That is why Alcoholics Anonymous insists that its members repeatedly tell themselves and others, "I am an alcoholic."

But generalizing in order to act on principle depends on coordination between the seat of planning and judgment in the prefrontal cortex and the centers of desire and reward in the medial forebrain bundle. In some people, especially antisocial personalities, this coordination may be poor from an early age. Instead of following rules to guide their actions, they tend to do what they want when they can. Since they are reluctant to choose among motives or delay the satisfaction of desires, they are highly likely to abuse alcohol and other drugs and eventually develop addictions that are especially

difficult to treat. More often, addiction itself impairs the coordination of judgment and desire by decreasing the value of all other experiences so much that the drug effect is preferred even as it becomes less and less rewarding. When an addict calls on reserves (presumably from pathways in the brain that remain intact), acknowledges the problem, and seeks treatment, it may be not just a means to recovery but a sign that recovery has already begun, because judgment is reassuming control over motivation. In fact, research has shown that most addicts do eventually find a way to quit on their own, although sometimes not before irreparable damage has been done to their health or their lives.

Is addiction a brain disorder?

Critics who are impressed by the role of rulers and voluntary action in the onset and progress of drug addiction question whether it should be regarded as a brain disorder. The risk, they say, is that underlying problems will be ignored, moral irresponsibility encouraged, or the choice of solutions unnecessarily limited. For the same reason that addicts are often ambivalent about their habits, the rest of us are unsure about how to cope with them. Should we be finding ways to treat an illness, or should we be using whatever means are necessary, including coercion, to persuade unhappy and troublesome people to abandon their bad behavior and reform their lives by acting on different motives? We make different choices in different contexts. We pay taxes to rehabilitate addicts, but they are also imprisoned for the possession and use of drugs, although it would be unthinkable to treat victims of any other disorder that way.

These contradictory attitudes and social policies are responses to different aspects of a complicated situation. Because motivation and desire can be disturbed in many ways, addiction does not have a single simple meaning. Different kinds of addiction have different causes and consequences. No single best method of prevention, management, or treatment exists for all hereditary proclivities, social conditions, states of mind, or personal characteristics that promote the development of overpowering and self-destructive habits. There are many roads to what the poet, philosopher, and opium addict Samuel Taylor Coleride called "insanity of the will", and a variety of potential escape routes, from counteracting chemicals to self-help groups, psychotherapy, religious experience, and social change.

For Further Reading

George Ainslie. Beyond microeconomics: Conflict among interests in a multiple self as a determinant of value. In: John Elster, ed. *The Multiple Self*, New York: Cambridge University Press, 1985.

Eliot L. Gardner. Brain reward mechanisms. In: Joyce H. Lowinson, Pedro Ruiz, Robert B. Millman, and John G. Langrod, eds. *Substance Abuse: A Comprehensive Textbook*, Third Edition. Baltimore: Williams & Wilkins, 1997.

Steven E. Hyman. Why does the brain prefer opium to broccoli? *Harvard Review of Psychiatry* 2:43–46 (May/June 1994).

George F. Koob and Eric J. Nestler Neurobiology of drug addition. *Journal of Neuropsychiatry and Clinical Neuroscience.* 9(3): 482–497 (1997).

Charles P. O'Brien. Recent developments in the pharmacotherapy of substance abuse. *Journal of Consulting and Clinical Psychology* 64:677–686 (August 1996).

Stanton Peele and Archie Brodsky. The Truth about Addiction and Recovery. New York: Simon & Schuster, 1991.

The Harvard Mental Health Letter (ISSN 0884–3783) is published monthly for $72 per year by the Harvard Medical School Health Publications Group, 164 Longwood Ave. Boston, MA 02115. Periodical postage paid at Boston, MA and additional mailing offices. Postmaster: Send address changes to The Harvard Mental Health Letter, P. O. Box 420448, Palm Coast, FL 32142–0448.

Cognition is central to drug addiction

Recent research shows that drug abuse alters cognitive activities such as decision-making and inhibition, likely setting the stage for addiction and relapse.

BY SIRI CARPENTER
Monitor staff

Most substance abuse researchers once believed that drug abuse and addiction are best explained by drugs' reinforcing effects. Pharmacological studies have long supported that view, showing that drugs of abuse powerfully affect the brain's dopamine system, which regulates emotional responses and plays a part in abuse by providing an emotional "reward" for continued use.

Increasingly, however, scientists are learning that the story is more complicated. Brain-imaging studies in humans and neuropsychological studies in nonhuman animals have shown that repeated drug use causes disruptions in the brain's highly evolved frontal cortex, which regulates cognitive activities such as decision-making, response inhibition, planning and memory.

"We now know that many of the drugs of abuse target not just those aspects of the brain that alter things like emotion, but also areas that affect our ability to control cognitive operations," says Herb Weingartner, PhD, of the Division of Neuroscience and Behavioral Research at the National Institute on Drug Abuse (NIDA).

The new findings hold promise for better understanding why only some drug users become addicted, why drug abusers so easily relapse even after long periods of drug abstinence and, ultimately, how prevention and treatment efforts can be tailored to people's individual vulnerabilities.

"In the past few years, people have begun to recognize that drug abuse is not a pharmacological disease—it's a pharmacological and behavioral disease," says Elliot A. Stein, PhD, a neuroscientist at the Medical College of Wisconsin. "The cognitive functions that sit in the frontal lobes play a role in drug abuse."

For treatment, he believes, that may suggest that it will be difficult to find a "magic bullet" to attack both the pharmacological and the behavioral parts of addiction.

Shifting tide

Since the 1980s, scientists have observed that many people who were addicted to drugs such as cocaine and marijuana appeared to have frontal cortex abnormalities. Such abnormalities, however, were long thought to be incidental side effects of drug abuse, explains Steven Grant, PhD, a program officer in NIDA's Division of Treatment Research and Development.

"We typically haven't thought of the influence of those processes on substance abuse and addiction," he says, "because we have been so focused on the role of reinforcement and the hedonic effects of drugs as being the driving force in drug abuse. That has been the dominant paradigm for the last two decades."

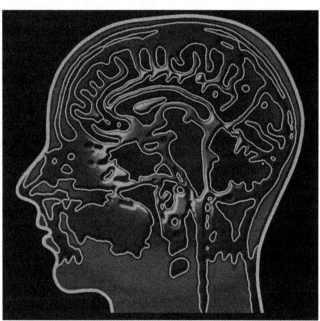

MEHAU KULYK/SCIENCE PHOTO LIBRARY
Brain-imaging and behavioral studies by psychologists and others have revealed that the frontal cortex, which controls much of higher cognition, is involved in addiction.

In the past five years, however, the tide has begun to turn. At a 1992 scientific conference, University of Iowa neuroscientist Antoine Bechara, MD, PhD, described research showing that patients with frontal cortex damage had impaired decision-making abilities, reflected in their performance on a laboratory gambling task.

Grant saw Bechara's presentation and made the connection to drug abuse, hypothesizing that disruptions in the frontal cortex might be responsible for impaired decision-making and behavioral inhibition in drug abusers—and that that could help explain the compulsive drug-seeking that is a hallmark of addiction.

Using Bechara's gambling task, Grant and his colleagues tested drug abusers' decision-making abilities. Last year, they reported in the journal *Neuropsychologia* (Vol. 38, No. 8) that drug abusers indeed made poorer decisions on the gambling task than did participants in a control group.

"Classically, people thought that drug addiction was a disease that involved the centers of pleasure—that people are taking the drug because it's pleasurable. But that's not the case—in fact, addicted people don't have as strong a pleasure response as people who aren't addicted. Recent data are showing us that addiction entails a basic disruption of motivational circuits."

Nora D. Volkow
Brookhaven National Laboratory

More recently, Bechara and his colleagues uncovered three subgroups of drug abusers. About one-third, they found, showed no decision-making impairment on the gambling task. About 25 percent, in contrast, responded exactly as patients with frontal lobe damage have been shown to do, almost invariably choosing a higher immediate reward even knowing that their strategy would be unprofitable in the long run. Finally, about 40 percent of Bechara's study participants appeared to be hypersensitive to potential rewards—no matter whether they were immediate or long-term.

Bechara suggests that these differences in decision-making impairment reflect different vulnerabilities to drug addiction. If so, he argues, they may help shed light on treatment strategies. Drug users who show no decision-making impairment may be at least risk for becoming addicted and may be able to stop if they want to, he suggests. In contrast, he says, for those with severe decision-making impairments, "There's probably nothing you can do. You can put them in jail, but in my opinion, they're unlikely to respond."

Finally, Bechara argues, for drug users who are sensitive to both the short- and long-term consequences of drug use, heightening awareness of the negative long-term consequences of abuse may be sufficient to tip the scales and help people quit using drugs.

In other studies, researchers have used two imaging techniques, positron emission tomography and functional magnetic resonance imaging, to measure drug abusers' brain activity during craving.

In 1996, Grant and NIDA colleagues David B. Newlin, PhD, Edythe D. London, PhD, and others reported in the *Proceedings of the National Academy of Sciences* (Vol. 93) that cocaine craving was linked to heightened activity in areas of the frontal cortex that regulate decision-making and motivation, but not in the brain's dopamine control centers. Those findings have since been replicated and extended in other laboratories.

"Classically, people thought that drug addiction was a disease that involved the centers of pleasure—that people are taking the drug because it's pleasurable," concludes Nora D. Volkow, MD, a research scientist at the U.S. Department of Energy's Brookhaven National Laboratory. "But that's not the case—in fact, addicted people don't have as strong a pleasure response as people who aren't addicted. Recent data are showing us that addiction entails a basic disruption of motivational circuits."

Seeking clues for treatment

Evidence that craving and drug cues can trigger abnormal activity in the frontal cortex—even in the absence of drugs—has led many researchers to believe that this brain area may be especially important in relapse. Grant suggests it may be in the frontal cortex that the residual effects of drugs manifest themselves, long after dopamine effects have disappeared.

"Without a properly functioning frontal cortex," he says, "one may be unable to look beyond drugs' immediate reinforcing or hedonic aspects and consider the long-term consequences of drug use."

Bechara adds, "I think there are two mechanisms playing in addiction. One is the pharmacological reward process that we've been studying for years. But the other is the behavioral process of controlling your behavior in the face of punishment."

The growing body of research on the roles that the frontal cortex and cognitive processes such as decision making and behavioral inhibition play in addiction raises many questions about treatment:

• What is the difference, in the brain, between drug use and addictive drug use?

• Do some people have pre-existing, subtle abnormalities in the frontal cortex that make them more vulnerable to drug use? If so, how can such dysfunction be identified and used for early interventions?

• What are the long-term brain consequences of drug use? Are they reversible?

• How can the recent findings of frontal cortex activation during drug craving be exploited to develop better ways to evaluate treatment effectiveness?

"Right now, the best tool for measuring success of drug treatment is recidivism—does the person show up in the hospital again?" comments Stein. "Compare that with a field like cardiology, where a physician would never release a heart attack patient without a stress test. In drug addiction, we send people out on the street without certainty that the treatment worked."

He hopes that someday, he'll be able to put people in a craving situation and measure their brain responses. "That," he says, "will help us know if the intervention blunted the craving response."

From the *Monitor on Psychology*, June 2001, pp. 34-35. © 2001 by the American Psychological Association. Reprinted by Permission.

HOW IT ALL STARTS INSIDE YOUR BRAIN

SCIENCE: New research on how cocaine, heroin, alcohol and amphetamines target neuronal circuits is revealing the biological basis of addiction, tolerance, withdrawal and relapse.

By Sharon Begley

One by one, each crack addict took his turn in the fMRI tube, its magnets pounding away with a throbbing bass. A mirror inside was angled just so, allowing the addict to see a screen just outside the tube. Then the 10-minute video rolled. For two minutes, images of monarch butterflies flitted by; the fMRI, which detects active regions in the brain, saw nothing untoward. Then the scene shifted. Men ritualistically cooked crack…an addict handed cash to a pusher…users smoked. It was as if a neurological switch had been thrown: seeing the drug scenes not only unleashed in the addicts a surge of craving for crack, but also triggered visible changes in their brains as their anterior cingulate and part of the prefrontal cortex—regions involved in mood and learning—lit up like Times Square. Nonaddicts show no such response. The fMRI had pinpointed physical changes in the brain that apparently underlie cue-induced craving, showing why walking past a bar, passing a corner crack house or even partying with the people you used to shoot up with can send a recovering addict racing for a hit. "The brain regions that became active are where memories are stored," says Dr. Scott Lukas

of McLean Hospital in Massachusetts, who led the 1998 study. "These cues turn on crack-related memories, and addicts respond like Pavlov's dogs."

"This is your brain on drugs": it's not just an advertising line. Through fMRI as well as PET scans, neuroscientists are pinpointing what happens in the brain during highs and lows, why withdrawal can be unbearable and—in one of the most sobering findings—how changes caused by addictive drugs persist long after you stop using. "Imaging and other techniques are driving home what we learned from decades of animal experiments," says Dr. Alan Leshner, director of the National Institute on Drug Abuse. "Drugs of abuse change the brain, hijack its motivational systems and even change how its genes function."

An addicted brain is different—physically different, chemically different—from a normal brain. A cascade of neurobiological changes accompanies the transition from voluntary to compulsive drug use, but one of the most important is this: cocaine, heroin, nicotine, amphetamines and other addictive drugs alter the brain's pleasure circuits. Activating this circuit, also called the reward circuit, produces a feel-

good sensation. Eating cheesecake or tacos or any other food you love activates it. So does sex, winning a competition, acing a test, receiving praise and other pleasurable experiences. The pleasure circuit communicates in the chemical language of dopamine: this neurotransmitter zips from neuron to neuron in the circuit like a molecular happy face, affecting the firing of other neurons and producing feelings from mild happiness to euphoria.

What happens to the circuit if you inject, inhale or swallow an addictive drug? To find out, Dr. Hans Breiter of Massachusetts General Hospital and colleagues recruited cocaine addicts who had been using for an average of seven to eight years and had used on 16 of the past 30 days. After making sure none had a heart problem or any other condition that would put them at risk, Breiter and colleagues gave each a "party" dose of cocaine, up to about 40 milligrams for a 150-pound man. An fMRI took snapshots of their brains every eight seconds for 18 minutes. At first, during the "rush" phase, the addicts described feeling "out of control," as if they were "in a dragster" or "being dangled 10 feet off the ground by a giant hand." They also felt a

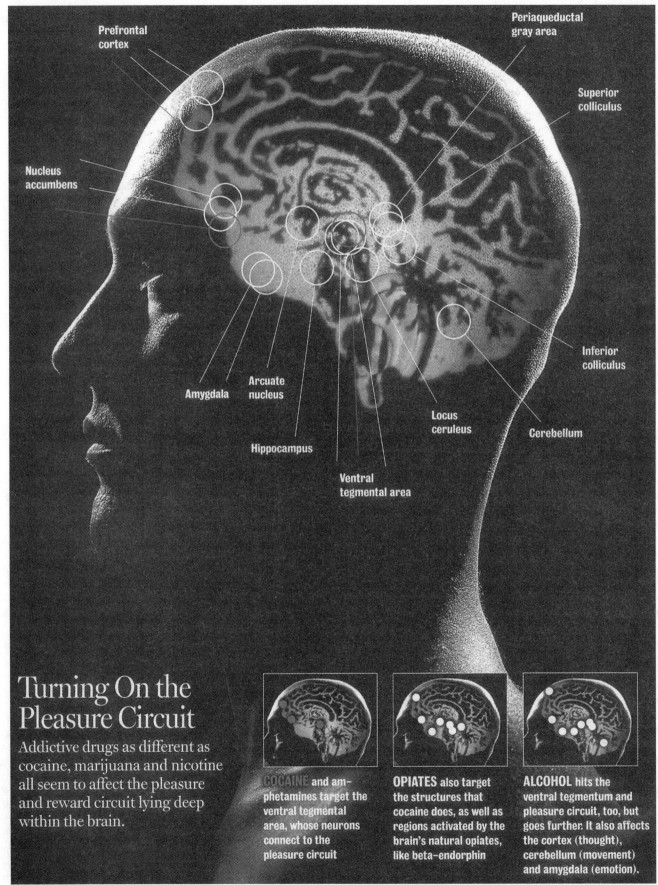

Prefrontal cortex

Periaqueductal gray area

Superior colliculus

Nucleus accumbens

Inferior colliculus

Amygdala

Arcuate nucleus

Hippocampus

Locus ceruleus

Cerebellum

Ventral tegmental area

Turning On the Pleasure Circuit

Addictive drugs as different as cocaine, marijuana and nicotine all seem to affect the pleasure and reward circuit lying deep within the brain.

COCAINE and amphetamines target the ventral tegmental area, whose neurons connect to the pleasure circuit

OPIATES also target the structures that cocaine does, as well as regions activated by the brain's natural opiates, like beta-endorphin

ALCOHOL hits the ventral tegmentum and pleasure circuit, too, but goes further. It also affects the cortex (thought), cerebellum (movement) and amygdala (emotion).

PHOTOGRAPHY BY HANS NELEMAN. SOURCE: NIDA

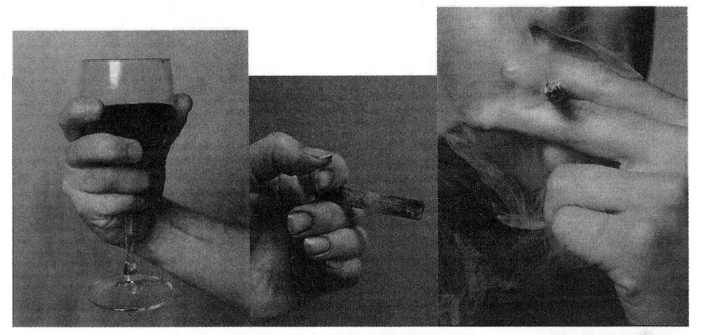

HOT BUTTONS Why is relapse so easy? In the addict's brain, even visual cues—glasses, crack pipes, cigarettes—trigger chemical cravings.

high, a surge of energy and euphoria. The fMRI showed why: cocaine made a beeline for the pleasure circuit, turning on brain areas called the sublenticular extended amygdala and nucleus accumbens and keeping them on.

How? "Drugs of abuse increase the concentration of dopamine in the brain's reward circuits," says Nora Volkow of Brookhaven National Lab. The drugs do that more intensely than any mere behavior, be it eating a four-star meal or winning the lottery. But each drug turns up this feel-good neurochemical in a different way:

• Cocaine blocks the molecule that ordinarily mops up dopamine sloshing around neurons. When all the seats on this so-called transporter molecule are occupied by cocaine, there is no room for dopamine, which therefore hangs around and keeps the pleasure circuit firing. The intensity of a cocaine high, Volkow found in 1997, is directly related to how much cocaine ties up the seats on the transporter bus.

• Amphetamines block the transporter, too. They also push dopamine out of the little sacs, called vesicles, where neurons store it. More dopamine means more firing of neurons in the pleasure circuit.

• Heroin stimulates dopamine-containing neurons to fire, releasing the neurochemical into the nucleus accumbens, a key region in the pleasure circuit. Nicotine does the same. Heroin also excites the same neurons that our brain's natural opioids do, but much more powerfully.

• Alcohol opens the neurotransmitter floodgates. It releases dopamine, serotonin (which governs our sense of well-being) and the brain's own opioids. It also disturbs levels of glutamate, which incites neurons to fire and helps account for the initial alcoholic high, as well as GABA, which dampens neuronal firing and eventually makes (most) drinkers sleepy.

After igniting these acute effects, an addictive drug isn't nearly through with the brain. Chronic use produces enduring changes. The most important: it reduces the number of dopamine receptors. Receptors are simply little molecular baseball gloves that sit on neurons, grab passing neurotransmitters like fly balls and reel them in. Animal evidence suggests that the more you take an addictive drug, the more dopamine receptors you wipe out, as the brain attempts to quiet down an overly noisy pleasure circuit. Having fewer dopamine receptors means fewer of those passing dopamines get caught, and the pleasure circuit calms down. But now the law of unintended consequences kicks in. With fewer dopamine receptors, a hit that used to produce pleasure doesn't. This is the molecular basis for tolerance. Drugs don't have the effect they originally did. To get the original high, the addict has to up his dose.

The only escape from irritability, anxiety and depression is to take more drug

But there's worse. The dearth of dopamine receptors means that experiences that used to bring pleasure become impotent. A good meal, a good chat, a good massage—none ignite that *frisson* of happiness they once did. The only escape from chronic dysphoria, irritability, anxiety and even depression, the user believes, is to take more drug. Initial use, in other words, may be about feeling good. But addiction is about avoiding abject, unremitting distress and despair.

The agony of withdrawal is also a direct result of drugs' resetting the brain's dopamine system. Withdrawal and abstinence deprive the brain of the only source of dopamine that produces any sense of joy. Without it, life seems not worth living. When a junkie stops supplying his brain with heroin, for instance, he becomes hypersensitive to pain, chronically nauseated and subject to uncontrollable tremors. "This is why addiction is a brain disease," says NIDA's Leshner. "It may start with the voluntary act of taking

45

drugs, but once you've got it, you can't just tell the addict 'Stop,' any more than you can tell the smoker 'Don't have emphysema.' Starting may be volitional. Stopping isn't."

Although the biological basis of tolerance, addiction and withdrawal is yielding some of its secrets, relapse is harder to explain. Why does an addict who has abstained for weeks, months or longer suddenly reach for the needle or the bottle? According to lab-animal studies, abstinence allows dopamine receptors to eventually return to normal, so after some period of withdrawal agony the brain should stop craving the drug. Yet addiction is practically the dictionary definition of a relapsing disease. One clue might lie in Scott Lukas's fMRI findings about cue-induced craving. The memories of drug abuse are so enduring and so powerful that even seeing a bare arm beneath a rolled-up sleeve reawakens them. And just as Pavlov's dog learned to salivate when he heard a bell that meant "chow time," so an addict begins to crave his drug when he sees, hears or smells a reminder of past use. Relapse might also reflect enduring genetic changes. Drugs can act as DNA switches, turning genes on or off. In lab animals, for instance, bingeing on cocaine turns down the activity of a gene that makes a dopamine receptor, finds Dr. Mary Jeanne Kreek of Rockefeller University. If that gene remains chronically inactive, it could lay the basis for relapse as an addict tries to compensate for a crippled pleasure circuit.

Genes may also explain, at least in part, why some people are at greater risk of drug addiction than others. It turns out that the same dopamine system that drugs activate can also be turned on by novel experiences, finds Dr. Michael Bardo of the University of Kentucky. That suggests that people driven to experience the Next New Thing may be trying to appease the same primal pleasure system as drug abusers—and that if they don't do it by, say, bungee jumping, they may try to do so with drugs. In fact, people who compulsively seek novelty also tend to abuse drugs more than people who are content with the same-old same-old. And novelty-seeking seems to have a genetic basis. That suggests that "there is a heritable component to addiction," says Kreek. But genes can also reduce the risk of addiction. Many Asians carry variants of genes that control the metabolism of alcohol. As a result, they suffer intense reactions—flushing, nausea, palpitations—from liquor. That could serve as a built-in defense against alcoholism, since people tend to avoid things that make them throw up. If only avoiding addiction were as easy for everyone else.

How Addictive Is Cigarette Smoking?

William M. London

Are cigarettes likelier to cause addiction than heroin? Are they more addictive than cocaine? The answers depend on how one defines "addiction."

The word "addict" traces to "addictus," the past participle of the Latin verb "addicere." "Addicere" combines the prefix "ad-," meaning "to or toward," and the verb "dicere." The standard meaning of "dicere" was "to say" (as exemplified in the words "dictate" and "dictionary," for instance), but its other senses were "to allot" and "to adjudge or give over." Thus, "addicere" meant "to give (oneself) over to"—i.e., "to give in or surrender to."[*]

Centuries ago, "to be addicted" meant to be devoted (to give oneself up) to a practice. Shakespeare wrote in *Othello:* "Each man to what sports and revels his addiction leads him." "The unhappy woman has ever been more addicted to the rites of her pagan ancestors than those of Holy Church," wrote the English statesman and poet Edward G. Bulwer-Lytton (1803–1873). In those days—long before 20th century theorists defined addiction in terms of the physiologic signs of discontinuance of the use of certain drugs—addictions were recognized not as bodily conditions, but rather as habitual behaviors with certain characteristics.

The headlines of some newspaper and magazine articles about potentially addictive behaviors other than drug taking (see box, "Headlines") clarify that in ordinary usage the word "addicted" continues to convey the meaning of "addicere." Acceptance of basing recognition of addiction on this meaning, rather than on

physical symptoms of withdrawal, has been growing. For example, in a 1997 edition of *The Washington Post,* Dr. Alan I. Leshner, director of the National Institute on Drug Abuse, stated in an editorial:

> ...[M]any of the most addicting and dangerous drugs do not produce severe physical withdrawal symptoms.... What matters most is whether a drug causes what we now know to be the essence of addiction: uncontrollable, compulsive drug seeking and use. This is how the National Academy of Sciences–Institute of Medicine, the American Psychiatric Association, and the American Medical Association all define addiction.

At bottom, one becomes addicted (devoted in a way that disrupts one's life) not to objects—drugs or television sets, for example—but rather to behaviors, like snorting drugs or watching telecasts. The expression "drug addiction" should be considered shorthand for "drug taking addiction."

EVALUATING ADDICTIVENESS

So I rephrase and combine this article's introductory questions: Is smoking cigarettes more addictive than shooting heroin into oneself or snorting (or smoking) cocaine? The 1998 Surgeon General's report *Health Consequences of Smoking: Nicotine Addiction* likened the phar-

macologic and behavior processes responsible for "tobacco addiction" to those responsible for addiction to heroin and cocaine. The Surgeon General acknowledged "tobacco addiction" not only on the basis of compulsive use but also because smokers often develop: (a) a withdrawal syndrome from not smoking, and (b) tolerance—in this case, the necessity of increasing nicotine intake to maintain one's response to the drug. The report did not, however, deal comparatively with the addictiveness of tobacco, heroin, and cocaine.

A psychiatrist who has done so is Yale University lecturer Sally Satel, M.D. In a 1996 *Wall Street Journal (WSJ)* editorial, she stated:

> Is it true that cigarettes are more addictive than heroin? This is ridiculous. When cigarettes are temporarily unavailable, smokers—as lousy as they may feel without a cigarette—don't initiate a crazed effort to find their next "fix." In contrast, people addicted to heroin commonly lie, cheat, or steal to get money to buy more, so distressing are the symptoms of heroin withdrawal. In the case of cocaine, the rush is so stimulating and the "crash" after a binge so wrenching that addicts will often do virtually anything to get more cocaine. Even alcoholics sometimes resort to desperate measures.

> Alcohol and illegal drugs can render users unable to cope with ordinary life. It's a vicious circle for many users, who turned to alcohol or drugs be-

cause they had trouble coping and the substance promised to numb their pain. By contrast, even the heaviest smokers don't forsake their families and jobs to pursue a nicotine habit. Cigarettes may shorten one's life, as sociologist James Q. Wilson has said, but they don't debase it.

Satel did not state the criteria she had used to judge the addictiveness of cigarette smoking relative to that of heroin use. Her implication that heroin addicts are likelier to lie, cheat, or steal to get heroin than are cigarette smokers to get cigarettes may well be correct—at least for American heroin addicts. If it is correct, however, the difference may be completely unrelated to differences in physiologic effects between shooting heroin and smoking cigarettes: In the United States, heroin addicts face sociolegal obstacles much more formidable than those that persons addicted exclusively to cigarette smoking face. And the more formidable such obstacles are, the likelier that an individual who decides to use a drug nonmedically will lie, cheat, and/or steal to get the drug. First, heroin addiction puts heroin addicts in danger of prosecution and coercion by courts to join treatment programs; by comparison, the legal risks of addiction to cigarette smoking are negligible. Second, a typical day's supply of heroin for an individual is much costlier than a typical day's supply of cigarettes. Third, heroin is available only through the black market, whereas anyone aged at least 18 years can easily and lawfully obtain tobacco.

Banning cigarettes would generate a cigarette black market and result in the inflation of cigarette prices; it would thus increase lying, cheating, and stealing among cigarette smokers. While many persons smoke less or quit smoking altogether when the sales tax on cigarettes increases, many others—even many for whom an extra weekly expenditure of a few dollars would be considerable—continue to smoke, unabatedly. After an 80-cent rise in the price of a pack of Pall Malls, a smoker with a physical disability told The New York Times in Febru-

ary 1999: "The President says he plans to raise the price of cigarettes another 55 cents. He does that, I'm going to make a gang, a wheelchair gang, and we're going to go out and steal money for cigarettes."

At bottom, one becomes addicted (devoted in a way that disrupts one's life) not to objects— drugs or television sets, for example— but rather to behaviors, like snorting drugs or watching telecasts.

Data from the most recent National Household Survey on Drug Abuse (NHSDA) suggest that most heroin users are not heroin addicts. In a 1998 edition of The New York Times, Satel herself conveyed information suggesting that heroin use is not as addictive as many persons suppose: "Two decades ago Lee Robins, a professor of psychiatry at Washington University in St. Louis, in a classic study of returning Vietnam veterans, found that only 14 percent of men who were addicted to heroin in Vietnam resumed regular use back home. The culture surrounding heroin use, the price and fear of arrest helped keep the rest off the needle."

Moreover, it is discernible from statistics on patterns of cocaine use that resisting cocaine is ordinarily not as difficult for cocaine users as Satel has implied. According to the aforementioned NHSDA, Americans who used cocaine occasionally (i.e., on 11 or fewer days) in 1997–1998 (approximately 2.4 million) outnumbered—by a factor of four—Americans who used it frequently (i.e., on at least 51 days). It is presumable that those who use cocaine often— the minority of cocaine users in the U.S.—are much likelier to use it addictively than are those who use it occasionally. Thus, cocaine addicts may take extraordinary steps to obtain cocaine, but most cocaine users

in the U.S. are not cocaine addicts. (Similarly, many persons addicted to imbibing resort to extremes to obtain alcoholic beverages, but most Americans who consume alcoholic beverages are not alcoholics.)

How Fast Can One Become Addicted to Cigarette Smoking?

In a 1998 study published recently in the British Medical Association journal Tobacco Control, scientists with the University of Massachusetts surveyed smoking habits among 681 youngsters, 95 of whom said they'd started smoking cigarettes occasionally (at least one per month) during the study. The researchers found that 63 percent of these 95 subjects had at least one of eight symptoms of addiction, and that these symptoms had arisen shortly after their first smoke. They further found that 25 percent of the symptomatic smokers had developed a symptom of addiction within two weeks of their first smoke. Sixty-two percent of the symptomatic subjects had said that they'd developed such a symptom before they'd started smoking daily or that the symptoms had set off their smoking daily.

—J.R

The summary of the NHSDA findings states: "Of the 23.1 million persons who used an illicit drug in the past year... 4.1 million were dependent on an illicit drug." This statement suggests that less than 20 percent of Americans who use illegal drugs are addicted to using them. But most of those respondents in the 1991–1992 NHSDA who said they had smoked cigarettes in the previous 30 days stated that they had: (a) smoked cigarettes daily for at least two weeks, (b) tried unsuccessfully to cut down on cigarettes, (c) felt dependent, and (d) felt sick when they'd refrained from smoking. None of these

HEADLINES OF ARTICLES ABOUT NON–DRUG-RELATED, POTENTIALLY ADDICTIVE BEHAVIORS

Buying lottery tickets

"The new breed of lottery addicts: Gambling on rise as states entice more to chase dreams, counseling groups say." *The Beacon Journal* (Akron), August 26, 1991.

Collecting

"Gathering trash or treasures is an addiction that can strike anyone. I should know." *Newsweek*, January 20, 1997.

Eating carrots

"Carrots good? Not if you're hooked on 'em." *The Beacon Journal* (Akron), August 2, 1992.

"Carrots hard to quit? Czech psychiatrists report carrot addiction in patients." *Record-Courier* (Ravenna, Ohio), August 2, 1992.

Eating chocolate

"Man looks for cure to chocoholism." *The Beacon Journal* (Akron), August 20, 1995.

Golfing

"Addicted to divots: Birdies and eagles not in columnist's vocabulary, but something about golf keeps him coming back," *The Beacon Journal* (Akron), August 29, 1991.

"Clinton misses chance to tell truth: He suffers addictive golfing disorder." *Florida Sun-Sentinel*, March 29, 1992.

"Househunting"

"'Don't mind me, I'm just looking': While researching his novel, Henry Sutton uncovered 'serial househunters'—people addicted to viewing, but who never buy." *Financial Times*, February 14, 1999.

Looking after pets

"'Cat dependent' book won't help you raise one." *The Beacon Journal* (Akron), January 26, 1992.

Lying

"Big-time liars try to reinvent lives: When truth is stretched beyond breaking point, compulsive lying sometimes creates a thrill that can be addictive, expert says." *The Beacon Journal* (Akron), March 16, 1993.

Playing games

"Bingo habit came close to wrecking a life: Canton woman found she was addicted to game, losing $400 a week when problem was at its worst." *The Beacon Journal* (Akron), August 6, 1991.

"Some clergy cancel the games, saying they can be addictive: But good causes, such as radio station for the blind, contend they couldn't survive without bingo profits." *The Beacon Journal* (Akron), August 6, 1991.

"Puzzling addictions." *Newsweek*, August 25, 1997.

"Clicking the habit: So it comes to this: Write books or play another round of hearts on the computer?" *The New York Times Magazine*, June 4, 2000.

Religious observance

"When religion becomes toxic: Addictive faiths wreak havoc in their followers, distorting aims, relate local man, three authors." *The Beacon Journal* (Akron), September 19, 1992.

Sexual activity

"Girls who go too far: Affection-starved teenagers are giving new meaning to the term boy crazy." *Newsweek*, July 22, 1991.

"Sex addict, husband to spend time apart." *The Beacon Journal* (Akron), February 4, 1992.

Shopping

"Compulsive shopping." *The Beacon Journal* (Akron), June 4, 1992.

"To shop, perchance nonstop: Compulsive spenders' payback time is nigh." *The New York Times*, December 29, 1996.

"The card-carrying angst of the dysfunctional shopper." *The New York Times*, December 20, 1998.

Skydiving

"It's flying, not falling, addicted sky diver says." *The Beacon Journal* (Akron), January 4, 1992.

Talking

"Addicted to talking: Cell phones are fast becoming the new cigarette." *The New York Times*, August 5, 2000.

Trading stock

"Can't stop checking your stock quotes? More compulsive investors are seeking help." *U.S. News & World Report*, July 10, 2000.

Undergoing cosmetic surgery

"Scalpel slaves just can't quit: Perpetual plastic surgery patients go from face-lift to face-lift in search of physical perfection." *Newsweek*, January 11, 1988.

Watching sport events

"Life is a camel race: A Broadway actor satisfies his sports addiction any way he can: Videotaped games, Internet recaps, even late-night updates from the desert." *The New York Times Magazine*, October 18, 1998.

Watching TV

"Oscar orgy is addictive." *The Beacon Journal* (Akron), March 29, 1992.

Web surfing

"They log on, but they can't log off: People are getting trapped in the Web. Should so-called Internet addicts get help—or just get a life?" *Newsweek*, December 18, 1995.

"Stuck on the Web: The symptoms of Internet addiction." *The New York Times*, December 1, 1996.

"Can we become caught in the Web? Psychologists and pundits hype 'Internet addiction.' My own online existence is more complex." *Newsweek*, December 6, 1999.

"Craving your next Web fix: Internet addiction is no laughing matter." *U.S. News & World Report*, January 17, 2000.

Other behaviors

"Addicted to perks: How America's elites rationalize their problem." *Newsweek*, July 8, 1991.

"Jackson finds campaigning addictive." *The Beacon Journal* (Akron), September 26, 1991.

"Support groups slash truancy, dropouts: Treating chronic class skippers as addicted to their behavior works for Springs High School." *Rocky Mountain News*, May 19, 1992.

"Addicted to sanctions: At this rate, the whole world will face U.S. penalties." *U.S. News & World Report*, June 15, 1998.

"Energy addicted in America." *The New York Times*, November 1, 1998.

---

signs of addiction were reported by most of those respondents who stated that they had used alcohol, cocaine, or marijuana in the previous 30 days.

In 1994, researchers examined data from the National Comorbidity Survey and made the estimates about prevalence indicated below.

- alcohol dependence anytime among consumers of alcoholic beverages: 15.4 percent

- heroin dependence anytime among heroin users: 16.7 percent

- dependence anytime on any drug other than alcohol and tobacco among drug users: 14.7 percent

In research interviews, persons who use more than one drug addictively tend to rate tobacco as their top drug need and as the drug most difficult to stop using.

In contrast, the researchers estimated the prevalence of tobacco dependence anytime among tobacco users at 31.9 percent. Indeed, they estimated the prevalence of tobacco dependence anytime among all Americans at 24.1 percent. Moreover, according to national surveys cited in the above-mentioned Surgeon General's report, 75–85 percent of cigarette smokers in the U.S. would like to quit smoking for good and have tried unsuccessfully to do so.

Satel's *WSJ* piece blurs the issue of addictiveness with the issue of socially disruptive eventualities from specific addictions. In research interviews, persons who use more than one drug addictively tend to rate tobacco as their top drug need and as the drug most difficult to stop using. Being "drug-free" is typically a requirement for participation in inpatient treatment programs for drug addicts. But cigarettes are not among the forbidden drugs in such programs. If they were, few drug addicts would be considered eligible for participation in them.

According to a 1994 edition of *The New York Times,* Dr. Jack E. Henningfield of the National Institute of Drug Abuse and Dr. Neal L. Benowitz of the University of California at San Francisco independently ranked alcohol, caffeine, cocaine, heroin, marijuana, and nicotine in terms of each of five categories:

- withdrawal symptoms;
- "reinforcement"—the likelihood that using the substance will result in its repeated use in preference to other substances;
- tolerance—the necessity of increasing use of the drug to maintain one's response to it;
- intoxication; and
- dependence—e.g., relative difficulty of discontinuing use of the drug.

Neither scientist ranked nicotine as the first among the six drugs in any of the above-mentioned categories except that of dependence—in which category both Henningfield and Benowitz ranked nicotine as first. And dependence of the kind they have defined is basically addiction of the "addicere" sort. This rank apparently holds across cultures.

THE BOTTOM LINE

Inherently, other drugs may have more "reinforcement" power than nicotine has; for example, they may please users more than nicotine pleases cigarette smokers. But addictive cigarette smokers smoke cigarettes more often than "drug addicts" use the drugs they favor. I consider cigarette smoking the most addictive form of drug taking.

---

* A word etymologically related to "addicere"—"abdicate," whose prefix means "away from"—also conveys the sense of giving up.

ACSH SCIENTIFIC ADVISOR WILLIAM M. LONDON, ED.D., M.P.H., IS A WALDEN UNIVERSITY FACULTY MENTOR

From *Priorities for Health,* 2000, Vol. 12, No. 3, pp. 11-15, 37. © 2000 by Priorities, a publication of the American Council on Science and Health (ACSH), 1995 Broadway, 2nd Floor, New York, NY 10023-5800. To learn more about ACSH visit us online at *www.asch.org.* Reprinted by permission.

Alcohol, the Brain, and Behavior

Mechanisms of Addiction

The actions of alcohol that cause intoxication, initiate and maintain excessive drinking behavior, and promote relapse during abstinence occur primarily in the brain. A thorough understanding of alcohol's effects on the mechanisms underlying brain function is essential to develop and improve alcoholism prevention and treatment strategies. This article is not an exhaustive overview of alcoholism neurobiology, but a sampling of the more significant recent advances in the field. KEY WORDS: neurobehavioral theory of AODU (AOD [alcohol or other drug] use, abuse, and dependence); brain; synapse; neuron; cell signaling; intracellular messengers; protein kinases; phosphorylation; AOD tolerance; AOD withdrawal syndrome.

The specific mental processes thought to underlie the development of alcoholism and its manifestations involve functions such as learning, attention, emotion, and cognition. The normal brain must orchestrate these functions simultaneously to perceive the environment, assess the significance of environmental stimuli in terms of survival, and initiate behavioral reactions. These activities require efficient communication among different regions of the brain and at multiple levels within those regions. This article considers alcohol's effects on three levels of communication within the brain: (1) the synaptic level, involving information transfer between individual nerve cells (neurons); (2) the systems level, representing the integrated activity of different brain regions; and (3) the intracellular

level, comprising signaling processes that occur within neurons.

ALCOHOL AT THE SYNAPSE: MODIFYING COMMUNICATION BETWEEN NEURONS

Within the brain, each neuron may communicate with many other neurons. Information is transferred by chemical messengers called neurotransmitters, which are released by one neuron and then bound by specialized proteins called receptors embedded in the outer membrane of another neuron. The tiny gap between communicating neurons is called a synapse. There are many neurotransmitters, each of which binds to a particular receptor. However, a given receptor may exist in multiple subtypes. Each subtype may produce a different response to the

same neurotransmitter, accounting for multiple effects of the same neurotransmitter in different brain regions or even in different locations on the same neuron (Weiner et al. 1997). Although a given neuron can release only one or two neurotransmitters it may possess different receptors. Thus, a neuron's response to information from other neurons depends on complex interactions of potentially conflicting messages arriving simultaneously (Charness 1990).

One of the most powerful effects of alcohol is to reduce the pace of brain activity in part by (1) decreasing the excitatory actions of the neurotransmitter glutamate at the NMDA subtype of glutamate receptor[1] and (2) boosting the inhibitory actions of the neurotransmitter gamma-aminobutyric acid (GABA) at the $GABA_A$ receptor (Diamond and Gordon 1997). These actions are among the reasons that alcohol is often thought of as a depressant.

The NMDA and GABA$_A$ receptors are linked to ion channels; that is, they function by opening a pore through the cell membrane to allow specific ions (electrically charged atoms) to enter the cell and affect the cell's electrical balance (Harris 1999). Other neurotransmitters of interest to alcohol researchers include dopamine, serotonin (5—HT), and a family of substances called opioid peptides. These neurotransmitters interact with their receptors to modulate the activity of the neuron on which they reside.

Dopamine's role in coordinating the execution of complex motor activities has long been recognized. Dopamine also appears to play a major role in motivational behavior (i.e., the pursuit of rewarding stimuli). Alcohol administration causes release of dopamine in a brain region (the nucleus accumbens) that is a key member of a group of linked structures associated with the development of addiction (Rassnick et al. 1992; Brodie and Pesold 1999).

Opioid peptides are a class of neurotransmitters that produce physiological effects similar to those of morphine and heroin. In humans, opioid peptides interact with other neurotransmitters to influence a broad range of physiological functions, including the control of pain. High blood levels of certain opioid peptides have been correlated with feelings of euphoria. Alcohol consumption affects the activity of opioid peptides, which in turn appears to increase the rewarding effects of alcohol (Roberts et al. 2000). The medication naloxone, which inhibits the function of opioid receptors, blocks the release of dopamine in the nucleus accumbens and has been shown to suppress alcohol consumption by laboratory animals (Benjamin et al. 1993).

Serotonin is involved in the regulation of mood, sleep, body temperature, appetite and a host of other physiological functions. Experiments in which mice have been genetically altered to lack specific serotonin receptor subtypes have suggested a role of serotonin on drinking levels. Alcohol-induced activation of specific serotonin-receptor subtypes can stimulate dopaminergic activity in the nucleus accumbens, potentially contributing to alcohol's rewarding effects. Other serotonin receptors have potential roles in tolerance,[2] withdrawal,[3] and intoxication (Valenzuela 1997).

ALCOHOL AND NEURONAL CIRCUITS: DETOURS ON THE INFORMATION HIGHWAY

Since the discovery in the late 1980s that alcohol at concentrations capable of producing intoxication in humans can inhibit the excitatory effects of the NMDA receptor and enhance the inhibitory function of the GABA receptor, much alcohol research has focused on identifying other specific receptors and ion channels that may be affected by alcohol. However, unlike most illicit drugs of abuse, alcohol does not have a specific neurotransmitter binding site in the brain. Moreover, the complex behaviors associated with alcohol use cannot be attributed to a limited number of specific chemical interactions. This realization sparked a closer look at alcohol's effects on pathways of neuronal communication that integrate the activities of multiple brain regions.

Reinforcement and Neuroadaptation

Two major processes that contribute to development of addiction are reinforcement and neuroadaptation. Reinforcement is when a rewarding stimulus (e.g. alcohol and other drug [AOD] induced euphoria) or relief of an unpleasant state (e.g., anxiety) increases the probability of a behavioral response (e.g., AOD use). Neuroadapt-ation refers to compensatory adjustments whereby the brain attempts to continue normal function despite the presence of alcohol. Occurring essentially simultaneously, reinforcement and neuroadaptation appear to underlie both the initial, short-term (acute) response to a drug and the establishment of the long-term (chronic) craving that characterizes addiction. Some neuroadaptive changes may be permanent, producing the persistent sense of discomfort that may lead to relapse long after a person stops drinking (Koob et al. 1993).

A common manifestation of neuroadaptation is the occurrence of an acute withdrawal syndrome following the abrupt cessation of a bout of heavy drinking. In response to the continued presence of alcohol, compensatory mechanisms attempt to overcome alcohol's inhibition of NMDA receptors by increasing overall NMDA function (upregulation). When alcohol leaves the synapse, the combination of upregulated excitatory transmission and downregulated inhibitory transmission results in the brain hyperexcitability characteristic of the acute withdrawal syndrome (Littleton 1998). Some brain damage occurs during acute alcohol withdrawal, and the severity of symptoms increases after repeated withdrawal episodes (Becker 1998). Withdrawal triggers the body's stress response, leading to elevated levels in the blood of the stress hormone cortisol. Excessive cortisol levels can kill neurons in the hippocampus, increase the risk of infectious diseases, alter energy metabolism, and promote disorders of mood and intellect (Adinoff et al. 1998).

Neuroadaptation is usually thought of in terms of counteradaptation—processes such as tolerance that are initiated to oppose the acute effects of drugs. However, neuroadaptation also includes sensitization, an *increased* response to a drug effect following repeated drug administration. If sensitization induces increased AOD consumption (as in the motivational state called "wanting" or craving, discussed later), it may contribute to addiction. Sensitization may be more likely to occur with intermittent, repeated exposure to AODs, whereas tolerance is more likely to occur with continuous exposure (Robinson and Berridge 1993).

Acute alcohol withdrawal includes motivational effects (Koob and LeMoal 1997). The neurological structures associated with the reinforcing actions of alcohol and other drugs may involve a common neural circuitry that forms a separate entity within the basal forebrain, the extended amygdala (Alheid and Heimer 1988). The term extended amygdala refers to a complex of several small structures near the base of the front of the brain that are similar in cell structure, function, and neural connectivity. This system has extensive connections to brain regions that play central roles in reinforcement and reward (Diamond and Gordon 1997).

Rats trained to self-administer alcohol during withdrawal show neurochemical and neuropharmacologic changes indicative of alterations in GABAergic, dopaminergic, and serotonergic function in specific components of the extended amygdala. One key structure encompassed by the extended amygdala is the nucleus accumbens, which has long been implicated in the rewarding properties of AODs. Other investigations have demonstrated selective activation of dopaminergic transmission in the shell of the nucleus accumbens in response to acute administration of virtually all major drugs of abuse (Tanda et al. 1997).

ALCOHOL AND MOLECULES: SABOTAGING THE COMMUNICATIONS INFRASTRUCTURE

Coordinated interneuronal communication can help account for relatively transient features of alcoholism, such as acute tolerance, physical withdrawal symptoms, and the initiation of reinforcement, which can lead to dependence. However, studying these processes alone does not provide a complete understanding of longer-term manifestations of alcoholism, such as the uncontrolled craving that may contribute to relapse years after cessation of drinking. The mechanisms underlying alcohol's chronic effects involve processes called intracellular signaling, the cell's internal biochemical response to receptor activation by extracellular chemical messengers.

Some Aspects of Normal Signaling

Intracellular signaling helps provide a link between the cell's initial response to alcohol and persistent alterations in neuronal function similar to the processes involved in memory. These processes may in-

volve the activation of genes that direct the synthesis of (i.e., express) specific proteins such as components of receptors or structural elements of the outer neuronal membrane. Such changes can strengthen information flow between neurons, helping close the loop between neurotransmitter activation and alcohol-related behavior. Intracellular signaling comprises a complex network of mutually interacting processes. Among the common themes that emerge is the regulatory role of protein-phosphorylating enzymes (e.g., protein kinases). Phosphorylation is the attachment of a phosphate group (a cluster of phosphorus and oxygen atoms) to a molecule. Phosphorylation can activate regulatory enzymes (e.g., G proteins), modify the function of ion channels, or activate transcription factors that initiate the expression of specific genes (Diamond and Gordon 1997).

The mechanisms underlying alcohol's chronic effects involve processes called intracellular signaling.

Many signaling pathways involve molecules called second messengers. These molecules may regulate short-term events (e.g., ion channel activity and neurotransmitter release) as well as longer-term processes (e.g., synaptic plasticity, memory, and learning). Some G proteins may influence shifts in alcohol sensitivity following chronic alcohol exposure by affecting the function of calcium-specific ion channels. Calcium itself can be a second messenger, and is required to stimulate many neuronal activities, including the release of neurotransmitters.

Alcohol's Effects on Protein Phosphorylation

Some protein kinases are located within the neuron, whereas others are attached to the inner surface of the neuronal membrane, where they chemically modify the structure of receptors to help regulate their function. Certain kinases appear to influ-

ence alcohol's effects on various NMDA and GABA receptor functions (Diamond and Gordon 1997).

The role of kinases in alcoholism has been studied using the techniques of genetic engineering. Null mutant, or knockout (KO), mice are made by replacing a normal gene with an inactive gene. Transgenic mice are created by permanently adding a foreign gene that may function differently than the animal's natural gene.

Schuckit (1998) has suggested that low initial sensitivity to alcohol's behavioral effects among sons of alcoholics is associated with increased risk of future alcoholism, possibly mediated in part by more rapid development of tolerance (Schuckit 1998). Knockout of a specific kinase that interacts with $GABA_A$ receptors in mice produces results consistent with Schuckit's observations in humans (Weiner et al. 1997).

Knockout of a different kinase in mice inhibits the function of hippocampal NMDA receptors, impairs the development of acute tolerance to alcohol, increases sensitivity to alcohol-induced sedation, and impairs spatial learning. Some evidence indicates that this kinase may modulate the activities of both NMDA and $GABA_A$ receptors to determine alcohol sensitivity (Yagi 1999).

NOTES

1. So called because the synthetic chemical N-methyl-D-aspartate (NMDA) also can activate this receptor subtype.

2. Tolerance, or the reduction in a drug effect after repeated use, may stimulate a user to take increasing doses of the drug in an attempt to reexperience its initial effect.

3. Acute withdrawal syndrome begins from 6 to 48 hours after the last drink and may include tremors, elevated blood pressure, increased heart rate, and seizures. Alcohol and other drug (AOD) withdrawal also includes changes in mental state (anxiety, depression, and craving) that may outlast the physiological symptoms and motivate renewed AOD consumption.

REFERENCES

Selected references are presented. For a full list of research cited, see the related article in the Tenth Special Report to the United States Congress on Alcohol and Health.

ADINOFF, B.; IRANMANESH, A.; VELDHUIS, J.; and FISHER, L. Disturbances of the stress response: The role of the hypothalamic-pituitary-adrenal axis during alcohol withdrawal and abstinence. *Alcohol Health & Research World* 22(1):67–71, 1998.

ALHEID, G.F., and HEIMER, L. New perspectives in basal forebrain organization of special relevance for neuropsychiatric disorders: The striatopallidal, amygdaloid, and corticopetal components of substantia innominata. *Neuroscience* 27(1):11–39, 1988.

BECKER, H.C. Kindling in alcohol withdrawal. *Alcohol Health & Research World* 22(1):25–33, 1998.

BENJAMIN, D.; GRANT, E.R.; and POHORECKY, L.A. Naltrexone reverses ethanol-induced dopamine release in the nucleus accumbens in awake, freely moving rats. *Brain Research* 621(1):137–140, 1993.

BRODIE, M.S., and PESOLD, C. Ethanol directly excites dopaminergic ventral tegmental area reward neurons. *Alcoholism: Clinical and Experimental Research* 23(11):1848–1852, 1999.

CHARNESS, M.E. Alcohol and the brain. *Alcohol Health & Research World* 14(2):85–89, 1990.

DIAMOND, I., and GORDON, A.S. Cellular and molecular neuroscience of alcoholism. *Physiological Reviews* 77(1):1–20, 1997.

HARRIS, R.A. Ethanol actions on multiple ion channels: Which are important? *Alcoholism: Clinical and Experimental Research* 23(10):1563–1570, 1999.

KOOB, G.F., and LEMOAL, M. Drug abuse: Hedonic homeostatic dysregulation. *Science* 278(5353):52–58, 1997.

KOOB, G.F.; MARKOU, A.; WEISS, F.; and SCHULTHEIS, G. Opponent process and drug dependence: Neurobiological mechanisms. *Seminars in the Neurosciences* 5:351–358, 1993.

From *Alcohol Research & Health,* Vol. 24, No.1, 2000, pp. 12-14.

Medical Consequences of Alcohol Abuse

Studies have shown that long-term alcohol abuse produces serious, harmful effects on a variety of the body's organ systems. Parts of the human body most affected include the liver and the immune, cardiovascular, and skeletal systems. Current research has examined some of these effects in an effort to better understand the medical consequences of alcohol use and abuse and to ultimately develop more effective treatments for responding to alcohol-induced bodily damage. This article discusses some of those findings. KEY WORDS: *chronic AODE (effects of AOD [alcohol or other drug] use, abuse, or dependence); alcoholic liver disorder; immune system; cardiovascular system; bone; breast; cancer; alcoholic cardiomyopathy; heart disorder; cardiac arrhythmia*

Long-term alcohol abuse is known to exert harmful effects on a number of the body's organ systems. Those most affected by alcohol abuse include the liver and the immune, cardiovascular, and skeletal systems. Many of the mechanisms involved in alcohol's effects on these systems are not yet completely understood. Consequently, recent research has examined some of alcohol's medical consequences in an effort to increase understanding and develop appropriate and effective treatments.

ALCOHOLIC LIVER DISEASE

The liver is a vital organ involved in processing fats, sugars, proteins, and vitamins and in regulating blood clotting. It plays a central role in the body's defenses, filtering toxins and microbes from the blood and marshaling an array of responses to trauma, stress, or inflammation.

Although the liver is capable of regeneration and repair, severe liver disease can be life threatening. Long-term, heavy alcohol use is the leading cause of illness and death from liver disease in the United States. The number of persons with alcoholic liver disease (ALD), which ranges in severity from fatty liver to end-stage cirrhosis, is conservatively

estimated at more than 2 million. Women, compared with men, develop alcoholic hepatitis and alcoholic cirrhosis after fewer years of drinking and from ingesting smaller daily amounts of alcohol. Rat studies confirm greater liver damage in females than in males at the same blood alcohol concentration (BAC).

There are three forms of ALD: fatty liver, which is usually reversible with abstinence; alcoholic hepatitis, characterized by persistent liver inflammation; and cirrhosis, characterized by progressive scarring of liver tissue. A person can have more than one type of liver disease. Patients with both cirrhosis and alcoholic hepatitis have a death rate of more than 60 percent over a 4-year period, with most deaths occurring within the first 12 months of diagnosis.

The major problem in developing new therapies for ALD has been a lack of understanding of the mechanisms for liver injury. However, much has been learned recently as a result of better technology and advances in research.

The Process of Inflammation

Long-term alcohol consumption has been shown to prolong the natural inflammatory responses of the liver. Inflammation functions to prevent the spread of localized injury or in-

fection while mobilizing the defense mechanisms of the immune system. An important aspect of liver inflammation is the production of chemical messengers called cytokines, which help regulate the inflammatory process. Cytokines attract and activate cells of the immune system, promote scar formation, and stimulate the production of additional chemical messengers, including more cytokines. However, if the increased levels of cytokines do not subsequently return to normal, they can cause chronic inflammation, leading to cell injury or cell death.

Cytokine production can be stimulated by endotoxin, a substance derived from the cell walls of certain bacteria that reside in the human intestine. Heavy alcohol consumption can increase the passage of endotoxin through the intestinal wall into the bloodstream. Specialized immune system cells (i.e., Kupffer cells) in the liver respond to blood-borne endotoxin by producing inflammatory cytokines. These cytokines further increase gut permeability, perpetuating a destructive cycle.

Another stimulus for excessive cytokine production is the generation of reactive oxygen species (ROS), toxic by-products of alcohol metabolism in the liver. Normally, ROS are quickly inactivated by antioxidants, protective molecules such as glutathione and vitamins A and E. However, if these defenses are impaired or if there is an overproduction of ROS, the result can be destruction of cell components and eventual cell death.

Persistent liver inflammation is characteristic of alcoholic hepatitis and usually precedes alcoholic cirrhosis. The hallmark of cirrhosis is cytokine-induced scarring that distorts the liver's internal structure and impairs its function. Imbalances in cytokine interactions impair the normal regeneration of tissue that typically follows liver injury.

Preventing Alcoholic Liver Injury

Researchers have devised several strategies to prevent or minimize alcoholic liver damage. In experiments using rats, alcohol-induced liver injury has been lessened by suppressing endotoxin-producing intestinal bacteria (e.g., through the use of antibiotics); administering substances that selectively destroy Kupffer cells or that inhibit the generation of ROS; and feeding antibodies that neutralize specific cytokines.

Experiments with a soybean extract, polyenylphosphatidylcholine (PPC), showed that it could prevent fibrosis and cirrhosis in alcohol-fed baboons. It also reduces the formation of scar tissue and may possess antioxidant properties as well. A study conducted by the U.S. Department of Veterans Affairs is currently evaluating the effects of PPC in humans with early ALD. Therapy with S-adenosyl-l-methionine (SAM) may lessen the depletion of the antioxidant glutathione in liver cells. Choline and methionine, dietary factors related to SAM, may help protect against endotoxin-induced liver injury in rats.

ALCOHOL'S EFFECTS ON THE IMMUNE SYSTEM

For 200 years physicians have observed that excessive alcohol consumption can lead to increased illness and death from infectious diseases. Alcohol abusers suffer from increased susceptibility to bacterial pneumonia, pulmonary tuberculosis, and hepatitis C (HCV). Patients with ALD are at high risk of having HCV, the leading cause of liver transplantation in the United States (National Institute on Alcohol Abuse and Alcoholism [NIAAA] 1998). Findings indicate that patients with ALD who are HCV positive have more severe liver disease and are younger than HCV-negative patients (NIAAA 1998). This increase in disease may reflect impaired immune function (i.e., immunodeficiency) caused by alcohol abuse.

Alcohol abusers may be at increased risk compared with nonabusers for infection with human immunodeficiency virus (HIV) from risky sex practices while intoxicated. Researchers also are investigating whether alcohol consumption itself may increase susceptibility to HIV infection or hasten the progression from HIV infection to full-blown AIDS.

In addition, some alcohol-related organ damage, as in ALD, may result in part from immune system overactivity in which the immune system attacks the body's own tissues (i.e., autoimmunity). Current research is examining the effects of heavy drinking on the immune system.

How the Immune System Works

The body's first line of defense against disease is inflammation, as described earlier. Inflammation is a nonspecific response, directed against all sources of damage. When nonspecific defenses are breached, an array of specific immune responses (see table) come into play. Specific immune responses may be broadly classified as either cell-mediated or humoral. Cell-mediated immunity involves direct contact between immune system cells and target cells (e.g., bacteria). Humoral immunity is provided by antibodies that circulate in the blood and lymph. Antibodies are specialized proteins designed to recognize and disable specific microorganisms or toxic substances. Antibodies that persist in the bloodstream may confer long-term immunity to a given disease.

Phagocytes are specialized cells that engulf invading microorganisms and cell debris through a process called phagocytosis. The first phagocytes to be activated are macrophages, which reside in tissues and organs throughout the body. White blood cells infiltrate the area, with neutrophils (a type of phagocyte) being the first to arrive, followed by monocytes. Monocytes are one of the types of cells that initially determine the "foreignness" of an invading agent and present it to other cells, which respond by producing appropriate cytokines. Various immune cells release chemical messengers to attract more cells, and within neutrophils and macrophages, the toxic oxygen-containing compounds ROS destroy phagocytosed microorganisms. Excess ROS, however, can damage liver cells.

Throughout the immune response, cytokines continue their regulatory functions. They include tumor necrosis factor (TNF) and a family of both inflammatory and anti-inflammatory substances called interleukins.

How Alcohol Affects the Immune System

Both chronic and acute alcohol administration can produce the loss of various types of immune responses in experimental animals. Administration of alcohol concentrations similar to those seen in binge drinkers impairs the function of cultured human monocytes and can temporarily reduce the numbers and activity of immune cells in mice. Alcohol inhibits neutrophil migration in humans and in experimental animals. However, an infiltration of neutrophils into the liver is observed in alcoholic hepatitis. Experiments with alcohol-fed rats showed that their neutrophils engulfed bacteria efficiently but did not kill all strains of pneumonia-causing bacteria with normal effectiveness.

Although inflammatory cytokine levels increase in ALD, endotoxin-induced secretion of inflammatory cytokines in the lung may decrease in alcohol-fed animals as well as in human alcoholics, potentially increasing susceptibility to pneumonia. Acute administration of alcohol to rats reduced ROS production by isolated lung macrophages after challenge with TB organisms.

Mediators of the Immune Response

Immune Response	Function
Humoral	
Antibody	A specialized protein that recognizes and disables specific microorganisms or toxic substances. When persisting in the bloodstream, it may help confer long-term immunity against a specific disease.
Cell-Mediated	
Phagocyte	A specialized cell that engulfs invading microorganisms and cell debris through a process known as phagocytosis.
Macrophage	A type of phagocyte that is the first to be activated during phagocytosis. It resides in tissues and organs throughout the body.
Neutrophil	A type of phagocyte that aids in the destruction of invading microorganisms, in part by releasing toxic compounds known as reactive oxygen species (ROS). Together with monocytes, neutrophils are commonly referred to as white blood cells.
Monocyte	A type of cell that is responsible for determining the "foreignness" of an invading agent and then presenting such agents to other cells for destruction. Monocytes release ROS to aid in the destruction process. They are also referred to as white blood cells.

Therapeutic Measures

Some proposed therapies include administration of such substances as antibodies against endotoxin or against specific cytokines, substances that would absorb excess cytokines or inhibit their function, and drugs that have a widespread effect (e.g., decreasing the permeability of the intestinal wall to the passage of endotoxin). Administration of growth hormone and related chemical messengers has been shown to improve some, but not all, measures of immune function in rats.

ALCOHOL'S EFFECTS ON THE CARDIOVASCULAR SYSTEM

Chronic heavy drinking is a leading cause of cardiovascular illness such as degenerative disease of heart muscle (cardiomyopathy); disorders associated with decreased blood supply to the heart muscle (coronary heart disease [CHD]); high blood pressure; heart rhythm disorders (arrhythmias); and stroke.

Alcoholic Cardiomyopathy

Long-term heavy drinking can cause the heart to become enlarged and lose some of its ability to contract, a condition known as alcoholic cardiomyopathy. These symptoms include shortness of breath and an insufficient blood flow to the rest of the body. Women may have a greater risk than men of developing alcoholic cardiomyopathy. The condition may be at least partially reversible with abstinence.

Alcohol's toxic effects on heart muscle may be mediated by increased ROS levels and decreased antioxidant enzyme activity. Another recent study found that alcohol may decrease the sensitivity of heart muscle to chemical messengers from nerve cells that regulate heart muscle metabolism and contraction.

Coronary Heart Disease

The blood that nourishes the heart muscle is delivered through the coronary arteries. Manifestations of CHD range from episodic chest pain to sudden death. Heart attacks, the most common serious manifestations of CHD, are usually triggered by the formation of a blood clot within a coronary artery already narrowed by deposits of cholesterol and other fatty substances. The resulting ischemia reduces the heart's pumping ability, often leading to permanent disability or death.

With few exceptions, worldwide epidemiologic data demonstrate a 20- to 40-percent lower CHD incidence among drinkers compared with nondrinkers. Heavy drinkers have an increased risk of death from heart disease. However, moderate drinkers exhibit lower rates of CHD-related mortality than both heavy drinkers and abstainers. This is confirmed by studies in which participants were interviewed about their drinking habits and life styles before the onset of disease. Such studies—representing a total population of more than 1 million men and women of different ethnicities followed for up to 24 years—confirm an association between moderate drinking and lower CHD risk. However, this association does not necessarily mean that alcohol itself is the cause of the lower risk.

In addition, different epidemiologic studies apply the term "moderate drinking" to a wide range of consumption levels, sometimes more than the amount defined by the Dietary Guidelines for Americans as moderate: two or fewer standard drinks per day for men and one less per day for women. In any case, the apparent benefits of moderate drinking on CHD mortality are offset at higher drinking levels through increasing risk of death from other alcohol-related causes.

Research has suggested several possible mechanisms by which alcohol may protect against CHD. For example, alcohol inhibits the deposition of fatty substances within the coronary arteries of mice and also may inhibit the formation of blood clots within already narrowed coronary arteries.

> *Intoxication can cause certain types of arrhythmia in both alcoholics and otherwise healthy persons.*

Epidemiologic data and results of studies on isolated animal hearts suggest that moderate alcohol consumption also may lower CHD mortality by improving survival after a heart attack. Further studies are needed to confirm this effect and to determine its applicability in humans.

Alcohol and Blood Pressure

An association between heavy alcohol consumption and increased blood pressure has been observed in more than 60 studies in diverse cultures and populations. The effects of moderate alcohol consumption on blood pressure are unclear.

Arrhythmias

The heart's ability to function effectively depends on regular, synchronous contraction of the heart muscle. Heavy drinking can disrupt the heart rhythm both acutely (during an episode of drinking) and chronically (due to long-term use). Intoxication can cause certain types of arrhythmia in both alcoholics and otherwise healthy persons. The development of arrhythmias with binge drinking—a condition seen most frequently around the holidays—is known as "holiday heart syndrome."

Sudden death attributable to arrhythmia is one of the causes of mortality in alcoholics with or without pre-existing heart disease. Such deaths often occur during periods of abstinence (Clark 1988), suggesting the development of arrhythmias during alcohol withdrawal.

Alcohol and Stroke

The relationship between alcohol consumption and stroke is similar to that seen with CHD. Moderate alcohol consumption appears to be associated with lower incidence of ischemic strokes, whereas heavy drinking may increase the risk of both ischemic and hemorrhagic strokes (i.e., bleeding within the brain).

ALCOHOL AND BONE

Epidemiologic studies have found a significant association between alcohol consumption and risk for bone fracture. In addition to increased risk of accidental injury through alcohol-induced impairment of gait and balance, alcoholics also may suffer from a generalized decrease in bone mass, making their bones more fragile. Heavy drinking may lead to osteoporosis, characterized by severe back pain, spinal deformity, and increased risk of wrist and hip fractures, although some recent studies suggest that moderate alcohol consumption may protect against osteoporosis.

Alcohol and Skeletal Development

Bone growth and remodeling during childhood and adolescence involves the coordinated activity of two types of cells: (1) osteoclasts, which break down (i.e., resorb) bone, and (2) osteoblasts, which form new bone.

Cyclic bone remodeling continues throughout adulthood to regulate and maintain bone mass. Adult bone formation and resorption rates are tightly coupled, with approximately 10 percent of bone undergoing the process at any given time. Between ages 20 and 40, a person's bone density begins to decline, resulting in a cumulative decrease in skeletal mass of up to 40 percent by age 70. Women experience accelerated decline in bone density following menopause and are most susceptible than men to osteoporosis.

Alcohol disrupts bone remodeling in animals and humans. Overall, studies in alcoholics suggest that alcoholic bone disease involves considerable suppression of bone formation

with essentially normal rates of resorption. The changes in bone turnover induced by alcohol can apparently be reversed by abstinence. The skeletal consequences of alcohol intake may be especially harmful during adolescence, when the rapid skeletal growth ultimately responsible for achieving peak bone mass occurs. By limiting peak bone mass attainment, the risk of developing osteoporosis later in life may increase and its onset hastened.

Potential Mechanisms of Alcohol-Induced Bone Disease

Long-term consumption of alcohol disrupts the processes of bone growth and bone tissue repair. A decrease in bone density, as well as an increased risk of bone fracture, may result. These effects of alcohol on bone may occur directly, with alcohol itself interfering with bone metabolism, or indirectly, with alcohol exerting its effects through a third party, such as hormones. The female reproductive hormone estrogen appears to affect bone metabolism, although its role with respect to alcohol consumption is uncertain.

A number of researchers have noted that alcohol can reduce osteoblast formation. Alcohol can inhibit osteoblast proliferation in culture at concentrations well within the drinking level observed in alcoholics. A concentration of alcohol equivalent to a blood alcohol level of 0.044 percent, about half the blood alcohol level that many States define as legally intoxicated, also resulted in a 20-percent decline. Alcohol also may depress osteoblast function by inhibiting the cell's response to insulin-like growth factors, chemical messengers that help regulate bone remodeling.

Studies of alcohol's effects on osteoclast numbers have provided conflicting results. However, alcohol increases levels of a specific interleukin (IL-6), which may contribute to the development of osteoporosis by stimulating osteoclastic activity.

BREAST CANCER

The lifetime risk for breast cancer among U.S. women is estimated to be as high as one in eight. Results of approximately 50 epidemiologic studies and analyses conducted since the 1970s point to an increase in breast cancer risk associated with alcohol consumption. Controversy remains over the interpretation of these studies, however. For epidemiologists, the actual numerical association between alcohol and breast cancer risk is considered relatively modest. In addition, some studies found no link between high alcohol intake and breast cancer risk.

Mechanisms of Alcohol-Related Breast Cancer

Scientists have identified plausible biological mechanisms for alcohol's actions. Research findings suggest a role for alcohol in breast cancer risk in both premenopausal and postmenopausal women. Cumulative lifetime exposure to estrogen is considered an important contributor to breast cancer risk. A number of studies have examined whether alcohol raises estrogen levels in premenopausal and postmenopausal women. Although some studies report such an effect, the evidence is not conclusive.

Alcohol may be capable of enhancing the progression as well as the initiation of cancer. Increased metastasis (proliferation beyond the site of origin) of implanted breast cancer cells was observed in rats given alcohol in a liquid diet. In addition, alcohol and its highly reactive metabolite acetaldehyde also have been linked to the body's inability to repair damage to the cell's genetic material (i.e., DNA) induced by cancer-causing agents. If unrepaired, damage to critical regions of DNA in breast cells could lead to mutations and the subsequent initiation of cancer. When rodents are fed alcohol, their levels of circulating protein—a hormone that can stimulate the growth of breast tissue—increase. In addition, ROS can contribute to tumor promotion. Alcohol intake also decreases the immune system's ability to detect and destroy cancer cells (Yirmiya and Taylor 1993).

REFERENCES

Selected references are presented. For a full list of research cited, see the related article in the Tenth Special Report to the United States Congress on Alcohol and Health.

Clark, J. Sudden death in the chronic alcoholic. *Forensic Science International* 36(1–2):105–111, 1988.

National Institute on Alcohol Abuse and Alcoholism. *Alcohol Alert No. 42: Alcohol and the Liver: Research Update.* Bethesda, MD: The Institute, 1998.

Yirmiya, R., and Taylor, A.N., eds. *Alcohol, Immunity and Cancer.* Boca Raton, FL: CRC Press, 1993.

From *Alcohol Research & Health,* Vol. 24, No. 1, 2000, pp. 27-31.

UNIT 3

The Major Drugs of Use and Abuse

Unit Selections

Key Points to Consider

• How is it that specific drugs evolve, develop use patterns, and lose or gain popularity over time?

• How does the manner in which a drug is ingested help define its respective user population?

• How does the manner in which a drug is used influence the severity of consequences related to that drug? Or does it?

• Why does the use of certain drugs encourage the use of other drugs?

 **Links: www.dushkin.com/online/**
These sites are annotated in the World Wide Web pages.

Drugs, Solvents and Intoxicants
http://www.termisoc.org/~harl/

QuitNet
http://www.quitnet.org

The following articles discuss those drugs that have prevailed historically as drugs of choice. Although pharmacological modifications emerge periodically to enhance or alter the effects produced by certain drugs or the manner in which various drugs are used, basic pharmacological properties of the drugs remain unchanged. Crack is still cocaine, ice is still methamphetamine, and black tar is still heroin. In addition, tobacco products all supply the drug nicotine, coffee and a plethora of energy drinks provide caffeine, and alcoholic beverages provide the drug ethyl alcohol. These drugs all influence how we act, think, and feel about ourselves and the world around us. They also produce markedly different effects within the body and within the mind.

To understand why certain drugs remain popular over time, and why new drugs become popular one must be knowledgeable about the effects produced by individual drugs. Why people use drugs is a bigger question than why people use tobacco. However, understanding why certain people use tobacco, or cocaine, or marijuana, or alcohol is one way to construct a framework from which to tackle the larger question of why people use drugs in general. One of the most complex relationships is the one between Americans and their use of alcohol. Some 76 million Americans have experienced alcoholism in their families. The most recent surveys of alcohol use estimate that 105 million Americans currently use the drug. About 45 million are estimated to have engaged in binge drinking (five or more drinks on one occasion), and currently there are 10.4 million drinkers between the ages of 12 and 20. Alcohol prevails as the most popular recreational drug of choice and its use is commonly associated with the use of most illicit drugs. Of the current 11.2 million heavy drinkers, 30 percent (3.3 million people) are illicit drug users. There is also a long-standing and significant relationship between the use of alcohol and the use of tobacco. An estimated 66.8 million Americans report current cigarette use. The majority consensus is that alcohol is used responsibly by most people who use it even though 10 percent of the American population is believed to be suffering from various stages of alcoholism. The use of alcohol is a powerful force within our national consciousness about drugs.

Understanding why people initially turn to the nonmedical use of drugs is a huge question that is debated and discussed in a voluminous body of literature. One important reason why the major drugs of use and abuse, such as alcohol, nicotine, cocaine, heroin, marijuana, amphetamines, and a variety of prescription, over-the-counter, and herbal drugs, retain their popularity is because they produce certain physical and psychological effects that humans crave. They temporarily restrain our inhibitions; reduce our fears; alleviate mental and physical suffering; produce energy, confidence, and exhilaration; and allow us to relax. Some also, albeit artificially, suggest a greater capacity to transcend, redefine, and seek out new levels of consciousness. And they do it upon demand. People initially use a specific drug, or class of drugs, to obtain the desirable effects historically associated with the use of that drug. Heroin and opiate-related drugs such as oxycontin and vicodin produce, in most people, a euphoric, dreamy state of well-being. Cocaine and related stimulant drugs produce euphoria, energy, confidence, and exhilaration. Alcohol produces a loss of inhibitions and a state of well-being. Nicotine and marijuana typically serve as relaxants. Various over-the-counter and herbal drugs all attempt to replicate the effects of more potent, and often prohibited or prescribed, drugs. Although effects and side effects may vary from user to user, a general pattern of effects is predictable from most major drugs and their analogs. Varying the dosage and altering the manner of ingestion will alter the drug's effects. Some drugs, such as LSD and some types of designer drugs, produce effects on the user that are less predictable and more sensitive to variations in dosage level and to the user's physical and psychological makeup.

Although all major drugs of use and abuse have specific reinforcing properties perpetuating their continued use, they also produce undesirable side effects that regular drug users attempt to mitigate. Most often, users attempt to mitigate these effects with the use of other drugs. Cocaine, methamphetamine, heroin, and alcohol have long been used to mitigate each other's side effects. A good example is the classic "speedball" of heroin and cocaine. When they are combined, cocaine accelerates and intensifies the euphoric state of the heroin, while the heroin softens the comedown from cocaine. One present popular trend is to mix energy drinks with alcoholic beverages to mitigate the drowsiness associated with drinking alcohol. Some alcoholic beverage companies are producing recipes to capitalize on this trend. Other related drug trends, availability, price, and the public's perception of the drug's safety often influence the degree to which some drugs remain popular.

Drug abuse in America spans the spectrum of legality. To associate only illegal drugs with abuse and criminality is shortsighted. In terms of drug-related social impacts, any discussion of major drugs could begin and end with the topics of alcohol and nicotine. The pursuit of drugs and the effects they produce may be influenced by, but not bound by, legal status. For the student of drug-related phenomena, an attachment to the concepts of legality or illegality for purposes of comprehensively rationalizing drug-related reality is inappropriate. For example, yearly alcohol-related deaths far outnumber deaths from all illegal drugs combined.

THE ANDEAN COCA WARS

A crop that refuses to die

Drug-fighters claim that a combination of repression and social engineering can eliminate coca cultivation, and so cocaine. It has not happened yet

PALMAPAMPA, PERU

MAXIMO ROJAS'S farm lies up a steep and muddy track on a hillside high above the Apurimac river, in eastern Peru. At this time of year, the river is a swirling brown torrent as it cuts through a broad tropical valley on its way to the Amazon. The track passes through a field of glossy young coffee bushes before ending at an open-sided thatched hut. There Mr Rojas and his family have spread soyabeans to dry on the ground. As well as coffee and soya, Mr Rojas has planted cacao, citrus, pineapples and maize on his eight hectares (20 acres) of land. In all this, he has been helped by agronomists from the United Nations Drug Control Programme. It is, he says proudly, a model farm that others can copy.

But does Mr Rojas also have any coca, the hardy Andean shrub from which cocaine is extracted? "A little," he says, shifting awkwardly, as if a little in fact means a lot. Even so, it is much less than it was. Until 1997, coca was Mr Rojas's only crop, as it was for most of his neighbours.

It brought in a good, reliable income, in an industry that had remained fairly stable since the 1970s. Coca was grown by farmers in Peru's eastern valleys and in Bolivia's Chapare lowlands. It was roughly processed into cocaine paste, and then taken to Colombia for refining and export to the United States and Western Europe.

By last December, however, the amount of land under coca in the Apurimac had fallen to just 8,100 hectares, from a peak of 21,000 hectares (52,000 acres) in 1995. The fall is part of a trend that has spread rapidly over the past four years. The State Department's annual report on international narcotics control, released this week, and unusually upbeat in tone, shows that land in coca production in Peru has fallen to 38,700 hectares, one-third of what it was in 1995. In Bolivia, there are no fewer than 10,000 hectares of coca left (excluding some 12,000 hectares planted with legal coca for traditional use, such as chewing and coca tea). Overall, the total amount of land under coca in the Andes has fallen by 15% since 1995.

Figures like these have emboldened officials in the United States and at the United Nations to talk seriously about the near-total eradication of coca, or at least its reduction to "residual" levels. One such optimist is John Hamilton, the United States' ambassador in Lima. "When I flew over the Upper Huallaga in 1986 for the first time and saw coca fields like Iowa corn fields, it was a sight for despair," he says. "Now, I'm becoming convinced that getting rid of it altogether is not a pipedream." In Peru, the government of Alberto Fujimori says that it hopes to achieve complete eradication by 2003. In Bolivia, President Hugo Banzer's administration is pledged to remove Bolivia from the cocaine trade by the end of its term in mid-2002.

For anti-drug warriors in the United States, all this is proof that the "war" on Andean cocaine declared by President George Bush in 1989 is at last starting to be won. So far, it has been a relatively cheap strategy, too. Action aimed at cutting the supply of drugs in producer countries accounted for only around 13% of the United States' $18 billion anti-drug budget last year.

The cost is higher in diplomatic terms. Critics complain that the United States has sacrificed more important policy goals in Latin America, such as support for democracy and human rights, to its drug crusade. Both the United States and European countries have more time these days for the Latin American argument that the cocaine industry would not exist without their demand for drugs and their supply of chemicals, firearms and money-laundering facilities. But Americans still cling to their heavy-handed and often unilateral strategy, symbolised by this week's "certification" ritual, an annual exercise mandated by law in which the United States delivers judgment on its neighbours' anti-drug efforts. On March 1st, as expected, the Clinton administration announced that all the Andean countries and Mexico were fully co-operating.

Has certification produced results? The figures for declining production, drawn up by the CIA on the basis of satellite monitoring and selected field visits, are not above challenge. Although they do not dispute the trend, some responsible drugwatchers believe the figures overstate the fall in coca production in Peru and Bolivia. And meanwhile the Andean drug industry has continued to diversify. Cultivation of opium poppies, unknown in Colombia in 1990, has risen sharply, to more than 6,000 hectares last year; now it has begun in Peru's northern Andes. Although the Andean countries supply less than 10% of world opium output, their share is rising, and their product, being extra-pure, is especially attractive.

There is also one notable exception to the trend of coca decline. Having previously underestimated the yield and potency of Colombian coca, the CIA said last month that it had more than doubled its estimate of that country's potential output of cocaine. Well it might. The amount of land under coca in Colombia has more than doubled since 1995, to 122,500 hectares. In other words, much of the coca has merely migrated north.

The Colombian exception

"Colombia is a drug disaster," says General Barry McCaffrey, the United States' director of national drug policy. Most of the new coca is in the departments of Putumayo and Caqueta, in southern Colombia, in areas controlled by the FARC, the country's main leftist guerrillas—just as, a decade ago, coca flourished in Peru's Huallaga and Apurimac Valleys under the protection of the now-defeated Maoist guerrillas of the Shining Path. Whereas, in Peru, coca is typically grown on small plots, in Putumayo there are plantations of up to 10,000 hectares, divided into blocks and carefully managed, according to an American official.

As a result of these shifts, the supply of cocaine remains more than adequate to meet demand. The wholesale price of cocaine in Miami and other entry points in the United States has remained broadly constant in nominal terms for more than a decade. By moving coca cultivation to Colombia, the drug makers have cut their costs and risks and increased their efficiency to "extraordinary levels", according to the State Department report. Those new large coca plantations are the ostensible reason for the Clinton administration's proposal, now before Congress, to give Colombia $1.6 billion in extra military aid over the next two years.

The FARC is not the only violent group in Colombia to be involved with the drug trade. General McCaffrey concedes that some right-wing paramilitaries own and operate cocaine-processing laboratories, whereas the FARC does no more than tax and protect the industry. But from that alone it earns perhaps $500m a year. This income has helped the FARC to grow. It now has 17,000 men under arms, giving it a military power which far outweighs its political support.

The main purpose of the proposed American aid is to train and equip three new army battalions to wrest military control of the southern coca-growing areas from the FARC. Once that is done, the Colombian police should be able to eradicate the coca fields by dumping herbicide on them from low-flying aircraft. The Colombian police already claim to spray some 50,000 hectares of coca a year, as well as 5,000 hectares of opium poppies. Critics doubt whether this has much effect. But General Rosso Jose Serrano, Colombia's police chief, says that without spraying, Colombia would have up to three times more coca. "If it weren't effective, they wouldn't have shot down five helicopters and four aircraft," he argues.

Ironically, the FARC's current strength owes much to the United States' decision to "decertify" Colombia two years running during the government of Ernesto Samper (1994–98), whose election campaign was alleged to have been boosted by drug money. That spurred Mr Samper into tougher action against the drug trade. But, thus distracted, his weakened government stood helpless as the FARC drove the armed forces from several bases in the south.

The United States' anti-drug warriors are now intent on helping the Colombian government to regain military control of its territory. Once that is done, they believe, coca production can be cut in Colombia just as it has been elsewhere. This assumes, however, that one set of policies fits sharply differing countries. It also raises the question of where coca will migrate to next.

Home-grown solutions

The steep fall in coca production in Peru and Bolivia has come about not only because of heavy-handed intervention from the United States. It has also been helped by changing policies and attitudes within those countries themselves. In recent years, a certain amount of give-and-take has been going on. At the urging of the United States, the present governments of the Andean countries have adopted far tougher measures than their predecessors tried. In return, the United States has been persuaded—often with difficulty—to give more money to help coca growers find other ways of earning a living.

This shift in attitudes among the Andean governments partly reflects a desire to avoid decertification. They have seen what it did to Mr Samper. His successor,

Andres Pastrana, is working closely with the United States in his efforts to pull Colombia out of its quagmire. In Peru, Mr Fujimori's co-operation over drugs makes the Americans reluctant to criticise his autocratic rule. Bolivia's government began forcible coca eradication in 1995, only after being warned that it would otherwise be decertified. American officials had become fed up with Bolivia. After a decade of alternative development and voluntary eradication, in which farmers were paid to pull up their coca, the overall amount of the crop had not diminished at all; the farmers were simply planting new coca elsewhere.

In addition, public opinion in the Andean countries is more hostile to the drug industry than in the past. That is partly because consumption has risen, though it remains low: drug abuse is no longer something that hurts only Americans and Europeans. But it is also because of public weariness at the violence and corruption that come with the cocaine industry.

In both Peru and Bolivia, the policy is to wield bigger sticks and bigger carrots than in the past. But the details vary. In Peru in the mid-1990s, Mr Fujimori ordered his air force to shoot down suspicious planes flying towards Colombia, and stepped up harassment of coca-processing points. This caused—or at least coincided with—a steep fall in the price of coca in Peruvian fields, as Colombian buyers stayed away. As prices fell below the cost of production, many growers abandoned their field. Last year the government also began forcible eradication, chopping down some 15,000 hectares of coca. This reversed a policy under which coca cultivation had been judged to be legal, lest coca farmers should be driven into the arms of the Shining Path.

In Bolivia, President Banzer, now a democrat but a military dictator in the 1970s, has cracked down on the powerful coca growers' unions in the Chapare. In 1998, 12 farmers were killed when troops and police cleared road blocks thrown up by the coca farmers' unions in protest at the government's decision to make eradication compulsory. The government is now using 2,000 troops and police to eradicate coca in the Chapare. It is also trying to stop the import of chemicals needed for processing cocaine. This reduces the drug's purity, and therefore its market value.

Repressive measures, however, are only part of the solution. Unless government and aid donors can also deter farmers

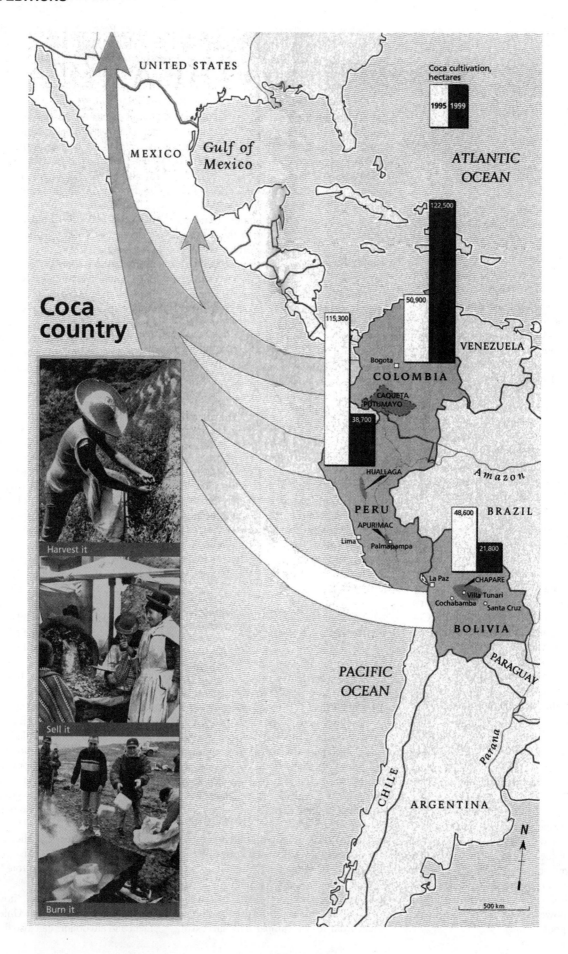

Coca cultivation, hectares

1995 | 1999

Coca country

Harvest it

Sell it

Burn it

UNITED STATES

MEXICO

Gulf of Mexico

ATLANTIC OCEAN

122,500

50,900

115,300

VENEZUELA

Bogota

COLOMBIA

CAQUETA
PUTUMAYO

38,700

HUALLAGA

Amazon

BRAZIL

PERU

APURIMAC

Lima

Palmapampa

48,600

21,800

La Paz

CHAPARE

Villa Tunari

Cochabamba

Santa Cruz

BOLIVIA

PACIFIC OCEAN

PARAGUAY

CHILE

Parana

ARGENTINA

N

500 km

from planting coca by offering economic alternatives, there is no chance of lasting success. But this is by far the trickiest part of the strategy. First, it is all but impossible for any legal alternative crops to match the income that coca can provide in normal market conditions. At December's price of $1.40 per kilo (2.2lb) of leaf, a well-run coca farm in the Apurimac can give a net annual profit of more than $2,000 per hectare: less than in the past, but almost double the profit from coffee. In Bolivia, a hectare of coca may yield up to three times the income of a hectare of bananas. So trying to drive down the coca price by harassing the traffickers is essential, if alternative development is to work.

Better, but poorer

Officials in charge of alternative development stress that they do not promise the farmer the same kind of income as coca offers. They can claim, perhaps, to offer a better quality of life. "We can give a decent income to the farmer, put in infrastructure, integrate these areas into the national economy. The trafficker brings credit and cash, but also violence, corruption, prostitution, and disorder," says Patrice Vandenberghe, the UN's anti-drug man in Lima.

But even providing a decent income is hard. Consider Bolivia's Chapare. If alternative development is ever to work, it will be there. The Chapare is a fairly compact, socially cohesive area; its farmers have decent-sized plots, of which coca used to occupy only a part; and it has seen nearly two decades of outside investment. Much of the money has gone on infrastructure: a (mainly) asphalted highway now runs through the area, linking it to the cities of Cochabamba and Santa Cruz. A network of secondary roads and bridges, and packing and storage plants, gives farmers "better access to markets than in any other part of the country," says Jose Deckers, the deputy minister for alternative develop-

ment. An electricity grid provides power for processing plants.

In 1980 Villa Tunari, the area's small administrative centre, was a roadside slum. Now it is neat and prosperous, with several good hotels (though the guests are mainly aid workers, and a big new golf resort being built across the river seems heroically ambitious). Where once coca reigned, legal commercial crops are taking over: they cover some 108,000 hectares now, almost three times as much as in 1986, and generated sales of $87m last year. One group of former coca farmers has begun exporting bananas to Buenos Aires, now only three days away by refrigerated truck; two local investors have set up plants to process hearts of palm. Some farmers are successfully growing black pepper, pineapples and passion fruit.

Yet there are plenty of problems. Coca is sturdy, easy to grow and to transport. Many of the alternatives are more demanding, and may be vulnerable to disease or local market gluts. The UN is now promoting "integrated agro-forestry", a scheme under which farmers hedge their bets (not least against mistakes by the aid agencies' army of well-meaning agronomists) by planting a bit of everything, as well as doing some selective and, it is hoped, sustainable, logging. Even so, one experienced aid official reckons that only 20% of the Chapare's cocaleros will become successful farmers; another 20% will leave the area, and the rest will scrape along, mixing odd jobs with marginal farming. The Chapare's population has already fallen: perhaps by as much as 50,000 people, to around 100,000.

In Peru, alternative development is less advanced; the United States has spent some $60m on it since 1995. Again, much has gone on infrastructure. In the Apurimac valley, which accounts for a third of the investment, roads have been improved and villages have big new schools. Aid workers have high hopes for cacao and especially coffee; they are working on quality and marketing. The United States

Agency for International Development has persuaded Nestlé and a rival maker of instant coffee to set up buying offices in the valley, and has arranged trial shipments to M&M Mars and Seattle's Best Coffee, two American companies. Already, some Apurimac coffee is exported through "fair trade" companies; more could be marketed as "bird-friendly", since the groves still have their shade trees.

Yet it all seems very fragile. In the apurimac, the price of coca leaf has tripled since mid-1998, to around $1.50 per kilo (the price has also risen elsewhere in Peru and in Bolivia). Traffickers have found new smuggling routes, to Brazil among other places, and are hoofing it over the Andes with mules to Lima, according to Colonel Oscar Oquendo, who commands a police anti-drug base newly installed in Palmapampa. Peruvian drug enterprises have emerged that are refining their own cocaine, rather than simply exporting coca paste to Colombia. "There's a lot of other possibilities, but unfortunately people here cling to coca. They think they have a right to it," says Colonel Oquendo.

They are not alone in thinking that. In Bolivia, the Chapare is split uneasily between those who have embraced the new ways and those who still follow the cocalero unions. Hugo Cabieses, an adviser to farmers in Peru's coca areas, argues that alternative development can work only if it is linked to government price supports and subsidised credit. The vagaries of agricultural markets are hard to cope with unaided, even for far better equipped farmers in richer parts of the world.

At the least, alternative development will require much more donor money—unless and until far more private investment can be attracted to often remote and difficult farming areas to make the process self-sustaining. American aid for the Chapare is due to end in 2002; in Peru, a year later. Expect the coca to be back in force if it does.

Drinking to get drunk

Campuses still can't purge bingeing behavior

BY DAVID L. MARCUS

The headlines from campuses in recent months are troubling: A 20-year-old student at Georgetown University dies in a fight after drinking. A fraternity member at the University of Michigan shoots a 19-year-old pledge with a pellet gun at a keg party. A party at Washington State University turns into a 500-student brawl.

College student's excessive drinking is still on the rise.
"Students used to drink to have fun."

—Richard Yoast

Despite unprecedented campaigns against alcohol abuse at colleges in the past few years, heavy drinking has actually increased. A survey by the Harvard School of Public Health, released last week, found that 23 percent of students are "frequent binge drinkers"—up from 20 percent when the first nationwide survey was conducted in 1993. And the number of binge drinkers has remained steady, at 44 percent of undergraduates. (Binge drinkers are considered those who have consumed at least five drinks in a row at one point during a two-week period; frequent binge drinkers downed that amount at least three times in two weeks.) "Students used to drink to have fun, and now they drink to get drunk," says Richard Yoast, director of drug abuse programs for the American Medical Association.

Who, me? The price of these drinking sprees is staggering. The Harvard researchers found that binge drinkers are seven times as likely to miss classes and 10 times as likely to damage property as are light drinkers. Drug Strategies, a nonprofit group, estimates that underage drinking costs $58 billion a year in traffic accidents, crimes, and treatment. The researchers also say that students drink a lot for a variety of reasons—from academic pressures to peer pressure—but that beer companies and bars exacerbate the situation by touting cheap drinks. Making matters worse, heavy drinkers on campus usually describe themselves as moderate drinkers. "If someone does not think they have a problem, they are unlikely to listen to messages directed at people who have that problem," says Henry Wechsler, the psychologist who oversees the Harvard study.

To provide alternatives to drinking, Florida State University shows free movies every night, and Louisiana State University organizes alcohol-free "family zones" at campus festivals. Scores of campuses have no-drinking dorms and fraternities. And researchers believe that this full-court press works: The Harvard survey of 14,000 students at 119 colleges found that the number of students abstaining from alcohol increased from 15 percent in 1993 to 19 percent last year.

Still, schools are finding that there is no quick way to curb heavy drinking. Last month, Florida education officials decided to crack down on drinking—but just two weeks later a drunk, unconscious University of Florida fraternity member was taken to the hospital; another was found partially clothed, tied to a tree.

"Students don't respond to messages that are too simplistic or too judgmental," says Duke University psychology Prof. Scott Swartzwelder, who is teaching a new course called Alcohol: Brain, Individual, and Society. He suggests exposing students to research, such as his studies showing that alcohol impairs the memory of college students more than that of adults. Swartzwelder's class discussions have special poignancy: Even as the course was being developed last fall, a 20-year-old Duke student got drunk at a party—and died after inhaling his own vomit.

THE DRUG THAT PRETENDS IT ISN'T

Car accidents, date rapes, domestic violence—
and it goes so well with Chinese food and pizza!

By ANNA QUINDLEN

SPRING BREAK IN JAMAICA, AND THE patios of the waterfront bars are so packed that it seems the crowds of students must go tumbling into the aquamarine sea, still clutching their glasses. Even at the airport one drunken young man with a peeling nose argues with a flight attendant about whether he can bring his Red Stripe, kept cold in an insulated sleeve, aboard the plane heading home.

The giggle about Jamaica for American visitors has always been the availability of ganja; half the T shirts in the souvenir shops have slogans about smoking grass. But the students thronging the streets of Montego Bay seem more comfortable with their habitual drug of choice: alcohol.

Whoops! Sorry! Not supposed to call alcohol a drug. Some of the people who lead anti-drug organizations don't like it because they fear it dilutes the message about the "real" drugs, heroin, cocaine and marijuana. Parents are offended by it; as they try to figure out which vodka bottle came from their party and which from their teenager's, they sigh and say, "Well, at least it's not drugs." And naturally the lobbyists for the industry hate it. They're power guys, these guys: the wine guy is George W's brother-in-law, the beer guy meets regularly with House Majority Whip Tom DeLay. When you lump a cocktail in with a joint, it makes them crazy.

And it's true: booze and beer are not the same as illegal drugs. They're worse. A policy-research group called Drug Strategies has produced a report that calls alcohol "America's most pervasive drug problem" and then goes on to document the claim. Alcohol-related deaths outnumber deaths related to drugs four to one. Alcohol is a factor in more than half of all domestic-violence and sexual-assault cases. Between accidents, health problems, crime and lost productivity, researchers estimate alcohol abuse costs the economy $167 billion a year. In 1995 four out of every 10 people on probation said they were drinking when they committed a violent crime, while only one in 10 admitted using illicit drugs. Close your eyes and substitute the word blah-blah for alcohol in any of those sentences, and you'd have to conclude that an all-out war on blah-blah would result.

Yet when members of Congress tried to pass legislation that would make alcohol part of the purview of the nation's drug czar the measure failed. Mothers Against Drunk Driving faces opposition to both its education programs and its public-service ads from principals and parents who think illicit drugs should be given greater priority. The argument is this: heroin, cocaine and marijuana are harmful and against the law, but alcohol is used in moderation with no ill effects by many people.

Here's the counterargument: there are an enormous number of people who cannot and will never be able to drink in moderation. And what they leave in their wake is often more difficult to quantify than DWIs or date rapes. In his memoir, "A Drinking Life," Pete Hamill describes simply and eloquently the binges, the blackouts, the routine: "If I wrote a good column for the newspaper, I'd go to the bar and celebrate; if I wrote a poor column, I would drink away my regret. Then I'd go home, another dinner missed, another chance to play with the children gone, and in the morning, hung over, thick-tongued, and thick-fingered, I'd attempt through my disgust to make amends." Hamill and I used to drink, when we were younger, at a dark place down a short flight of stairs in the Village called the Lion's Head. There were book jackets covering the walls, jackets that I looked at with envy, books by the newspapermen and novelists who used to drink there. But then I got older, and when I passed the Head I sometimes thought of how many books had never been written at all because of the drinking.

Everyone has a friend/an uncle/a co-worker/a spouse/a neighbor who drinks too much. A recent poll of 7,000 adults found that 82 percent said they'd even be willing to pay more for a drink if the money were used to combat alcohol abuse. New Mexico and Montana already use excise taxes on alcohol to pay for treatment programs. It's probably just coincidence that, as Drug Strategies reports, the average excise tax on beer is 19 cents a gallon, while in Missouri and Wisconsin, homes to Anheuser-Busch and Miller, respectively, the tax is only six cents.

A wholesale uprising in Washington against Philip Morris, which owns Miller Brewing and was the largest donor of soft money to the Republicans in 1998, or against Seagram, which did the same for the Democrats in 1996, doesn't seem likely. Home schooling is in order, a harder sell even than to elected officials, since many parents prefer lessons that do not re-quire self-examination. Talking about underage drinking and peer pressure lets them off the hook by suggesting that it's all about 16-year-olds with six-packs. But the peer group is everywhere, from the frogs that croak "Bud" on commercials to those tiresome folks who behave as if wine were as important as books (it's not) to parents who drink to excess and teach an indelible life lesson.

Prohibition was cooked up to try to ameliorate the damage that drinking does to daily life. It didn't work. But there is always self-prohibition. It's not easy, since all the world's a speakeasy. "Not even wine?" Hamill recalls he was asked at din-ner parties after he stopped. Of course children should not drink, and people who sell them alcohol should be prosecuted. Of course people should not drink and drive, and those who do should be punished. But 21 is not a magic number, and the living room is not necessarily a safe place. There is a larger story that needs to be told, loud and clear, in homes and schools and on commercials given as much prominence and paid for in the same way as those that talk about the dangers of smack or crack: that alcohol is a mind-altering, mood-altering drug, and that lots of people should never start to drink at all. "I have no talent for it," Hamill told friends. Just like that.

From *Newsweek,* April 10, 2000, pp. 88. Reprinted by permission of International Creative Management, Inc. © 2000 by Anne Quindlen.

SPEED DEMONS

METHAMPHETAMINES ARE RIPPING ACROSS ASIA, SEDUCING THE YOUNG WITH A PROMISE OF A FAST, CLEAN HIGH. KARL TARO GREENFELD VISITS ONE OF THE REGION'S WORST DRUG SLUMS AND COMES TO TERMS WITH THE DEADLY DOSE THAT NEARLY DESTROYED HIS OWN LIFE

JACKY TALKS ABOUT KILLING HIM, SLITting his throat from 3 till 9 and hanging him upside down so the blood drains out of him the way it ran from the baby pigs they used to slaughter in her village before a funeral feast. He deserves it, really, she says, for his freeloading, for his hanging around, for how he just stands there, spindly legged and narrow chested and pimple faced with his big yearning eyes, begging for another hit.

She has run out of methamphetamine, what the Thais call *yaba* (mad medicine), and she has become irritable and potentially violent. Jacky's cheeks are sunken, her skin pockmarked and her hair an unruly explosion of varying strands of red and brown. She is tall and skinny, and her arms and legs extend out from her narrow torso with its slightly protuberant belly like the appendages of a spider shortchanged on legs.

Sitting on the blue vinyl flooring of her Bangkok hut, Jacky leans her bare back against the plank wall, her dragon tattoos glistening with sweat as she trims her fingernails with a straight razor. It has been two days—no, three—without sleep, sitting in this hut and smoking the little pink speed tablets from sheets of tinfoil stripped from Krong Tip cigarette packets. Now, as

the flushes of artificial energy recede and the realization surfaces that there's no more money anywhere in her hut, Jacky is crashing hard, and she hates everyone and everything. Especially Bing. She hates that sponging little punk for all the tablets he smoked a few hours ago—tablets she could be smoking right now. Back then, she had a dozen tablets packed into a plastic soda straw stuffed down her black wireframe bra. The hut was alive with the chatter of half a dozen speed addicts, all pulling apart their Krong Tip packs and sucking in meth smoke through metal pipes. Now that the pills are gone, the fun is gone. And Bing, of course, he's long gone.

This slum doesn't have a name. The 5,000 residents call it Ban Chua Gan, which translates roughly as Do It Yourself Happy Homes. The expanse of jerry-built wood-frame huts with corrugated steel roofs sprawls in a murky bog in Bangkok's Sukhumvit district, in the shadow of 40-story office buildings and glass-plated corporate towers. The inhabitants migrated here about a decade ago from villages all around Thailand. Jacky came from Nakon Nayok, a province near Bangkok's Don Muang airport, seeking financial redemption in the Asian economic miracle. And for a while in the mid-'90s, conditions in

this slum actually improved. Some of the huts had plumbing installed. Even the shabbiest shanties were wired for electricity. The main alleyways were paved. That was when Thailand's development and construction boom required the labor of every able-bodied person. There were shopping malls to be built, housing estates to be constructed, highways to be paved.

Around the same time, mad medicine began making its way into Do It Yourself Happy Homes. It had originally been the drug of choice for long-haul truck and bus drivers, but during the go-go '90s, it evolved into the working man's and woman's preferred intoxicant, gradually becoming more popular among Thailand's underclass than heroin and eventually replacing that opiate as the leading drug produced in the notorious Golden Triangle—the world's most prolific opium-producing region—where Myanmar (Burma), Thailand and Laos come together. While methamphetamines had previously been sold either in powdered or crystalline form, new labs in Burma, northern Thailand and China commoditized the methamphetamine business by pressing little tablets of the substance that now retail for about 50 baht ($1.20) each. At first only bar girls like Jacky smoked it. Then some of the younger guys who hung out with the girls tried it. Soon a few of the housewives began smoking, and finally some of the dads would take a hit or two when they were out of corn whiskey. Now it has reached the point that on weekend nights, it's hard to find anyone in the slum who isn't smoking the mad medicine.

When the *yaba* runs out after much of the slum's population has been up for two days bingeing, many of the inhabitants feel a bit like Jacky, cooped up in her squalid little hut, her mouth turned down into a scowl and her eyes squinted and empty and mean. She looks as if she wants something. And if she thinks you have what she wants, look out. She slices at her cuticles with the straight razor. And curses Bing.

But then Bing comes around the corner between two shanties and down the narrow dirt path to Jacky's hut. He stands looking lost and confused, as usual. Jacky pretends he's not there. She sighs, looking at her nails, and stage whispers to me that she hates him.

Bing, his long black hair half-tied into a ponytail, stands next to a cinder-block wall rubbing his eyes. Above his head, a thick trail of red army ants runs between a crack in the wall and a smashed piece of pineapple. He reaches into his pocket and pulls out a tissue in which he has wrapped four *doa* (bodies, slang for speed tablets). Jacky stops doing her nails, smiles and invites Bing back into her hut, asking sweetly, "Oh, Bing, where have you been?"

This mad medicine is the same drug that's called *shabu* in Japan and Indonesia, *batu* in the Philippines and *bingdu* in China. While it has taken scientists years to figure out the clinical pharmacology and neurological impact of ecstasy and other designer drugs, methamphetamines are blunt pharmaceutical instruments. The drug encourages the brain to flood the synapses with the neurotransmitter dopamine—the substance your body uses to reward itself when you, say, complete a difficult assignment at the office or finish a vigorous workout. And when the brain is awash in dopamine, the whole cardiovascular system goes into sympathetic overdrive, increasing your heart rate, pulse and even your respiration. You become, after that first hit of speed, gloriously, brilliantly, vigorously awake. Your horizon of aspiration expands outward, just as in your mind's eye your capacity for taking effective action to achieve your new, optimistic goals has also grown exponentially. Then, eventually, maybe in an hour, maybe in a

day, maybe in a year, you run out of speed. And you crash.

In country after country throughout Asia, meth use skyrocketed during the '90s. And with the crash of the region's high-flying economies, the drug's use has surged again. The base of the drug—ephedrine—was actually first synthesized in Asia: a team of Japanese scientists derived it from the Chinese *mao* herb in 1892. Unlike ecstasy, which requires sophisticated chemical and pharmaceutical knowledge to manufacture, or heroin, whose base product, the poppy plant, is a vulnerable crop, ephedrine can be refined fairly easily into meth. This makes meth labs an attractive family business for industrious Asians, who set them up in converted bathrooms, farmhouses or even on the family hearth.

THERE IS SOMETHING FAMILIAR TO ME about Jacky and her little hut and her desperate yearning for more speed and even for the exhilaration and intoxication she feels when she's on the pipe. Because I've been there. Not in this exact room or with these people. But I've been on speed.

During the early '90s, I went through a period when I was smoking *shabu* with a group of friends in Tokyo. I inhaled the smoke from smoothed-out tinfoil sheets folded in two, holding a lighter beneath the foil so that the shards of *shabu* liquefied, turning to a thick, pungent, milky vapor. The smoke tasted like a mixture of turpentine and model glue; to this day I can't smell paint thinner without thinking of smoking speed.

The drug was euphorically powerful, convincing us that we were capable of anything. And in many ways we were. We were all young, promising, on the verge of exciting careers in glamorous fields. There was Trey, an American magazine writer, like me, in his 20s; Hiroko, a Japanese woman in her 30s who worked for a Tokyo women's magazine; Delphine, an aspiring French model; and Miki, an A. and R. man for a Japanese record label. When we would sit down together in my Nishi Azabu apartment to smoke the drug, our talk turned to grandiose plans and surefire schemes. I spoke of articles I would write. Delphine talked about landing a job doing a Dior lingerie catalog. Miki raved about a promising noise band he had just signed. Sometimes the dealer, a lanky fellow named Haru, would hang around and smoke with us, and we would be convinced that his future was surely just as bright as all of ours. There was no limit to

what we could do, especially if we put our speed-driven minds to work.

It's always that way in the beginning: all promise and potential fun. The drug is like a companion telling you that you're good enough, handsome enough and smart enough, banishing all the little insecurities to your subconscious, liberating you from self doubts yet making you feel totally and completely alive.

I don't know that it helped me write better; I don't believe meth really helps you in any way at all. But in those months, it became arguably the most important activity in my life. Certainly it was the most fun. And I looked forward to Haru's coming over with another $150 baggie of *shabu*, the drug resembling a little oily lump of glass. Then we would smoke, at first only on weekends. But soon we began to do it on weekdays whenever I had a free evening. At first only with my friends. Then sometimes I smoked alone. Then mostly alone.

THE TEENS AND TWENTYSOMETHINGS IN Ban Chua Gan also like to smoke *yaba*, but they look down on Jacky and Bing and their flagrant, raging addictions. Sure, the cool guys in the neighborhood, guys like Big, with a shaved head, gaunt face and sneering upper lip, drop into Jacky's once in a while to score some drugs. Or they'll buy a couple of tablets from Bing's mother, who deals. But they tell you they're different from Bing and the hard-core users. "For one thing," Big alibis, "Bing hasn't left the slum neighborhood in a year. He doesn't work. He doesn't do anything but smoke." (Bing just shrugs when I ask if it's true that he hasn't left in a year. "I'm too skinny to leave," he explains. "Everyone will know I'm doing *yaba*.") Big has a job as a pump jockey at a Star gas station. And he has a girlfriend, and he has his motorcycle, a Honda GSR 125. This weekend, like most weekends, he'll be racing his bike with the other guys from the neighborhood, down at Bangkok's superslum Klong Toey. That's why tonight, a few days before the race, he is working on his bike, removing a few links of the engine chain to lower the gear ratio and give the bike a little more pop off the line. He kneels down with a lighted candle next to him, his hands greasy and black as he works to reattach the chain to the gear sprockets. Around him a few teenage boys and girls are gathered, smoking cigarettes, some squatting on the balls of their feet, their intent faces peering down at scattered engine parts. The sound is the clatter of adolescent boys. Whether the vehicle in question is a '65 Mustang or a '99 Honda GSR motorcycle, the posturing of the too cool motorhead trying to goose a few more horse-power out of his engine while at the same time look bitchin' in front of a crowd of slightly younger female spectators is identical whether in Bakersfield or Bangkok.

The slang for smoking speed in Thai is *keng rot*, literally racing, the same words used to describe the weekend motorcycle rallying. The bikers' lives revolve around these two forms of *keng rot*. They look forward all week to racing their bikes against other gangs from other neighborhoods. And while they profess to have nothing but disgust for the slum's hard-core addicts, by 4 a.m. that night on a mattress laid on the floor next to his beloved Honda, Big and his friends are smoking *yaba*, and there suddenly seems very little difference between his crowd and Jacky's. "Smoking once in a while, on weekends, that really won't do any harm," Big explains, exhaling a plume of white smoke. "It's just like having a drink." But it's Thursday, I point out. Big shrugs, waving away the illogic of his statement, the drug's powerful reach pulling him away from the need to make sense. He says whatever he wants now, and he resents being questioned. "What do you want from me? I'm just trying to have fun."

In Jacky's hut, Bing and a few bar girls are seated with their legs folded under, taking hits from the sheets of tinfoil. As Jacky applies a thick layer of foundation makeup to her face and dabs on retouching cream and then a coating of powder, she talks about how tonight she has to find a foreign customer so she can get the money to visit her children out in Nakon Nayok. Her two daughters and son live with her uncle. Jacky sees them once a month, and she talks about how she likes to bring them new clothes and cook for them. When she talks about her kids, her almond-shaped eyes widen. "I used to dream of opening a small shop, like a gift shop or a 7-Eleven. Then I could take care of my children and make money. I used to dream about it all the time, and I even believed it was possible, that it was just barely out of reach."

Jacky was a motorbike messenger, shuttling packages back and forth through-out Bangkok's busy Chitlom district until she was laid off after the 1997 devaluation of the baht. "Now I don't think about the gift shop anymore. Smoking *yaba* pushes thoughts about my children to the back of my mind. It's good for that. Smoking means you don't have to think about the hard times." Bing nods his head, agreeing:

"When I smoke, it makes everything seem a little better. I mean, look at this place—how can I stop?"

Bing's mother Yee slips off her sandals as she steps into the hut, clutching her 14-month-old baby. She sits down next to her son, and while the baby scrambles to crawl from her lap, she begins pulling the paper backing from a piece of tinfoil, readying the foil for a smoke. Her hands are a whir of finger-flashing activity—assembling and disassembling a lighter, unclogging the pipe, unwrapping the tablets, straightening the foil, lighting the speed and then taking the hit. She exhales finally, blowing smoke just above her baby's face. Bing asks his mother for a hit. She shakes her head. She doesn't give discounts or freebies, not even to her own son.

I ask Yee if she ever tells Bing he should stop smoking *yaba*. "I tell him he shouldn't do so much, that it's bad for him. But he doesn't listen."

Perhaps she lacks credibility, since she smokes herself?

"I don't smoke that much," she insists.

"She's right," Bing agrees. "Since she doesn't smoke that much, I should listen to her."

"And he's only 15 years old," Yee adds.

Bing reminds her he's 17.

"I don't know where the years go," Yee says, taking another hit.

For the countries on the front lines of the meth war, trying to address the crisis with tougher enforcement has had virtually no effect on curtailing the numbers of users or addicts. Asia has some of the toughest drug laws in the world. In Thailand, China, Taiwan and Indonesia, even a low-level drug-trafficking or -dealing conviction can mean a death sentence. Yet *yaba* is openly sold in Thailand's slums and proffered in Jakarta's nightclubs, and China's meth production continues to boom. Even Japan, renowned for its strict antidrug policies, has had little success in stemming speed abuse. Most likely, these countries and societies will have to write off vast swaths of their populations as drug casualties, like the American victims of the '80s crack epidemic.

Asia's medical and psychiatric infrastructure is already being overwhelmed by the number of meth abusers crashing and seeking help. But in most of the region, counseling facilities are scarce, and recovery is viewed as a matter of willpower and discipline rather than a tenuous and slow spiritual and psychological rebuilding process. Drug-treatment centers are usually run like a cross between boot camp and

prison. Beds are scarce as addicts seek the meager resources available. In China, for example, the nearly 750 state-run rehab centers are filled to capacity; in Thailand the few recovery centers suffer from a chronic shortage of staff and beds. While the most powerful tools for fighting addiction in the West—12-step programs derived from Alcoholics Anonymous—are available in Asia, they are not widely disseminated and used.

WHAT STARTED OUT AS A DIVERSION FOR me and my Tokyo crowd degenerated in a few months into the chronic drug use of Jacky and her crowd. I began to smoke alone to begin my days. In the evening I'd take Valium or halcyon or cercine or any of a number of sedatives to help me calm down. When I stopped smoking for a few days just to see if I could, a profound depression would overcome me. Nothing seemed worthwhile. Nothing seemed fun. Every book was torturously slow. Every song was criminally banal. The sparkle and shine had been sucked out of life so completely that my world became a fluorescent-lighted, decolorized, saltpetered version of the planet I had known before. And my own prospects? Absolutely dismal. I would sit in that one-bedroom Nishi Azabu apartment and consider the sorry career I had embarked upon, these losers I associated with compounding the very long odds that I would ever amount to anything.

These feelings, about the world and my life, seemed absolutely real. I could not tell for a moment that this was a neurological reaction brought on by the withdrawal of the methamphetamine. My brain had stopped producing dopamine in normal amounts because it had come to rely upon the speed kicking in and running the show. Researchers now report that as much as 50% of the dopamine-producing cells in the brain can be damaged after prolonged exposure to relatively low levels of meth-amphetamine. In other words, the depression is a purely chemical state. Yet it feels for all the world like the result of empirical, clinical observation. And then, very logically, you realize there is one surefire solution, the only way to feel better: more speed.

I kept at that cycle for a few years and started taking drugs other than methamphetamine until I hit my own personal bottom. I spent six weeks in a drug-treatment center working out a plan for living that didn't require copious amounts of meth-amphetamines or tranquilizers. I left rehab five years ago. I haven't had another hit of *shabu*—or taken any drugs—since then. But I am lucky. Of that crowd who used to gather in my Tokyo apartment, I am the only one who has emerged clean and sober. Trey, my fellow magazine writer, never really tried to quit and now lives back at home with his aging parents. He is nearly 40, still takes speed—or Ritalin or cocaine or whichever uppers he can get his hands on—and hasn't had a job in years. Delphine gave up modeling after a few years and soon was accepting money to escort wealthy businessmen around Tokyo. She finally ended up working as a prostitute. Hiroko did stop taking drugs. But she has been in and out of psychiatric hospitals and currently believes drastic plastic surgery is the solution to her problems. Miki has been arrested in Japan and the U.S. on drug charges and is now out on parole and living in Tokyo. And Haru, the dealer, I hear he's dead.

Despite all I know about the drug, despite what I have seen, I am still tempted. The pull of the drug is tangible and real, almost like a gravitational force compelling me to want to use it again—to feel just once more the rush and excitement and the sense, even if it's illusory, that life does add up, that there is meaning and form to the passing of my days. Part of me still wants it.

AT 2 A.M. ON A SATURDAY, BIG AND HIS fellow bikers from Do It Yourself Happy Homes are preparing for a night of bike racing by smoking more *yaba* and, as if to get their 125-cc bikes in a parallel state of high-octane agitation, squirting STP performance goo from little plastic packets into their gas tanks. The bikes are tuned up, and the mufflers are loosened so that the engines revving at full throttle sound like a chain saw cutting bone: splintering, ear-shattering screeches that reverberate up and down the Sukhumvit streets. The bikers ride in a pack, cutting through alleys, running lights, skirting lines of stalled traffic, slipping past one another as they cut through the city smog. This is their night, the night they look forward to all week during mornings at school or dull afternoons pumping gas. And as they ride massed together, you can almost feel the surge of pride oozing out of them, intimidating other drivers to veer out of their way.

On Na Ranong avenue, next to the Klong Toey slum, they meet up with bikers from other slums. They have been holding these rallies for a decade, some of the kids first coming on the backs of their older brothers' bikes. *Ken rot* is a ritual by now, as ingrained in Thai culture as the speed they smoke to get up for the night of racing. The street is effectively closed off to non-motorcyclists and pedestrians. The bikers idle along the side of the road and then take off in twos and threes, popping wheelies, the usual motorcycle stunts. But souped up and fitted with performance struts and tires, these bikes accelerate at a terrifying rate, and that blast off the line makes for an unstable and dangerous ride if you're on the back of one of them. It is the internal-combustion equivalent of *yaba*: fast, fun, treacherous. And likely to result, eventually, in a fatal spill. But if you're young and Thai and loaded on mad medicine, you feel immortal, and it doesn't occur to you that this night of racing will ever, really, have to end.

THERE ARE STILL MOMENTS WHEN EVEN hard-core addicts like Jacky can recapture the shiny, bright exuberance of the first few times they tried speed. Tonight, as Jacky dances at Angel's bar with a Belgian who might take her back to his hotel room, she's thinking that she'll soon have enough money to visit her children, and it doesn't seem so bad. Life seems almost manageable. A few more customers, and maybe one will really fall for her and pay to move her to a better neighborhood, to rent a place where even her children could live. Maybe she could open that convenience store after all.

By the next afternoon, however, all the promise of the previous evening has escaped from the neighborhood like so much exhaled smoke. Jacky's customer lost interest and found another girl. Even the bike racing fell apart after the cops broke up the first few rallying points. And now, on a hazy, rainy Sunday, Jacky and a few of the girls are back in her hut. They're smoking, almost desperately uploading as much speed as possible to ward off this drab day and this squalid place.

Jacky pauses as she adjusts the flame on a lighter. "Why don't you smoke?" she asks me.

She tells me it would make her more comfortable if I would join her. I'm standing in the doorway to Jacky's hut. About me are flea-infested dogs and puddles of stagnant water several inches deep with garbage, and all around is the stench of smoldering trash. The horror of this daily existence is tangible. I don't like being in this place, and I find depressing the idea of living in a world that has places like this in it. And I know a hit of the mad medicine is the easiest way to make this all seem bearable. Taking a hit, I know, is a surefire way of feeling good. Right now. And I want it.

But I walk away. And while I hope Jacky and Bing and Big can one day do the same, I doubt they ever can. They have so little to walk toward.

Cocaine Colonialism

A version of this article first appeared in Third World Network Features.

Coca, one of the most significant plants in the world, grows in South America. It is cultivated in warm and humid valleys, known in the local Aymara language as yungas. Andean peasants chew it while working and resting and even treat their guests with it. The habit of chewing—not only accepted but widely spread among millions of inhabitants in countries such as Colombia, Ecuador, Peru, Bolivia, Argentina and Chile—has an economic basis. For peasants coca is a most beneficial crop because of its ability to yield three to four harvests a year, in non-arable soils. In fact, a detailed description of its leaf concludes that, due to its richness in amino acids and vitamins, the coca plant is the Earth's most complete plant in non-proteinic nitrogen. This kind of nitrogen eliminates toxins and pathogens from the human body, also hydrating and regulating the nervous system.

At present, the US market almost entirely absorbs Latin American drug production. Drug consumers in that country amount to 20 million, but in order to solve this domestic problem, the US policy is to fight it abroad.

History

Andean peasants praise coca for its profitability, in comparison with other crops. Its very specific farming technique is well adapted to the valleys through the construction of stone or walled ground platforms. Raising coca in the Andean valley is an ancestral custom. Since about 2000 BC, the leaf has been intertwined with local life. Andeans not only utilised it for conveying friendship, repaying services or simply as a coin, but also considered it sacred. Besides discovering its medicinal powers, they employed the leaf, mixed with certain oils, to soften rocks.

When the Incas politically centralised the area, plantations were located all across the empire in order to maintain a stable production, the Incas being the sole proprietors of sacred harvests. Later on, once the Spaniards imposed themselves in the area, the Spanish Crown distributed these plantations among some colonos under the encomiendas regime, and payment with coca leaves was authorised.

When the Spaniards conquered the continent and discovered coca's energising properties, they encouraged consumption in order to increase the productivity of the natives they forced to work in the Potosi mines. As a result, the coca trade became an important revenue source for the Spanish Crown, second only to mine exploitation. Tithes on coca contributed almost all of the Andean Catholic Church's funds.

In this way, coca entered the market economy, and colonial society adopted the plant, fully incorporating it in its habits and manners to the extent that physicians employed it as a medicine for asthma, haemorrhages, toothache, vomiting and diarrhoea.

Criminalisation

Nevertheless, despite its early assimilation by colonial society, Spaniards were not reluctant to blame the natives' ritual use of the coca leaf for delaying their conversion to Christianity—thus beginning the long fight against its consumption. When decolonisation brought independent states in the region, the plant was once again accused, this time of blocking the natives' assimilation into 'white' society.

Towards the end of the 19th century, cocaine consumption extended through the upper classes and the artistic circles of both Europe and the US.

However, it was the emergence of cocaine—one of the 14 alkaloids of the plant—which ignited the black history of this bush. Soon after being isolated in 1884, cocaine began to be used as an anaesthetic in surgery, with the likes of Sigmund Freud recommending it as a relief for nervous stress and fatigue. Towards the end of the 19th century, cocaine consumption extended through the upper classes and the artistic circles of both Europe and the US. Vin Mariani, a tonic based on the coca extract, was prescribed by every physician as a cure for several diseases. In this, its origins were similar to those of Coca-Cola—patented in 1895 as a stimulant and headache reliever which originally contained cocaine.

But in 1906, the US authorities made cocaine illegal by officially declaring it was a narcotic and then prohibiting its import, together with the coca leaves. In spite of the prohibition—or eventually because of it—all through the century cocaine has become highly appreciated and consumed.

The UN Convention for Narcotics placed cocaine on its toxic drugs first page, listing it as 'psychotropic' in 1961. But the truth is that its rocketing price makes cocaine one of the most profitable businesses on Earth. In financial, artistic and political milieus from Western Europe and the US, cocaine is regarded as synonymous with opulence and distinction, also being consumed in Japan, Eastern Europe and Latin America, though to a lesser degree.

Cocaine's desirability has launched a fabulous business—more lucrative than oil, and second only to the warfare business— known as narcotraffic.

Narcotraffic

Cocaine's desirability has launched a fabulous business—more lucrative than oil and second only to the warfare business— known as narcotraffic. This word defines the entire process of illegal production, transportation and selling of illegal and controlled drugs. In this transnational game, each one plays its role.

The USA, Europe and France sustain a strong demand, while Andean countries like Peru, Bolivia and Colombia supply the product. In these latter countries, coca consumption still differs from the one developed in the North. While the use of cocaine paste expands among the young floating population, the natives and peasants— while disliking the paste—still preserve the habit of daily chewing.

The coca-producing regions have been transformed by this trade into developing zones, because drug cartels extend credit and insurance to the groups that produce cocaine. Coca-planting peasants have increased their incomes: raising the leaf means much more profit than raising any other crop. In Bolivia, coca and its by-products generate a revenue of $600 million a year, and provide jobs for 20 per cent of the adult labour force. In Peru, the coca industry occupies 15 per cent of the active labour force and reports a yearly income of $1 billion.

In Colombia, the drugs trade provides a revenue of $1 billion, a sum higher than coffee exports. The main gain, however, belongs to the consumer countries, where the money laundering is undertaken, chemicals for cocaine production are supplied and weapons to sustain drug dealers are sold.

Hypocrisy

The basic point about this amazing business seems to be its hypocrisy. In the US, more than $100 billion has been spent on arrests, imprisonment, education and other action since President Ronald Reagan initiated his "war against drugs" in 1983. But, in the period from 1983 to 1993, the death by drug abuse rate doubled, while assassinations linked to drug-trafficking trebled. Statistics reveal that in 1992, in the US, 12,000 people died from drug abuse and 2,000 more from drug-related murders.

The worst statistics for drug casualties are for adults between 35 and 50 years old, who in 1983 accounted for 80 per cent of the total drug casualties. Ten years later, the risk of dying by drug abuse was 15 times greater for people in their forties than for university students. And yet US authorities in charge of the fight against drugs give no explanation for these figures. They just present statistics showing an increase in the relatively low rate of teenagers who smoke marijuana.

At present, the US market almost entirely absorbs Latin American drug production (as well as a third of the world's heroin and 80 per cent of its marijuana). Drug consumers in that country amount to 20 million, but in order to solve this domestic problem, the US policy is to fight it abroad. This exclusively domestic issue of drug consumption has been turned into one of the favourite excuses for US intervention abroad, the creation of the Drug Enforcement Agency (DEA) in July 1973 being one of the fundamental steps to institutionalise this. This cocaine colonialism has led to a disregard for other countries' sovereignty. A 1992 US Supreme Court judgement, legalising the kidnapping of drugs suspects in other countries, carries with it a very serious threat to human rights, and mocks international law.

The US approach to the popularity of cocaine is a classic example of misrepresenting the real problem. Drug consumption has become the object of a crusade, projecting the evil onto the producer and not onto the consumer—onto the 'other' and not onto oneself. Today, many respectable voices can be heard proposing that drugs such as cocaine should be legalised, as a first step to solving some of the problems created by the prohibitions—such as the high price, which often leads to corruption and violence, or the bad quality of the final product, that endangers health. Such a move would not only remove the carpet from beneath the feet of the corrupt, but would decriminalise large sections of a society wracked by many more serious problems.

Drug War Aids Heroin Trade

Colombian police diverted to crack down on coca

By Will Weissert
ASSOCIATED PRESS

BOGOTA, Colombia—Washington's $1.3 billion war on Colombian cocaine has had an unexpected consequence: It has forced the scaling back of efforts to stop this country's flourishing heroin trade.

Strikes against poppy plantations high in the Andes have been on hold since December because airplanes and helicopters used in aerial eradication missions were reassigned to the U.S.-financed push against coca crops.

U.S. officials are calling the suspension temporary, but the halt is frustrating Colombian police and angering some U.S. lawmakers concerned about the increasing heroin production in the country.

The world's leading cocaine producer, Colombia now exports more heroin than Asian producers Thailand and Pakistan and supplies 70 percent of an expanding U.S. heroin market, according to the U.S. Drug Enforcement Administration.

At a hearing in Washington last week, Rep. Benjamin Gilman, R-N.Y., raised questions about the poppy suspension. He warned that "more American youngsters caught up in the current heroin crisis here at home will die needlessly for lack of an effective U.S. heroin strategy directed at Colombia."

> *"More American youngsters caught up in the current heroin crisis here at home will die needlessly."*
>
> REP. BENJAMIN GILMAN

DEA Administrator Donnie Marshall said successful efforts to battle heroin in Asia and years of battling cocaine in Columbia has unwittingly pushed Colombian traffickers into a booming U.S. heroin market.

Colombia still produces nearly 100 times as much cocaine as heroin—it accounts for about 90 percent of the U.S. market and 75 percent of the world market.

But U.S. heroin use has doubled in the last five years, while casual cocaine use has dropped 70 percent in the last decade, according to the White House Office of National Drug Control Policy.

Concern about heroin could dampen the enthusiasm over what U.S. officials are calling a successful start to coca eradication under Washington's $1.3 billion aid package. The United States is providing troop training and combat helicopters to escort crop dusters over southern coca plantations that are often guarded by armed rebels.

By early February, some 62,000 acres—nearly a fifth of Colombia's estimated coca crop—had been sprayed with chemical herbicides, U.S. officials say.

Gen. Gustavo Socha, head of Colombia's anti-narcotics police force, complained that the aggressive attack on coca is undercutting the war on heroin.

Whereas his forces wiped out a record 22,700 acres of opium plants last year, Socha says he'll be lucky to kill more than 15,000 acres this year—a drop of more than a third.

A State Department official, who spoke on condition of anonymity, acknowledged that poppy eradication has been temporarily halted because aircraft were needed in coca-growing areas and due to bad weather. He said the program would resume by early May.

Critics off the U.S.-backed fumigation policy say even a renewed poppy eradication program will do little good.

The changing face of marijuana research

Studies on marijuana withdrawal have helped ignite interest in developing effective treatments.

BY SIRI CARPENTER
Monitor staff

New research in nonhuman animals and humans is showing that marijuana withdrawal can produce symptoms such as irritability, anxiety and depressed appetite. The findings provide the most compelling evidence yet that people can become physically dependent on the drug—perhaps contributing to continued use.

"For many years, there was resistance to the whole notion of marijuana dependence," says Columbia University psychologist Margaret Haney, PhD. "Neither society nor scientists viewed marijuana as an important drug of abuse. It paled in comparison to cocaine or heroin. I think that resistance has now lessened."

But the research also indicates that physical dependence on marijuana is far from universal, even among longtime users. Although withdrawal is only one indicator of drug dependence, findings like these may nonetheless help resolve some of the confusion and controversy over whether marijuana is a drug of dependence and how psychologists can develop treatments for substance abusers, researchers say.

> "People have this simple-minded idea that the risk of becoming dependent on marijuana is the same for every user, and that's really not the case. It varies, and we have to understand the reasons for that in order to tailor prevention and treatment efforts to particular groups' needs."
>
> *Denise B. Kandel*
> *Columbia University*

"People have this simple-minded idea that the risk of becoming dependent on marijuana is the same for every user, and that's really not the case," says Columbia University epidemiologist Denise B. Kandel, PhD. "It varies, and we have to understand the reasons for that in order to tailor prevention and treatment efforts to the needs of particular groups."

Indeed, the emerging evidence of a marijuana withdrawal syndrome in humans, along with similar findings in studies of rats and mice, has helped spur interest in developing effective treatments for marijuana abuse.

"We know that a small but significant percentage of people who ever try marijuana become dependent and may need treatment," says clinical psychologist Robert S. Stephens, PhD, of the Virginia Polytechnic Institute and State University. "Yet there have been very few randomized, controlled trials to evaluate the effectiveness of different treatment approaches—but that's finally beginning to change."

A withdrawal syndrome emerges

The studies that have sparked excitement in scientific quarters are based on the 1991 finding in rats that animals' brains possess abundant receptors for a class of chemicals known as cannabinoids—one of which is delta-9-tetrahydrocannabinol (THC), the psychoactive compound in marijuana. The receptors, subsequent research revealed, are part of an internal, or endogenous, cannabinoid system whose evolved purpose is not yet well understood.

The discovery of the cannabinoid receptors presented a new opportunity for studying marijuana withdrawal. A complication in conducting research in this area has been that THC metabolizes slowly, making subtle withdrawal effects difficult to detect. In 1995, building on the discovery of the cannabinoid receptors, Brown University and Virginia Commonwealth University researchers independently found the first clear evidence of cannabinoid withdrawal in rats.

Studying animals that had been chronically administered THC, the researchers used a procedure called precipitated withdrawal to chemically block cannabinoid receptors in the animals' brains, abruptly stopping the drug's action. The animals suffered a range of withdrawal symptoms, including paw tremors, "wet-dog shakes" and other disorganized behavior.

Following up, researchers at Virginia Commonwealth University recently learned that withdrawal effects subside when animals whose cannabinoid receptors are blocked are then given more THC. Those results, not yet published, bolster the notion that people continue to take marijuana in part to avoid withdrawal effects. Such neurobiological findings have raised a range of questions—about just how the endogenous cannabinoid system operates, what purposes it evolved to serve and how it can be exploited in medicine.

The animal studies also reignited behavioral scientists' interest in quantifying withdrawal symptoms in humans. In a 1999 study, Haney and colleagues at Columbia University gave chronic marijuana smokers alternating courses of marijuana or a placebo for 21 days, each for several days at a time.

While abstinent during placebo phases of the experiment, participants experienced anxiety, irritability, stomach pain and decreased appetite. Most withdrawal symptoms peaked on the third or fourth day and abated when participants again received marijuana. In two subsequent studies, Harvard University psychologist Elena M. Kouri, PhD, and colleagues found similar ef-

fects with marijuana smokers who were abstinent for 28 days. Kouri emphasizes, however, that many people who smoke marijuana regularly do not become dependent on the drug. In her studies, for example, about 40 percent of participants experienced no withdrawal symptoms, despite having smoked marijuana for an average of 22 years.

Columbia's Kandel echoes the sentiment. Her research, examining nationally representative samples of marijuana smokers, has indicated that the risk of dependence is different for different population groups. For example, males are more likely to become dependent than are females and adolescents are at greater risk than are adults.

Testing treatment options

The evidence that marijuana use can lead to dependence—coupled with concern over the high and growing prevalence of marijuana use, especially among youth—has underscored the societal need for effective treatment. In the first controlled study of marijuana treatment, published in 1994, Stephens and colleague Roger A. Roffman, DSW, of the University of Washington, compared the effectiveness of two treatment approaches, both of which took place in group therapy sessions.

One approach applied cognitive-behavioral treatment principles to help people identify and prevent situations in which they are most likely to use marijuana. The second approach simply provided social support to people who wanted to quit. In the study, about 60 percent of the 212 participants in both treatment groups successfully quit smoking marijuana. One year later, about 25 percent remained abstinent.

In a follow-up study involving 291 participants, Stephens's group compared a 14-session cognitive-behavioral treatment approach with a two-session "motivational enhancement" intervention, in which a therapist helped participants review their reasons for wanting to quit smoking marijuana, helped them set goals and provided written materials describing coping skills.

The results, published last year, showed that participants in both

treatment conditions were more successful at quitting marijuana than were participants in a control group—and equally so. As in the first study, one year after treatment ended about 25 percent of participants were abstinent.

Although that study suggested that a brief treatment works as well as longer treatment, a recent large, multisite study funded by the federal Center for Substance Abuse Treatment (CSAT) has indicated otherwise.

That study compared 450 chronic marijuana users who were randomly assigned to a two-session motivational enhancement program or to a nine-session program that involved both cognitive-behavioral therapy and motivational enhancement. Participants who received more treatment reduced marijuana consumption by about 60 percent on average, the results showed, compared with 30 percent for those in the brief-intervention condition.

Although the reasons for the treatment differences remain uncertain, University of Connecticut psychologist Thomas F. Babor, PhD, one of the study's lead investigators, says the results are heartening.

"Consistent with earlier findings," he observes, "the CSAT study suggests that treatments for marijuana dependence are effective, even for people who are long-time, chronic marijuana users."

Another recent CSAT-funded study addressed marijuana treatment for youth. The study, involving 600 adolescents, evaluated the effectiveness of five different treatment strategies currently in use. They included brief and extended cognitive-behavioral and motivational treatments as well as programs that supplemented such therapy with discussions about family dynamics, community-reinforcement programs or family therapy.

Preliminary results released last fall indicate that all five treatment strategies are equally effective. After six months, about 70 percent of teen-agers had reduced their marijuana use and about 50 percent had reduced consumption by half or more. After one year, more than one-third of participants were abstinent.

"All five of the treatments did two- or three-fold better than evaluations of existing practice and cost less than current treatment options," says lead investigator Michael L. Dennis, PhD, a research psychologist at Chestnut Health Systems in Bloomington, Ill. The results were so encouraging, in fact, that CSAT plans to release manuals for all five treatment methods in the coming months.

But, cautions Dennis, "Let's not kid ourselves. Two-thirds of these teens were not out of the woods 12 months after treatment. There's lots of room for improvement."

In a departure from traditional cognitive-behavioral and motivational enhancement approaches, clinical psychologist Alan J. Budney, PhD, and colleagues at the University of Vermont have tested another strategy for treating marijuana dependence. The treatment, modeled after programs they and others have used to treat cocaine and opiate addiction, hinges on an old behavioral standby: reinforcement for positive behavior.

In a 1999 study, the Vermont group examined the effectiveness of supplementing traditional motivational and behavioral therapy with voucher incentives, rewarding people for marijuana abstinence. They found that participants who were randomly assigned to the therapy-plus-voucher condition remained abstinent for longer than did those who received only motivational or behavioral therapy, or both.

Another recent study, reported in the *Archives of General Psychiatry* (Vol. 58, No. 4) in April, explored a new method of treating marijuana dependence by chemically blocking people's cannabinoid receptors, dulling the effects of the drug.

In the study, Marilyn A. Huestis, PhD, and colleagues at the National Institute on Drug Abuse gave 63 participants either a "cannabinoid antagonist" known as SR141716 or a placebo. Two hours later, participants smoked a marijuana cigarette. Results showed that the participants who had received the cannabinoid antagonist reported feeling less

"high" after smoking the marijuana than did participants who had been given a placebo. In addition, they showed less increase in heart rate after smoking the marijuana than did participants in the control group.

Such findings are promising, to be sure. But one of the most instructive findings in the treatment literature so far, many researchers observe, has concerned not treatment outcomes, but treatment *turnout*. In the past, few treatment programs specifically addressed marijuana dependence, and researchers were initially uncertain whether many people would seek treatment for marijuana use. That question can now be put safely to rest.

When his group began recruiting participants for its first treatment study, Stephens remembers, "We were almost overwhelmed by people coming out of the woodwork who wanted treatment for marijuana. I think it was very useful for these people to realize there were other people seeking treatment."

WELCOME TO
METH COUNTRY

Toxic waste from clandestine drug labs in the rural West is
being dumped on the land and into streams, sewage systems, and landfills.

BY MARILYN BERLIN SNELL

WHEN SHERIFF'S DEPUTIES IN SPARSELY POPULATED NORTH-eastern Arizona received a tip about a stolen vehicle in 1999, they figured they'd be able to make a bust near the town of Show Low and be back at Apache County headquarters in St. Johns in time for lunch. Instead, they stumbled into one of the largest clandestine methamphetamine labs found in the state that year. The easy part was arresting the three suspects—brothers ages 56, 62, and 64, who lived on the property and had in their possession 39 weapons, including a fully automatic Mac-10 with a 50-round magazine and a 30 aught-six rifle with a spotting scope. Then the dangerous work began.

Known variously as ice, speed, crank, go, and the poor man's cocaine, meth is a highly addictive central-nervous-system stimulant and one of the few controlled substances people without any chemistry expertise can manufacture on their own. Of the 32 chemicals that can be used in varying combinations to make or "cook" meth, one-third are extremely toxic. Many of these chemicals are also reactive, explosive, flammable, and corrosive. Of the 1,654 labs seized nationwide in 1998—mostly in the western United States—nearly one in five were found because of fire or explosion.

Law enforcement officers have to take samples of all the chemicals for prosecution purposes, and must wear hermetically sealed moon suits and self-contained breathing apparatuses for protection. Hazmat (hazardous-materials) teams then come in to clean up the mess. And it's a big mess: For every pound of meth produced, between five and six pounds of highly toxic waste is generated. For big cooks like the one in Apache County, which was capable of making fifteen pounds of meth a day, cleanup costs often exceed $100,000. Yet even with these measures, there's no guarantee that the location will ever be fit

to reinhabit. The chemicals and fumes that permeate the walls, carpets, plaster, and wood of meth labs, as well as the surrounding soil, are known to cause cancer, short-term and permanent brain damage, and immune and respiratory system problems. In fact, because of the environmental and liability risks, counties don't even bother to confiscate the property. In a sign of just how risky ownership of this type of hazardous-waste site is, a $70,000 lien was put on the Apache County property, but since no one else wanted anything to do with it—including the bank and the county—the land is now back in the hands of the three brothers.

"I would rather investigate a homicide than a meth lab," says a frustrated Lieutenant Andrew Tafoya, who led the Apache County investigation. "These labs are a logistical and environmental nightmare." The lab sites also act as toxic springs that wend their way into nearby streams and groundwater.

It took three days and more than $100,000 to clean up the contaminated soil, destroy the buildings, and cart off the toxic chemicals.

When Tafoya got into law enforcement 13 years ago, the last thing on his mind was being done in by toxic fumes or cancer-causing chemicals. Apache County is cattle country, and although officers there were not at first thrilled to be talking to someone associated with the Sierra Club—which has strongly criticized grazing practices in the Southwest—Tafoya and others were eager to discuss what has become one of the most hazardous aspects of their job: clandestine meth labs.

A 1998 NATIONAL HOUSEHOLD SURVEY ON DRUG ABUSE estimated that 4.7 million Americans have taken meth. Though it's always difficult to get an accurate reading of illegal drug use, a few meth statistics confirm its growing popularity: In a national survey that measured the prevalence of drugs among U.S. adolescents, meth use among high school seniors more than doubled between 1990 and 1996; in San Diego in 1994, there were more admissions to treatment facilities for meth than for alcohol; and in Contra Costa County near San Francisco, police found that meth was involved in 89 percent of the reported domestic dispute cases in 1998.

Until the 1990s, meth production was concentrated primarily in the West and Southwest and controlled by outlaw motorcycle clubs that kept a tight lid on their secret recipes. But in the mid-'90s, after a cooking method showed up on the Internet that called for an ingredient widely available in farming communities—a type of fertilizer—small-scale meth labs took hold and flourished in the Midwest as well. Today, California, Arizona, and Missouri vie for the dubious honor of meth capital of America—though in terms of sheer volume, California has always been and remains Numero Uno. According to Drug Enforcement Administration testimony before Congress, of the 71 "super labs" seized by DEA agents nationwide in 1998—a super lab can produce between 10 and 100 pounds of meth in a single batch—57 were in California.

At the Apache County site, Tafoya and his team discovered massive amounts of iodine crystals, hidriotic acid, and red phosphorus. The suspects had been using a cooking method known as the pseudoephedrine/ephedrine reduction method, which mixes toxic chemicals to convert the drug ephedrine—a stimulant that acts on the body like the hormone adrenaline—into meth. Pure ephedrine is a regulated chemical (meaning the DEA has reporting requirements for its sale and movement), but the synthetic version is available in over-the-counter decongestants and diet pills. The federal government places a limit of eight packages per person on Sudafed and other medications containing pseudoephedrine—because of their use in the manufacture of meth—but the determined meth cook need only visit less vigilant stores to fill his basket with this key ingredient.

Iodine is mostly used by ranchers, in miniscule amounts, to treat thrush on horse hooves. As a rule, most meth cooks don't have horses. Instead, they use gallons of the chemical—which in large amounts is toxic to the gastrointestinal system and the thyroid gland, not to mention the environment—in the initial stages of the pseudoephedrine/ephedrine cooking process.

Oil refineries use hidriotic acid to test crude oil for sulfur content. One or two gallons can last a refinery an entire year. So, what does a guy living out in the middle of nowhere need with 50 gallons of the stuff? As the principal chemical in the pseudoephedrine reduction process, hidriotic acid breaks down the pseudoephedrine molecules to create meth.

Red phosphorus can be found at the end of every matchstick in your house, and also in road flares. Needless to say, it's highly flammable. The Apache County lab had 550 pounds of red phosphorus on site—about 549.99 pounds more than anyone in their right mind would need to light their backyard barbecue.

In the pseudoephedrine reduction process, if red phosphorus and iodine are heated and improperly vented by the amateur chemist, a lethal and odorless gas called phosphene is created. "If we don't know it's a lab when we go in," says Tafoya, "the immediate danger is that we don't have breathing apparatuses on and we inhale toxic gases that can kill us or fry our lungs."

In 1999, Arizona found 473 labs. The year 2000 was on track to exceed that number. The majority were small-scale operations (called "Beavis-and-Butthead" labs by DEA agents) located in urban areas. Makeshift labs have been found in motel rooms, homes and apartments on quiet, cactus-lined streets in Phoenix, and even in car trunks. Jim Molesa, the DEA's public-affairs officer for Phoenix, says that the average small lab costs between $3,000 and $4,000 to clean up. "The small urban labs make a couple ounces," he says, just enough to feed the cook's addiction—with leftovers sold to buy over-the-counter chemicals for the next batch. "But there's still a horrible environmental component with these labs," Molesa adds. "They're almost like a mini-hazardous-waste site."

Special Agent William Etter works with the DEA in Northern California and deals with urban labs almost daily. According to Etter, these labs are an ever-increasing micro problem: In 1995, 52 percent of the lab seizures nationwide were in metropolitan areas. "With urban labs, there are levels of contamination that hit you where you live," says Etter. "When I think of the environment, it's not just about the birds, bees, and trees. How about the urban environment? Knowing what I know about meth, I'd never move into a house that had been a lab."

Scott Logan, who heads Envirosolve, the company contracted by the DEA to clean up meth labs in Arizona, agrees. "The small labs contain flammable solvents, chlorinated solvents, acid bases," says Logan. "We find just about every toxic food group." When it comes to the environmental costs of meth, urban blight and rural blight—micro labs and macro ones—blur into one Superfund-size problem.

The "trunk labs," where all the makings for meth are piled into the trunk of a car, present their own special problems since they're essentially mobile hazardous-waste sites. Recently, a trunk lab was discovered in the Apache National Forest in the southern sector of Apache County. Rocky Gardom, a supervisory law enforcement officer for the U.S. Forest Service, was involved in the raid. "They were in a little side canyon and had been cooking right next to the vehicle," he says. "They had set up tents and had everything laid out. It looked like they planned to be there a while." Gardom adds that he often finds tree-kills around the labs. "We had one mobile-home lab that had been operating for several years on private land within the boundaries of the Sitgreaves National Forest," he says. "We found some large ponderosa pines that were a hundred and fifty years old killed off by the fumes."

Gardom also says he's seeing more labs in his forest than he did ten years ago, and attributes the increase both to a sharp rise in the drug's popularity during the 1990s and to intensified law enforcement in urban areas. "This stuff is easier to detect in the city," says Gardom, "and so they're moving onto Bureau of Land Management and national forest land that's more remote." The cooking process smells to high heaven—one law enforcement officer describes it as a mix between battery acid and rotten eggs—but the smaller labs can conceal the stench by using a hose to run the fumes from glass cooking flasks through kitty litter before it's piped outside. Larger-scale operations can't control the smell, so they need a lot of wide-open space without nosy, complaining neighbors. The Southwest, with its vast tracts of rural and public lands, is perfect for the bigger cooks.

Remote areas also offer easier disposal of the toxic by-products of the manufacturing process. Lab operators routinely dump hazardous waste on the land, into streams, and into landfills and sewage systems. The cooks at the lab in Apache County used their land and a nearby ravine as a toxic-waste dump. The county, a 12,000-square-mile area with only 65,000 residents, has two lab-certified officers—both trained at the DEA center in Quantico, Virginia—and they're training a third. When a lab is discovered, these officers are called in, along with hazmat teams from Phoenix. Two buildings were demolished at the Apache County site, since all surfaces were contaminated with toxic chemicals. Tons of contaminated soil were also removed. Along with the red phosphorus, iodine crystals, and hidriotic acid, 500 pounds of other chemicals, including acetone and Red Devil lye, were carted off, as well as $15,000 worth of glassware used in the meth-making. Envirosolve trucked off seven semi loads of toxic material, though it left behind the dead shaggy bark juniper and piñon pines that had been poisoned by fumes from the lab.

"I would rather investigate a homicide than a meth lab," says one officer. "These labs are a logistical and environmental nightmare."

"These guys had their own breathing apparatuses to use while cooking," says Apache County's narcotics agent Clifford Thorn, adding that the Phoenix Fire Department had to donate breathing devices to the county because it couldn't afford them. The trees had to fend for themselves.

Born and raised on a ranch, Agent Thorn still works cattle on 11,000 acres near the lab site. He notes that downstream from the site, on a ranch adjoining the property, 20 head of cattle turned up dead. "As a rancher, I found that highly unusual," says Thorn. "These guys were filtering their chemicals and then dumping the toxic residue right into the drainage." Autopsies on the cows found high levels of toxicity but the results were inconclusive. The report said the cattle had extensive kidney and liver damage, but that this was consistent with damage caused by jimson weed as well as some of the chemicals found at the site. "But you've got to wonder," Thorn adds. "Jimson only grows in the spring and these cows all died at once, in September."

Across the state from Apache County, near the California border, lies the desert outpost of Kingman, Arizona. The town made headlines in 1995 when it was discovered that Oklahoma City bomber Timothy McVeigh had been living there right before his fateful road trip to the heartland. This vast and desolate region in western Arizona is also meth country. In fact, McVeigh's lawyer made an argument during the trial that his client was a practicing, paranoid, delusional "tweaker," or meth addict, whose judgment had been irreparably impaired by his drug use. Mohave County law enforcement officers don't like to be reminded of their infamous former resident, but they're more than willing to confirm that they have a serious meth-lab problem. The county's percentage of meth labs per capita has earned it a High Intensity Drug Trafficking Area designation from the federal government.

In 1998, a super lab using the "Nazi" cooking method was found near Kingman. Named for the process used to make meth during World War II in Germany to energize Wehrmacht troops, the recipe was taped to the lab wall when officers and a hazmat team from Phoenix arrived. "In this county there's no industry besides prisons and agriculture," says Mohave County DEA agent Jeff Sandberg. "But there are a lot of remote areas that make a great place to do meth business." According to both state and federal narcotics agents in Mohave County, meth labs are their biggest problem.

Last February, Mohave County law enforcement raided a super lab in a scrub-brush-and-chaparral rural subdivision 18 miles east of Kingman. Emmett Sturgill, the Narcotics Unit supervisor for the Arizona Department of Public Safety in Kingman, says that as cattle grazing operations go under, the land is being subdivided and sold dirt-cheap. "For $250 down you can buy a 40-acre parcel, so all these low-life jerks who don't have much money grab these deals, go out there and put a camper down, and start cooking meth." The lab, on Cedar Ridge Road, was in full swing when officers converged on the trailer. It took three days and more than $100,000 to clean up the contaminated soil, destroy the buildings, and cart off the toxic chemicals. "We didn't find much waste in containers at the site," says Detective Ernie Severson, who was in charge of the Cedar Ridge raid and cleanup. "But there are miles and miles of desert where they probably dumped it."

"I have an 11-month-old baby," Severson adds. "Because of the chemicals I track through at these labs I've got to keep my boots away from him. In a real sense, I have to worry about taking my work home."

MARILYN BERLIN SNELL *is* Sierra's *writer/editor.*

From *Sierra*, January/February 2001, pp. 50-54. ©2001 by Sierra. Reprinted by permission.

UNIT 4
Other Trends in Drug Use

Unit Selections

Key Points to Consider

- How have the drug use increases of the 1990s suggested valid new worries about drug use by the young?

- What factors cause drug-related trends and patterns to change?

- How are drug-related patterns and trends related to specific subpopulations of Americans?

- How significant is socioeconomic class in influencing drug trends?

 **Links: www.dushkin.com/online/**
These sites are annotated in the World Wide Web pages.

Marijuana as a Medicine
http://mojo.calyx.net/~olsen/

Rarely do drug-related patterns and trends lend themselves to precise definition. Identifying, measuring, and predicting the consequences of these trends is an inexact science, to say the least. It is, nevertheless, a very important process.

Some of the most valuable data produced by drug-related trend analysis identify subpopulations whose vulnerability to certain drug phenomena is greater than that of the wider population. These identifications may forewarn of the implications for the general population. Trend analysis may produce specific information that may otherwise be lost or obscured by general statistical indications. For example, tobacco is probably the most prominent of gateway drugs with repeated findings pointing to the correlation between the initial use of tobacco and the use of other drugs. Currently, about 16 percent of youths 12 to 17 years of age are users of cigarettes and about 19 percent report using alcohol at least once in the

past month. Research suggests that among boys aged 12 to 17 years of age, who have no other problem behaviors, those who report drinking alcohol and/or smoking cigarettes at least once in the previous month are 28 times more likely to use marijuana than those who did not smoke or drink. The relationship is even higher for girls. There are similar findings when researchers study the use of marijuana by youth and its implications for the use of harder drugs. Thus, the analysis of specific trends related to youth smoking is very important, as it provides a threshold from which educators, health care professionals, parents, and young people may respond to significant drug-related health threats and issues.

Historically popular depressant and stimulant drugs, such as alcohol, tobacco, heroin, and cocaine, produce statistics that identify the most visible and sometimes the most constant use patterns. Other drugs such as marijuana, LSD, Ecstasy and other "club drugs" often produce patterns widely interpreted to be associated with cultural phenomena such as youth attitudes, popular music trends, and political climate. Still other drugs, such as methamphetamine, suggest potential use patterns of cocaine-like proportions.

One of two emerging drug trends that are expressing alarming consistencies concerns the use of club drugs such as: MDMA (ecstasy), GHB (grievous bodily harm, easy lay), Rohypnol (roofies, r-2, forget me drug), Ketamine (jet, special k, honey oil), PMA (death, mitsubishi double-stack), Nexus (venus, bromo, toonies), and PCP (angel dust, rocket fuel). Often, these drugs are perceived as less dangerous and less addictive than mainstream drugs such as heroin and cocaine. Unfortunately, however, the quality of these drugs varies significantly and often substitute drugs are sold in their place. Since distribution networks associated with club drugs are unpredictable, users are subject to a constant menu of "look-alikes" or analogs. Rohyponol exists as one good example as supplies are limited by a significant government effort to curtail its availability. The government's Drug Abuse Warning Network (DAWN) that tracks

drug related emergency room visits is reporting drastic increases in emergency room treatment for overdoses of Ecstasy and GHB.

The other emerging and alarming trend concerns the abuse of prescription drugs. An estimated 4 million Americans a year are abusing prescription drugs more than ever before. Opiate related drugs such as Codeine and Oxycontin, Benzodiazepines such as Valium and Xanax, and stimulants such as Ritalin are among the most abused. More surprising is that many of the abusers are older Americans, adolescents, and women.

Information concerning drug use patterns and trends obtained by a number of different investigative methods is available from a variety of sources. On the national level, the more prominent sources are the Substance Abuse and Mental Health Services Administration, the National Institute on Drug Abuse, the Drug Abuse Warning Network, the National Centers for Disease Control, the Justice Department, the Office of National Drug Control Policy, and the Surgeon General. On the state level, various justice departments, including the attorney general's office, the courts, state departments of social services, state universities and colleges, and public health offices maintain data and conduct research. On local levels, criminal justice agencies, social service departments, public hospitals, and health departments provide information. On a private level, various research institutes and universities, professional organizations such as the American Medical Association and the American Cancer Society, hospitals, and treatment centers, as well as private corporations, are tracking drug-related trends. Surveys abound, with no apparent lack of available data. As a result, the need for examination of research methods and findings for reliability and accuracy is self-evident.

The articles in this unit provide information about some drug-related trends occurring within certain subpopulations of Americans. While reading the articles, it is interesting to contemplate whether the trends and patterns described are confined to specific geographical areas.

Playing With
PAIN KILLERS

Over the past decade, doctors have focused new energy on managing their patients' pain, and sales of prescription painkillers have tripled since 1996. For most people, these drugs are a blessing. For some, they're a nightmare.

By Claudia Kalb

IT ALL STARTED INNOCENTLY ENOUGH. Three years ago, when Michelle Brown got pregnant, her doctor wrote her a prescription for Lortab, a potentially addictive painkiller similar to Vicodin, for relief from migraine headaches. Her migraines eventually got worse; the Lortab made her life bearable. But it had a devastating side effect: "Slowly," says Brown, who is from Sanford, Maine, "I started to get addicted." She became a classic "doctor shopper," hopping from one physician to the next to get multiple prescriptions. She discovered Percocet, and soon she was mixing Lortab with OxyContin, a new, superstrength pain-killer she got through a dealer. By early last year, Brown, 25 years old, and the mother of two small children, worked up the nerve to commit fraud. Pretending to be phoning from her doctor's office, she called her local pharmacy, read her physician's identification number off a prescription bottle and won, she says, "my key to the palace."

For millions of Americans, painkillers are a godsend. Cancer patients suffer the agony a little bit more easily. People battling severe arthritis can, for the first time, take walks and play with their grandchildren. Realizing that for years doctors neglected to include pain management in patient care, the medical establishment has, over the past decade, taken a new, more aggressive approach to treating pain. In January a national accrediting board issued new standards requiring doctors in hospitals and other facilities to treat pain as a vital sign, meaning that they must measure it and treat it as they would blood pressure or heart rate. Even Congress has gotten into the act, last fall passing a law declaring the next 10 years the "Decade of Pain Control and Research."

In this environment, pharmaceutical companies are experimenting with new formulations of painkillers, and existing painkillers themselves are more widely distributed than ever before. While the pharmaceutical market doubled to $145 billion between 1996 and 2000, the painkiller market tripled to $1.8 billion over the same period. Yet at the same time, the incidence of reported first-time abuse of painkillers has also surged. Many of these painkillers aren't new, and "there's not necessarily something wrong with" the increase in controlled substances, says Michael Moy in the Drug Enforcement Administration's Office of Diversion Control. "But once you put something into the food chain, someone's going to want to bite."

Although there are no perfect statistics on how many people misuse or abuse prescription drugs, in 1999 an estimated 4 million Americans over the age of 12 used prescription pain relievers, sedatives and stimulants for "nonmedical" reasons in the past month, with almost half saying they'd done so for the first time. According to the DEA, the most-abused prescription drugs include the oxycodone and hydrocodone types of painkillers, which contain potentially addictive opioids (the two drugs differ slightly in chemical structure, but both work similarly on the body). And emergency-room data suggest that certain drugs have seen dramatic spikes in abuse in recent years. ER visits involving hydrocodone medications like Vicodin and Lortab jumped from an estimated 6,100 incidents in 1992 to more than 14,000 in 1999, oxycodone painkillers like Percodan and OxyContin rose from about 3,750 to 6,430 and the anti-anxiety drug Xanax (including generic formulations) increased from 16,500 to more than 20,500. Illegal drugs, abused in much higher numbers, also increased: cocaine from 120,000 to 169,000 and heroin and morphine from 48,000 to 84,400.

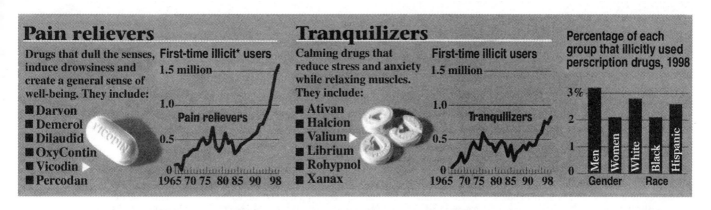

Pain relievers

Drugs that dull the senses, induce drowsiness and create a general sense of well-being. They include:

- Darvon
- Demerol
- Dilaudid
- OxyContin
- Vicodin ▶
- Percodan

First-time illicit* users

Pain relievers

1965 70 75 80 85 90 98

Tranquilizers

Calming drugs that reduce stress and anxiety while relaxing muscles. They include:

- Ativan
- Halcion
- Valium ▶
- Librium
- Rohypnol
- Xanax

First-time illicit users

Tranquilizers

1965 70 75 80 85 90 98

Percentage of each group that illicitly used perscription drugs, 1998

Gender: Men, Women
Race: White, Black, Hispanic

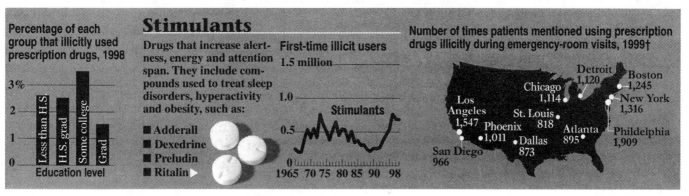

Percentage of each group that illicitly used prescription drugs, 1998

Education level: Less than H.S., H.S. grad, Some college, Grad

Stimulants

Drugs that increase alertness, energy and attention span. They include compounds used to treat sleep disorders, hyperactivity and obesity, such as:

- Adderall
- Dexedrine
- Preludin
- Ritalin ▶

First-time illicit users

Stimulants

1965 70 75 80 85 90 98

Number of times patients mentioned using prescription drugs illicitly during emergency-room visits, 1999†

- Detroit 1,120
- Boston 1,245
- Chicago 1,114
- New York 1,316
- Los Angeles 1,547
- St. Louis 818
- Phoenix 1,011
- Dallas 873
- Atlanta 895
- Philedelphia 1,909
- San Diego 966

* "ILLICIT" REFERS TO NONMEDICAL USE. †DRUGS INVOLVED: XANAX, CLONAZEPAM, HYDROCODONE AND D-PROPOXYPHENE, AT SELECT HOSPITALS.
SOURCES: THE SUBSTANCE ABUSE & MENTAL HEALTH SERVICES ADMIN., NATL. INSTITUTE ON DRUG ABUSE, DRUG ENFORCEMENT ADMIN.
RESEARCH BY JOSH ULICK. PILL PHOTOGRAPHS BY DAVID N. BERKEWITZ.

Reports of painkiller abuse from Hollywood catch the attention of the public more than any statistic ever will. In the last six months, Melanie Griffith and Matthew Perry each checked into rehab, publicly acknowledging their addiction to prescription painkillers. TV shows fill their scripts with the problem: on "ER," Dr. John Carter gets hooked on painkillers after he's stabbed, and on the new show, "The Job," Denis Leary plays a detective who takes painkillers on a stakeout. Even Homer Simpson battles a compulsion for the drugs in a season-ender where he's catapulted into a surreal celebrity existence. After looking at the data and following the news reports, the National Institute on Drug Abuse (NIDA) will announce next week a major public-health initiative about prescription-drug abuse. "Once you get into millions of people [abusing]," says Dr. Alan Leshner, NIDA's director, "you have a serious public-health issue on your hands."

Addiction to prescription drugs is not a new problem. Remember "Valley of the Dolls"? The uppers, the downers, the sleeping pills? But some of today's drugs are far more sophisticated than anything Jacqueline Susann could have envisioned. OxyContin, which hit the market in 1996, is by far the most powerful: it's a 12-hour time-release incarnation of the molecular compound oxycodone, the active ingredient in older drugs like Percodan and Percocet. Unlike drugs in the hydrocodone category, OxyContin and several other oxycodones don't contain acetaminophen, which can damage the liver in high doses and limits the extent to which those drugs can be safely used. OxyContin allows patients to swallow fewer pills, and offers pain relief three times longer than earlier versions. But when the drug is crushed and snorted, eliminating its time-release feature, it's a huge narcotic rush to the brain. "You feel vitalized, like you can do whatever you want," says Eric, 38, of Portland, Maine, who has spent as much as $525 a week buying the drug from a street dealer. Abuse of OxyContin has gotten so bad that in some areas users are robbing pharmacies to get the drug—just last month, Hannaford, a major chain in Maine, decided that "for the safety of our associates and customers," it would no longer stock the drug on its shelves.

When it comes to prescription painkillers, there is no typical abuser. Police departments say they've seen every variety, from teenagers to stay-at-home moms to executives who started taking drugs for their tennis elbow. Particularly at risk are chronic substance abusers who may divert to prescription drugs when their preferred poisons, like heroin, run out. In Hollywood clubs, cocaine and ecstasy still dominate, one 30-year-old actor says, but people also share Vicodin, Xanax and Valium, then wash them down with alcohol. Health-care professionals, with easy access to drugs, often succumb. Among arrests in Cincinnati, which carefully tracks prescription-drug abuse, 30 percent of cases involve medical employees. Landon Gibbs, a Virginia state police officer, says his department arrested a doctor last year who would "write a prescription, drive that person to the pharmacy and then split the pills."

Prescription painkillers are appealing in part because users think of them as "safe." They're FDA approved, easy to take on the sly and don't have the same stigma as illegal drugs. Cindy Mogil started taking Valium at 20 to ease the trauma after a car accident, and "liked

How One TOWN GOT HOOKED

Hazard, Ky., has seen its share of hard times. But nothing prepared the gritty hamlet for the onslaught of the drug OxyContin. Now the abuse is an epidemic.

By Debra Rosenberg

NO ONE COULD BLAME JOSHUA COOTS for wanted to escape. Bored and frustrated, the pale, soft-spoken teen felt trapped in the tiny town of Hazard, Ky. The place didn't offer him many options. Left behind by the economic boom, the town of 5,500 still depends largely on the aging coal and timber industries. Empty storefronts dot the depressed Main Street. Highway strip malls are about the only places left to go for a night out. Coots couldn't imagine a lifetime hauling logs or toiling in the mines, where his father once worked. Instead, he took a job as a telemarketer. In his off hours he hung out with friends in the park, smoking pot and popping pills. The drugs were a mild distraction, but did little for his mood. Then someone gave him the powerful prescription painkiller OxyContin. When crushed, the pills delivered a euphoric, heroinlike punch. "I don't know how to explain the buzz," says Coots, now 21. "It's just this utopic feeling. You feel like you can conquer the world... It's a better high than anything else."

Coots was hooked. He started out with a modest 20mg, but before long, he says, he needed 400mg just to make it through the day. And that took money. OxyContin is known as the poor man's herion, but at a street price of $1 per milligram it can be anything but cheap. Coots quit his job and spent all his time in pursuit of the precious pills. Each morning began with an orange 40mg tablet, which he downed before getting out of bed. "I couldn't hardly walk if I didn't have it." At first he crushed and snorted the pills, after sucking on them to remove the time-release coating. Later he dissolved the powder in water and injected it for a quicker buzz. He floated through the days in a dreamlike stupor, not even bothering to eat. His waist dropped from 42 inches to 36 inches in two months. As his cravings got worse, he found creative ways to get hold of the pills. Sometimes he would fake back pain and get a shady local doctor to write him an Oxy prescription. Once, he even stole the pills from his grandfather, who was taking them to dull the pain from a fractured spine. "I had to have more and more," he says.

These days, nearly everyone in Hazard has an OxyContin horror story to tell. In the last year, local officials say, the drug has swept through the small town, wrecking lives and destroying families. Precise statistics are hard to pin down, but the number of local addicts runs in the hundreds. Oxy abuse cuts across income and age lines. Teens meet for Oxy parties in the park. Miners blow their paychecks to feed their addictions. Even grandmothers peddle their prescriptions for quick cash. In February police rounded up more than 200 Oxy dealers in Hazard and surrounding counties, the largest drug bust in state history. Hazard's crime rate has soared; the jail is packed with Oxy-addicted inmates. In nearby Harlan, Judge Ron Johnson sentenced a woman to 10 years in prison for selling just four of the pills. OxyContin is "a pure scourge upon the land," he fumed from the bench. It is, he said, "demonic fire."

Hazard isn't the only place struggling to quell the flames. Oxy has taken hold in other rural Appalachian states and in New England, places where it's tougher to get more familiar street drugs like heroin and crack. The drug's maker, Purdue Pharma, says it is appalled by the widespread abuse of the drug, a form of synthetic morphine. "When this drug is used properly, it has the potential to save lives. When it's abused, it has the potential to take lives, just like any other strong medication," says Dr. J. David Haddox, Purdue Pharma's medical director. In an effort to stem the damage, Purdue has held workshops for doctors and met with the DEA and officials from five states. The company is even researching new drugs that would be more tamperproof and less addictive. But those efforts are years away from pharmacy shelves. Hazard isn't willing to wait. In recent months police and community activists have joined forces to get OxyContin off the streets, and out of their town.

Getting tough:
A judge in nearby Harlan sentenced a woman to 10 years in prison for selling four pills. Oxy is 'a pure scourge upon the land,' he fumed.

That could prove difficult. Hazard has a long tradition of self-medication. Moonshine and marijuana, grown in its fertile soil, have long helped to blot out depression, boredom, even physical pain. Eastern Kentucky has one of the nation's highest cancer rates, and many residents suffer from chronic mining and timber injuries. OxyContin seemed like the most potent antidote yet to the local despair. "If there's ever been a drug made that will knock depression out for the short term, it's OxyContin," says therapist Mike Spare. "The euphoria sucks you in."

When the then police chief, Rod Maggard, first heard about Oxy in the summer of 1999, he had to ask his pharmacist what it was. But by spring, he knew all too well what the drug was doing to his town. Burglaries and domestic-violence reports were up. Overdoses were mounting at the local hospital. (State police count 19 OxyContin-related deaths in Kentucky this year alone. Purdue Pharma disputes the number.) Maggard, 57, who retired as police chief in March, was flooded with hundreds of calls from families begging him to help get a son or daughter off the drug. "I have never seen anything take off like this did," says Maggard, a square-shouldered, gray-haired cop. "It has mushroomed." On the wood-paneled wall above him hangs a prized painting called "The Protector"—an image of Jesus with his hand on the hood of a flashing police cruiser.

Maggard was especially outraged that the town's sole refuge, leafy, peaceful Perry County Park, had become an open-air drug market. Clusters of teens and young adults jammed the parking lot near the Little League fields, lining up to buy Oxy. "Nobody wanted to get stoned. Nobody wanted to get drunk. Everybody wanted to go get an OC and sit in the park," says Holly, a recovering addict who's now 21. Girls carried ceramic bathroom tiles in their purses so they could be ready to crush a pill anywhere, any time. In a futile effort to control the trade, Maggard patrolled the grounds in his unmarked car, installed surveillance cameras and had the park gates locked late at night. Nothing seemed to work. When addicts started referring to the park as "Pillville," Maggard called in the Feds for help. The DEA and other law-enforcement agencies set up an undercover task force.

By then Hazard was in the throes of a crime wave sparked by Oxy addicts searching for a fix. James Wallace, a baby-faced 20-year-old, was locked in the dilapidated Perry County Jail for receiving stole property. Leaning on a blue plastic picnic table in the jail's smoky visitors' lounge, Wallace admits he stole televisions, guns, knives—all to earn money for Oxy. Sometimes he'd even go into stores and claim the soda machine outside had taken his dollar. "You'll do everything and anything," he says. In Hazard, whatever he got his hands on could be traded for the drug. Addicts even lifted grocery-store steaks. At one Hazard fruit stand, you could swap food stamps for the pills.

Down in Pillville:
'Nobody wanted to get stoned. Nobody wanted to get drunk. Everybody wanted to go get an OC,' says Holly, a 21-year-old recovering addict.

Throughout the fall, Maggard's undercover task force quietly plugged away. Police eventually seized 10,000 OxyContin pills and bought an additional 3,500 in sting operations. As they worked, Maggard and his team traced the drug's route to Hazard. Most of the pills came through a disturbingly convenient pipeline: the local pharmacy. Dealers would fake injuries or visit a few unscrupulous doctors willing to write prescriptions for a $100 fee. Several doctors have already been charged, and Joseph Famularo, U.S. attorney for the eastern district of Kentucky, hints his next round of indictments may target health-care workers explicitly. Though Kentucky has a computer system designed to track narcotics prescriptions, Hazard was close enough to five other states that "doctor shoppers" could easily cross borders. Many users paid cash for the pills. Others were bold enough to get Medicaid or private insurance to pick up the tab. Police even found some elderly patients who rationed their own pain pills and sold the rest. "People were selling what they should be taking," says Maggard.

The task force got tips from an unlikely source: local churches. Late last fall pastors found themselves conducting funeral services for a growing number of Oxy overdose victims. One October evening the weekly Bible-study session at Petrey Memorial Baptist Church became a virtual OxyContin support group, as congregants spontaneously began sharing their stories about the drug. The Rev. Ronnie (Butch) Pennington launched a faith-based group, People Against Drugs. When he called a communitywide meeting on Oxy, so many people responded that he had to move the location twice to find a room large enough for the crowd. In the end, more than 400 people showed up. After the meeting participants called in 60 tips about possible Oxy dealers.

Police put them to use. As the sun rose on Feb. 6, more than 100 officers fanned out across eastern Kentucky with a sheaf of arrest warrants. By evening, Operation Oxyfest 2001 had rounded up 207 dealers. But a month later people wondered if the arrests had even made a dent. Frustrated, Kentucky prosecutor John Hansen has vowed to file murder charges against Oxy-overdose survivors, including family, friends and dealers.

With the whole town focused on catching the dealers, Hazard's addicts have largely been left to fend for themselves. The town still has no rehab program. Joshua Coots bottomed out about a year and a half ago. He'd lost his car, declared bankruptcy and wound up getting arrested for stealing the family truck. One day he collapsed on his parents' kitchen floor. "Mom and Dad, I'm on Oxy and it's killing me," he sobbed. At a religious revival meeting, a visiting pastor preached about evil in people's lives. He seemed to be looking straight at Coots, who wept steadily, tears dripping off his mustache and down his chin. Was he ready to step into a new life? the preacher asked. Coots was. He quit Oxy cold turkey. "It was miraculous," he says.

Today, Main Street in Hazard has one fewer boarded-up storefront. In the building that once housed a campaign office, Coots and his father, Pastor Donnie Coots, refer Oxy addicts to private rehab programs out of state. In Pillville, police are still rounding up dealers and users on weekends. The hundreds of busts have managed to decrease the supply, making the drug more expensive. Yet the Oxy market continues to thrive. Too many people in Hazard, it seems, are willing to pay any price.

the feeling of euphoria." As a manager in a health clinic, she had easy access to sample pills, then found her way to Vicodin and Percodan, visiting different doctors to get her supply. "Boy, it's so easy," says Mogil, who lives in suburban Atlanta. "I'd walk in and tell them I had a migraine; that's all I had to say." Her family never questioned the pills: "They think

you're taking it for medical reasons." Finally, after two decades of abuse, Mogil collapsed—her face numb, her speech slurred—and checked into rehab. "I was no better than a street addict," she says.

All pain passes through the brain. Pills like Vicodin and OxyContin lock onto a cell receptor called *mu*, found most prominently in the brain, spinal cord and

gut. When the drug connects to the receptors in the spinal cord, pain signals from nerves are blocked; in the brain, the receptors seem to promote an overall sense of well-being; in the gut, they have the unfortunate side effect of constipation. While any patient who takes an opioid painkiller or any other addictive drug over a long period will develop a physical dependence—meaning the body adjusts to the chemicals now swirling about and thinks that's normal—that dependence can be properly managed. When it's time to go off the drug, a good physician will taper the prescription so there's no withdrawal or rebound effect. But a genetic tendency, an underlying mental illness, a history of substance abuse or a combination of factors may lead a small group of patients to go beyond just physical dependence. They become compulsive about taking the drug, even when it threatens their health or social and professional lives.

Once you're hooked, getting more becomes an obsession. Many abusers, like Michelle Brown, become doctor shoppers. Others buy their fix on the street: one Vicodin goes for about $6, Percocet and Percodan, up to $8, and an 80mg OxyContin for as much as $80. Tales of cunning and desperation abound—the weekend visits to the ER claiming a toothache, the stolen prescription pads. Dr. Sheila Calderon, an internist in Dallas, says a former employee used her name to call in a prescription for Vicodin (she was never charged). Cathy Napier, a former Percodan addict and now head of the chemical-dependency program at Presbyterian Hospital in Dallas, says she knows women who go to real-estate open houses, "then go through the medicine cabinets and steal the Lortab."

So who's to blame for the misuse of these drugs? Many abusers point the finger at doctors, who they say tend to prescribe medications too quickly without warning patients that certain drugs can be highly addictive. But once patients begin deceiving doctors and pharmacists by phoning in fake scripts or seeking prescriptions from multiple doctors, they become the culprits. Seventeen states currently have prescription-monitoring programs, which vary widely—some track drugs like OxyContin (a schedule II drug, deemed "high potential for abuse"), but not Vicodin (schedule III, "some potential"). But many states don't dedicate resources to full-time oversight. Nor does the DEA, which is largely watching out for abuse by health professionals. If abusers are caught, they're charged with fraud—a misdemeanor in some states and a felony in others. Brown says she is "so thankful" for the DEA agent who handled her case after a suspicious pharmacist called the police. "He knew I needed help. He told my family everything. And it just blew open from there." Now, says Brown, she's in treatment, taking methadone to ease her off her addiction and finally "learning how to live a normal life."

With all the focus on abusers, pain specialists worry that legitimate patients will suffer. Too many doctors succumb to "opiophobia," fear of prescribing much-needed medications for appropriate patients who suffer moderate to severe pain, says Dr. Russell Portenoy, chair of pain medicine at New York's Beth Israel Medical Center. Dr. Kenneth Pollack, a pain specialist in Des Moines, Iowa, says he recently prescribed OxyContin for a woman who had suffered painful nerve tumors in her feet for 11 years and could barely stand up. Last time Pollack saw her, "she was practically in tears," he says. "She said, 'Thank you for giving me my life back'." Says David E. Joranson, director of the Pain & Policy Studies Group at the University of Wisconsin:

"My fear is that some patients and doctors are going to start looking at this stuff like it's nuclear material. There is a real risk of losing recent gains made in pain management."

Pharmaceutical companies acknowledge that misuse is a problem. Pharmacia, which manufactures Xanax, says "all of our peer-group companies realize there is a potential for abuse here." They say they educate as many people as possible about the importance of taking the drug safely under a doctor's care; the drug is also marketed generically by other companies. Abbott Labs, which manufactures Vicodin, offers symposiums for prescribers and pharmacists to teach about abuse potential. And Purdue Pharma, which manufactures OxyContin, has been actively addressing the problem through education sessions and meetings with the DEA and the FDA.

Maryann Timmons, 51, says she needs her medication. After lifelong ear infections and a broken eardrum, Timmons, 51, of Concord Township, Ohio, takes Vicodin to dull the pain. Initially, she says, her doctor didn't want to prescribe the pills; he ultimately did, but told Timmons to use them sparingly because of their addictive potential. "I felt like a criminal," she says. "It shouldn't be a battle to get help with pain relief." Pain relief and criminal activity. The new challenge for doctors and public-health officials is to provide one without advancing the other.

With JOAN RAYMOND, ELLISE PIERCE, SAM SMITH, JAY P. WAGNER, JEANNE GORDON-THOMAS *and* ALAN WIRZBICKI

ARE YOU MAN ENOUGH?

**Testosterone can make a difference in bed and at the gym.
And soon you'll be able to get it as a gel. But it's a risky substance.
And is it really what makes men men?**

By RICHARD LACAYO

WHATEVER ELSE YOU MAY THINK about testosterone, you can tell it's a hot topic. Every time you mention that you happen to be writing about it, the first thing people ask is "Can you get me some?" (Everybody, even the women.) Maybe that's not so surprising. If there is such a thing as a bodily substance more fabled than blood, it's testosterone, the hormone that we understand and misunderstand as the essence of manhood. Testosterone has been offered as the symbolic (and sometimes literal) explanation for all the glories and infamies of men, for why they start street fights and civil wars, for why they channel surf, explore, prevail, sleep around, drive too fast, plunder, bellow, joust, plot corporate takeovers and paint their bare torsos blue during the Final Four. Hey, what's not to like?

Until now, it was easy to talk about testosterone but hard to do much about it. About 4 million men in the U.S. whose bodies don't produce enough take a doctor-prescribed synthetic version, mostly by self-injection, every one to three weeks. But the shots cannot begin to mimic the body's own minute-by-minute micromanagement of testosterone levels. So they can produce a roller coaster of emotional and physical effects, from a burst of energy, snappishness and libido in the first days to fatigue and depression later. The main alternative, a testosterone patch, works best when applied daily to the scrotum, an inconvenient spot, to put it mildly. Some doctors recommend that you warm that little spot with a blow dryer, which may or may not be fun.

All of that will change this summer when an easy to apply testosterone ointment, AndroGel, becomes generally available for the first time by prescription. The company that developed it, Illinois-based Unimed Pharmaceuticals, promises that because AndroGel is administered once or more a day, it will produce a more even plateau of testosterone, avoiding the ups and downs of the shots. Though the body's own production of this hormone trails off gradually in men after the age of 30 or so, not many men now seek testosterone-replacement therapy (not that they necessarily need to) or even get their T levels tested. But replace the needles and patches with a gel, something you just rub into the skin like coconut oil during spring break at Daytona Beach, and suddenly the whole idea seems plausible.

And besides, there's the name: testosterone! Who can say no to something that sounds like an Italian dessert named after a Greek god?

Testosterone, after all, can boost muscle mass and sexual drive. (It can also cause liver damage and accelerate prostate cancer, but more on that later.) That makes it central to two of this culture's rising preoccupations: perfecting the male body and sustaining the male libido, even when the rest of the male has gone into retirement. So will testosterone become the next estrogen, a hormone that causes men to bang down their doctor's doors, demanding to be turned into Mr. T? Do not underestimate the appeal of any substance promising to restore the voluptuous powers of youth to the scuffed and dented flesh of middle age. If you happen to be a man, the very idea is bound to appeal to your inner hood ornament, to that image of yourself as all wind-sheared edges and sunlit chrome. And besides, there's the name: testosterone! Who can say no to something that sounds like an Italian dessert named after a Greek god?

But testosterone is at issue in larger debates about behavioral differences between men and women and which differences are biologically determined. A few Sundays ago, the New York *Times* Magazine ran a long piece by Andrew Sullivan, 36, the former editor of the *New Republic*, in which he reported his own experience with testosterone therapy. In two years he has gained 20 lbs. of muscle. And in the days right after his once-every-two-weeks shot, he reports feeling lustier, more energetic, more confident and more quarrelsome—more potent, in all senses of the word.

Looking over the scientific research on testosterone, Sullivan speculated on the extent to which such traits as aggression, competitiveness and risk taking, things we still think of as male behavior, are linked to the fact that men's bodies produce far more testosterone than women's bodies. His answer—a lot—was offered more as an intuition than a conclusion, but it produced a spate of fang baring among some higher primates in the media and scientific world, since it implies that gender differences owe more to biology than many people would like to believe. Three researchers wrote the *Times* to complain that Sullivan had overstated their thinking. In the online magazine *Slate*, columnist Judith Shulevitz attacked Sullivan for favoring nature over environment in a debate in which nobody knows yet which is which. In the days that followed, Sullivan fired back at Shulevitz in *Slate*, she attacked again, and other writers joined in. If testosterone use becomes a true cultural phenomenon, expect the conversations about its role in gender differences to become even more, well, aggressive.

So just what does testosterone actually do for you? And to you? And how does it figure among the physical and environmental pressures that account for headbanging aggression, or even just the trading pit on Wall Street? One reason testosterone enjoys a near mythical status is that myth is what takes over when conclusive data are scarce. Though testosterone was first isolated in 1935, hormone-replacement therapy is one of the few areas of medicine where research on men lags behind that on women.

What we do know is that testosterone is an androgen, as the family of male sex hormones are called, and these hormones, in turn, are made up of the fat known as steroids. Both men and women produce testosterone in their bodies, men in the testes and adrenal glands, women in the adrenal glands and ovaries. But men produce much more—the average healthy male has 260 to 1,000 nanograms of testosterone per deciliter of blood plasma. For women the range is 15 to 70. But because men differ on how effectively their bodies process the substance—for instance, some have more receptors around their body that absorb it—a man on the low end of the normal range can still have all the testosterone he needs for normal sex drive and other benefits. In healthy men, levels also vary during the day, peaking around 8 a.m., which is why men commonly awaken in a state of sexual arousal, and dropping as much as half before bedtime.

Testosterone is the substance that literally turns boys into boys in the womb. In the first weeks after conception, all embryos are technically sexless. Around the sixth week of gestation, the presence of the

Y chromosome in males triggers a complex set of signals that cause a surge in testosterone. Among other things, that sets in motion the formation of the penis and testes. In adolescence, boys undergo another eruption that deepens their voices, causes hair to form on their bodies and allows their muscles to enlarge. Testosterone in the blood of teenage boys can jump to as high as 2,000 nanograms, which helps explain teenage boys.

One possible danger of easy-to-use testosterone is that it might become a temptation to younger males looking to bulk up at the gym. Not many of them would be able to demonstrate the diminished T counts that would allow them to get it legally from their doctors, but the potential for a black market in AndroGel is not hard to imagine among teens and guys in their 20s—and older—who hear stories about a new substance stronger than the supplements available over the counter and easier to use than anabolic steroids that are injected. For teens in particular, the dangers of testosterone overload are not just acne and breast development but a shutting down of bone growth—though they may be at an age that makes them almost deaf to the risks. For older men, studies indicate that high levels of T do not necessarily cause prostate cancer but do fuel the growth of tumors once they occur, which is why chemical castration is one means of treating the disease in the advanced stages.

Gay men may have been one of the first populations to talk up testosterone replacement, which is often part of the treatment regimen for HIV-positive men like Sullivan, author of the *New York Times Magazine* piece. They produced a buzz about increased sex drive and better results at the gym, things that happen to be of interest to a lot of straight men too, especially middle-age baby boomers looking to put themselves back in the driver's seat as far as their sex drive is concerned. "These men already come in asking for [testosterone]," says Dr. Louann Brizendine, co-director of the program in sexual health at the University of California, San Francisco. "This generation came out of the sexual revolution. They really identify themselves as sexual beings. And they don't want to give that up."

At 66, Gene Teasley, who operates a family business that makes banners in Dallas, is a decade older than the baby boomers, but he gets the idea. About nine years ago, he went to his doctor complaining of less interest in sex. Since then, he has been getting testosterone shots once

every two weeks. "I've enjoyed the results not just in the sexual way but also in a broader way of feeling healthier. I have more of a desire to work out, be outdoors and do more athletic things," he says. "Everybody wants to feel like they felt in their 20s and 30s."

Some researchers are taking seriously the still controversial notion of "male menopause," a constellation of physical changes, including fatigue, depression and drooping libido, that they believe can be traced to the decline of hormones, including testosterone, in men over 50. Others are not so sure. "One thing we have to recognize is that the decline in testosterone is also intertwined with changes, such as decrease in blood flow, and psychological and social changes too," says Dr. Kenneth Goldberg, medical director of the Men's Health Center in Dallas. "Simply expecting to take men who are androgen deficient and expecting testosterone to fix it all—it just can't be."

Yet even the passage of time doesn't guarantee that a particular man's testosterone will decline to a level that much affects how he feels, at least not by middle age. Middle-age men who preserve the body weight they had in their 20s may have no falloff at all, while overweight adult men of any age tend to have lower testosterone levels. This means that a couple of the *goombahs* on *The Sopranos* are probably deficient, though maybe I should let you be the one to tell them that.

Once you get past the proven links between testosterone, libido and muscle mass, the benefits of having higher levels of testosterone become harder to prove, though no less interesting to hear about. Just how much of a role does this play in producing behaviors such as aggression, competitiveness and belligerence? Men who take testosterone by injection routinely report that in the first days after the shot, when their T counts are especially high, they feel increased confidence, well-being and feistiness—what you might call swagger. They also describe feeling snappish and fidgety.

Jim—not his real name—is a family therapist who was 40 when he started taking the shots because of fatigue and a so-so interest in sex, which had led him to get his T levels tested. The first day or two after the shot, he says, he's on pins and needles. "My fiancé knows to steer clear. I tend to be short-tempered, more critical, and I go around the house looking for problems. I live out in the country, so right after I get

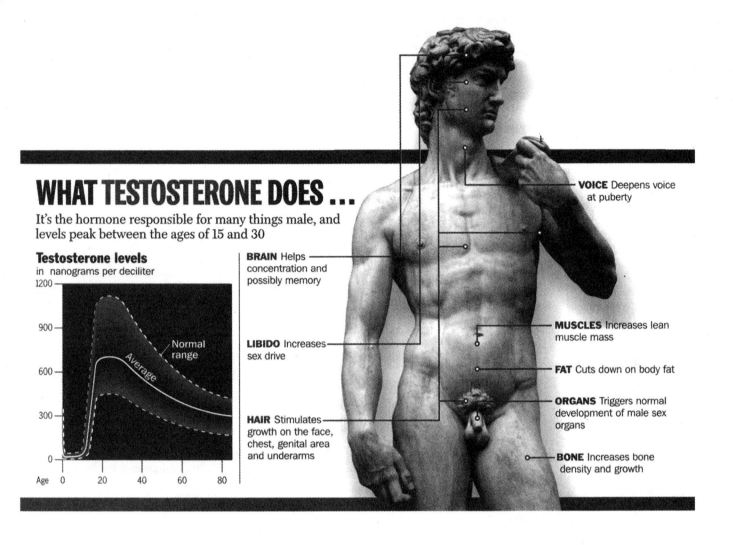

WHAT TESTOSTERONE DOES ...

It's the hormone responsible for many things male, and levels peak between the ages of 15 and 30

Testosterone levels
in nanograms per deciliter

BRAIN Helps concentration and possibly memory

LIBIDO Increases sex drive

HAIR Stimulates growth on the face, chest, genital area and underarms

VOICE Deepens voice at puberty

MUSCLES Increases lean muscle mass

FAT Cuts down on body fat

ORGANS Triggers normal development of male sex organs

BONE Increases bone density and growth

... AND HOW IT IS ADMINISTERED

Taking the hormone in steady, small doses is safest, but not always convenient. A gel form, due in pharmacies this summer, may become the method of choice for boosting testosterone counts.

Injection
HOW OFTEN Every 7 to 30 days
DOSE 100 mg to 350 mg
WHERE Muscle

BENEFITS High doses of testosterone

PROBLEMS Testosterone levels are not steady; high in first few days after injection, they fall back down at the end of a cycle

RISKS Surge of testosterone carries risk of liver problems, blood thickening, acne and breast development and may accelerate growth of existing prostate tumors

Patches
HOW OFTEN Daily
DOSE 4 mg to 6 mg
WHERE Scrotal tissue, back, abdomen or thighs

BENEFITS Controlled, steady delivery of testosterone that mimics natural cycles

PROBLEMS Best absorbed when applied to scrotal skin with a hair dryer. But scrotal skin contains enzymes that break down testosterone too quickly. Possibility of allergic reactions to patch

RISKS May spur growth of existing prostate tumors

Gel
HOW OFTEN Once to several times a day
DOSE 10 mg to 40 mg
WHERE Hairless skin

BENEFITS Controlled, steady delivery of testosterone that mimics natural cycles

PROBLEMS Variable effects. Not long-lasting

RISKS May cause faster growth of existing prostate tumors

Pill
HOW OFTEN 2 to 4 times a day
DOSE 40 mg to 80 mg
WHERE Mouth

BENEFITS Steady levels mimic natural cycles of testosterone

PROBLEMS Liver breaks down most testosterone before it can work. Not commercially available in U.S.

RISKS May increase bad cholesterol and decrease good cholesterol levels. Risk of liver damage the shot I get out the weed whacker and the chain saw, and I just go crazy."

Gee. Even putting aside for a moment the much increased danger of prostate cancer, do we really want men to turn later life into a hormonal keg party? The thought could be mildly exasperating to women, who might be forgiven for greeting the news with the same feelings china shopkeepers have for bulls. But this is the point at which the discussion of testosterone veers into the metaphysical.

Outside the bedroom and the gym, just what does testosterone do for you? Studies in animals have repeatedly shown that testosterone and aggression go hand in hand. Castrate species after species, and you get a pussycat. Boost the testosterone with injections and the castrated animal acts more like a tiger. In one study of men, when the testosterone levels were suppressed (in this case by researchers using medications) libido and dominant behaviors dropped. But when a mere 20% of the testosterone was added back, libido and domination climbed to the levels where they had started. Which suggests that men do not need much of the stuff to go on doing whatever it is they have already learned to do.

Other studies have shown that men with naturally higher testosterone levels are more aggressive and take-charge than men with slightly lower levels. When two sports teams meet, both teams will show an increase in testosterone during the game. "In the face of competition, levels of testosterone will rise," says Alan Booth, a sociologist at Penn State University. "This prepares the competitor and may help increase the chances for a win. It could be that the rise in testosterone has physical benefits, such as visual acuity and increased strength. But only the winning team continues to show high testosterone after the game."

For this exercise, you don't even have to picture the Packers vs. the Vikings. The T boost also happens during nonphysical competitions, like chess games and trivia contests. Whatever the game, in evolutionary terms this makes sense. Among the primates from whom we are descended, the victorious male in any encounter may have needed to maintain high testosterone levels in the expectation that his position in the pecking order would be challenged by the next guy coming up.

But here it gets complicated. Does higher testosterone produce more aggressive behavior? Or does the more aggressive male—whose aggression was learned, say, at home or in school or in the neighborhood or on the team or in the culture at large—call for a release of testosterone from within himself for assistance? And if testosterone really does determine male behaviors like aggression, then what are we to make of the fact that although testosterone levels are pretty equal in prepubescent children, boys and girls already demonstrate different behaviors?

What we know for certain is this: aggressive behavior and testosterone appear in the same place. And aggressive behavior seems to require some testosterone in your system. But researchers have yet to show conclusively that adding a little more in males who already have a normal range of the stuff does much to make them more aggressive or confrontational. In one study, Dr. Christina Wang of UCLA found that men with low testosterone were actually more likely to be angry, irritable and aggressive than men who had normal to high-normal levels of testosterone. When their testosterone was increased during hormone-replacement therapy, their anger diminished and their sense of well-being increased. "Testosterone is probably a vastly overrated hormone," says Robert Sapolsky, a Stanford University biolo-

gist and author of *The Trouble with Testosterone*.

All the same, there are social implications connected to the one area in which we know for a fact that testosterone matters—sex drive. Married men tend to have lower testosterone. It's evolution's way of encouraging the wandering mate to stay home. (In newly divorced men, T levels rise again, as the men prepare to re-enter the competition for a mate.) If aging men start to routinely boost their testosterone levels, and their sexual appetite, to earlier levels, will they further upset the foundations of that ever endangered social arrangement called the family? "What happens when men have higher levels than normal?" asks James M. Dabbs, a psychology professor at Georgia State University. "They are just unmanageable."

Dabbs, the author of *Heroes, Rogues and Lovers*, a book about the importance of the male hormone, is another researcher who believes that T counts for a lot in any number of male moods and behaviors. "It contributes to a boldness and a sense of focus," he insists. It's possible for the scientific community to come to such disparate conclusions on the stuff, not just because the research is slim but because the complexities of human behavior are deep. If we're verging on a moment when testosterone will be treated as one more renewable resource, we may soon all get to focus more clearly on just what it does. But if men, in a culture where the meaning of manhood is up for grabs, look to testosterone for answers to the largest questions about themselves, they are likely to be disappointed. One thing we can be sure of is that the essence of manhood will always be something more complicated than any mere substance in the blood.

—Reported by Lisa McLaughlin and Alice Park/New York

the future of **drugs**

Recreational Pharmaceuticals

Finding new party drugs like K and ecstasy won't be easy

By JOHN CLOUD

IN THE PAST FEW MONTHS, IT'S BECOME nearly impossible to buy Ketaset in New York City's underground drug market. Made by Fort Dodge, an Iowa-based pharmaceutical firm, Ketaset is a brand of ketamine, a compound that blocks certain neuroreceptors, causing hallucinations in high doses and, in lower doses, a fuzzy dissociation—like the warmth of a couple of Jim Beams. Legally, it's used as an anesthetic. Illegally, one snorts ketamine because the fuzziness lasts half an hour and doesn't produce bourbon's four-Advil hangover.

Ketaset's scarcity dates back to August 1999, when the U.S. Drug Enforcement Administration, acting on preliminary evidence that ketamine may lead to dependence, subjected its legal purveyors to strict security rules. But K, as users call it, had already won so many devotees that traffickers were smuggling off-label brands from Mexico. Today Manhattan dealers sell a gram of K for $80, up 100% from 1998.

The recent history of K limns a well-established law of recreational drug use:

once users find a substance they like, they will snort or shoot or drop whatever version is available, whatever the cost. Which is why you must look to the market to understand the future of drugs used for anything other than doctor-approved healing. That market can be divided into three groups: the partyers, who just want to have fun (and who sometimes become addicts); the shrinks and shamans, who believe drugs can expand your consciousness; and the scientists, who suspect that illegal drugs—or their chemical cousins—may have marketable legal uses. These groups are distinct but tightly linked: scientific research leads to new drugs, which shamans discover and use in their quests, which often turn out to be as much fun as spiritual. The use of drugs in party settings eventually leads to government crackdowns.

But as a rule, the partyers don't pursue the new drugs; they tend to find a potion and stick with it, sometimes until it kills them. Today's popular party drugs are derived from ancient medicinal herbs: marijuana from hemp, cocaine from coca leaf, prescription painkillers from poppies. It's

the shamans who aggressively seek out new substances. Recent additions to the U.S. market include ayahuasco, a plant long used in religious ceremonies in Brazil for its mind-manipulating qualities, and *Salvia divinorum*, a soft-leaved plant native to Mexico that is chewed or smoked for hallucinogenic effects.

New compounds do occasionally come from underground drug labs or, like MDMA (ecstasy), are rediscovered after years of being ignored in scientific literature. In this world, no one is held in greater esteem than Alexander Shulgin.

Shulgin is a biochemist who once studied psychedelics for Dow Chemical. Now 75, Shulgin has synthesized hundreds of compounds in the smelly lab in the woods behind his California home. He and his wife Ann, a therapist, have published two books that are the bibles of underground drug research: *PIHKAL* (Phenethylamines I Have Known and Loved) and *TIHKAL* (Tryptamines I Have Known and Loved). Many of the drugs that have emerged from underground labs can be traced to well-thumbed copies of the Shulgins' books.

It was they who helped popularize MDMA—a signal event in the history of recreational drugs. Ecstasy is easily the biggest advance since LSD. It changed not only the party world but the shaman world, where it was used by psychologists who believed it had therapeutic value. Since MDMA was banned in 1986, scientists have looked for compounds that have the same effects without damaging neurotransmitters, as MDMA can. They haven't had much success.

So today's nonmedical drug research tends to focus on new uses for old substances. That effort is led by Richard Doblin, who runs the Multidisciplinary Association for Psychedelic Studies out of his Belmont, Mass., home. Founded the year MDMA was outlawed, the association uses its $530,000 yearly budget to assist scientists who, with government permission, study the risks and benefits of a wide variety of nonmedical uses for psychedelic drugs and marijuana. Such research is highly political, however, and it can take years for a research protocol to be approved.

The new drugs that appear on the market usually do so after underground chemists read scientific papers and decide to cook something up. Scientists studying how cocaine works in the brain, for example, have developed a version 100 times more powerful. The recipe is available in academic journals, waiting to be exploited.

But the chemicals needed to synthesize such drugs are tracked by authorities, a change from the Shulgins' day. And even if the ingredients were widely available, the scientific expertise is not. According to David Nichols, a student of Shulgin's who is now a professor of chemistry at Purdue, "The underground chemist is typically not going to discover a completely new psychoactive substance. The kinds of things that are easy to make, by and large, have been made."

Scouting a Dry Campus

Concerned about binge drinking at college, more parents and prospective students are checking out anti-alcohol policies.

BY DANIEL MCGINN

T HEY ARE STORIES that make every parent's heart ache. On Nov. 10, University of Michigan sophomore Byung Soo Kim celebrated his 21st birthday by trying to drink 21 shots of whisky. He downed 20, then passed out, turned blue and stopped breathing. As Kim lay dying in a Michigan hospital later that next night, seven college students hopped into a Jeep 500 miles away on the campus of Colgate University. Moments later, the driver, a Colgate student who authorities say was dangerously intoxicated, veered off the road and struck a tree, killing four of the passengers. And by the time Monday classes began, five proud families who'd sent their children away to school were busy planning their funerals.

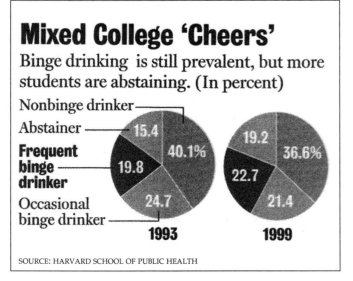

Mixed College 'Cheers'
Binge drinking is still prevalent, but more students are abstaining. (In percent)

Nonbinge drinker

Abstainer

Frequent binge drinker

Occasional binge drinker

1993: 15.4, 40.1%, 19.8, 24.7

1999: 19.2, 36.6%, 22.7, 21.4

SOURCE: HARVARD SCHOOL OF PUBLIC HEALTH

As tragedies like these fill the evening news, they're increasing the anxiety for parents of college-bound students. While this year's seniors winnow through applications, experts see families beginning to consider campus alcohol abuse as a factor in college selection. Surveys show that just under half of all college students drink excessively (defined as five drinks for males and four for females in a single sitting—a proportion that

hasn't budged despite a decade of work to reduce it. Even for families who trust their children to abstain, steering clear of campuses with rampant abuse can still be smart, since sober students can suffer from the assaults, sex crimes and poor academic environments that go with heavy drinking. Finding out just how much drinking goes on at different schools isn't easy, but a variety of organizations are trying to help. Says Bill Modzeleski of the U.S. Department of Education: "We're trying to get families to understand there are schools out there focusing on these issues, so they can factor that into their college selection."

That's a message Cat O'Shaughnessy already understands. As the relative of a recovering alcoholic, she was determined to find a college where she didn't have to drink to fit in. That resolve grew after visiting schools that seemed awash in liquor. "You'd walk down the dorm hallways on Saturday afternoon and people would still be puking," she says. O'Shaughnessy didn't consider schools where fraternities dominated social life. On campus tours she grilled students about the party scene. She liked what she found at George Washington University. "The urban environment in Washington, D.C., made her feel like the campus extended beyond tailgating and Friday-night parties," says Andrew Bryan, a college consultant who helped with her search. O'Shaughnessy, now a freshman, has sipped a few drinks, but she happily spends most weekend nights at dance clubs or watching DVDs.

Reliable school-by-school data on student drinking isn't readily available. The best-known ranking of "party schools," done by The Princeton Review, is based on student opinions, and its editor admits it's not scientific. Experts offer other rules of thumb. Schools with large fraternity systems traditionally harbor more excessive drinkers. Some studies also show heavier drinking at rural colleges, which have fewer off-campus entertainment options. Not surprisingly, Christian and women's colleges have less drinking. More definitive data are on the way. Last month Mothers Against Drunk Driving approved plans to begin ranking colleges based on how well they curb student drinking. Its list could be published as soon as next fall.

Until then, parents can do their own sleuthing. During campus tours, watch for posters touting cheap drinks at bars, or too many empty beer cans in dorms. Time visits to see how students behave when they're not studying. "Go on Thursday or Friday and stay over," says Dr. Henry Wechsler, a Harvard professor who studies student drinking. Stroll the campus near midnight and gauge the raucousness. Ask admissions officials about alcohol policies, such as whether they notify parents of students caught with alcohol. Schools that take alcohol abuse seriously are willing to talk about it, so be wary of vague or evasive answers.

Some schools have signed on to national programs to combat heavy drinking. Ten schools, including Lehigh and the University of Vermont, take part in a program called A Matter of Degree, which tries to change campus cultures to cut drinking. Some schools are studying whether they're scheduling too few classes on Fridays, which might spur Thursday-night partying. They're also restricting tailgating and stadium beer sales. The U.S. Department of Education has begun highlighting innovative antidrinking practices; high-school guidance offices now have a brochure listing model schools. Other colleges are trying a "social norms" approach, spreading the message to students that their peers drink less than they think, in an attempt to make heavy drinking less socially acceptable.

As families begin focusing on campus drinking, schools that crack down can win applicants. After years of rampant alcohol abuse at the University of Rhode Island, administrators went on the offensive, banning alcohol from campus parties and toughening penalties for students caught drinking. To really change campus culture, officials discourage heavy drinkers from applying. "I'm very direct," says president Robert Carothers. "I tell parents and kids that if they're looking for a place to abuse alcohol, don't come here—you won't be happy."

No matter which school a family chooses, there's no guarantee bad things won't happen to good kids. "Any individual on any particular night can make bad choices," says Wesley Perkins, a Hobart and William Smith Colleges sociologist. The best protection is to talk to kids about sensible drinking long before they depart for college. When it comes to alcohol, a concerned parent can be a better teacher than anyone with a Ph.D.

Convenience-Store High:
How Ordinary Cough Medicine Is Being Abused for its Mind-Altering Effects

By Lee Burcham

If you think your home is free of addictive drugs, you might want to think again. The potential for drug abuse could lie as near as the cough syrup or cough caplets in your family medicine cabinet. You may be surprised to find that these medicines contain a drug that can produce dissociation (a sense of disconnection from the body and surrounding environment), sensory enhancement, and hallucinatory effects when taken in sufficient quantity. Its name is Dextromethorphan, or DXM.

Familiar Sources

Dextromethorphan is a semisynthetic narcotic related to opium and found in many over-the-counter cough suppressants in the United States and most countries. DXM is contained in any drug whose name includes "DM" or "Tuss."

The drug comes in various forms. Most common are cough suppressants in caplet or liquid form, including Robitussin, Vicks Formula 44, Drixoral, Delsym, Pertussin, and several generic brands.

(A caution: Not all medicines under these brands contain the drug since most brands put out several formulations. Look on the label for "DM," "Tuss," or "Maximum Strength.")

This FDA approved and presumably safe substance is being scrutinized by parents, health care professionals, and community leaders in light of scientific studies of abuse in Houston and Minneapolis, St. Paul, as well as recent incidents involving abuse in Plano, TX, and the hospitalization of four teenagers in Newark, NJ, and an incident in Pennsylvania involving four teenage girls who entered the hospital with complaints of short breath and racing hearts after taking the drug.

Less publicized and more easily obtained than the more well-known drug ecstasy, DXM's legal status and familiarity may lure some kids into taking it, despite the dangers it poses of addiction, injury, and death. "It's not an ugly drug. It's much less intimidating than snorting a powder or injecting a strange substance," said William Bobo, M.D., a psychiatrist who, along with Shannon Miller, M.D., is conducting an exhaustive review of the scientific literature on DXM.

Anyone, including minors, can buy these medicines at a local convenience mart or drugstore. And since the Food and Drug Administration (FDA) approves DXM for sale in over-the-counter medicines, those seeking a high, and especially teens, may assume it's "safe." "It's a very familiar substance, in short," said Bobo, and thus "it is felt to be benign by abusers."

This underestimation of the drug's dangers and abuse potential is not limited to abusers, explained Miller. "Many clinicians simply aren't asking these questions—and certainly when they are faced with someone using it, they tend to minimize it."

A Risky High

DXM is related to opiates in its make-up, and it produces mind-altering highs. Those hoping to achieve a high often exceed the recommended safe dosage, a daunting prospect for anyone who's ever gagged on a mere two tablespoons of cough syrup. Misuse of the drug creates both depressant and mild hallucinogenic effects. It also acts as a dissociative anesthetic, similar to PCP and ketamine. Sought-after effects include:

- Hallucinations
- Dissociation
- Euphoria
- Mania-like symptoms such as thoughts racing

- Heightened perceptual awareness
- Lethargy
- Perceptual distortion

Depending on the dose, DXM's effects vary. Users report "a set of distinct dose-dependent 'plateaus' ranging from a mild stimulant effect with distorted visual perceptions at low doses… to a sense of complete dissociation from one's body," reports the *National Institute on Drug Abuse Research Report Series: Hallucinogens and Dissociative Drugs*. The high, however, presents distinct risks to health. Adverse effects are many:

- Confusion
- Impaired judgment and mental performance
- Blurred vision
- Slurred speech
- Loss of coordination
- Rigid motor tone and involuntary muscle movement
- Tremor
- Dizziness
- Nausea, abdominal pain, vomiting, vomiting of blood
- Dysphoria (sadness)
- Paranoia
- Headache
- Decreased ability to regulate body temperature
- Excessive sweating
- Reduced sweating and increased body temperatures, or hot flashes
- Irregular heartbeat
- High blood pressure
- Numbness of fingers or toes
- Redness of face
- Loss of consciousness
- Dry mouth and loss of body fluid, from the anti-cholinergic effect of the drug
- Dry itchy skin and occasional patches of flaky skin
- Death (rarely)

A phenomenon that is sometimes called "rave-related heat stroke" occurs when DXM is "taken in a dance-club setting, accompanied by vigorous physical activity (dancing, etc.) and poor air circulation," according to the Indiana Prevention Resource Center Factline on Non-Medical Use of Dextromethorphan.

Emergency rooms increasingly report DXM overdoses and DXM-related crises. In the rare cases where DXM overdose has resulted in death, the precise cause of death is unclear, but respiratory failure appears to be a good candidate in several instances. (Emergency procedures for overdose of DXM can be found on the Web site of former U.S. Surgeon General C. Everett Koop.

Associated Health Risks

Another major concern is the risk incurred when abusers get high and engage in activities requiring reasonable judgment and quick reactions, like driving or swimming. The effects induced by overdose of DXM can make these activities deadly. The story told by one teenager illustrates the profound disconnection with reality and inability to exercise caution caused by this drug. This teenage boy got high on DXM, spent most of the night being half-carried, half-dragged by friends through the woods, while drifting in and out of consciousness, and woke at home the next day to discover over 100 ant bites on his body. Apparently, he had fallen into an ant bed the previous night and not even noticed.

DXM is not the only danger in the over-the-counter cough preparations taken for the DXM in them. Abusers may experience toxic side effects due to other ingredients in these preparations. They may contain combinations of drugs, including acetaminophen (an analgesiac pain reliever used in the popular brands Tylenol and Panadol), guaifenesin (an expectorant), ephedrine (an appetite suppressant and stimulant) and/or pseudoephedrine (an antihistamine with stimulant-like properties), and chlor-pheniramine maleate (an antihistamine with anticholin-ergic (drying) and sedative side effects), reports the Indiana Prevention Resource Center Factline. Of particular concern is the ingredient acetaminophen, which can result in severe liver damage when taken in excessive quantities. The risk of these side effects escalates as users exceed the dosage recommendations on the medicine package.

In spite of these serious potential adverse effects of DXM, the dangerous behavior it induces, and the ingredients ingested along with DXM-containing cough medicines, abusers keep returning because of the drug's legal status and easy access. But the drug is not taken in a social vacuum. Abusers introduce other abusers to it, and they do so most often where teenagers gather, mingle, and take illicit drugs like ecstasy.

DXM and the Club Drug Culture

While DXM can be abused by anyone at any age or station in life, it is an emerging problem among school-aged youth and young adults in the United States. Its use is becoming more prevalent in dance clubs and at dance events called "raves," where it is sometimes used as an alternative for the more well-known drug ecstasy. Adolescent youth easily can obtain the drug because stores sell it over the counter, with no prescription required. Its street names include:

- DXM
- robo
- skittles
- Vitamin D
- dex
- tussin

Users are sometimes called "syrup heads." Swallowing large doses of cough syrup is known as "robodosing" or "robo-tripping." The staggering gait caused by the drug is known as the "robo-walk," and users speak of the groggy feeling it often induces as feeling "drippy."

A growing subculture has developed around the use and glorification of DXM, with several music groups such as Nightchild, Dr. Max, and Oedipus Complex producing music purportedly made under the drug's influence, and multiple Web sites devoted to perpetuating DXM use.

The imaginative scenarios and distortionary colors and graphics found on these sites often mimic the mental and sensory effects produced by DXM. Here, users and sellers can also obtain information about purchase, production, levels of dosage amounts and levels of dosage-dependent intoxication, or "plateaus." One such Web site features detailed descriptions of each "plateau"—how to attain it, its subjective characteristics, the activities compatible and incompatible with that level (such as socializing, dancing, and swimming), the adverse effects, and even the risks involved.

Many sites supply information about the ready availability of DXM in bulk powder form directly from manufacturers—since the drug is not regulated—and techniques for making it into tablets or caplets of various attractive shapes and colors, which are then handed out at raves and dance clubs. But the clandestine labs that produce these often have no quality control, making accurate dosing to unsuspecting patrons impossible.

Potential Addictive Properties

While scientific debate continues over the subject, the chemical and mental reactions caused by ingestion of DXM highlight its potential for addiction and abuse. They can be placed into three categories:

- Chemicals involved. Two main chemicals are involved: dextromethorphan (DXM), and dextrorphan. Only DXM is ingested into the body. Dextrorphan, by contrast, is a metabolite, or bodily derivative, that the body creates as it processes DXM.
- Interaction with bodily receptors. Chemically and structurally, DXM is related to the opiates, particularly codeine, and it is active at sigma-type opiate receptors in the body. However it is Dextrorphan, said Dr. Miller, that carries the real punch and that may cause addiction. "We have good, hard scientific studies showing that on the molecular level, on the receptor level, it does similar things that PCP does," he said, and it may also have "the specific chemical qualities that put it at higher risk of turning on the addiction neurobiology in the brain."
- Mental effects. Dextromethorphan (DXM) has sedative-like qualities, and Dextrorphan has hallucinogenic and dissociative qualities. These dissociative effects experienced by the mind—separate from how the drug interacts with the bodily receptors as discussed above—also illustrate the drug's similarity to addictive drugs such as PCP and ketamine.

The full potential for abuse and addiction is not yet known due to insufficient study of this relatively new drug. However, the properties discussed above strongly suggest the possibility of addictive qualities and warrant further research of DXM.

Challenged Prevention Efforts

Most States have few or no legal restrictions on DXM. The history of attempts to limit the availability of it illustrates the extreme difficulty of dealing with the abuse of a drug that is legal, and completely safe when taken in the recommended dosage.

The World Health Organization published a report in 1970 that concluded the drug needed no special monitoring and posed no concern for public health.

However, an outbreak of adolescent DXM abuse in Utah in the 1980's led that State to begin a policy of stocking medications containing DXM behind the counter so that pharmacists could exercise more discretion, especially in its sale to minors.

The Pennsylvania Drug Device and Cosmetic Board and the United States Food and Drug Administration's (USFDA) Drug Advisory Committee in 1990 made inquiries into Dextromethorphan's abuse potential. Although they expressed concern about press reports of DXM abuse and official reports from several States, they ultimately found lacking the data on the problem and retained the drug's status as an over-the-counter medicine.

Education the Main Tool

This difficulty in limiting the drug's availability, combined with the lack of data on abuse in the population, makes the standard prevention-based method of treatment much more difficult. What's more, although testing can detect the drug, the standard tests for illicit drugs administered by most corporations, institutions and drug treatment facilities don't target it. Bobo and Miller therefore suggest a two-pronged approach. First, traditional treatment programs can play a limited role, but they should observe several precautions:

- The addiction treatment professional should be fully educated about the drug's nature, mechanism, and history.
- The addiction treatment professional and facility should actively test for the drug since standard drug tests don't screen for it.
- The patient should make the selected sponsor aware that their problem is with DXM and that it is a rather unconventional drug of abuse.

However, because the abuser of DXM will so seldom appear in the traditional treatment environment, the second prong of the approach is the more important. Education about the problem is needed for all people involved, including:

- Abusers and potential abusers
- Physicians
- School personnel
- Parents
- The drug prevention and treatment community.

The American Medical Association (AMA) in 1997 took up the issue and resolved, according to Miller and Bobo, that the AMA should launch a physician education process to educate doctors, particularly pediatricians and primary care physicians, on the risks of DXM abuse by young people.

Information about DXM is gradually becoming more available, particularly on the Web sites of drug abuse prevention and health-related organizations. It is crucial that all those involved be aware of the drug and become as educated as possible on its dangers, potential for abuse, symptoms of intoxication, and surrounding drug culture.

The most important knowledge for everyone is simply to be aware that the problem exists. Parents should look for signs of abuse such as a child bringing home his or her own box, or an unexplained dwindling of the family's stock. Doctors can look for signs of abuse and send patients to

treatment providers. Treatment providers need to be aware of the special considerations outlined above. And abusers should know that the drug is dangerous and has addictive properties.

The legal status and easy availability of DXM challenge efforts to detect its misuse, let alone deal with it. As Bobo said, when most people think of cough syrup they probably think of "your mom spooning it into your mouth and taking care of you as a kid." We should not let that innocent image block our view of the reality of the drug's abuse.

Shannon Miller, M.D., is a staff psychiatrist at Andrews Air Force Base and currently chief of the Tri-Service Addiction Recovery Center. William Bobo, M.D., is currently completing his residency in psychiatry and works for the U.S. Navy. Dr. Bobo has made presentations of their review findings at the Substance Abuse and Mental Health Services Administration's (SAMHSA) National Clearinghouse for Alcohol and Drug Information (NCADI) center in Rockville, MD, and at the Walter Reed U.S. Army Medical Center.

From the *NCADI Reporter (National Clearinghouse for Alcohol and Drug Information)*, June 12, 2001.

Natural Hazards

*Tonic or toxic? Americans are gobbling up nature's remedies for
everything from obesity to depression*

BY AMANDA SPAKE

Sara Sullivan woke up one Sunday with a searing pain in her chest. When the paramedics arrived, they thought Sullivan was suffering a heart attack. Her heart was racing so fast that it couldn't pump enough blood and oxygen to her brain. In the ambulance, she felt herself passing out. "I thought about my five kids," the 34-year-old housewife recalls, "and then I said to myself, 'This is it. I'm going to die.'"

When Sullivan regained consciousness, emergency room physician Rebecca Bigoney walked into her room with a bottle of diet pills that Sullivan's husband had shown the doctor, a popular ephedra-based supplement. "You know this stuff can kill you?" Bigoney asked.

Labeling on the product warned her to "seek advice" from her doctor if she had "heart or thyroid disease," but her physician did not think the herbal remedy would harm her. Even though she'd had surgery five years earlier to fix a rapid and irregular heartbeat, Sullivan had been symptom free ever since.

That's no longer true. "It's not certain, but Sara's history suggests that the ephedra caused a recurrence," says Bigoney. Since her scare in 1999, she has been back to the emergency room six times because of chest pain,

a racing heart, loss of consciousness, or other cardiac symptoms. "Her heart," says her attorney, Mary Ann Barnes of Charlottesville, Va., "has never returned to normal."

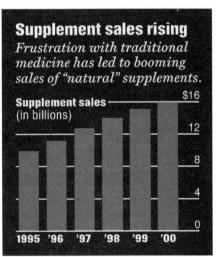

SOURCE: NUTRITION BUSINESS JOURNAL

Sullivan is one of an estimated 123.5 million Americans who try herbs, vitamins, minerals, enzymes, amino acids, and thousands of other "natural" potions and products to treat a variety of ills. Many, like Sullivan, are trying to lose weight, but supplements are also being marketed to prevent cancer, lift mood, build muscle, and improve sleep,

joints, memory, concentration, immune function, and sex.

Not since the early 1900s, when tonics and elixirs made from alcohol, opiates, cardiac depressants, and other toxic substances were sold as "natural" cures for ailments like meningitis, have so many bought so much with so little sound science behind it. The U.S. Food and Drug Administration has over 2,900 adverse-event reports about ephedra, ginkgo, St.-John's-wort, ginseng, and thousands of other supplements; these include 104 deaths. For every adverse event in its files, the FDA estimates 100 more go unreported.

Congress's General Accounting Office estimates that consumers spent about $31 billion in 1999 on dietary supplements and "functional foods," like AriZona Rx Memory Mind Elixir or Kava Kava Corn Chips. A recent survey shows that 63 percent of consumers took a vitamin, mineral, or herbal supplement in the past three months. Many take all of them at once. What's more, only about a third of patients tell their doctors they're taking supplements. Even if they do, laments Stephen Piscitelli, a drug researcher at the National Institutes of Health, "We don't know *anything* about these products in terms of their pharmacology."

SPORTS & SEX

Performance in a capsule

Matt Coda was a fanatic about his body. So his mother, a nurse in Pittsburgh, was mystified when the 26-year-old was rushed to the hospital in a coma in July 1999. Patricia Trovato-Ragano told the doctors her son had been taking only a body-building supplement.

Like many medical professionals, Trovato-Ragano was unfamiliar with the class of highly addictive solvents that are turned by the body into GHB, a central nervous system depressant that can cause coma and death. GHB precursors were key ingredients in many supplements—with names like Verve, Thunder, Invigorate, and Serenity—promoted to athletes to build mus-cle, improve mood and sleep, and even enhance sexual performance.

The Drug Enforcement Administration has logged 1,343 similar life-threatening incidents and 71 deaths, figures agency officials consider just the tip of the iceberg. After several ineffective FDA pleas to supplement makers to remove the products from shelves, Congress passed a law in April outlawing the use of GHB precursors in all products sold for human consumption.

New tactics. But the new legal restriction has simply inspired innovative marketing strategies. Writing recently in the *New England Journal of Medicine*, Deborah Zvosec and Stephen Smith of the Hennepin County Medical Center in Minneapolis report on eight patients who have suffered overdoses.

Some suppliers have set up mail-order operations in Canada. Other companies are now selling "all-natural cleaning products"—legally— with some of the same names as the former supplements.

The supplement of choice for athletes is creatine, a synthetic version of a substance made naturally by the body for intense bursts of energy. Science has, so far, failed to demonstrate that creatine supplements improve performance. But aggressive marketing—even in school athletic programs—increased creatine sales by 600 percent between 1995 and 1998. While some studies, particularly of weightlifters, show creatine increases fat-free body mass and muscle, others indicate it causes water retention and cramping during endurance sports. In a 52-person study of college athletes taking creatine, 31 percent had diarrhea and 25 percent, muscle cramps. Rats on creatine have also experienced kidney failure.

Creatine's popularity is due in part to its use by home-run king Mark McGwire, who at one time also swore by androstenedione, a "natural" alternative to anabolic steroids. A 1999 study of "andro" use by young men showed the supplement did *not* increase testosterone, as advertised, nor enhance strength. It lowered high-density lipoprotein, or HDL—the good cholesterol—and estrogen blood levels of *estrogen*—an unexpected finding. Among older men, it increased coronary risk without any benefit.

After Matt Coda's autopsy and funeral, his mother phoned the FDA, the DEA, and the Pennsylvania attorney general. "He OD'd on the damn supplement," she told officials. Several agents came to see the family. But in the end, she says, "They never followed up."

—*A.S.*

That's because, unlike with prescription drugs, the FDA requires no scientific studies on safety and effectiveness before dietary supplements are put on the market. Michael McGuffin, president of the American Herbal Products Association, argues that premarket testing is unnecessary. "These products are tested by years and years of use," he contends.

BROKENHEARTED. Sara Sullivan can no longer do housework or even attend her kids' school events without becoming exhausted. "I'm 34 years old, and I feel like I'm 80."

In some cases that may be true, but a growing number of doctors are concerned about consumers mixing and concentrating vitamins, herbs, and traditional remedies for daily use. Rossanne Philen of the Centers for Disease Control and Prevention cites the case of chaparral, a therapeutic tea used safely by American Indians. But when supplement makers put the plant's leaves in capsules as an antioxidant, chaparral can become a potent liver toxin. Equally problematic is what one scientist calls "a total lack of quality control" in the industry. Though some in the industry have adopted quality standards, remedies adulterated with unapproved drugs, pesticides, heavy metals, and carcinogens do end up on store shelves.

Short-handed. The FDA has a tough time getting even demonstrably harmful supplements off the market. The agency's dietary supplement effort, says the FDA's Joseph Levitt, "operates on a shoestring." Congress, which benefits mightily from the nutrition industry (box, "Lobbying for Nature"), has been stingy with funds, making meaningful oversight unmanageable.

Ephedra products have been among the most controversial—and lucrative—of all supplements. More than 1,200 complaints about the hundreds of ephedra products on the market fill FDA files, including reports of 70 deaths. Supplement trade groups counter that 2 billion to 3 billion doses of ephedra are taken yearly—evidence, they say, that the vast majority is being used safely.

Others aren't so sure. Michael Hoffstetter, a Virginia neurologist, says he has seen four patients in the past year who had catastrophic reactions to these diet supplements. Three patients suffered strokes; one, a 24-year-old woman, is still in rehab, and another in her 40s is seriously disabled; one died. The fourth, Veronica Golmon, was 17 years old when she began taking several ephedra products, recommended by three high school-age friends. She blacked out while driving and hit a utility pole, the result, says Hoffstetter, of cardiac irregularities. "I thought I was burning fat," Golmon says.

Most consumers are a lot like both Golmon and Sullivan. A survey by *Prevention* magazine shows that their major sources of information are—in this order—friends and family, magazines, product labels, and advertising. Doctors are low on the list. More than half of those surveyed are confident that labels are accurate.

More or less. It's a false confidence. The University of Arkansas College of Pharmacy studied the labeling of ephedra supplements and found that half the products varied by more than 20 percent from the amount of ephedrine alkaloids listed on the label. More disturbing, says Bill Gurley, associate professor of pharmacy, was their variability. "Some bottles were subpotent and others superpotent," he says. Gurley also found that three contained only ephedrine—impossible, he says, if the supplements really came from herbs. "If you're making a product from synthetic ephedrine, then you're making a drug."

That's exactly what the FDA believed Chemins Co. was making when it produced a weight-loss product called Formula One. The company and CEO James Cameron were fined $4.6 million, and Cameron is now serving a 21-month jail sentence for spiking supposedly "all natural" Formula One with synthetic ephedrine and caffeine, both drugs. At least nine deaths were linked to Formula One, which Chemins stopped producing in 1994, after a number of lawsuits against the product.

Lawsuits abound, in fact, when it comes to ephedra. Last week, a $4 million settlement was reached in a Texas case against Next Nutrition, brought on behalf of a young man who, after using what he said was "Ultimate Orange," suffered a stroke, had a portion of his brain removed, and remains permanently disabled. James Frantz, a California attorney, recently sued on behalf of 13 clients who suffered strokes, brain damage, seizures, and death, allegedly related to the popular ephedra supplement Metabolife 356.

ASLEEP AT THE WHEEL. Veronica Golmon used ephedra to diet. She blacked out while driving and crashed her car. "I thought I was burning fat."

"No merit." "There's no medical evidence that shows Metabolife is anything but safe and effective when used as directed," says Tony Knight, a spokesperson for the company, which had sales of $1 billion in 1999. "These claims are baseless and these lawsuits have no merit." The company cites a just completed study of 167 people done by Carol Boozer, director of energy metabolism at New York's Obesity Research Center and endocrinologist Patricia Daly of York, Pa. Over six months the subjects who took a generic ephedra/caffeine supplement lost twice as much weight as the group taking a placebo. Some supplement takers had small blood pressure increases and higher heart rates, but no arrhythmias, says Boozer.

The FDA recently asked five independent physicians to evaluate 140 of its adverse-event reports. These reports, submitted by consumers, have been criticized by the GAO and the supplement makers because data in them are incomplete. Among those 140 cases, Georgetown University's Raymond Woosley found 104 descriptions of strokes, heart attacks, seizures, hypertension, and more that were likely or probably related to ephedra. There were 10 reports of cardiac arrest and sudden death. Woosley concluded that, given these side effects, ephedra supplements shouldn't be used without medical supervision.

Medical supervision means, among other things, availability by prescription only—a suggestion that turns ephedra executives apoplectic. "People are allergic to peanut butter, too, but should peanut butter be sold with a prescription?" asks Metabolife's Mike Rothmiller. "People can make informed decisions."

But some of FDA's experts wonder if that's true. In a recent article in the *New England Journal of Medicine*, Neal Benowitz of San Francisco General

Hospital and an FDA reviewer noted that nearly half of the FDA's serious cases were cardiovascular events; 26 percent of all the cases led to permanent disability or death. "These findings indicate the need for a better understanding of individual susceptibility to the adverse effects of such dietary supplements," Benowitz concludes.

Benowitz's article has been attacked by the industry. "The only cases I know where people [who took ephedra] died, they had severe coronary artery disease or they took overdoses," says San Francisco pathologist Steven Karch, who has been a consultant to the Ephedra Education Council. What concerns the FDA reviewers, however, is the unknown number of people with underlying or undiagnosed medical conditions who take ephedra and suffer catastrophic health events as a result.

Ephedra supplements are raising the greatest worry in the medical community right now, but other natural remedies also concern scientists. Among them:

St.-John's-wort. Andrea started taking this herbal antidepressant after a friend sent her a magazine article about its benefits. And she did

Food for thought

The herbal ingredients in these "functional foods" may be too minimal to have any effect.
Their safety as food additives, however, has not been proved.

Ginkgo Biloba Rings: A Memory Snack
CLAIM: Ginkgo biloba has been shown to increase blood flow to the brain.
BUT: Ginkgo acts as a blood thinner; if taken with certain drugs, it may cause bleeding or stroke.

Mango Passion Crisp
CLAIM: Herbal de-stress cereal… to support emotional and mental balance
BUT: Contains St.-John's-wort, which can interfere with prescription drugs, and kava kava, a sedative.

Fire
CLAIM: Provides the body with a natural energy boost
BUT: It's mostly caffeine plus herbs that thin the blood.

AriZona Rx Memory Mind Elixir
CLAIM: Mind enhancing; a safe and certain tonic
BUT: Contains ginkgo biloba and panax ginseng; in diabetics, these herbs may affect insulin secretion and lower blood sugar.

Oh, Happy Day
CLAIM: Fruit juice that will "lift the spirits"
BUT: St.-John's-wort, added as an antidepressant, may interfere with drug metabolism and cause nerve damage in sun worshipers.

JEFFREY MACMILLAN FOR *USN&WR*

Herbs, dollars, and lawmakers

Despite their image as a cottage industry serving a handful of health nuts, nutritional product companies have become significant players in campaign finance ever since the passage of the Dietary Supplement Health and Education Act in 1994.

A survey based on Federal Election Commission records, compiled for *U.S. News & World Report* by the nonpartisan FECInfo, shows that nutritional companies and their executives have donated more than $10.9 million to candidates, parties, and political action committees over the past five years.

Contributions more than doubled, from $2.42 million in the 1995–96 elections to $5.61 in the 1999–2000 cycle. Several of President George W. Bush's "Pioneers," who raised $100,000 or more for his campaign, own supplement companies or lobby for them.

Top contributors, 1995–2000:
- Bristol-Myers Squibb Co.: $3.61 million
- Florida Crystals, and Flo-Sun Inc.: $2.07 million
- American Home Products Corp.: $1.25 million
- Metabolife Int'l. Inc.: $793,400

Top recipients, 1995–2000:
- Sen. Orrin Hatch (R-Utah) $107,100
- Rep. Robert Wexler (D-Fla.) $81,512
- Rep. Dan Burton (R-Ind.) $79,249
- Sen. Tom Harkin (D-Iowa) $58,250
- Texas Gov. George W. Bush $52,750 —A.S.

indeed feel less depressed while taking the herb. But one sunny day she went for a bike ride and the skin on her legs began to hurt. "It was almost like needles in them," she recalls. As the days got warmer, her pain worsened.

Geoffrey M. Bove, a pain expert at Beth Israel Deaconess Medical Center in Boston, suspected her symptoms might be the result of nerve damage. He knew St.-John's-wort could interact with sunlight, producing oxygen molecules that damage the myelin wrapped around nerves. If myelin is damaged, nerves can produce electrical activity, which feels like tingling, needles, or pain. Bove suggested she stop taking the herb. Within three months, Andrea's pain was gone, "consistent with how long it takes myelin to regenerate," Bove says.

Scientists are only beginning to understand how this popular mood-elevator works in the body. Preliminary evidence suggests that the herb may interact with other drugs, rendering them ineffective. Researchers at GlaxoSmithKline reported in June that St.-John's-wort appears to affect a particular enzyme used by the body to process drugs. The enzyme, which is turned on like a faucet by St.-John's-wort, flows into the liver, eliminating many prescription drugs twice as fast as normal—and greatly reducing their curative effects.

These interactions can be life threatening under certain circumstances. Organ transplants, for example, have been rejected because of low levels of cyclosporin, an immunosuppressor, which St.-John's-wort apparently eliminates too rapidly from the body. And a recent study indicates that St.-John's-wort interferes with Indinavir, a drug critical to many HIV patients' health. Scientists suspect that the drugs affected by St.-John's-wort may include everything from oral contraceptives and analgesics to cancer drugs and antibiotics. The American Herbal Products Association is recommending that St.-John's-wort carry a warning to avoid sunlight and to consult a physician before mixing with prescription drugs.

Ginkgo and ginseng. Other herbal supplements also appear to interfere with the management and treatment of disease. In fact, studies show that 15 to 20 million Americans each year may be risking drug-supplement interactions that could harm their health. University of Maryland professor of pharmacology Magaly Rodriguez de Bittner, who runs a diabetes clinic, says that ginkgo—a popular memory enhancer—can affect insulin secretion and ginseng can reduce blood sugar among diabetics. There is some evidence that a ginkgo-ginseng combination may lead to modest memory and cognitive improvement, but de Bittner is worried about the packaging and marketing of the herbs. Some are now packaged as orange-flavored treats and have moved from the vitamin shelves to the high-profile candy displays at supermarket checkout stands. But these products cannot be used like mints or chewing gum, says de Bittner. Diabetics on prescription medication may take the herbs for memory and not know their blood sugar is plummeting. "They can go into a coma, not be found, and die," says de Bittner, who is very concerned about elderly diabetics using these popular herbs.

Indeed, older consumers may be experiencing a disproportionate share of the drug interaction risks, in part because they take many prescription medications. Patients have suffered cerebral hemorrhages and other bleeding that their doctors attributed to using ginkgo with aspirin, warfarin, or Coumadin—drugs often prescribed to prevent blood clots after surgery or for heart ailments. In one recent Oregon case, a man who was taking Coumadin began using ginkgo for his memory, according to his family, and died of a cerebral hemorrhage.

As serious as drug-supplement interactions may be, the real threat is lack of quality assurance, says Purdue University's Varro Tyler, a leading expert on herbs. "There's so much junk out there." Among 21 ginseng products tested by ConsumerLab.com, for example, nearly half contained high levels of toxic pesticides or lead, and seven provided less than the listed amount of ginseng. Some scientists estimate as many as 25 percent of supplements aimed at "men's health," particularly some of the "herbal Viagra" products, contain bovine or other animal organs, tissues, and extracts, which are not covered under regulations that protect U.S. consumers from animal products that harbor "mad cow" disease.

Phytoestrogens. Even if products are pure, herbal experts are troubled by the use of "natural" remedies in "unnatural" ways. "Take soybeans," says Adriane Fugh-Berman, a clinical professor at George Washington School of Medicine. Soy in its natural state may protect against cancer and heart disease, she says. "But what happens when you take genistein, the largest group of phytoestrogens in soybeans, concentrate it into 100-milligram tablets, and sell it as a 'natural' alternative to hormone replacement? We have no idea whether these pills cause uterine growth, breast growth, or tumors."

In fact, new research on concentrated genistein shows the compound increases both the size and number of malignant tumors in mice. University of Missouri nutritional scientist Ruth MacDonald, who conducted some of the genistein studies, says, "Lifelong consumption of soy foods may decrease breast cancer risk," as it appears to do among Asian women. But the phytoestrogen supplements "are not really 'natural.' You are taking far in excess of what you get if you were eating soy—it could be 1,000- or even 10,000-fold." At that dose, she believes, cancer risk may increase.

Functional foods. The CDC's Philen agrees with MacDonald. "We're taking these products out of their original context. Another good example is putting dietary supplements in things like snack chips." Last July, the watchdog group Center for Science in the Public Interest urged the FDA to halt the sale of more than 75 "functional foods" produced by Snapple, Procter & Gamble, R. W. Knudsen Family, and other food giants. Last week the FDA wrote to functional food manufacturers stressing that some herbal ingredients being added to foods have not been approved as additives and are not "generally recognized as safe." The products, some labeled as "supplements," contain St.-John's-wort, ginkgo biloba, ginseng, kava kava, echinacea, dong quai, and others. "They shouldn't be added to foods any more than Viagra or Prozac," says CSPI's Bruce Silverglade.

Many scientists are open to the idea of functional foods—when their claims can be validated. Calcium-fortified orange juice, cereals with folic acid to prevent birth defects, oat bran and psyllium approved to reduce cholesterol—these, says Silverglade, are truly functional foods. "But these other products are really modern-day snake oil."

So what's to be done? Certainly, there is a need for a better understanding of the pharmacology of the supplements in widespread use. NIH's National Center for Complementary and Alternative Medicine is performing clinical trials of St.-John's-wort for depression, ginkgo for memory loss, saw palmetto for the treatment of benign prostate problems, and glucosamine sulfate and chondroitin for osteoarthritis. A study on glucosamine released last week in the *Lancet* showed that among a small group of patients with osteoarthritis, the supplement reduced some pain and slowed joint degeneration. Next year, NIH will begin trials of ephedra.

But studies will not help Sara Sullivan. She and her husband of 17 years recently bought their first home. Suddenly, they find themselves buried under a mountain of medical bills, and Sullivan is afraid to look to the future. "It's a funny feeling to wake up and think, 'Is this the day I'm going to die?'"

Recognizing the Dangers of GHB

By Trinka Porrata, Pasadena, California

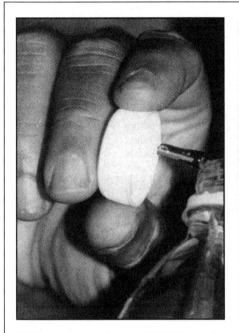 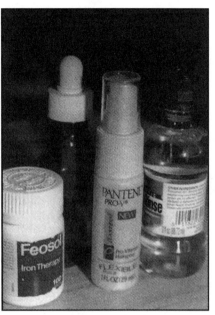

GHB is most commonly seen in liquid form and may be encountered in any container that will hold a liquid —water bottles, sports drink bottles, purse-size hair spray containers, mouthwash bottles, vitamin or other pill containers, eyedroppers, children's bubble solution containers, liquid candy containers, vanilla or food coloring bottles, etc. Smaller containers, such as breath mint or eye drop containers may also contain GHB.

GHB is typically dispensed and sold by the capful or by the sip, at from $5 to $20 per dose. It is colorless, unless colored to match the container's actual product, and essentially odorless (with a mild chemical smell if good quality or a strong smell if poor quality). It has a salty taste, but can be hidden in fruity drinks or strong alcoholic beverages. Sometimes the bad taste is explained as a sports supplement tonic, which commonly has an odd taste.

Gamma-hydroxybutyrate—GHB. Many police officers still have never heard of it. With resources already strained handling other drug-related problems—methamphetamine abuse, the upsurge in black tar heroin, ongoing problems with cocaine, marijuana and other drugs of abuse—law enforcement has not focused on the abuse of certain trendy drugs. Groups that use trendy drugs generally do not come to law enforcement's attention and take drugs most officers have never been trained to recognize.

Recognizing and responding to the growing problem of designer and club drugs is a slow process, given the need to focus on street level drug dealing and related crime. Teenagers often use drugs for the first time at rave parties. When law enforcement is called to these parties, it is generally for traffic and crowd control instead of to address the possibility of the parties being a drug smorgasbord. GHB has become particularly common at rave parties. It is also found in strip clubs and exotic dancing clubs because many dancers feel that low doses enable them to perform more sensually. It is increasingly common in the "high-end" club scene more affluent people frequent, and it is used in drug-facilitated rapes. It remains most common among bodybuilders, who may become addicted because of their regimented daily use of the drug. Withdrawal from GHB addiction is now recognized to be life endangering.

Although this article focuses on GHB, other drugs such as flunitrazepam (known as "roofies" or by the trade name Rohypnol), ketamine (Special K), MDMA (Ecstacy or the "hug drug") and other drugs produced outside of the United States are descending on this country. These drugs bring with them personal abuse tragedies, drug-induced rapes, black-out crimes, assaults and batteries, illicit drug laboratory dangers, drug overdoses and deaths. Without knowledge of these drugs, where they come from, how they are made and imported, how they are packaged and distributed, who uses them and why, symptoms of their use and testing issues, law enforcement is in a difficult position when faced with a drug-affected person since many do not show the traditional signs of drug use.

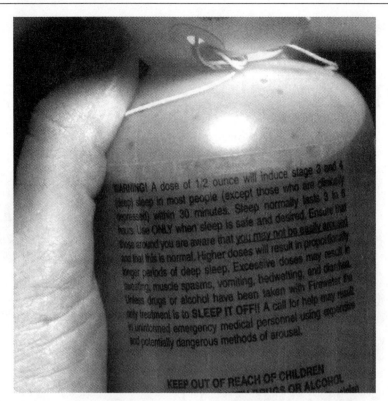

WARNING! A dose of 1/2 ounce will induce stage 3 and 4 (deep) sleep in most people. (except those who are clinically depressed) within 30 minutes. Sleep normally lasts 3 to 6 hours. Use ONLY when sleep is safe and desired. Ensure that those around you are aware that you may not be easily aroused and that this is normal. Higher doses will result in proportionally longer periods of deep sleep. Excessive doses may result in sweating, muscle spasms, vomiting, bedwetting, and diarrhea. Unless drugs or alcohol have been taken with Firewater the only treatment is to SLEEP IT OFF!! A call for help may result in uninformed emergency medical personnel using expensive and potentially dangerous methods of arousal.

KEEP OUT OF REACH OF CHILDREN

Analogs of GHB (chemical cousins with the same effects as GHB) are marketed over the Internet despite warnings from the Food and Drug Administration. Many of the deaths documented by the DEA are from these products which the body converts into GHB.

What is GHB?

GHB is also known as Easy Lay, G, Liquid Ecstasy, Liquid X, Scoop, Grievous Bodily Harm, Georgia Home Boy, Water, Salty Water, Everclear and Jib. It is of particular concern because it is an easy drug to make and obtain and hard for law enforcement to recognize.

GHB can be made by combining floor stripper or degreasing solvent with sodium hydroxide (drain cleaner, lye or baking soda) and shaking. Heating is optional.

It is a clear liquid, slightly thicker than water, but it may be diluted and colored. The odor may be rank, but most commonly is very mild and nondistinct. It may also be seen in powder for or in capsules. Because it is hydroscopic (absorbs moisture from the air), the powder may have a moist appearance or be in chunks or paste.

GHB has been found in vanilla and food-coloring bottles, purse-size hair spray containers, kids' bubble solution containers, shampoo bottles and cleaning solvent bottles. In some areas of the country it is commonly mixed with beer. As a sexual assault facilitator, it is slipped into fruity or strong mixed drinks such as margaritas and Long Island iced teas. Or it may be passed off as a sports tonic to get the victim past the salty, somewhat unpleasant taste.

GHB leaves the blood and its effects usually dissipate in approximately four hours. Its effects may resolve instantly at the four-hour mark if no other drugs or alcohol are present. This lack of hangover is part of the enticement of GHB. It also leaves no trace in urine after approximately 12 hours.

GHB generally is considered a behavioral depressant, but some researchers consider it a central nervous system excitant. In low doses it stimulates sexual conduct and aggression. Male GHB users in clubs may become aggressive, grab women's breasts, and attack security officers who intervene. Extreme GHB reactions may mimic the aggression and bizarre conduct of PCP reactions. Average party-scene users and rape victims are likely to experience rapid, giddy intoxication. This may be followed by vomiting, seizures and unconsciousness—even an unarousable, near-death coma.

GHB overdose victims should be kept on their side, not lying on their backs or face down. They can drown in their own vomit or choke because of GHB overdose can suppress the gag reflex. Presently, there is no antidote for this drug. In the hospital, overdose victims are simply put on life support until the episode passes in approximately four hours.

As of March 1, 2000, at least 66 people had died after using GHB, and approximately 40 more deaths are being reviewed for possible inclusion in the tally. More than 15 of these deaths occurred in 1999 and nearly all of the 40 under investigating occurred in 1999. That is likely just the tip of the iceberg, as most coroners are still unaware of it or may not know when to test for it. Three overdose victims were only 15 years old.

Analogs of GHB

Gamma butyrolactone (GBL) is an analog—a chemical cousin with the same, similar or stronger effects—of GBH, GBL, or 2 (3H) furanone dihydroxy, has been sold over the counter and through the Internet under many names. Another active analog, 1,4 Butanediol (also known as tetramethylene glycol), has also surfaced. Other analogs may surface soon.

Chemists may disagree about whether GBL is a chemical cousin of GHB, because one is a closed ring and one is an open ring. But GHB and GBL exist in equilibrium and GHB molecules swing from open to closed on their own. As one expert put it, a shoelace is a shoelace, tied or untied. In fact, the body converts any of the several known GHB analogs into GHB.

A series of products equally as dangerous as GBL are sold through the Internet and over the counter as sports or nutritional supplements, sleep aids, weight-loss aids or sexual stimulants. Names include Blue Nitro, Renewtrient, Revivarant, Remforce, Firewater, Enliven, Serenity, Rivitalize Plus, Thunder Nectar, Weight Belt Cleaner, SomatoPro, NGR3, GHRE, Invigorate and Serenity. These products may also be labeled as degreasing or cleaning products but in reality are intended for human consumption. The names keep changing, but the dangers are the same.

These and similar products also appear in powder and capsule form. Some of the Internet sites promoting these products admit that there is no scientific evidence to back up the safety and beneficial effects they claimed. Some note that their product is manufactured in an FDA-approved lab, but then admit that this does not mean the FDA has approved the product itself. Many list their main ingredient as 2 (3H) furanone dihydroxy, 1,4 butanediol or tetramethylene glycol and claim that they do not contain GHB or any other illegal substance.

In fact, possession of 1,4 butanediol is not illegal. Depending on the state, however, any action rendering GBL for human consumption (such as sticking a straw in the bottle or pouring the liquid into a water, vitamin or mouthwash bottle) may be illegal.

Some state laws define an analog as "a substance that has, is represented to have or is intended to have effects on the central nervous system that are substantially similar to or greater than the controlled substance itself." Some also stipulate that the analog must have a substantially similar chemical structure. Some states require that one of those conditions be met, but others require both conditions be met for a chemical to be considered an analog. Federally, and in most states with analog laws, analog statutes apply only to Schedule I and II drugs.

The analog status of 1,4 butanediol needs to be clarified in every state, and ad-

Editors Note

Since this article was written, GHB has been placed on the federal Schedule 1 of controlled substances. Following is a summary of the rule from the Federal Register, Vol. 65, No. 49, Monday, March 13, 2000.

Department of Justice Drug Enforcement Administration
21 CFR Parts 1301 and 1308
[DEA-200F]

Schedules of Controlled Substances: Addition of Gamma-Hydroxybutyric Acid to Schedule 1
   Agency: Drug Enforcement Administration, Department of Justice.
   Action: Final rule.
   Summary: This is a final rule issued by the Deputy Administrator of the Drug Enforcement Administration (DEA) placing gamma-hydroxybutyric acid (GHB) and its salts, isomers and salts of isomers into Schedule 1 of the Controlled Substances Act (CSA) pursuant to Public Law 106-172. Public Law 106-172 also imposes Schedule III physical security requirements for storage on registered manufacturers and distributors of GHB when it is manufactured, distributed or possessed in accordance with Food and Drug Administration (FDA)-authorized Investigational New Drug (IND) exemptions under the Federal Food, Drug and Cosmetic Act (FFDCA). In addition, this final rule places FDA-approved products containing GHB into Schedule III, if or when they are approved.
   Effective Date: March 31, 2000.

For further information, contact Frank Sapienza, Chief, Drug and Chemical Evaluation Section, Office of Diversion Control, Drug Enforcement Administration, Washington, DC 20537, 202-307-7183.

equate training given to law enforcement and prosecutorial agencies. Agencies should study their state laws to determine whether or not GHB has been controlled, whether an analog law exists, and what products any such law covers.

For states that have not controlled GHB, analog issues can be attacked using

state food, drug and cosmetics laws, which are usually misdemeanors. The products have to be treated as misbranded or mislabeled drugs. Demonstrating that they are drugs is easily done, and then the products cannot be labeled legally unless the FDA approves the label wording. There is no approved drug-label wording for 1,4 butanediol or gamma butyl lactone.

When the Internet is the source of the product and when the location of the source can be determined, prosecution may be possible either under that state's laws or under the provisions of the Department of Justice, Office of Consumer Litigation.

Investigating Suspected GHB Abuse

GHB is changing sexual-assault investigations. Law enforcement agencies that take only blood samples from rape victims need to begin collecting urine samples as well. Because GHB remains in the urine only 2 to 15 hours, protocols need to be established to ensure that urine samples are taken as quickly as possible. When GHB or an analog is suspected in sexual assault and DUI cases, officers must specifically request that tests be performed on blood and urine samples for GHB and other drugs not included in standard toxicology screening. Recovered samples of GHB analogs may not test positive for GHB, but blood or urine may test positive because the body converts analogs into GHB. Labs must be capable of identifying the analogs in recovered samples.

Witnesses' statements about victims' and suspects' behaviors are more important than ever. Expert witnesses are often necessary for prosecution and will need as many details as possible regarding symptoms and a time line. Search warrants take on a new significance in cases of drug-facilitated rapes. Officers making initial investigations and executing search warrants need training on these drugs and who uses them.

Partygoers call it "carpeting out" when someone on GHB is dancing happily into the night, only to collapse and "hit the carpet" heading for a fit of vomiting, twitching or a coma. That may not sound like an exciting way to spend an evening, but the dissociative effect of GHB "protects" users from remembering some of the effects they have undergone. GHB abuse continues to grow at a staggering rate.

Heroin trade helped fuel bin Laden's rise

Sales have supported the Taliban and money from Western users has funded the Islamic jihad.

By James Rosen
BEE WASHINGTON BUREAU

WASHINGTON—Long before he became Public Enemy No. 1, Osama bin Laden was waging a different kind of war on Americans and their Western allies.

Since the mid-1990s, while the spotlight shone on cocaine cartels in Latin America, bin Laden fortified a drug-trafficking network that provided major revenues for Afghanistan's Taliban regime—and financed his al Qaeda network of terrorism.

The renegade Saudi's commerce in narcotics helped make Afghanistan the world's leading exporter of heroin, some 2,200 pounds of which reached the United States last year, according to the U.S. State Department.

Worth at least $260 million in street value, some of the proceeds from the American heroin sales found their way back to bin Laden, who stands accused by President Bush of orchestrating the Sept. 11 suicide hijack attacks on the World Trade Center and the Pentagon.

"What better way to poison the Western world than through drugs?" said Donnie Marshall, who headed the U.S. Drug Enforcement Administration from July 1999 through June of this year. "It's another weapon in their arsenal."

Yoseff Bodansky, author of a 1999 biography of bin Laden and director of the congressional Task Force on Terrorism and Unconventional Warfare, said the terrorist kingpin takes a 15 percent cut of the drug trade money in exchange for protecting smugglers and laundering their profits.

"The Afghans are selling $7 (billion) to $8 billion dollars (worth) of drugs in the West a year," Bodansky said. "Bin Laden oversees the export of drugs from Afghanistan. His people are involved in growing the crops, processing and shipping. When Americans buy drugs, they fund the jihad (holy war)."

Bin Laden is the son of a Saudi construction magnate, and estimates of his wealth vary widely. Some intelligence experts say his family cut him off after the Saudi government expelled him in 1992 for organizing violent protests against its alliance with the United States in the Gulf War. Many experts believe that bin Laden needs few personal assets because he oversees a large stream of income from a web of legitimate businesses, donations from wealthy Muslims throughout the Middle East, drug trafficking and ties to other organized crime.

Rachel Ehrenfeld, who tracks international money laundering and drug trafficking as director of the Center for the Study of Corruption in New York, said bid Laden recycles the drug proceeds through businesses, in Europe and the Far East.

"The drug trade is a triple-pronged weapon for bid Laden and the Taliban," she said. "It finances their activities. It undermines the enemy. And it proves that the enemy is corrupt, which they then use in their own recruiting propaganda."

Heroin is produced in labs through a chemical process from opium gum, a thick sap scraped from the scored flower bulbs of poppy plants.

Ten pounds of opium produces 1 pound of pure heroin, which is dried, pulverized into white powder, cut with cornstarch and other substances, then sold on the street in varying degrees of purity.

Afghanistan's Taliban rulers announced a ban on poppy plant cultivation 14 months ago. Before the Sept. 11 attacks, they complained that the ban had not succeeded in easing economic sanctions the United Nations imposed on Afghanistan in 1998 for harboring terrorists and drug traffickers.

"We have done what needed to be done, putting our people and our farmers through immense difficulties," Abdol Hamid Akhondzadeh, director of the Taliban's High Commission on Drug Control, said in May. "We expected to be rewarded for our actions, but instead were punished with additional sanctions."

But a five-person panel of United Nations experts concluded that 10 months after the ban, stored opium was being sold to buy arms, "finance the training of terrorists and support the operation of terrorists in neighboring countries and beyond."

The U.N. panel also noted that Afghanistan was still importing large quantities of acetic anhydride, the main chemical used in heroin production.

Many Western experts suspect the Taliban of stockpiling opium gum and heroin, which unlike cocaine have long shelf lives and can be stored for years if securely packaged.

"They have reduced poppy cultivation over the last year or two, but I think that was largely a sham," said Marshall, the former DEA chief. "There is a lot of evidence that they have stockpiled opium gum and that limiting cultivation is not going to have any impact because they have been preparing for several years to do that."

Indeed, wholesale opium prices have plummeted in recent days, signaling to Marshall and other experts that the Taliban has started to dump its stockpiles before the possible outbreak of war in Afghanistan.

Robert Brown, deputy director of supply reduction in the White House Office of National Drug Control Policy, said the Taliban raises revenue by taxing opium cultivation and heroin production.

"A substantial percentage of the Taliban's government proceeds comes from the opium trade," Brown said. "There has been really no significant reduction in the outflow of drugs from Afghanistan despite the cultivation ban."

Afghanistan and Burma were the only two countries the United States failed to certify in March in its annual assessment of foreign nations' cooperation in fighting illegal drugs. Congress passed a law in 1986 requiring two dozen countries to get annual anti-trafficking certification as a condition for getting U.S. aid.

"Traffickers of Afghan heroin continued to route most of their production to Europe, but also targeted the United States," the State Department says in its report. "Those in positions of authority have made proclamations against poppy cultivation, but they have had little or no effect on the drug trade, which continues to expand."

The Bee's James Rosen can be reached at (202) 383–0014 or jrosen@ mcclatchydc .com.

From *The Sacramento Bee,* September 30, 2001, p. A19. © 2001 by The Sacramento Bee. Reprinted by permission.

UNIT 5
Drugs and Crime

Unit Selections

Key Points to Consider

- What role do the media play in influencing drug-related crime?

- Explain why you believe drug-related crime is either overrepresented or underrepresented.

- Survey your class to determine what percentage have been victims of crime. Determine what percentage of those were victims of drug-related crime.

- Consider the costs of drug-related crime on the criminal justice, health care, and educational systems in your community.

- How is the fear of crime continuing to change the way we live?

 **Links: www.dushkin.com/online/**
These sites are annotated in the World Wide Web pages.

Drug Enforcement Administration
http://www.usdoj.gov/dea/
The November Coalition
http://www.november.org
TRAC DEA Site
http://trac.syr.edu/tracdea/index.html

Crime is intrinsic to the world of illegal drugs. The relationship is strong and enduring. The type of crime associated with this world varies according to the type of drugs involved and certain environmental factors associated with them. For example, patterns of violent crime consistently accompany the trafficking of both cocaine and methamphetamine. The lucrative nature of the market, the fierce competition it generates, and the tendency for street dealers to be users of the product all serve to perpetuate violence. The repeated use of cocaine and methamphetamine produces a loss of judgment, paranoia, and psychosis in the user, promoting aggressive and irrational behavior. This behavior is associated with an increased risk of becoming a victim or perpetrator of crime and being present at a place where crime is occurring. Many illicit drugs fall into similar categories due to their associated black market economy or their pharmacology.

The use and abuse of legal drugs, although not as publicly sensational, also produce a significant relationship with crime. The most notable one is alcohol, which studies repeatedly connect to crimes ranging in severity from shoplifting to rape, homicide, and child abuse. The high percentage of perpetrators as well as victims using alcohol before and during the offense is a long-established criminological phenomenon. One study reported that violence was ten times more likely to occur during the commission of a crime if the offender had been drinking. Another recent study suggested that alcohol-related deaths of young people occur at rates 6.5 times higher than those caused by all illegal drugs combined. The best evidence suggests that the relationship between drugs and crime is developmental rather than causal and varies by the nature and intensity of drug use.

Ample evidence exists supporting the strong relationship between drug use, criminal activity, and being arrested. Over half of the crime in this country is committed by persons under the influence of drugs. Research suggests that 80 percent of men and women behind bars in the United States are seriously involved with alcohol and other drugs. Crime increases as drug use increases. Criminal activity is reported to be two to three times higher among frequent users of heroin and cocaine as compared to the criminal activity of irregular users. In most cities surveyed, over 68 percent of arrestees reported recently using drugs. Three out of four arrestees reported drug use in their lifetime. Two out of three state prison inmates reported using drugs once a week or more before their arrest and incarceration.

Juvenile crime related to drugs continues to be a major concern for students, parents, school districts, and the nation. In the aftermath of the tragic 1999 Columbine High School shootings, new controversies arose from the concerns of many mental health professionals about the tremendous numbers of school-age youth (approximately 6 million) taking prescribed psychotropic medication for mental disorders. Some are questioning the possible connection between these drugs and violence. In the Columbine shootings as well as in several that followed, some or all of the suspects were being treated for psychological disorders with drugs such as Luvox, Ritalin, and Prozac. The DEA reports that the United States buys and uses 90 percent of the world's Ritalin. The International Control Board, an agency of the United Nations, reported in 1995 that "10 to 12 percent of American boys between the ages of 6 and 14 had been treated with Ritalin."

Another different but remarkable dimension of the drugs/crime relationship concerns the expanding relationship between drug use and sexual assault. More than 430,000 sexual assaults occur annually in the United States and many of these involve drug and alcohol use on the part of the victim as well as the offender. In the mid- and late '90s, however, an alarming phenomenon involving new rape-facilitating drugs became distinctly apparent in reports to police and rape crisis centers. The primary drug culprits identified in these attacks are Rohypnol, a benzodiazepine, and GHB, a drug most commonly used in Europe as an adjunct to anesthesia. The secret administration of one of these drugs into the drink of a victim can create a situation in which assailants do not have to overcome resistance, use force, make threats, or attract attention. These drugs immobilize and silence the victim. The drugs may also produce amnesia preventing recall and disqualifying victims' statements in court. One victim was told, "He has his memory, you don't have yours. There is no evidence. The case is closed." It is an error to limit the discussion of drug use and crime to suspects and perpetrators. Sexual assault, domestic violence, and child abuse have long established the relationship between drug use and victimization. One must remain aware of how the use and abuse of drugs have often caused disproportionate tolls on specific populations of people.

Currently, no discussion of large-scale drug-related crime and trafficking is possible without recognizing the emergence of powerful Mexican cartels. In addition to purchasing cocaine and heroin directly from Colombian traffickers for sale in the United States, Mexican traffickers now manage the largest methamphetamine manufacturing and distribution network in the hemisphere. According to the Drug Enforcement Administration, Mexican syndicates now control 80 to 90 percent of the methamphetamine distribution in the United States, 33 percent of the cocaine distribution, and 20 percent of the heroin distribution. In fiscal year 2001/02 more than $600 million was committed to target the Colombian production of cocaine and heroin and its subsequent crossing of the southwest U.S. border.

The articles in unit 5 help illustrate the wide range of criminal activity associated with the manufacture, trafficking, and use of some illicit drugs. As you read, consider the significance of drugs as they relate to the most pervasive fear in this country—the fear of crime.

Organized Crime in Narcotics Trafficking

By Julie Salzano and Stephen W. Hartman

The effects of drug trafficking were never understood in the United States because it has been viewed primarily as a domestic, criminal justice, and public health problem. This viewpoint was articulated during the 1973 establishment of the Drug Enforcement Administration (DEA).[1] As the DEA came on-line, a coup in Chile brought the Pinochet government to power. General Augusto Pinochet had drug traffickers arrested. This crackdown enabled Colombians to seize control of approximately eighty percent of the cocaine processing—providing for a cocaine boom.

Over the next eight years, cocaine trafficking moved from a relatively small criminal activity to an international criminal industry. By 1980 Bolivia became the first *narcocracy* under General Garcia Meza, serving as the template for the growth and development of cocaine trafficking in Central and South America.

By late 1982 and into 1983 hundreds of manual laborers were recruited to construct three separate camps and a landing strip in Colombia capable of accommodating large aircrafts, as well as six smaller airstrips. With help American-Colombian minister of Justice Rodrigo Lara Bonilla decided to destroy the complex. With electronic transmitters secreted in 55-gallon drums of precursor chemicals bound for the island, the DEA and Colombian forces were able to track the route. They destroyed the drug labs and took $1.2 billion dollars worth of narcotics and dumped it into the river turning the Yari River white. After the raid, Justice Bonilla was ambushed and killed.

The Bonilla assassination showed the scope of power which cocaine traffickers had acquired in Colombia including their willingness to exercise that power; the complicity of members of the Colombian government, and, finally, the inability of the Colombian government to respond to their challenge.[2] The thrust of the attack was economic which undermined the nation-states through corruption, and was cemented with the selective application of violence.

The Colombian cocaine industry is the Third World's first truly successful multinational enterprise, being the most profitable business in the world. The Colombians use the term "Mafia," (*La Empresa Coordinadora*—the Coordinating Enterprise) as a classification which more accurately describes the familiar business aspect of their organization.[3]

Rather than having a well-structured corporate bureaucratic configuration, like the La Cosa Nostra (LCN) in the United States, La Empresa is a loose associative or confederated model rooted in familiar and patron-client relationships, as in fact are many units in Italian LCN organized crime.

La Empresa Coordinadora has been recognized as a major interest group that Colombia must account for in the development and implementation of public policies. The infrastructure should be thought of as snap-links. Each link can stand alone, but has the ability of being together. At times, five or six leaders may choose to associate their organizations, or independently become partners in one or more enterprises that require large sums of capital, or involve such economies of scale that a limited partnership may be justified. There are at least 100 separate drug trafficking organizations in Colombia.[4]

The United States has been evolving a somewhat haphazard policy of drug interdiction spread over many different agencies. Operations under various names have been set in motion at the U.S. border just to be abandoned months later because of a lack of coordination and the inability to stop the flow of narcotics into the country. At a 1990 Operation Alliance Joint Command Group Meeting (17 Federal, State and Local law enforcement agencies including military support) a feasibility study was created to determine what intelligence exchange and management might be supported by member agencies. In April 1991 the study was published finding that out of 1,741 state law enforcement agencies and 15 federal agencies only 29% responded. The majority of survey respondents were not satisfied with the present situation, characterizing information/intelligence exchange as being "hit or miss" with the actual "intelligence business" being conducted on a case-by-case basis. There is unwillingness amongst law enforcement agencies to share intelligence regarding drug trafficking. This may be due to the many corruption investigations that have plagued the southwest border.

El Paso Intelligence Center (EPIC) was created in 1975 as an interagency clearinghouse for the analysis of acquired information and timely intelligence to support and facilitate international U.S. border and domestic interdiction. Such a mission is impossible to execute. According to EPIC officials, the center has been flooded with too much intelligence data. The truth of the matter is that it was never designed as an operational intelligence production center.[5]

Today the U.S. Department of Defense (DOD) is playing a larger role in intergovernmental drug interdiction programs. The DOD counter-drug budget for fiscal year 1997 was $808 million, most of which was spent on U.S.

domestic programs to detect and interdict the flow of illicit drugs intended for U.S. consumers.[6]

Federal seizures of cocaine in the Southwestern United States more than doubled from 1990 to 1992. During 1994, the annual cash surplus reported by the Los Angeles branch of the Federal Reserve Bank tripled to $9.3 billion from $3.4 billion in 1990. In January 1996 the numbers continue to rise. El Paso and San Antonio are among the top five districts in the country reporting surpluses.[7] Trafficking in cash has become as big a problem as the narcotics itself.

The money transfer industry is essential in understanding money laundering. Due to the global trend of rapidly increasing electronic commerce the U.S. market for money transmission services has grown steadily over the last ten years. U.S. money transmitters remit upwards of $10.8 billion, exclusive of fees, each year, through approximately 43,000 locations nationwide. The industry is highly concentrated: two companies, Western Union and MoneyGram, handle the vast majority of fund transfers. Most of the money transmission outlets are concentrated in six major states: California, New York, Texas, New Jersey, Florida, and Illinois.[8] More drug money either originates or flows through the United States than anywhere else in the world. The DEA estimates that at least three quarters of Latin American drug proceeds are laundered through New York City alone.[9]

In addition, a new growth industry in Colombia is the rise of "Peso Brokers." These brokers play a very important role in the laundering of Colombian drug cartel money. In exchange for clean pesos, the cartels give the (Peso) brokers mounds of $1, $5, and $20 bills from stash houses in cities such as Houston, New York, and Los Angeles. Peso brokers inject the cash into the U.S. financial system by using runners known as *smurfs*.[10]

Typically unemployed Latin Americans, the smurfs then begin transferring money into U.S. bank accounts in amounts less than $10,000 to avoid triggering bank audits. Puerto Rico has also emerged as a major transshipment point for drug trafficking and money laundering in the Caribbean area in the early 1980s. In 1982 the Federal Reserve Bank and the Internal Revenue Service (IRS) noticed a majority of the banks in Puerto Rico were sending more currency to the Federal Reserve than they were receiving from it. Based on this discrepancy, a federal task force initiated an investigation to determine the origin of the cash surplus. The investigation, named Operation Greenback, uncovered a money laundering scheme controlled by local financial institutions and illegal lottery ticket leaders.[11]

Because of their proximity to Latin America, both San Juan and Miami continue to be major ports of entry for drug trafficking. There is increasing evidence that airport and seaport workers are actively involved in drug smuggling in the airports and seaports at both of these locations.

Whether drugs have been smuggled into a port of entry by airplane or by ship, it is often transported to its final destination by truck as concealed cargo. On land drug smuggling via tractor-trailer has been in existence for decades. But using this transport system, the amounts of narcotics being transported into the United States have reached staggering proportions.[12] The use of cover loads by drug traffickers to conceal their shipments can be extremely effective.[13] On a case-by-case informant type of police investigation, only four percent of the containers entering U.S. ports are targeted as high-risk smuggling.

In North America, South Africa and Europe, particularly in Amsterdam, Netherlands, there has been an increase in theft of motor freight carriers over the past five years. Internationally metropolitan areas having a high volume of cargo shipments frequently become high narcotic traffic zones. Coincidentally, these areas have also experienced a steadily increasing rate of cargo losses.[14]

U.S. Border Patrol officer uncovers cocaine stash at Mexican border. More than 200 tons of cocaine flows to US through Mexico each year.

While cargo smuggling can be exceedingly difficult to detect, the smugglers are extremely well organized and sophisticated. Truck cargo is the ideal transport methodology for the smuggler who often uses hijacking and theft to complete the delivery. Trucks are inherently designed to be mobile and easily driven which makes the job of a potential hijacker, thief or smuggler that much easier.

Since the predominant type of cargo crime is theft either from a truck or cargo container, it is considered a low priority property crime. There is no FBI crime category for reporting cargo theft crime. It is grossly under reported or interrelated with other crime categories. There is an additional problem in lost cargo containers and trucks as manufacturers do not want to report losses since it would give some indication as to the amount of illicit merchandise currently in the market. As a rule of thumb, the U.S. Attorney's Office will not prosecute any cargo crimes where the loss is less than $50K.[15] However, this hides the real shipment, which are narcotics masked as an insignificant cargo loss. Even if the cargo is located, the drugs, of course, have disappeared. This leaves a situation where no theft is reported and the major drug shipment is totally undetected. The shippers, including trucking and sea cargo companies, do not want to report cargo theft since this would discourage manufacturers from using their services.

The lack of a centralized cargo tracking system and a uniform cargo crime reporting system cause related problems. Losses are reported to the local police or port authorities. It leads to long delays before missing cargo is discovered and subsequently reported generating jurisdictional disputes at the local level, state and federal levels. This compounds the difficulty in recovering lost cargo. The FBI estimates that nationwide cargo loss is at the $3 billion level while "a coalition of freight and security interests, the Washington-based National Cargo Security Council, puts the annual losses at $10 billion."[16]

Mexico is a major port of entry for drug shipments into the United States. Despite stepped-up border inspections since 1995, U.S. officials concede that more than ninety percent of the cocaine and heroin shipped through Mexico from South America gets past them. Since the North American Free Trade Agreement (NAFTA) began, Mexican exports to the United States have more than doubled and at least eighty-five percent moves by truck through fifteen border crossings between Brownsville, Texas, and San Diego. Nearly two million trucks per year enter at Laredo alone.[17]

In addition NAFTA (euphemistically termed the "North American Drug Trade Agreement") has been so successful in promoting business between the United States and Mexico, that Federal law enforcement is having difficulty in discerning what are and are not legitimate money transfers. Thus, money laundering, or the transfer of billions of narco-dollars back and forth across the U.S. and Mexican border, cannot be stopped because of the sheer velocity of modern capital flow. It is estimated that seventy percent "of the more than 200–400 tons of cocaine consumed in the U.S. each year is shipped through Mexico."[18]

If a drug trafficker or money launderer were asked what are the optimum conditions for conducting their operations, the answer would be low trade barriers, deregulation, relaxed international banking standards, border-erasing technology, and weak rule of law. Those are the prevailing trends or conditions in the world today, and every means the worlds of business and finance have to offer, linked by wireless and fax transmissions, are today used by traffickers and the managers of their illicit proceeds.[19]

The bombardment of narco-dollars has moved into a crisis situation. U.S. law enforcement officials are not able to prosecute individuals transporting large sums of U.S. currency into the country who claim it is from legitimate means without establishing a clear nexus to drug trafficking.

The Mexican *narcotrafficantes* bought a huge piece of the Del Monte Corporation.[20] In May 1997 a tractor-trailer load of commercial size cans of Del Monte tomatoes were opened in the DEA lot in New York City finding sealed bundles of cash in the tomato sauce.[21] *Narcotrafficantes* are opening up tile factories in Canada.[22] They are moving into the trucking industry and in import/export businesses.

The Mexican drug industry alone is estimated at 30 billion dollars a year in profits, a sum that is quadruple the revenues from its largest export, oil, and a sum sufficient to service Mexico's entire $160 billion governmental and private foreign debt.[23] In addition, "authorities believe that at least ten percent of that is earmarked for police and politician payoffs."[24]

The Cali Cartel can be expected to focus more on their legitimate holdings managed with the help of the high-powered business managers they have cultivated from among the world's best business schools. Illegal drugs will still be a profitable part of the ledger, but at a reduced and less ostentatious level. The "new cartel" will not be easy to attack. It is believed that they own 100 legitimate companies in the United States that are involved in everything from car sales to pharmaceuticals.[25]

Overall, the dimensions of drug trafficking and money laundering have become staggering. They have become so enmeshed with everyday commerce and financial transactions in a globalized economy that it has become nearly impossible to distinguish the illicit from the legitimate. Drugs now find their way to market commingled with other commodities in vast networks of airfreight and container shipping by sea and land. Today, there are more than five hundred companies worldwide transporting containers in giant seagoing vessels, with more than twenty million container slots available per year. Customs agencies in the industrialized world are overwhelmed, and most in the developing world have been corrupted by traffickers to one degree or another.[26]

Latin America is a main point of origin for a great proportion of the total drug traffic entering the United States. This is particularly true with cocaine and marijuana. However, Europe and Turkey are major trafficking points for heroin, opium and hashish. Turkey essentially acts as a bridge between Europe and Asia. It has long served as a crossroads for heroin and hashish smugglers. But the volume of narcotics trafficked through Turkey has grown substantially during the past decade, as rising demand in

Western countries has boosted drug trade profits. Between 1993 and 1996, the amount of heroin seized annually by Turkish authorities doubled, to more than four metric tons. The DEA estimates up to six metric tons of heroin—equal to 75 percent of Western Europe's consumption of the drug—leave Turkey every month.[27]

Drug trafficking, in short, is a growing international problem involving enormous amounts of money presenting a tremendous concern for governments around the world. Even in Turkey trucks are the preferred mode of land transportation as "most of the (Turkish) heroin is hauled to Western Europe along the so-called Balkan route through Bulgaria and Romania, often hidden in trucks carrying legitimate export products."[28]

Obviously, then, the key to understanding the growth of the drug problem throughout the world is drug trafficking. Drug traffickers have created a highly sophisticated system that combines latest technology with highly developed transportation systems sustained by corruption and keen knowledge of the operations of drug enforcement agencies throughout the world. Its dangers are very real and could well mean the collapse of modern government and society.

References

1. William O. Walker III, *Drug Control in the Americas* (Albuquerque: University of New Mexico Press, 1981), p. 193.
2. Paul Eddy, Hugo Sabogal, and Sara Walden, *The Cocaine Wars* (New York: Bantam Books, 1988), p.26.
3. "The Kingdom of Cocaine," *The New Republic* (November 21, 1989), pp. 27–28
4. J. F. Hold en-Rhodes, *Sharing the Secrets: Open Source Intelligence and the War on Drugs.* (Westport, CT: Praeger), p. 49.
5. *Narcotics Control Digest*, September 12, 1991, p. 10.
6. Barracks, *Loc. Cit.*, p. 115.
7. WN, Federal Reserve/Banking Institutions, July 1995.
8. Raymond W. Kelly, "The New York Money Transmitter Geographic Targeting Order." Testimony before the subcommittee on General Oversight and Investigations, House Committee on Banking and Financial Services, Washington, DC, March 11, 1997.
9. Payne, *Loc. Cit.*, p. 62.
10. Mike France and Victoria Burnett, "Corporate America's Colombian Connection," *Business Week* (December 1, 1997), p. 170.
11. Alfredo Montalvo-Barbot, "Crime in Puerto Rico: Drug Trafficking, Money Laundering, and the Poor," *Crime and Delinquency* Vol., 43, Issue 4 (October, 1997), p. 534.
12. Personal interview with Janet Waugh, Special Agent for the Justice Department's Drug Enforcement Administration (May, 1997).
13. Julienne Salzano "The Pipeline: The South American/ Caribbean Drug Connection." Presented at the Academy of Criminal Justice Sciences, (March 1997), Louisville, Kentucky.
14. Interview with Robert DeBellis, Special Agent in Charge of Cargo Crime, FBI, Newark, NJ (June 12, 1996)
15. Federal Bureau of Investigation, Violent Crimes and Major Offenders Section, Interstate Theft Unit, "Cargo Theft" (April, 1995) p. 3.

16. Ken Cottrill, "National Cargo Crime Database Launched," Traffic World (November 27, 1995), p. 34.
17. Payne, *Loc. Cit.*, p. 59.
18. Jeff Builta, "Mexico, Corruption, Crime, Drug Trafficking & Political Intrigue," *Crime & Justice International* (February, 1997), p. 5.
19. *Ibid.*
20. Bowden, *Loc. Cit.*, p. 252.
21. Waugh, *Loc. Cit.*
22. Bowden Charles, "The Killer Across the River," *(April, 1997) GQ Magazine*, p. 212.
23. Builta, *Loc. Cit.*, p. 5.
24. National Narcotics Intelligence Consumers Committee, *The NNICC Report: 1994. The Supply of Illicit Drugs to the United States* (Washington, D.C.: Drug Enforcement Administration, 1995).
25. Payne, *Loc. Cit.*, p. 60.
26. John Doxey, "Losing the Battle and the War Against Drugs," *Middle East* (October, 1997), p. 21.
27. Robert D. Kaplan, "Was Democracy Just a Moment?" *The Atlantic Monthly* (December, 1997), p. 69.

Julie Salzano in an Associate Professor at St. Johns University and Stephen W. Hartman is an Associate Professor at the New York Institute of Technology.

Previously appeared in *Crime and Justice International*, Vol. 15, No. 26, March 1999, pp. 15-19. © 1999.

PERSPECTIVES

Drugs, Crime, Prison and Treatment

by Charles Blanchard, chief counsel, White House Office of National Drug Control Policy (ONDCP); former Arizona state senator and CSG Toll Fellow, class of '91

Talk to any police officer, judge or probation officer, or visit any prison. One fact becomes abundantly clear: there is a clear link between crime and drug use. While no one factor can explain criminal behavior, it is undeniable that drug addiction is an important factor in explaining crime and violence. Study after study confirms this link:

• Over half of the crime in this country is committed by individuals under the influence of drugs. The National Institute of Justice's ADAM drug-testing program found that more than 60 percent of adult male arrestees tested positive for drugs. In most cities, over half of young male arrestees are under the influence of marijuana. Importantly, the majority of these crimes result from the effects of the drug—and do not result from the fact that drugs are illegal.

• According to a study by the National Center on Addiction and Substance Abuse (CASA) at Columbia University, 80 percent of the men and women behind bars—about 1.4 million inmates—are seriously involved with alcohol and other drug abuse.

• A study published in the *Journal of the American Medical Association* last year indicated that nondrug users who live in households where drugs (including marijuana) are used are 11 times as likely to be killed as those living in drug-free households. Drug abuse in a home increased a women's risk of being killed by a close relative by 28 times.

Despite this strong link between drugs and crime, few probationers and inmates receive drug or alcohol treatment. While states estimate that 70 to 85 percent of their inmates need some substance abuse treatment, only 13 percent of these inmates received any treatment in 1996. Sadly, even in those state prisons that do offer quality treatment, only a relatively small percentage of offenders take advantage of it.

It is time for state and federal leaders to take a closer look at funding substance abuse treatment in criminal

justice systems. And, it is time to become more creative in using the coercive power of the criminal justice system (a system with many opportunities for rewards and punishments) to induce offenders to seek and remain in treatment.

Fortunately, in recent years many state and local governments and the federal government have experimented with drug treatment programs in the criminal justice system. Thanks to the evaluations of these innovative programs, we now have good evidence that using the coercive power of the criminal justice system to force probationers and inmates into treatment is a cost-effective means of reducing crime. Recent evaluations of a myriad of criminal justice treatment programs—ranging from diversion programs such as drug courts and the Brooklyn Drug Treatment Alternative-to-Prison program, and institutional drug treatment programs such as those in Delaware and the Federal Bureau of Prisons—have found that drug treatment reduces crime. These studies show that quality treatment programs of sufficient length that include transition services in the community reduce drug use and future criminal behavior.

Among inmates who completed residential drug treatment, only 3.3 percent were rearrested in the first six months, compared with 12.1 percent of inmates who did not receive treatment.

As a result of the Violent Crime Control and Law Enforcement Act of 1994, the Federal Bureau of Prisons now provides drug treatment to all eligible inmates prior to their release from custody. Last Spring, the Bureau of Prisons announced its first analysis of the success of this program. It shows that institution-based drug treatment can make a difference. Among inmates who completed residential drug treatment, only 3.3 percent were rearrested in the first six months, compared with 12.1 percent of inmates who did not receive treatment. Similarly, the Delaware Department of Corrections conducts outstanding drug treatment programs. A study of the Delaware program found that those inmates who received both institutional drug treatment and transitional support services had far fewer arrests and far less drug use after release than those inmates who had no such treatment. Eighteen months after arrest, 71 percent of the treated inmates were arrest-free, and 76 percent were drug-free. In contrast, only 30 percent of those inmates who had no treatment were arrest-free and only 19 percent were drug-free.

Perhaps the most innovative treatment programs, however, have not been in institutional settings. Instead, thanks in large measure to the ideas of scholars such as Mark Kleiman, several state and local leaders have begun to build treatment programs for offenders outside the prison system that are based on the concept of coerced abstinence. The idea is a simple one: use the coercive power of the criminal justice system to induce nonviolent offenders into treatment. Sadly, even when treatment is available, only a small number of offenders enter and remain in treatment. To remedy this problem, coerced abstinence programs use a "carrot and stick" approach—using drug testing, graduated sanctions and treatment—to induce offenders to take treatment seriously.

Surprisingly to some, these coerced abstinence programs work just as well as voluntary treatment programs in reducing the drug use and criminal activity of their graduates. Importantly, however, these coerced abstinence programs are more successful than voluntary programs both in inducing offenders to participate in treatment and in retaining offenders in treatment. For example, Charles J. Hynes, the Kings County (Brooklyn) District Attorney, has built a coerced treatment program known as the Drug Treatment Alternative-to-Prison (DTAP) program. Evaluations of the DTAP program found that the overall retention rate for offenders in the DTAP program was 64 percent—at least two times higher than the retention rate for most residential treatment programs. Moreover, after one year, DTAP offenders had less than half the arrest rate of drug offenders sent to prison.

Similarly, preliminary evaluations of drug courts have been encouraging. There are now about 300 drug courts in operation, with drug courts located in virtually every state. Using drug testing, treatment, and graduated sanctions, drug courts offer non-violent offenders the hope of a dismissal of charges if they successfully complete drug treatment. During the program, graduated sanctions (such as jail time) are used to punish offenders who test positive for drugs or who otherwise fail to participate in treatment. Offenders who fail the program altogether face time in prison. This combination of positive and negative incentives appears to work. Studies of the drug court programs in Brooklyn, Maricopa County (Arizona), the District of Columbia, Portland (Oregon), and Dade County (Florida) all found high retention rates, low rearrest rates and lower drug use. Participants in these programs had arrest and drug use rates far lower than similar offenders who did not participate in the program.

Substance abuse treatment of offenders will pay for itself. Indeed, the CASA study concluded that if just ten percent of inmates given one year of residential treatment stay sober and work during the first year after release, prison-based drug treatment would more than pay for itself in one year. This is because the costs of continued drug use by released offenders is tremendously expensive to society. By ensuring the availability of treatment in the entire continuum of criminal sanctions—from diversion programs to probation to prison—states can reduce crime, reduce arrest and prosecution costs, reduce incarceration costs, reduce drug-related emergency room visits, and increase employment.

Of course, states must carefully construct quality treatment programs that are based on models—such as the Delaware prison treatment program and Brooklyn's DTAP program—that work. If they do so, however, there is every indication of a large payoff. By breaking the cycle of drugs and crime, we will have fewer victims, more productive citizens, and safer communities.

More information on criminal justice treatment programs can be found on the ONDCP web site: http://www.whitehousedrugpolicy.gov.

From *Spectrum*, Winter 1999, pp. 26-27. © 1999 by The Council of State Governments. Reprinted with permission from Spectrum.

Women in Jail: Is Substance Abuse Treatment Enough?

Objectives. This study examined the self-reported needs of women in jail who indicated a need for drug abuse services.

Methods. A total of 165 interviews were conducted of women held in a large urban county jail in Ohio in May 1999.

Results. Drug-abusing women were more likely to report a need for housing, mental health counseling, education, job training, medical care, family support, and parenting assistance when released from jail.

Conclusions. The provision of drug abuse treatment referrals to women in jail may not break the continual cycle of drug and incarceration if other needs cannot be addressed. (*Am J Public Health.* 2001; 91:798–800)

Sonia A. Alemagno, PhD

That the number of women in America's prisons is increasing has been well documented in the literature since the early 1980s.[1] A growing population of concern includes women who are incarcerated in local jails. There are more than 3000 short-term confinement jails in the United States housing more than half a million inmates, including offenders convicted in misdemeanors serving relatively short sentences, felony offenders waiting assignment to long-term confinement facilities, and sentenced offenders serving time in local jails owing to overcrowded prisons. Since 1990, the nation's jail population on a per capita basis has increased over a third. On average, the adult female jail population has grown 7.0% annually since 1990, while the adult male jail population has grown 4.5%. Although women compose only 11% of the US jail population, the rate of incarceration is rising faster among women than among men, and female arrestees are more likely than male arrestees to be found drug positive. It is estimated that about two thirds of female arrestees use illicit drugs.[1]

Since jails historically have held predominantly men, facilities and services have not been developed to meet the special needs of women in jail.[2,3] Women offenders with histories of substance abuse present complex clinical profiles with a range of medical, psychological, educational, vocational, and social problems.[4–7] Effective programs for substance-abusing women need to address physical concerns,[7,8] psychological issues,[5,8] Vocational preparation,[5,9–11] family issues,[6,9,12] child care issues,[11] and educational needs.[3,6] Studies have bee primarily based on the observations of clinicians. Few studies, however, have examined women's self-reported hierarchy of needs.

Methods

During May 1999, interviews were conducted with 165 women incarcerated in a large, urban county jail in Ohio. We recruited women to the study by asking for volunteers within the female housing unit. There was no opportunity to perform random sampling owing to considerable transition and court appointments; therefore, this study reports on a convenience sample. Because of transition within this unit and the anonymity of respondents, we are unable to report he participation rate. There was no compensation other than coffee and snack provided at the time of the interview. Research assistants in a private setting just outside the jail pod conducted interviews.

Respondents were asked questions about demographics, services used in the past year, and their general history. By means of a checklist and a series of open-ended questions, respondents described services that they would need when they were released from jail. The checklist categories had been developed in a prior project on the basis of open-ended responses. Women were asked to rank their reported needs, including those offered in the open-ended questions. The objective of the interview was to determine what self-perceived spectrum of needs the women in jail would elaborate. For this study, women requesting a need for drug abuse services were compared with women who did not.

TABLE 1—Demographic Characteristics of Respondents to Survey of Self-Reported Needs of Women in Jail: Ohio, 1999	
Characteristic	%
Race/ethnicity	
African American	72
White	23
Other	5
Age, y	
18–29	30
30–39	48
40–49	19
≥50	3
Education	
<9th grade	3
Some high school	41
High school graduate	56
No. children	
0	<1
1	23
2	23
3	24
≥4	29
Arrest charge	
Drugs	32
Parole/probation vio-lation	23
Theft	14
Assault	10
Warrants	4
Solicitation	4
DUI	3
Contempt of court	2
Murder	1
Other charges	7
Times in jail	
First time	25
2	19
3–5	29
>5	27

Note. DUI = driving under the influence (of alcohol). Percentages adjusted for missing data.

Results

Demographic characteristics of the sample are presented in Table. Most respondents were African American (72%) and aged 30 to 40 years. More than half of the women had graduated from high school (56%). Almost all of the women reported having children.

The sample included women in all phases of the judicial process. Most women had considerable experience within the criminal justice system. Only one quarter reported that this was their first time in jail. The women had been charged with a spectrum of offenses.

In this sample, the 50% of women (n = 83) who reported a need for substance abuse services were compared with the women who did not. There were no significant differences between the 2 groups by age, race/ethnicity, or education.

Table 2 indicates that women who self-reported the need for drug treatment services were more likely to report fair or poor health status and having been hospitalized in the past year than were women who did not report a drug problem. Further, although almost half of the treatment-seeking women had been in some kind of substance abuse treatment in the past year (44%), they were much more likely to report continued family problems due to substance abuse. These women were more likely to have been in jail multiple times in the past year, to have a drug-related charge, and to be unemployed.

The treatment-seeking group in this sample was more likely to need housing, Medical care, education, mental health services, family support, and parenting assistance. The need most often expressed was for housing (84%). In fact, when asked to self-report the most important need on release, 40% of the treatment-seeking group indicated a priority need for housing (vs 26% in the comparison group).

When we further examined housing status, women in the treatment-seeking group were more likely to indicate a lack of stable housing (staying in a hotel, boarding house, on the street or homeless, or in a shelter) before their arrest (17%, vs 7% in the comparison group). Women in the treatment-seeking group also reported more transition in their living situation in the past year (35% moved 3 or more times in the past year, compared with 10% in the comparison group). More than one quarter of the treatment-seeking group indicated that they did not know where they would

go on being released from jail (vs 11% in the comparison group).

Discussion

There are several limitations to the study. The sample reflects a convenience sample selected from 1 county jail; the project should be replicated across a number of county jails with a larger sample. Further, this study did not validate the self-reported needs of the women. The results may indicate local issues.

Even so, there are possible treatment policy implications. Drug policy in the United States appears to be shifting from a "get tough on crime" emphasis (incarcerating drug offenders) to expansion of drug treatment opportunities. However, even if services are offered in jail, the women in this sample may not be able to follow through on referrals without stable housing or a legal source of income when they are released. Many women had already been through drug treatment within the past year only to find themselves in jail again.

This study supports previous work indicating that successful drug treatment of released jail detainees must go beyond addressing pathology alone. Efforts to manage the cases of women released from jail will require careful consideration of the *multidimensional* needs of these women. Most of the women had children and reported having no health insurance. A treatment referral may seem like a low priority to women faced with challenges such as homelessness.

Recent US drug policy has recommended treatment for drug-dependent offenders in all phases of the criminal justice system. Is treatment enough? From the responses of the 165 women interviewed, the answer appears to be no. Regardless of the matrix of services offered, treatment must serve as a bridge to a new way of life, likely to include a new living arrangement.

Acknowledgements

This project was supported by National Institute on Drug Abuse grant DA00245.

The author gratefully acknowledges the cooperation of the Cuyahoga County Corrections Department staff and the assistance of Robert B. Pace, Director of Corrections. Research assistants for this project included graduate students Kathy Petsko, Visobe Simfukwe, Lynn Gannon,

TABLE 2—Profile and Needs of Women in Jail Requesting Drug Abuse Service: Ohio, 1999

	Need Drug Abuse Services, % (n=83)	Do Not Need Drug Abuse Services, % (n=82)	Total (n=165)	χ^2	df	P
Profile						
Self-reported health fair or poor	57.4	34.1	45.7	13.96	2	.003*
Used substance abuse services in past year*	43.9	16.0	30.1	15.04	1	.000*
Used mental health services in past year	32.1	22.0	27.0	2.13	1	NS
Hospitalized in past year	32.9	19.5	26.2	3.81	1	.038*
Ever arrested for drinking/drugs	85.4	31.7	58.5	48.64	1	.000**
Family problems due to drinking/drugs	85.4	36.6	61.0	41.00	1	.000**
Unemployed at time of arrest	63.4	28.0	45.7	20.67	1	.000**
Drug charge at arrest	43.9	19.5	31.7	13.66	1	.000**
Assault or theft charge at arrest	13.4	32.7	20.7	4.54	1	.005*
In jail 3 or more times in past year	22.0	3.7	12.8	15.90	2	.001**
Self-Reported Needs on Release						
Housing/place to stay	84.1	45.1	64.6	27.32	1	.000**
Medical care	80.5	51.9	66.3	14.96	1	.000**
Education/training	62.0	37.0	49.4	9.99	1	.001**
Mental health services	61.5	24.4	42.5	22.57	1	.000**
Family support	51.9	34.6	43.2	4.93	1	.019*
Parenting assistance	46.9	22.0	34.4	11.26	1	.001**
Legal help	45.1	35.4	40.2	1.62	1	NS

Note. NS = not significant.
*P<.05; **P<.01.

Brian Stowder, Eric Dodson, and Karen Bailey.

References

1. *Prison and Jail Inmates at Mid-Year 1998.* Washington, D.C.: US Dept of Justice, Bureau of Justice Statistics; January 1999.

2. Henderson DJ. Drug abuse and incarcerated women: a research review. *J Subst Abuse Treat.* 1998; 15: 579–587.

3. Taylor SD. Women offenders and reentry issues. *J Psychoactive Drugs.* 1996; 28: 85–93.

4. Haller DL, Knisley JS, Dawson KS, Schnoll SH. Perinatal substance abusers: psychological and social characteristics. *J Nerv Ment Dis.* 1993; 181: 509–513.

5. Sheridan MJ. A proposed intergenerational model of substance abuse, family functioning, and abuse/neglect. *Child Abuse Negl.* 1995; 19: 519–530.

6. Weiner HD, Wallen MC, Zankowski GL. Culture and social class as intervening variables in relapse prevention with chemically dependent women. *J Psychoactive Drugs.* 1990; 22: 239–248.

7. Yang SS. The unique treatment needs of female substance abusers in correctional institutions: the obligation of the criminal justice system to provide parity of services. *Med Law.* 1990; 9: 1018–1027.

8. Singer MI, Bussey J. Song LY, Lunghofer L. The psychosocial issues of women serving time in jail. *Soc Work.* 1995; 40: 103–113.

9. Wellish J. Anglin MC, Prendergast ML. Number and characteristics of drug-using women in the criminal justice system: implications for treatment. *J Drug Issues.* 1993; 23: 7–30.

10. Lanehart RE, Clark HB, Kratochvil DI, Rollings JD, Fidora AF. Case management of pregnant and parenting female crack and polydrug users. J Subst Abuse.] 1994; 6: 441–448.

11. De Leon G. Jainchill N. Residential therapeutic communities for female substance abusers *Bull NY Acad Med.* 1991; 67: 277–290.

12. Reed BG. Drug misuse and dependency in women: the meaning and implications of being considered a special population or minority group. *Int J Addict.* 1985; 20: 13–62.

The author is with the Institute of Health and social Policy and the Department of Public Administration and Urban Studies, University of Akron, Ohio.

Requests for reprints should be sent to Sonia A. Alemagno, PhD, Institute for Health and Social Policy, University of Akron, Polsky 5th Floor, Akron, OH 44325–1915 (e-mail:salemagno@aol .com).

This brief was accepted July 21, 2000.

From *American Journal of Public Health,* May 2001, pp. 798-800. © 2001 by The American Public Health Association. Reprinted by permission.

Cracking down on ecstasy

Law enforcement is treating the 'hug drug' as if it were the next cocaine. Is it?

BY CHITRA RAGAVAN

In September 1999, two young case agents at the Drug Enforcement Administration and Federal Bureau of Investigation in Los Angeles asked federal prosecutor Jean Mohrbacher for a favor. The agents had gotten a tip that a low-level street dealer was selling ecstasy, the hot drug among America's teens, and they wanted Mohrbacher to tap his phone. They got the bug. But instead of nailing a small-time dealer, they stumbled upon a major international ecstasy and cocaine distribution syndicate. And all of a sudden, ecstasy—until then considered small potatoes in the drug world—popped on to the government's radar screens—big time.

In this case, the suspected ringleader was Tamer Adel Ibrahim, 26, a naturalized American who was born in Egypt and moved to the States as a teenager. The feds say they discovered in a 15-month investigation that Ibrahim, a jet-setting, high-rolling playboy, was buying cocaine from the Mexicans and Colombians, selling it for megabucks to Europeans, and then using those profits to buy millions of ecstasy tablets from the Netherlands to hawk in the United States. Last July, the U.S. Customs Service at Los Angeles International Airport seized 16 Federal Express packages containing 2.1 million ecstasy tablets (1,096 pounds) with an estimated street value of at least $41 million. Authorities say the Customs Service was tipped off by the DEA and the FBI, which knew about the shipments from wiretaps. Ibrahim, who knew the feds suspected him, fled first to Mexico and later to Amsterdam, where he was allegedly in the midst of arranging another big deal when Dutch authorities arrested him last September. "This is a snapshot of what the new emerging trafficking groups look like," says Michele Leonhart, head of the DEA's Los Angeles division.

Red tide. Law enforcement officials say that the bust, dubbed Operation Red Tide, is the largest seizure of ecstasy in the United States and that Ibrahim was probably the largest alleged wholesaler of the drug to date. The case has raised the curtain on an alarming new development in the drug wars: the rise of newly formed international, mostly Israeli and Russian, organized crime syndicates aggressively marketing ecstasy to Americans, mainly in their teens and 20s.

> "The Europeans . . . tell us that we are the worst abusers of [ecstasy]."

Ecstasy was originally prescribed by marriage counselors in the 1970s because of its supposed ability to bring out the warm and fuzzy feelings that couples had for each other (hence its nickname: "the hug drug"). The federal government banned it in 1985 after discovering that it was becoming popular as a recreational drug and was potentially harmful if misused. But that didn't stop the burgeoning illicit market. In fact, some say it may have encouraged it. "The Europeans... tell us that we are the worst abusers of it," says Joseph Keefe, DEA's chief of operations.

Young users. What's most worrisome, say officials, is that younger and younger Americans are trying it. Today, the use of ecstasy is growing faster than any other illegal drug in the United States, according to the White House drug czar's office. A University of Michigan survey conducted last year indicates that 1.3 million of the nation's students in grades eight through 12 have tried ecstasy at least once and that almost 450,000 students currently use it.

Users like to say the drug is risk free. Not so, say experts, who point to some serious side effects (see box, "The Dangers"). The problem is that researchers have yet to definitively determine whether there are any long-term medical ills. Critics of U.S. drug policy grumble that the recent crackdown is little more than a PR stunt designed to make the feds look good

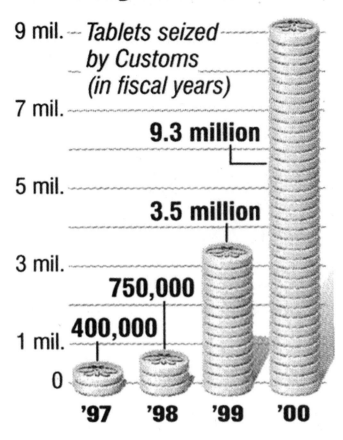

Ecstasy seizures

USN&WR
Source: U.S. Customs Service

9 mil. — *Tablets seized by Customs (in fiscal years)*

9.3 million

7 mil.

5 mil.

3.5 million

3 mil.

750,000

400,000

1 mil.

0

'97 '98 '99 '00

to help them wring more money out of Congress. "I don't want to make it sound like ecstasy is innocuous, but I fear there is far too much alarmism regarding it," says Michael Massing, a freelance journalist and author who has been covering the drug wars for a decade.

But law enforcement officials aren't taking any chances. "It could be worse than cocaine. We just don't know," says Christopher Giovino, head of the DEA's Long Island, N.Y., district office. Giovino worries that the DEA, until now consumed by cracking down on methamphetamine, cocaine, and heroin traffic, may have missed crucial early signs. So far, unlike heroin and crack cocaine, there's no evidence that ecstasy is addictive or so expensive that it prompts violent crimes by users desperate for money to buy more. Ecstasy also seems to have a pacifying, happy-time effect, so users don't generally stand out like hyped-up crack users or nodding heroin addicts. Consequently, Giovino says, ecstasy—which costs as little as $7 a pill but can run as high as $50 a pop at big-city

raves—had already become the drug of choice among young partygoers, especially in raves or dance clubs, by the time the feds caught on.

In the past two years, DEA agents in New York nabbed some big ecstasy dealers—but none as allegedly big-time as Ibrahim. "We've had to learn quick lessons of Israeli and Russian crime groups 101," says Los Angeles DEA agent Michael Braun. Ibrahim and his cohorts, mostly young Egyptian, Syrian, Russian, Israeli, and Korean men, allegedly ran a state-of-the-art global operation. Authorities say they would ship loads of ecstasy from Amsterdam to Los Angeles by way of France, Korea, and Mexico, usually via Federal Express. Ibrahim would then allegedly monitor the drug shipments on the Internet using FedEx's package tracking system.

Floating labs. According to DEA sources, more than 90 percent of the ecstasy on the U.S. market comes from the Netherlands and Belgium, where the drug is also illegal, although Romania and Poland now are be-

coming players. The tablets are manufactured in makeshift mobile labs set up inside 18-wheeler trucks or on floating barges; they're transported by criminal syndicates, many run by Israeli nationals, based in Europe, Israel, and America. "That is the ecstasy triangle," says Robert Gagne, a DEA agent on Long Island. Many of these Israeli nationals are Russian émigrés; many have prior convictions for cocaine and heroin smuggling. Gagne says many are also involved in diamond smuggling from Antwerp, Belgium, which for centuries has been the world's diamond-polishing capital. "The unification of Europe has helped ecstasy dealers as much as NAFTA has helped the Mexicans with free trade," says Gagne.

Recent DEA investigations show how these reputed syndicate heads frequently use couriers or "mules" to carry the drugs. An Israeli who came to the attention of authorities, Oded Tuito, allegedly recruited female American strippers from dance clubs. Authorities say one of his flunkies was Sean Erez, who moved to Amsterdam after Tuito's arrest on drug charges in 1999.

THE DANGERS

Ecstatic? Maybe. But not without risks

The mood-mellowing pill known as "X" seems like a drug that's too good to be true. It probably is. As its popularity soars, users and parents are beginning to worry about the health risks. The problem is, nobody knows for sure what they are—at least, not yet. But that hasn't stopped concerned government agencies from issuing stern warnings about ecstasy's potentially damaging effects. Nor has it kept ecstasy fans, like those featured in a recent *New York Times Magazine* article, from touting its supposed risk-free virtues.

"The problem with any drug is that the glorification of it puts one in the position of saying, 'No, no, no, no, it's horrible,'" says Alan Leshner, head of the National Institute on Drug Abuse in Bethesda, Md. "You don't want to be hyperbolic, but you do want to say it's a risk."

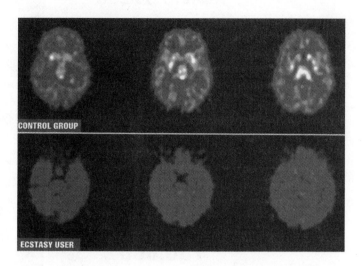

Studies show that ecstasy drains seratonin from brain cells.
• *"Ecstasy, taken alone can cause death."*

The facts: not clear, say scientists who are meeting in San Francisco this week to discuss the drug's possible downsides. What is known is that emergency-room admissions related to ecstasy have skyrocketed since 1997—the same indicator that heralded increasing cocaine abuse two decades ago. But doctors say some of those incidents—including liver failure, seizures, brain bleeding from heightened blood pressure, and heart palpitations—may stem from "lookalike" or fake ecstasy pills that contain other ingredients like paramethoxyamphetamine (PMA), which makes body temperatures dangerously high.

But that's not to say the real thing is safe. "Ecstasy, taken alone, can cause death," says Stephen Kish of the Centre for Addiction and Mental Health in Toronto, who has identified four such deaths in the past year likely caused by ecstasy overdoses. But it's the more subtle effects that proliferate: depression, memory loss, and insomnia in the days after a binge. Researchers say these symptoms develop because ecstasy drains the brain chemical serotonin out of cells. But they differ on the long-term impact.

Scientists George Ricaurte and Una McCann of the Johns Hopkins Medical Institutions say studies they've conducted over the past decade show that ecstasy damages serotonin neurons in both rodents and monkeys; a brain imaging study they did in 1998 indicates that humans might suffer similar effects. Other research suggests that people who used ecstasy at least 25 times had lowered serotonin levels for as long as a year after quitting.

Others point to flaws in current studies. For instance, some scientists say the research ignores whether users had prior serotonin or memory deficits. Even the drug's biggest cheerleaders, though, admit that more research is needed on both the benefits and the dangers.

Marriage therapists claim the drug can enhance couples' empathy toward each other. Scientists in Spain are now testing ecstasy as a possible therapy for post-traumatic stress disorder, and psychiatrist Charles Grob at the Harbor-UCLA Medical Center wants to test it as a treatment for end-stage breast cancer. Ant then there are the young partygoers who swear it makes them happier. "You'd have to have your head in the sand not to see that the effects these kids are describing sound interesting," says Ricaurte. Evidence suggests that perhaps some day a designer drug based on ecstasy may be developed that could provide potential psychological benefits—without the scary side effects. —*Nell Boyce*

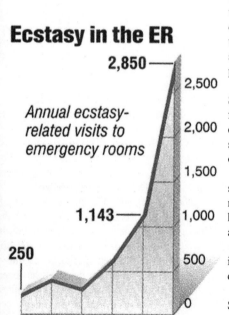

Ecstasy in the ER

Annual ecstasy-related visits to emergency rooms

2,850
2,500
2,000
1,500
1,143 — 1,000
250
500
0

'94 '95 '96 '97 '98 '99

Sources: Left: USN&WR, Drug Abuse Warning Network; Right: The Lancet/NIDA(2)

(Tuito was released last October, never convicted, after being held in a French prison for nearly two years.) In Amsterdam, Erez allegedly built a giant ecstasy smuggling ring using more than a dozen young Hasidic Jews as his couriers because their innocent demeanor and conservative appearance got them past airport security. Erez, who now is in a Dutch prison, has lost all his extradition appeals and could be returned to the United States as early as this week. Law enforcers say he will be the first ecstasy dealer to be prosecuted as head of a continuing criminal enterprise under a drug statute mimicking the famous RICO statutes used to take down organized crime families. If convicted, he faces a likely sentence of 20 years in prison. "We're hoping this sends a shock wave through the smuggling community," says Giovino.

Nouveau riches. But DEA officials aren't confident that it will. There's so much money in ecstasy that agents say smugglers don't seem to care about the risks, often even flaunting their wealth. Take the case of Michel Devalck, a Belgian who, according to authorities, believed he was delivering 150,000 ecstasy tablets to a distributor waiting for him at Miami Beach on December 13. Devalck arrived in a 2001 Mercedes SUV that he leased for a whopping $70,000. Even the feds waiting to nab him were impressed.

As the government cracks down, ecstasy cases are beginning to clog some courts. In New York, so many Hasidic Jews are being arrested as couriers that a federal judge in Brooklyn blew a gasket during a March sentencing hearing for one Hasidic teenager who was involved in the giant smuggling ring allegedly run by Erez. The judge upbraided dozens of Hasidic men and women who had come to court to offer testimony on behalf of the teen. "I don't know where this community was while all of this was going on," Judge I. Leo Glasser admonished from the bench. Law enforcers want to make sure they won't be asked the same question down the road.

From *U.S. News & World Report,* February 5, 2001, pp. 14-17. © 2001 by U.S. News & World Report, L.P. Reprinted by permission.

UNIT 6

Measuring the Social Cost of Drugs

Unit Selections

Key Points to Consider

- What do you believe to be the greatest drug-related threat facing our nation? Explain.

- How do drug-related threats and impacts differ from city to city and state to state? Why?

- It is often argued that Americans overreact and overemphasize the harm from illegal drugs while ignoring or underrepresenting the harm from legal drugs, namely alcohol and nicotine. Do you agree or disagree with this argument, and why?

- Has there been a significant shift in public concern over the abuse of legal drugs? Support your answer.

- Explain whether or not the harmful impacts from the abuse of drugs are greater today than they were a decade ago.

 **Links: www.dushkin.com/online/**
These sites are annotated in the World Wide Web pages.

DrugText
http://www.drugtext.org
The National Organization on Fetal Alcohol Syndrome (NOFAS)
http://www.nofas.org
National NORML Homepage
http://www.natlnorml.org

The most devastating effect of drug use in America is the magnitude with which it affects the way we live. Much of its influence is not measurable. What is the cost of a son or daughter lost, a parent imprisoned, a life lived in a constant state of fear? The emotional costs alone are incomprehensible.

The social legacy of this country's drug crisis could easily be the subject of this entire book. The purpose here, however, can only be a cursory portrayal of drugs' tremendous costs. More than one American president has stated that drug use threatens our national security and personal well-being. The financial costs of maintaining the federal apparatus devoted to drug interdiction, enforcement, and treatment are staggering. Although yearly expenditures vary due to changes in political influence, strategy, and tactics, examples of the tremendous effects of drugs on government and the economy abound. The federal budget for drug control exceeds $19 billion and includes $624 million for Colombia and the Andean region. The Department of Justice commits over $8 billion to antidrug efforts, the Department of Health and Human Services over $3.6 billion, and the Department of Defense over $1 billion. Over $20 million is committed to state and local authorities to clean up toxic methamphetamine labs. Drugs are the business of the criminal justice system. The United States incarcerates more of its citizens than almost any other nation and the financial costs are staggering. At the end of 1998 more than 1.8 million Americans were incarcerated; one in every 117 men in the United States was incarcerated. Including parolees, there are almost 300,000 felons under California Department of Corrections jurisdiction alone. When one considers the relationship between violent crime and drug use and property crime and drug use, the resulting picture is numbing.

In addition to the highly visible criminal justice–related costs, numerous other institutions are affected. Housing, welfare, education, and health care provide excellent examples of critical institutions struggling to overcome the strain of drug-related impacts. In addition, annual loss of productivity in the workplace exceeds well over $100 billion per year. Alcoholism, alone, causes 500 million lost workdays each year. Add to this the demographic shifts caused by people fleeing drug-impacted neighborhoods, schools, and businesses, and one soon realizes that there is no victimless public or private institution. Housing and welfare departments struggle to distinguish between drug-related and nondrug-related assistance requests. Educational systems struggle to counter the availability of drugs and its associated victimization and fear. Teachers struggle to overcome the time sacrificed to drug-related disruptive behavior. Health-care systems struggle to treat drug-exposed newborns, at annual estimates of between 375,000 and 739,000 infants. Prenatal exposure to polydrug use exacts tremendous costs, and no amount of debating, arguing, or denying the specific cause-and-effect scenarios really means much in the face of reality. Language acquisition delay, regardless of the degree to which it can be mitigated, is expensive. And it is just one of many problems that may arise when a child is exposed prenatally to drugs. Add injured, drug-related accident and crime victims, along with demands produced by a growing population of intravenous-drug users infected with AIDS, and a failing health-care system frighteningly appears. A universally affordable health-care plan capable of addressing drug-related impacts of such vast medical consequences may not be possible. Health-care costs from drug-related ills are overwhelming. One of every $5 that Medicaid spends on hospital care is attributable to substance abuse.

It should be emphasized that the social costs exacted by drug use infiltrate every aspect of public and private life. The implications for thousands of families struggling with the adverse effects of drug-related woes may prove the greatest and most tragic of social costs. Children who lack emotional support, self-esteem, role models, a safe and secure environment, economic opportunity, and an education because of a parent on drugs suggest costs difficult to comprehend.

As you read the following articles, consider the costs associated with legal and illegal drugs. However, before joining the debate on which is the greater harbinger of pain and suffering, consider the diversity of impacts to which legal and illegal drugs contribute. Combining pharmacological, environmental, legal, and the multitude of other factors influencing drug-related impacts with cause-and-effect propositions soon produces a quagmire of major proportions. Although it is tempting to generalize while considering and lamenting the impacts of drug use on our society, it seldom produces the most salient observations. An incremental approach to assessing drug-related impacts and costs may produce a greater understanding of how to measure social costs than an attempt to make a case for a combination of impacts generated because of issues such as the legal status of a drug. For example, annual alcohol-related deaths far exceed those related to cocaine, but to say the reason for alcohol's disproportionate toll stems solely from alcohol's legal status is shortsighted. Certainly, the legality of a drug will enter the process of assessing drug-related impacts and their causes, but it is still just one component within an equation of many.

Lastly, as you read and think about the different articles in this unit, keep in mind the pervasiveness of drug-related impacts affecting American families. Subsequent reflection reveals that we don't just "change schools," "move to a different town," or flee drug-related issues, and that the most critical component of defense against drug ills, the family, is the most mercilessly pursued target. Most people recognize that the world's most powerful institutions merely buy time in hopes that family institutions will come together, endure, and prevail against drugs.

129

The wrong race, committing crime, doing drugs, and maladjusted for motherhood: the nation's fury over "crack babies"

Enid Logan

Introduction

DURING THE 1990S, WOMEN WHO USE ILLICIT drugs during pregnancy became the subject of intense public attention and social stigmatization. They are regarded as incapable of responsible decision-making, morally deviant, and increasingly, unfit for motherhood. In recent years, the civil courts have terminated the parental rights of thousands of women whose infants tested positive for drug exposure at birth (Beckett, 1995). Women have also faced criminal prosecution for prenatal drug use, under statutes including criminal child abuse, neglect, manslaughter, and delivering substances to a minor. For the most part, the women targeted by the courts and the media have been black, poor, and addicted to crack cocaine (Roberts, 1991; Krauss, 1991; Beckett, 1995; Neuspiel et al., 1994; Greene, 1991).

I argue here that the phenomenon of the "crack-baby" is not produced simply by a tragic interaction between illicit substances and a growing fetus. The "crack-baby," rather, has resulted from a broader conjunction of practices and ideologies associated with race, gender, and class oppression, including the war on drugs and the discourse of fetal rights. In the late 1980s and early 1990s, the image of trembling, helpless infants irrevocably damaged by their mothers' irresponsible actions became a potent symbol of all that was wrong with the poor, the black, and the new mothers in the post-women's movement, post-civil rights era. Crack-babies provided society with a powerful iconography of multiple social deviance (nonmarital sexuality, criminality, drug addiction, aberrant maternal behavior), perpetrated upon the most innocent, by the least innocent: women who are in fact "shameless" and "scandalous" (Irwin, 1995).

Below I will discuss the issue of prenatal substance abuse, focusing on women addicted to crack and their children. As I will illustrate, the social, legal, and political trends that comprise the nation's response to this problem have been largely inspired by racial, gendered, and socioeconomic imperatives, rather than by the blind hand of justice.

The Media and the Crack-Baby in the Popular Imagination

In the 1980s, a crack cocaine epidemic exploded in the U.S., sweeping through low-income black communities with a vengeance (Roberts, 1991). Perceiving a dramatic rise in the number of boarder babies and children born to women abusing drugs, the media began to present the public with reports on a drug like no other, crack, and on appearance of a "different" kind of child—the crack-baby. The narrative of the crack-baby interwove specific messages about crack, pregnant addicts, and crack-exposed children. Crack cocaine, journalists wrote, was a drug like no other previously on the streets. Crack was more potent, more addictive, and more likely to lead its users to acts of violence, crime, and desperation.

Among its most desperate and debased users were pregnant women. One of the most harmful effects of crack was said to be that it literally destroyed the maternal instinct in the women who used it (Irwin, 1995; Hopkins, 1990; Appel, 1992; Elshtain, 1990; Debettencourt, 1990). Utterly irresponsible and incompetent, addicted mothers were seen as "inhuman threats to the social order" who willingly tortured their helpless fetuses (Irwin, 1995: 635). One California doctor was quoted as saying, "with every hit the mother plays Russian roulette with the baby's brain" (Hopkins, 1990: 108). Only concerned with feeding their addictions, mothers on crack were said to be incapable of taking care of their children or even caring about the irreparable harm that smoking crack would do to their unborn fetuses. A Rolling Stone article reported that the crack epidemic had left some social service workers "nostalgic" for the heroin mothers who "could buy groceries occasionally and give the kid a bath." "Crack," on the other hand, "leaves nothing to chance. It makes babies that only a mother could love, and wipes out that love as well" (Ibid.: 71).

The press often spoke of the frustration or anger that many health care workers felt toward pregnant addicts. The Economist, for example reported that:

> Heartbreaking as it is for the doctors and nurses who care for the babies [to see them suffer]… they find it even more distressing to return the babies to mothers for whom drugs remain the dominant feature of life (Economist, April 1, 1989: 28).

In a 1990 People magazine interview, Katherine Jorgensen, head nurse in the neonatal intensive care unit at Boston City Hospital, explained that the hardest part of her job "is when new mothers come to look in on their children." Seeing women come to visit their babies "with their pimps" or "while they are high," she said, made her "want to slug them" (Plummer and Brown, 1990: 85).

In the eyes of the media, the inhumane actions of addicted mothers often produced children who were almost beyond the pale of humanity. Crack-exposed babies were "supposedly doomed to a life of suboptimal intelligence, uncontrollable behavior, and criminal tendencies" (Neuspiel et al., 1994: 47). According to People, some crack-babies "shake so badly they rub their limbs raw" (Plummer and Brown, 1990: 85). In Rolling Stone we read, "During a crying jag their rigid little arms flap about, which makes them even more frantic: They seem to believe their arms belong to someone else, a vicious someone who relentlessly flogs them" (Hopkins, 1990: 71). Pictures of children who tested positive for exposure to drugs at birth most often showed them crying, "shrieking like cats" or staring, bug eyed into space for hours. According to the logic of the crack-baby narrative, the variety of physical and emotional problems faced by these children could be attributed to a single cause: prenatal exposure to crack cocaine (Greider, 1995; Griffith, 1992).

Children exposed to crack in the womb, it was reported, were likely to suffer from any number of serious medical conditions. Among the most frequently cited were cerebral hemorrhaging and intercranial lesions, prematurity, birth defects, genitourinary and cardiac abnormalities, prenatal strokes, heart attacks or death, fine motor disorders, low birth weight, and neonatal growth retardation (Hopkins, 1990; Sexton, 1993; Hoffman, 1990; Plummer and Brown, 1990;

Langone, 1988; Zitella, 1996). Fetal exposure to cocaine was also said to greatly increase the risk of postnatal neurological complications, such as extreme sensitivity to external stimuli, unpredictable mood swings, high-pitched "cat-like" crying, tremulousness, and difficulty interacting with others (Appel, 1992; Sexton, 1993; Hopkins, 1990; Economist, April 1, 1989). Even in the mildest cases, crack-exposed children would likely suffer grave emotional and cognitive abnormalities. Crack babies, we read, were generally unable to concentrate, prone toward violence and destructive behavior, and were averse to light, touch, and affection (Zitella, 1996; Hopkins, 1990).

From the inner cities, a new breed of child was being produced, one that was loveless, tortured, and demented. In the words of one pediatric researcher, "You can't tell what makes these children happy or sad. They are like automatons" (Hopkins, 1990: 72; emphasis added). Even in the "best case scenario" crack-exposed children were somehow fundamentally "different" from the rest of us— somehow less human. As Doctor Judy Howard told Newsweek, "in crack-babies the part of the brains that makes us a human being, capable of discussion or reflection has been wiped out" (Greider, 1995: 54). Similarly, another piece asserted that crack cocaine "robbed [exposed] children of 'the central core of what it is to be human'" (Irwin, 1995: 633).

Worst of all, the damage done to these children by their crack-smoking mothers was believed to be permanent and irreparable. In the chilling words of one journalist, "crack damages fetuses like no other drug… [and] the damage the drug causes… doesn't go away" (Hopkins, 1990: 68). Though the press was generally sympathetic to the plight of crack-exposed children, it typically portrayed them as damaged goods, largely beyond hope or salvation, and damned by the actions of their irresponsible mothers. One article read "for [some] people this is truly a lost generation, and neither love nor money is ever going to change that…. Love can't make a damaged brain whole" (Ibid.: 68–69).

State Response to Prenatal Cocaine Use: Prosecute and Terminate

The moral indignation, shock, and pity that such media imagery aroused in the American public were accompanied by an aggressive state response. Policy initiatives addressing the crack-baby phenomenon have been concentrated in the legal and social service arenas.

Legal Prosecution of Pregnant Addicts

In the later part of the 1980s, the country witnessed the emergence of a new and unprecedented legal strategy: the criminal prosecution of pregnant drug addicts. Due to the successful lobbying of the ACLU and medical, health, and women's organizations, no state has passed laws that make prenatal substance abuse an independent crime (Beckett, 1995; Lieb and Sterk-Elifson, 1995; Neil, 1992). Therefore, prosecutors have used "innovative" applications of existing laws to bring cases against pregnant addicts. Women have been charged under statutes for child abuse, neglect, vehicular homicide, encouraging the delinquency of a minor, involuntary manslaughter, drug trafficking, failure to provide child support, and assault with a deadly weapon (Mariner, Glantz, and Annas, 1990; Beckett, 1995; Sexton, 1993; Paltrow, 1990; Roberts, 1991; Greene, 1991).

In July 1989, Jennifer Johnson, a poor, 23-year-old African-American woman, became the first person convicted in the U.S. for giving birth to a drug-exposed infant. She was charged and found guilty of delivery of a controlled substance to a minor. Florida prosecutor Jeff Deen argued that this had taken place in the 30 to 90 seconds after the birth of the infant and before the cutting of the umbilical chord (Dobson and Eby, 1992).

Johnson received a 15-year sentence, including 14 years of probation, strict supervision during the first year, mandatory drug treatment, random drug testing, and mandatory educational and vocational training (Sexton, 1993; Logli, 1990; Neil, 1992). Johnson was further prohibited from "consuming alcohol, socializing with anyone who possessed drugs, and going to a bar without first receiving consent from her probation officer" (Sexton, 1993: 413). The court also ruled that if Johnson ever intended to again become pregnant, she must inform her probation officer and enroll in an intensive "judicially approved" prenatal care program (Logli, 1990; Sexton, 1993). Under Florida state law, she could have received a 30-year prison sentence (Curriden, 1990). Prosecutor Deen believed that prosecution "was the only way to stop her from using cocaine" and that Johnson "had used up all her chances" (Ibid.: 51). The case, Deen claimed, served to send the message "that this community cannot afford to have two or three cocaine babies from the same person."

Another highly publicized case was that of Kimberly Ann Hardy, also a poor, single young black woman addicted to crack cocaine. Hardy's case first came to the attention of the Department of Social Services in Muskegon County, Michigan, when the local hospital reported that her newborn had tested positive for cocaine at birth. Hardy's urine was tested for drugs because she had been identified as a "high-risk pregnancy" upon admission to the hospital: she had received no prenatal care and delivered six to eight weeks early (Hoffman, 1990).

Eleven days after she left the hospital, county prosecutor Tony Tague ordered Hardy arrested on the charge of delivering drugs in the amount of less than 50 grams—one generally used in prosecuting drug dealers (Ibid.). Though Hardy's case did not result in a conviction,

district attorney Tague felt that the prosecution served to fulfill several important goals: it got Hardy into treatment and gave other pregnant crack addicts a strong warning to get clean or face jail and the loss of their children. Muskegon County Sergeant Van Hemert stated that adopting the hard line in prosecuting mothers is "a form of caring." Speaking with anger that many seem to hold toward pregnant addicts, he adds: "If the mother wants to smoke crack and kill herself I don't care. Let her die, but don't take that poor baby with her" (Ibid.: 34, emphasis added).

These two cases are fairly typical. The prosecutors are white males, the defendants are young black women, the drug is crack, and the rationale is safeguarding the health of babies. By 1992, 24 states had brought criminal charges against women for use of illicit drugs while pregnant. All of the defendants in these cases were poor and most were nonwhite (Beckett, 1995; Lieb and Sterk-Elifson, 1995). Nearly all of the convictions obtained in criminal prosecutions for perinatal substance abuse have been overturned (including Jennifer Johnson's), on the grounds that the charges against the defendants were not congruent with legislative intent (Beckett, 1995; Logli, 1990). Despite this fact, district attorneys continue to bring pregnant women up on criminal charges for substance abuse. As Beckett (1995: 603) has stated, "the continuation of these efforts reflects their political utility in our cultural climate."

Polls taken in the last few years have found that a large and growing proportion of the American public (71% in one survey) believes that women who use drugs while pregnant should be held criminally liable (Curriden, 1990; Sexton, 1993; Hoffman, 1990). The prosecutions of Johnson, Hardy, and others have boosted the careers of the attorneys who put them on trial, who some have heralded as "crusaders" in the war against drugs.

"Protective Incarceration"

Protective incarceration is another legal tactic that is becoming increasingly popular (Appel, 1992). In these cases, judges send pregnant women convicted of charges unrelated to their drug use to jail to "protect" their fetuses. At the 1988 sentencing of a pregnant addict convicted of writing bad checks, the judge stated: I'm going to keep her locked up until that baby is born because she's tested positive for cocaine.... She's apparently an addictive personality, and I'll be darned if I'm going to have a baby born that way (Roberts, 1991: 1431, fn. 55).

Other addicts have been sent to jail for violations of their probation, in lieu of a probationary sentence, or for longer periods than is standard (Lieb and Sterk-Elifson, 1995; Schroedel, Reith, and Peretz, 1995; Appel, 1992).

Hospital Policy

Currently, at least 13 states require that public hospitals test women "suspected" of drug abuse and that they report those who test positive to social services or the police (Sexton, 1993). As in the Hardy case, mandatory reporting is often what triggers prosecution. Yet, drug screening conducted at public hospitals regularly takes place without women's consent or their being informed of possible legal ramifications.

In South Carolina, one hospital's testing and reporting policy (which stipulated that the police be notified of positive prenatal drug toxicologies) landed it a three million dollar lawsuit on the grounds that it violated patients' civil rights and discriminated on the basis of class and color. At the Medical University of South Carolina in Charleston, six lower-income women (five black and one white) who tested positive for drug use were "taken out of their hospital beds, handcuffed, and sent to jail without their babies" within days or hours after delivery (Furio, 1994: 93). At least one of the women "arrived at the jail still bleeding from the delivery; she was told to sit on a towel" (Paltrow, 1990: 41). The white woman was "detained for three weeks, put into a choke hold, and shackled by police during her eighth month of pregnancy... then placed against her will in a psychiatric hospital" (Furio, 1994: 93).

In September 1994, the case ended with a settlement and the requirement that the hospital abandon its practices. By that time, however, several hundred women had faced criminal prosecution under the reporting policy. Further, many other states continue to bring criminal or civil charges against women on the basis of drug tests performed without their consent.

Social Services—Unfit for Motherhood

The most frequent penalty for a mother's prenatal drug use is permanent or temporary removal of the newborn and/or other children. Based upon the results of drug screening, infants may be removed from their mothers right after birth, often without trial or hearing (Young, 1995). In today's political climate "positive neonatal toxicologies raise strong presumption of parental unfitness" (Roberts, 1991: 1431). Increasingly, civil courts agree that prenatal use of drugs constitutes neglect and is sufficient evidence for termination of parental rights (Beckett, 1995). In the last decade, literally thousands of women have permanently lost custody of their children as a result of their addiction. Upon appeal, the lower and appellate family courts have generally upheld these decisions (Ibid.).

Representative Kerry Patrick of Kansas introduced legislation that would require female addicts to have Noroplant capsules inserted in their arms or else go to jail. Patrick says of his plan: "I've gotten a lot of support from nurses who deal with crack-babies. Once you see one, you don't care about the rights of the mother" (Willwerth, 1991: 62). Others echo his anger. One employee of the Los Angeles County Department of Health says: "Damn it, babies are dying out there!... You get someone with a terrible family history, stoned, no parenting skills—and we keep giving back her babies because we don't want to look racist or sexist" (Ibid.: 62).

Assumptions Behind the Crack-Baby Narrative and Punitive Treatment of Addicted Women

The intensity of legal, civil, and journalistic activity centering on babies born addicted to crack cocaine has been undergirded by three main sets of assumptions: about the effects of crack cocaine on fetal and child development, about the pregnant addicts targeted by the courts and the press, and about the efficacy of prosecution and punishment. The following section explores each of these assumptions and shows that despite their power, they are not substantiated by empirical evidence. Their tenacity comes not from their basis in fact, but from their ideological resonance with popular beliefs about drugs, crime, race, and motherhood.

The Medical Effects of Crack Cocaine on Fetal Health

The first assumption fueling the crack-baby scare is that crack is far more dangerous to fetal health than any other drug. As new evidence has emerged in the last five to six years, it has become apparent that early reports as to the impact of crack cocaine on fetal development were grossly exaggerated, and that what was painted as the norm is most likely the worst-case scenario. Perhaps the primary shortcoming of the early research was that it failed to disentangle the effects of cocaine from the effects of other chemical and environmental factors (Appel, 1992; Greider, 1995; Science News, November 19, 1991; Gittler and McPherson, 1990; Neuspiel, Markowitz, and Drucker, 1994). This was a particularly serious flaw given the population of drug users under study. Women who use crack are more likely to smoke cigarettes, drink alcohol, use other drugs, and to be malnourished; they are also less likely to obtain adequate prenatal care (Greider, 1995; Feldman et al., 1992; Griffith, 1992; Appel, 1992; Debettencourt, 1990; Neuspiel, Markowitz and Drucker, 1994). Each of these factors has been documented to seriously impair fetal development—in the absence of cocaine (Appel, 1992; Neuspiel, Markowitz, and Drucker, 1994; Science News, November 19, 1991; American Journal of Nursing, May 1995).

Moreover, the presence of post-natal risk factors has also confounded the results of many studies. Cocaine-exposed children, like many poor black American children, are exposed to a higher-than-average level of violence, neglect, and abuse in their daily environments. Some scientists claim that "the social context of crack cocaine use, or more commonly polydrug use, is more likely to be related to the poor medical and developmental outcomes than to the actual drug exposure of the fetus" (Lieb and Sterk-Elifson, 1995: 690; emphasis added).

Despite these and other shortcomings, it was fairly easy for researchers to get this type of research published; conversely, it has been difficult to publicize findings that crack's effects on fetal development were minimal or nil (Greider, 1995; Pollitt, 1990; Beckett, 1995). Scientists whose work refuted the alarmist findings of the earliest published reports on crack cocaine and fetal development were often confronted with the disbelief, censure, and anger of their colleagues. In the words of one researcher, "I'd never experienced anything like this.... I've never had people accuse me of making up data or being an incompetent scientist or believing in drug abuse" (Greider, 1995: 54).

Dr. Ira Chasnoff has been a leading scientist in the field of prenatal cocaine exposure research since 1985. When Dr. Chasnoff recognized that his research was primarily being used to stigmatize and punish the women and children for whom he considered himself an advocate, however, he was appalled. In 1992, he stated that on average, crack-exposed children "are no different from other children growing up." Indicating his disgust with the popular rhetoric on "crack-babies," Dr. Chasnoff added, "they are not the retarded imbeciles people talk about.... As I study the problem more and more, I think the placenta does a better job protecting the child than we do as a society" (Sullum, 1992: 14).

Developmental psychologist Dan Griffith (formerly a member of Chasnoff's research group) has also sought to rectify the misimpressions concerning "crack-babies" so prevalent in the public imagination. Griffith notes that the most common assumptions about crack-kids—"(1) that all cocaine-exposed children are severely affected, (2) that little can be done for them, and (3) that all the medical, behavioral, and learning problems exhibited by these children are caused directly by their exposure to cocaine"—are false. Dr. Griffith cautions that far too little research has been conducted to allow scientists "to make any firm statement about the long-term prognosis" for cocaine-exposed children (Griffith, 1992: 30). However, his own research indicates that with early intervention and the reduction of other risk factors, most coke-exposed children "seem completely normal with regard to intellectual, social, emotional, and behavioral development though age three" (Ibid.: 31).[1]

Recent studies, which attempt to "smoke out" crack's unique impact on fetal development, tend to agree that cocaine increases the risk of low birth weight and prematurity in infants (Greider, 1995; Feldman et al., 1992; Barone, 1994; Beckett, 1995). Scientists have also found that receiving adequate prenatal care and curtailing drug usage significantly improves developmental outcomes for cocaine-exposed infants (Appel, 1992; Griffith, 1992). The extent to which cocaine alone causes neurobehavioral and other abnormalities is still up for debate. However, the consensus is that the average harm posed to infants by cocaine is far less than previously feared. Prematurity and low birth weight are indeed dangerous conditions for an infant and each significantly contributes to the high rates of infant mortality and morbidity among African-Americans.[2] Yet these two primary effects are a far cry from the cranial hemorrhages, severe retardation, and lack of "human" qualities said to be typical of children born exposed to crack cocaine.

Current evidence also suggests that the effects of crack are not so different from those of tobacco or some other common street drugs. Comparison of scientific data on the effects of several chemical factors on fetal development demonstrates that the selection of pregnant crack-addicts in particular for censure and prosecution "has a discriminatory impact that cannot be medically justified" (Roberts, 1991: 1435). It may make no more sense, then, to speak about "crack-babies" than it does to speak of "cigarette-babies," "pot-babies," or "speed-babies." Most crack-exposed children will not suffer permanent pharmacologically induced brain damage and are not, medically speaking, beyond "hope." Whatever developmental delays or antisocial behavior they appear to express in later life may have more to do with poisons in their postnatal environment than in the fetal one.

Pregnant Addicts Targeted by Courts

The crack-baby mythology is also powerfully buttressed by a set of assumptions and stereotypes concerning the pregnant addicts who have been targeted by the courts and the media. Despite popular mythology to the contrary, empirical evidence shows that rates of prenatal drug use are consistent across race and class lines (Neuspiel et al., 1994; Lieb and Sterk-Elifson, 1995; Beckett, 1995; Appel, 1992). Stated otherwise, white middle-class women are no less likely to abstain from the use of illicit substances during pregnancy than are poor minority women. Ira Chasnoff's 1989 study of patterns of prenatal drug use and reporting policies in Pinellas County, Florida, clearly documented this trend.

In a toxicological screen for evidence of alcohol, marijuana, cocaine, and/or opiate use, 14.8% of women in the study tested positive overall. Chasnoff found that "there was little difference in the percentage of drug detection between women seen in public clinics (16.3) and those seen in private offices (13.1), or between blacks (14.1) and whites (15.4)" (Neuspiel, 1996: 48). There were, however, significant racial differences in the drug of choice. A higher percentage of pregnant black women (7.8) used cocaine than did pregnant white women (1.8);

and pregnant white women (14.4) evidenced significantly higher usage of marijuana than their black counterparts (6.0). A more striking finding of the study concerned the discrepancy in the rates of reporting. In the state of Florida, health care providers are required by law to report both marijuana and cocaine use to authorities. Chasnoff discovered that "despite similar levels of use, black women were reported at 10 times the rate for white women" and that poorer women were reported more often than middle-class women were (Ibid.: 48, emphasis added).

If not substance abuse rates themselves, then what explains the overwhelming race/class discrepancy in reporting and prosecution of prenatal drug use? This discrepancy has its roots in the fact that "the process in which pregnant women are suspected of substance abuse, diagnosed, and prosecuted is suffused with enormous discretion" (Lieb and Sterk-Elifson, 1995: 691). As the data indicate, this discretion quite often translates into pernicious discrimination along lines of race and class.

The Health Care Profession: Should We Test? Should We Report?

There are many loci where discretion is exercised and discrimination occurs. It begins with the decision whether to test a woman for substance use. State guidelines for mandatory reporting and testing are often vague and underspecified, leaving the implementation of policies up to individual doctors, clinics, or hospitals. The criteria for determining likelihood of prenatal drug use vary tremendously, but most "risk factors" are associated with socioeconomic status (Beckett, 1995) and race. Physicians often decide whether to order a newborn urine screen based upon whether the mother received timely and adequate prenatal care. Since black women as a group "are twice as likely as white women to begin prenatal care late or not at all" (Krauss, 1991: 528), and poor women are often unable to afford adequate prenatal care, this testing criterion tends to discriminate by both race and by class.

Health care providers also may act upon the basis of straightforward prejudice. As Krauss (Ibid.: 527) writes, suspicions of substance abuse may be informed by stereotyped assumptions about the identities of drug addicts.... [These stereotypes are] reinforced by studies in medical journals which list, with questionable accuracy, the characteristics of those presumed to be at risk.

Florida's reporting policy "does not require documentation of maternal drug use, but only a 'reasonable cause to suspect it'" (Ibid.: 527). Therefore, regardless of actual drug history, all women who appear to "fit the profile" are at risk of being subjected to particular scrutiny by social services and the police.

The fact that most testing is conducted at public hospitals that service low-income communities also means that poor women of color are more likely to face drug screening than are women protected by race and class privilege. In private hospitals, pregnant women are usually not tested for drug use, even if drug use is suspected (Beckett, 1995). Furthermore, even if they present a positive drug toxicology or admit drug use to their physicians, most women seen in private facilities are not reported to the authorities. Prenatal drug use by women who are affluent and/or white may often be viewed by private and public physicians as an exception, a lapse in judgment, or as incidental. Prenatal drug use by poor black women, however, is often viewed as endemic, typical, and evidence of their unfitness for motherhood.

Prosecutorial Discretion

Once prenatal drug use is reported, the authorities must then decide what, if any, course of action to take. Dwight Green argues that the unchecked discretion of prosecutors, who are overwhelmingly white and male, means that prenatal drug cases are often based not upon "unbiased law enforcement," but on "pluralistic ignorance" and race, gender, and class discrimination (Greene, 1991). Prosecutors must first decide what statutes, if any, apply to the offense at hand. As mentioned, prosecutors brought prenatal drug abuse trials into existence by stretching the interpretations of existing laws.

Having found an appropriate statute under which to press charges, prosecutors then decide whether to take a given case to trial. There are many intervening factors that go into this decision, often colored by considerations of race and class. Women who drink alcohol or ingest marijuana are quite unlikely to face criminal sanctions for prenatal drug use, even when they are reported to the police (Hoffman, 1990). Greene (1991: 745, fn. 28) writes,

If long-term harm to children was the triggering event, this would present the unlikely image of affluent pregnant white women being subject to arrest at their country clubs or in the suburban home of a friend for having a drink.

The relative influence of a potential defendant may also influence the decision whether to press charges. Suspects in "white collar" crimes, for example, are often able to: hire well-paid criminal defense lawyers with social, political, and professional access to the prosecutor's office to argue at case screening conferences against instituting criminal charges or to lessen the seriousness of the crimes to be charged (Ibid.: 755).

Even after initiating a criminal case, the prosecutor still has the option to discontinue prosecution. Although prosecuting a poor black crack-addict can boost a district attorney's reelection chances, taking an expectant socialite to trial for popping a handful of barbiturates with a glass of wine may only bring him embarrassment or ridicule.

The Efficacy of Criminal Punishment

The oft-repeated rationales for taking punitive action against pregnant substance abusers are to force them to enter drug treatment and to safeguard the health of their fetuses. The reality is that taking such action does not ensure, and may often be counterproductive to, the realization of these goals.

Threatening women with jail time in no way ensures that treatment services appropriate for pregnant addicts will be available (Beckett, 1995). One of the great ironies of the criminalization of prenatal drug use is that as a "general rule," substance abuse programs do not accept pregnant women (Sexton, 1993). A 1989 study of 78 treatment programs in New York City found that 54% refused all pregnant women, 67% refused pregnant women on Medicaid, and 87% would not accept pregnant women on Medicaid who were addicted to crack (Appel, 1992; Hoffman, 1990; Roberts, 1991). Few addiction programs provide prenatal or obstetrical care and therefore most turn women away rather than risk treatment without these services (Lieb and Sterk-Elifson, 1995; Roberts, 1991).

Drug treatment programs designed primarily to serve men can also be alienating and ineffective for women. Appel (1992: 141) writes, "most treatment approaches are based on the characteristics and dynamics among male populations and comparatively little has been done to define the unique nature of addiction to women." Many female addicts, for example, "turned to drugs because they were sexually abused or raped as children, and they need help repairing the damage" (Willwerth, 1991: 63). According to one estimate, 80 to 90% of female alcoholics and drug addicts have been victims of rape or incest (Paltrow, 1990). A program that does not address the special issues facing pregnant addicts will doubtlessly have high rates of withdrawal and relapse. Yet the focus on punishment has generally not been accompanied by a correspondingly intense drive to increase the availability of services geared toward the needs of pregnant addicts.[3]

Instituting criminal sanctions for perinatal substance abuse is also counterproductive to the goal of helping women and children because it serves to deter pregnant addicts from seeking medical attention. Medical evidence (cited above) indicates that receiving adequate prenatal care and/or curtailing drug consumption can significantly improve developmental outcomes for cocaine-exposed infants. Yet many women will avoid seeking the information and treatment they need if they realize that a positive urine screen could result in their children being placed in foster care or land them in jail (Krauss, 1991).[4]

Putting women in jail for evidence of drug use upon delivery will not undo whatever harm was done to their newborns in utero. Sending women to prison while pregnant is unlikely to ensure the health of their fetuses either. While incarcerated, pregnant women "face conditions hazardous to fetal health, including overcrowding, poor nutrition, and exposure to contagious disease" (Ibid.: 537). Prison health facilities generally provide little or no prenatal care and are ill-equipped to handle the medical needs of pregnant women, especially those with drug histories. Like other inmates, pregnant addicts may also be able to obtain illegal drugs while imprisoned (Paltrow, 1990; Schroedel and Peretz, 1995). Moreover, if the supply of drugs is suddenly cut off, the physiological changes that immediate withdrawal brings about in the mother and the fetus can be dangerous to the health of both (Schroedel and Peretz, 1995; Appel, 1992).

Criminalizing prenatal substance abuse punishes women for failing to obtain treatment that is generally unavailable and may prevent them from seeking prenatal care. Because of the harm that it is likely to cause, prominent sectors of the medical community have taken a stand against this policy. In a paper published in 1988, the American Medical Association stated that:

> the current policy of prosecuting women who use drugs during pregnancy is irrational because it does not further the state's purpose of preventing harm to infants…. [D]rug addiction is an illness, which like any illness, is not due simply to a failure of individual willpower (Lieb and Sterk-Elifson, 1995: 693).

Similarly, in 1991, the American Nurses Association characterized the imposition of criminal sanctions against pregnant addicts as "extreme, inappropriate, and ineffective" (Sexton, 1993:420–421).

Race, Crime, Drugs, Motherhood

If, as I have argued, the three primary sets of assumptions that have rationalized prosecuting crack-addicted mothers are false, then what is this really about? If not the neutral exercise of justice, what is the driving force behind the imposition of criminal sanctions for prenatal drug use? Why are prosecutors, judges, the press, and much of the American public now so eager to demonize and imprison drug-addicted mothers? Why is it that crack addicts and poor black women are targeted for reproach and condemnation? If it does not help mothers or protect their babies, what societal goal does punishing pregnant addicts serve?

The crack-baby phenomenon, it seems, has arisen from a particular confluence of contemporary ideas about race, crime, drugs, and motherhood. These ideas and practices have their most proximate roots in the Reagan/Bush era "war on drugs" and the discourse on "fetal rights." In each of these discourses, the civil rights of "offenders" (pregnant women or drug users/dealers) are increasingly seen as an impediment to the realization of social justice (Mariner, Glantz, and Annas, 1990; Willwerth, 1991; Krauss, 1991).

War on Drugs: War on Communities of Color

The late 1980s witnessed the emergence of an aggressive anti-drug crusade, waged on several fronts. This crusade defined as criminal the use and sale of illicit substances. The federal government appropriated millions of dollars in public monies for the pursuit, arrest, and conviction of dealers and users (Beckett, 1995; Irwin, 1995). In response to federal initiatives, state legislatures wrote tougher drug laws and imposed stiffer penalties for their violation. The courts, in turn, sent more and more drug offenders to jail, for longer terms. Currently, one-third of the state prison population is composed of individuals convicted on drug-related charges (Beckett, 1995). The United States now has the highest incarceration rate in the world, with .4 percent of its population behind bars at any given time (Neuspiel et al., 1994).

Besides law enforcement, special interest groups, politicians, and news agencies turned their attention to the evils of illicit substances (Irwin, 1995). Through the popular press, these groups articulated "a language of intolerance and a rhetoric of contempt" for those who used drugs (Ibid.: 632). Pregnant addicts were subject to special scorn in the media and viewed as particularly deficient in morals (Ibid.; Lieb and Sterk-Elifson, 1995). According to the discursive arm of the war on drugs, increasing rates of drug usage were somehow responsible for much of the social disorder, moral decay, poverty, and decadence of the late 20th century.

Not all drugs received equal attention in the war on drugs: crack most firmly captured the nation's imagination. With crack's emergence in the mid-1980s, journalists "bombarded the public with frightening images of crack cocaine as a unique 'demon drug' different from any other… highly potent, instantly addictive, and conducive to systemic violence and moral decadence" (Lieb and Sterk-Elifson, 1995: 687). Crack cocaine was declared Time magazine's "issue of the year" in 1986 (Time, September 22, 1986). According to Newsweek, the devastation wrought by crack was "as newsworthy as the Vietnam War, the fall of Nixon's presidency, and the American civil rights movement" (Irwin, 1995: 633). With the issue of crack-babies, the war on drugs and the media's sensationalistic stories reached new heights.

Despite the sudden burst of alarmist press and the appearance of the war on drugs, the overall prevalence of drug use in the U.S. did not increase in the 1980s (Beckett, 1995). What did occur during this period was that "the practice of smoking cocaine, formerly restricted to the middle and upper-classes, spread into the inner-city with the increased availability of [crack], a new, less expensive form of smokable cocaine" (Ibid.: 599). The war on drags received its greatest intensity and its moral urgency from the fact that a new drug had found its way to the "lower colored classes."

Periods of public alarm over the drug use of nonwhites have occurred repeatedly throughout the social history of the United States. During these drug scares, "'moral entrepreneurs' seek to blame a wide variety of social problems on chemical substances and those who imbibe them" (Ibid.: 597). In the 1870s, whites in California claimed that the state's economic depression could be attributed to the presence of Chinese immigrants and, in particular, to their usage of opium. The image of opium-smoking Chinese in this period "became synonymous with immorality and depravity" (Ibid.: 598). Such racist scapegoating led to the passage of laws that made the use of opium illegal for Chinese-Americans, but not for those defined as white (Neuspiel et al., 1994).

In the 1930s, anti-Mexican sentiment was successfully exploited in the campaign to criminalize marijuana. Many whites in this period believed that "reefer mad Mexican bandits" were largely to blame for the era's skyrocketing rates of unemployment and general social upheaval (Ibid.; Beckett, 1995). Several decades earlier, Jews and Italians were believed to be threats to the moral character of the nation due to their predisposition toward drug addiction (Neuspiel et al., 1994). At the turn of the century, the fear of "the cocainized black" coincided with Southern attempts to strip African-Americans of the political and social gains of the Reconstruction era. The racially motivated anti-drug crusades of the previous 100-odd years share much in common with the war on drugs of the 1980s and 1990s. As in the past, customary use of a certain drug [has come] to symbolize the difference between [a minority group] and the rest of society…. [It is thought that] eliminating the drug might alleviate social disharmony and preserve the old order (Musto, 1973, as quoted in Neuspiel et al., 1994: 52).

In many respects, the Reagan/Bush-era war on drugs has been a war on communities of color. Racism in current U.S. drug policy is reflected in several arenas. Most notable are the rates of arrest and conviction for drug trafficking and drug usage. Concordant with the Reagan administration's mandate to combat "street crime," law enforcement officials have placed greatest emphasis upon the arrest and conviction of "low-level street dealers," who are disproportionately African American (Beckett, 1995; Neuspiel et al., 1994). Further, though 80% of drug users are white, the majority of those arrested and convicted for drug use are African American (Beckett, 1995). Increased police presence in inner-city neighborhoods, "ostensibly for the drug war—has resulted in a general increase of arrests and terror directed against people of color" (Neuspiel et al., 1994: 49). The rhetoric of "warfare" and portrayal of those who use and sell drugs as immoral social scum has legitimized the escalation of police brutality and harassment in inner-city communities, as well as the abrogation of the civil rights of suspected drug offenders.

Lastly, the tremendous discrepancy in federally mandated minimum sentences for the sale of powder cocaine and for crack (rock cocaine) is a clear manifestation of the targeting of black drug offenders by the U.S. legal system. In 1986, Congress amended the Comprehensive Crime Control Act (CCCA) of 1984, such that gram for gram, mandatory sentences for possession or sale of crack are 100 times greater than those for offenses involving powder cocaine (Neuspiel et al., 1994; Lieb and Sterk-Elifson, 1995). A federal defendant currently faces five years in prison for the sale of 500 grams of powdered cocaine, 100 grams of marijuana, or only five grams of crack. As one scholar has noted, the CCCA constitutes "an excellent example of institutional racism" (Beckett, 1995: 599).

The war on drugs has helped to legitimize the dismantling of the welfare state and the government's abandonment of the poor and the nonwhite. During the 1980s, the polarization of wealth in the United States reached an all time high; while the rich got richer, the poor only got poorer. With the restructuring of the economy and the disappearance of industrial wage labor, unemployment rates soared in urban communities. The income gap was further exacerbated by the Reagan administration's attempt to stimulate the economy by giving tax breaks to businesses while slashing social service programs that might have provided a safety net for disadvantaged Americans (Irwin, 1995).

At this time, anti-drug rhetoric "provided the ideological explanation of why certain segments of the population experienced hardship [while] select privileged groups were amassing more and more wealth" (Ibid.: 632). The message that increasing drug use was responsible for the declining economic and social welfare of the black community diverted attention from the role of factors such as global economic transformations, domestic social policy, and institutional racism (Roberts, 1991; Irwin, 1995; Neuspiel et al., 1994). Politicians found that "criminalizing the poor" was more "politically expedient" than examining the deep social roots of urban problems, creating a national health care system, or investing in the public school system (Beckett, 1995; Neuspiel et al., 1994). Through increased police surveillance and violence, discrimination in drug arrests and sentencing, and locking up pregnant addicts, the U.S. government has waged a war on communities of color and has been able to exert a powerful mechanism of social control over those most likely to rebel against it (Neuspiel et al., 1994).

Fetal Rights—Rescuing Fetuses from Pregnant Women

The second political current that has deeply influenced the nation's response to the problem of prenatal drug use is the fetal rights movement. Improvements in scientific knowledge and technology provided the medical foundation for the development of a discourse of fetal rights. In the mid-1800s, doctors began to position themselves as pregnancy experts, wresting control of that domain away from female midwives and pregnant women themselves (Krauss, 1991; Beckett, 1995). As the status and power of the medical profession has increased, so has its tendency to distrust the ability of women to make childbirth and pregnancy decisions on their own (Krauss, 1991). Major advances in biomedical technology in the last 40 years have made it possible to view fetuses in the womb and greatly improved our understanding of fetal developmental needs (Boling, 1995). Yet these developments have also legitimated a vision of the fetus as a "second patient" and reanimated the old patriarchal notion of the mother as "vessel," who merely provides a host environment for the growing embryo (Beckett, 1995; Boling, 1995). Pro-life ideology has contributed considerably to fetal rights discourse as well. The argument that abortion is murder rests upon the notion that the unborn are human beings who should be accorded a moral and legal status equal to that of the mother (Beckett, 1995).

The language of fetal rights implies that pregnancy is an adversarial relationship involving a "conflict of rights between a woman and her fetus" (Ibid.: 593). Advocates of fetal rights assert that the state has an affirmative duty to protect the unborn from potential (or likely) harm at the hands of the mother, and that once a woman has made the decision to carry a pregnancy to term, she should be legally liable for actions that could result in harm (Krauss, 1991; Pollitt, 1990). The image of women as the loving protectors of their unborn has been supplanted by "the image of the negligent mother whose willingness to support her fetus must be enforced by medical and legal professionals" (Beckett, 1995: 597). Once models of self-sacrifice, pregnant women are now believed to be selfish, confused, potentially violent, and incapable of making responsible choices (Pollitt, 1990). In addition, while women are being sent to prison for their alleged crimes against the unborn, "doctors, judges, prosecutors, and politicians are lining up as fetal advocates and authorities" (Beckett, 1995: 588).

Scholars have observed that as the rights of fetuses have expanded, those of mothers have diminished (Pollitt, 1990; Sexton, 1993). Both in and out of the courtroom, fetal rights are seen to take precedence over those of pregnant women. In some cases, the needs or wants of the mother are treated as an impediment to the more legitimate needs of the fetus.

In addition to legitimizing the imprisonment of pregnant drug addicts, fetal rights arguments have been used to force or coerce women into medical treatment. In the name of their unborn children, women have been made to undergo cesarean sections and other obstetrical interventions. The great majority of pregnant women forced to undergo unwanted medical treatment have been poor, nonwhite, or foreign born. According to a national study of women subjected to court-ordered cesarean sections, intrauterine transfusions, or detained in hospitals against their will, 81% were of black, Asian-American, or Latin American descent, and 25% were non-native speakers of English (Krauss, 1991). Doctors and judges may decide whether to override a pregnant woman's medical wishes based in part upon their assessments of her competency. This assessment of competency (like the assessment of likelihood of prenatal drug usage) may often be based upon racial, cultural, and class stereotypes. In one case, when a Bedouin woman, believing that she would die, objected to cesarean delivery, a team of physicians explained that the woman's refusal "resulted from the mother's ignorance and prejudice, which prevented her from arriving at an intelligent decision" (Ibid.: 532).

The concept of fetal rights has been attacked from many angles. The most basic critique is that it violates women's rights during pregnancy, and specifically the right to bodily integrity (in the case of court-ordered medical treatment) and the right to privacy, which includes the decision to bear a child (in the case of pregnant drug addicts) (Krauss, 1991; Garcia and Segalman, 1991; Neil, 1992). During pregnancy, it is argued, fetal rights reduce women to "second-class citizen[s] with constitutional rights inferior to those of men and non-pregnant women" (Krauss, 1991: 539).

Other critiques have been leveled at the very concept of granting rights to fetuses. The centerpiece of the theory of fetal rights is the notion that from the time a woman decides to carry her pregnancy to term, she has a special "duty of care" to her fetus. She must act in such a manner as to ensure the health of her unborn child, or risk legal punishment. The danger in this increasingly prevalent line of argumentation is that, potentially, a pregnant woman could be held legally responsible for any behavior that could harm her fetus. As Lynn Paltrow (1990: 42) of the ACLU points out, "prosecutions of pregnant women cannot be restricted to illegal behaviors because many legal behaviors cause damage to developing babies." In 1980, the Michigan Supreme Court ruled that "a mother who had taken prescription medication for her own health could be held criminally liable for failing to provide 'proper prenatal care'" (Beckett, 1995: 594). Other pregnant women have faced charges for consumption of alcohol, failing to follow doctor's orders, and taking non-prescription valium (Paltrow, 1990; Pollitt, 1990). As long as the rights of fetuses are believed to be morally superior to, and in

fundamental conflict with, those of their mothers, pregnant women who are obese, who take aspirin, travel by air, smoke cigarettes, change their cats' litter boxes, eat junk food, have sex, or fail to stay off their feet "could all be characterized as fetal abusers" (Pollitt, 1990; Schroedel and Peretz, 1995; quote from Paltrow, 1990: 42). In calling for increased governmental regulation of prenatal behavior, the "duty of care" standard seriously threatens to undermine women's reproductive autonomy.

There are many reasons to suspect that "fetal rights" is driven not by a concern for healthy children, but by a desire to control women (Pollitt, 1990). A universe of factors other than maternal behavior can jeopardize fetal health outcomes; but curiously, fetal rights activists have no interest in them. Outrage at pregnant women who use crack has not been accompanied by a corresponding level of outrage at the fact that many do not have health insurance, or that their children will be forced to live in roach-infested housing, or about the fact that many businesses have abandoned the inner cities. Fetal rights advocates have not campaigned for the building of day care centers in low-income communities, to increase the availability of prenatal care to poor mothers, or to expand eligibility for the WIC food vouchers program.

Fetal rights theorists also ignore male behavior. Though a woman's duty to her fetus may be "virtually limitless," the men in their lives have no corresponding duty of care. This is true despite the fact that a partner or spouse's drug abuse may itself contribute to neonatal mortality, low birth weight, learning disabilities, and abnormal newborn behavior (Krauss, 1991; Schroedel and Peretz, 1995).[5] Male battering is also a common and serious threat to fetal health. Approximately one out of 12 women are beaten during pregnancy and pregnant women as a group are more likely than non-pregnant women to be beaten by their partners or spouses (Pollitt, 1990; Schroedel and Peretz, 1995).

Furthermore, men who beat pregnant women often aim their assault directly at the woman's abdominal region, perhaps out of anger at, or jealousy of, the fetus. Battering can cause stillbirths, miscarriages, and other complications. In 1981, Lancet cited a case in which a baby was born "with bruises on its arms, neck, and shoulder, a swollen eye, and intraventricular hemorrhaging," as a result of prenatal battering (Schroedel and Peretz, 1995: 94). The baby subsequently died from its injuries. In 1990, Dianne Pfannenstiel, a pregnant woman from Laramie, Wyoming, went to the police to file a claim against her husband after being beaten severely. The police brought no charges against her husband, yet Pfannenstiel herself was charged with child abuse upon admitting that she had been drinking (Pollitt, 1990; Paltrow, 1990). As Pollitt (1990: 416) writes, "the threat to newborns is interesting only when it can, accurately, or fancifully, be laid at the women's doorstep.... If the mother isn't to blame, no one's to blame." Male violence, malnutrition, lead paint, poverty, and racism, are immaterial to fetal rights advocates because they lie outside of the implicitly patriarchal and racist parameters of the fetal rights discourse.

Devaluation of Black Children and Degradation of Black Motherhood

In evaluating the motivations behind fetal rights actions, we must also consider the history of interactions between the government and their most preferred objects of salvation: poor black children. The record of "overwhelming state neglect" of African-American children casts doubt upon the sincerity of claims that the state is only looking out for their best interests in prosecuting their mothers (Roberts, 1991). Until the 1930s, black children were routinely excluded from eligibility for most child welfare services, including adoption and foster care (Hill, 1977). Currently, the slashing of social service programs, lack of concern about the notoriously high rate of black infant mortality (unless it can be attributed to black women's prenatal drug consumption) and the underfunding of the public school system are indicators of the U.S. government's continuing disregard for black children. Furthermore, the drive to incarcerate rather than to educate black youth and the iconography of fear of black males that dominates popular imagery reveal society's disgust for the teenagers that these children will become.

Implied in the extreme demonization of crack-addicted mothers is the unlikely presumption that in-utero exposure to drugs is the greatest harm that drug-exposed children will face in their lives. Prenatal drug prosecutions allow the government to appear concerned about the welfare of black children "without having to spend any money, change any priorities, or challenge any vested interests" (Pollitt, 1990: 410–411). These prosecutions place the blame for the plight of black children and the black community at the feet of African-American women and absolve the white middle class of responsibility or guilt.

Fetal rights discourse champions the rights of the black unborn, but not those of black children, adolescents, or adults. It is particularly not a discourse of empowerment for black mothers. Fetal rights, in fact, "seeks to punish women who fail to act according to idealized concepts of motherhood" (Beckett, 1995: 589). Women who are poor and nonwhite (or homosexual) are the least able to conform to white middle-class standards of motherhood (Roberts, 1991).

The tendency to blame black women for the problems of the black community has a long history in American society. The most notable example in recent years is the infamous "Moynihan Report." In this 1965 essay, sociologist Daniel Patrick Moynihan argued that domineering, matriarchal black mothers created emasculated black men who would fail in school, abandon their families, and be unable to succeed economically. Patricia Hill Collins writes that the black matriarchy thesis:

> allows the dominant group to blame Black women for the success or failure of Black children... diverts attention from the political and economic inequality affecting Black mothers and children, and suggests that anyone can rise from poverty if he or she only received good values at home (Collins, 1990: 74).

The image of the black matriarch has lately been supplanted by that of the single black mother. With his 1984 book, Losing Ground, sociologist Charles Murray helped to validate stereotypical perceptions of the black "welfare mother" who "breeds" babies in order to increase the size of her government check and to avoid having to work. At the close of the 1990s, such images of black motherhood are as prevalent as ever. Patricia Williams argues that "the signifying power of the black single mother... as poor, drug addicted, and natally absent... is integral to the public articulation of fetal harm and abuse" (Bower, 1995: 144). On television talk shows such as Riki Lake, Jenny Jones, Richard Bey, and Jerry Springer, young women of color are routinely characterized as irrational, immature baby machines, who practice irresponsible sexuality and are scarcely fit for parenthood. Their multiple illegitimate children, it is frequently claimed, place a severe drain on the welfare system and thus heavily burden the nation's economy. According to contemporary imagery, the fertility and sexuality of poor black women are "unnecessary and even dangerous" to the nation (Collins, 1990: 76), and associated with disease, "pollution," and the downfall of Western civilization (Bower, 1995).

In this vein, scholars have argued that what many poor black women are being punished for is not any actual harm done to fetuses, but the crime of getting pregnant while addicted (Paltrow, 1990; Roberts, 1991; Krauss, 1991). It is the addict's decision to carry her pregnancy to term that results in criminal liability (Young, 1995). If she obtained an abortion, or had never been pregnant, there would be no case against her. Further, women who do not habitually engage in prenatal behaviors deemed actionable by the state do not face the prospect of jail upon conception. What appears as outrage that pregnant women use crack, then, is in fact outrage that crack addicts bear children.

According to Roberts (1991: 1472), "the value we place on individuals determines whether we see them as entitled to perpetuate themselves in their children." Like enforced sterilization, fetal endangerment prosecutions reflect society's judgment that poor, addicted African-American women do not deserve to become mothers (Ibid.). American society stigmatizes the pregnancies of all poor black women and it criminalizes those of poor black crack-addicts. In selecting crack-addicts for special punishment, the courts, health care providers, and the press are saying: "We don't particularly need any more of these people or their offspring. They are utterly unfit for motherhood and the damaged, subhuman children they produce will most likely become the nation's financial burden and later its criminal element."

It is curious to note that many of those who lament the tragedy of drug-exposed children apparently care nothing about the tragedy of their mothers. Yet, pregnant women who are drinking excessively, abusing drugs, smoking, or eating inadequately are first and foremost hurting themselves…. In our rush to blame women for their failure to take care of others we are missing the point that they have never been encouraged to "selfishly" care for themselves (Paltrow, 1990: 45).

In deciding that the best way to deal with the problem of drug-addicted babies is not to empower, but to punish their mothers, society is blind to the fact that their fates are inextricably intertwined. Locking a woman behind bars and castigating her in the press does little to prevent her child from having to face the same conditions (poverty, racism, gender oppression, and sexual violence) that likely contributed to her addiction. Who is to say that the addict's daughter will not have the same fate and become a scorned and degraded pregnant addict herself? When and why does that black girl child change from being among the most innocent to among the most guilty?

The primary utility of stigmatizing and punishing poor drug-addicted black women lies not in the prevention of fetal harm, but in the defense of normative standards of gender and motherhood, the resuscitation of public innocence concerning the plight of the black poor, and the legitimization of a status quo characterized by continuing oppression and inequality. With reflection upon the real imperatives driving the criminal prosecution of crack-addicted mothers, policymakers might begin to devise programs that empower pregnant addicts and allow them to be good mothers to their children. The policies pursued thus far have done little good for crack-exposed babies and have only helped undermine the fragile world into which they were born.

NOTES

1. All mothers in the study used cocaine and most also used other drugs during their pregnancies. Griffith's recent research was conducted with a study population in which several prenatal risk factors had been eliminated: while pregnant, expectant mothers received prenatal care, nutritional counseling, and therapy for chemical dependency.

2. Infants born prematurely have increased risk of breathing difficulties, brain hemorrhage, and mental defects. Babies born underweight are 40 times more likely to die than are normal-weight babies and 10 times more likely to have cerebral palsy (Appel, 1992). The black infant mortality rate in 1987 was 17.9 deaths out of 1,000, compared to a white infant mortality rate of 8.6 per 1,000 (Roberts, 1991).

3. As of 1993, the states of Georgia and New York had instituted mandatory reporting requirements, yet had allocated no funding for treatment of perinatal addiction (Sexton, 1993).

4. In 1988, Minnesota became the first state to include perinatal drug use in its legal definition of child abuse. Since that time, observers have claimed that despite the fact that the revised law does not call for criminal sanctions against prenatal drug abusers, it has deterred pregnant addicts from seeking drug treatment and from disclosing their drug use to their doctors (Sexton, 1993; Paltrow, 1990).

5. This is primarily by adversely affecting the quality of the sperm and through the mother's inhalation of second-hand smoke from cigarettes or illegal drugs.

REFERENCES

Appel, Deborah 1992 "Drug Use During Pregnancy: State Strategies to Reduce the Prevalence of Prenatal Drug Exposure." University of Florida Journal of Law and Public Policy 5 (Fall): 103–148.

Barone, Diane 1994 "Myths About 'Crack Babies.'" Educational Leadership 52 (October): 67–68.

Beckett, Katherine 1995 "Fetal Rights and 'Crack Moms': Pregnant Women in the War on Drugs." Contemporary Drug Problems 22 (Winter): 587–612.

Boling, Patricia 1995 "Introduction." Patricia Boling (ed.), Expecting Trouble: Surrogacy, Fetal Abuse, and New Reproductive Technologies. Boulder: Westview Press.

Bower, Lisa 1995 "The Trope of the Dark Continent in the Fetal Harm Debates: 'Africanism' and the Right to Choice." Patricia Boling (ed.), Expecting Trouble: Surrogacy, Fetal Abuse, and New Reproductive Technologies. Boulder: Westview Press.

Collins, Patricia Hill 1990 Black Feminist Thought: Knowledge, Consciousness, and the Politics of Empowerment. Boston: Unwin Hyman.

Curriden, Mark 1990 "Holding Mom Accountable." ABA Journal (March): 50–53.

1986 "Crack: A Cheap and Deadly Cocaine Is a Spreading Menace." Time (September 22).

Debettencourt, Kathleen B. 1990 "The Wisdom of Solomon: Cutting the Chord That Harms." Children Today 19 (August): 17–20.

Dobson, Tracy and Kimberly K. Eby 1992 "Criminal Liability for Substance Abuse During Pregnancy: The Controversy of Maternal v. Fetal Rights." Saint Louis University Law Journal 36,3 (Spring): 655–694.

1986 "Drug Treatment in City Is Strained by Crack, a Potent New Cocaine." New York Times (May 16).

Elshtain, Jean Bethke 1990 "Pregnancy Police: If You're an Addict It's Now a Crime to Give Birth." The Progressive 54 (December): 26–28.

Feldman, Joseph G., Howard L. Minkoff, Sandra McCalla, and Martin Salwen 1992 "A Cohort Study of the Impact of Perinatal Drug Use on Prematurity in an Inner-City Population." American Journal of Public Health 82 (May): 726–728. 1995 "Fetal Harm Greater from Cigarettes than Cocaine." American Journal of Nursing 95 (May): 56.

Furio, Joanne 1994 "Women Fight Civil Rights Abuse in South Carolina." Ms. 5 (November/December): 93.

Garcia, Sandra Anderson and Ralph Segalman 1991 "The Control of Perinatal Drug Abuse: Legal, Psychological, and Social Imperatives." Law and Psychology Review 15 (Spring): 19–64.

Gittler, Josephine and Dr. Merle McPherson 1990 "Prenatal Substance Abuse." Children Today 19 (July/August): 3–7.

Greene, Dwight L. 1991 "Abusive Prosecutors: Gender, Race, and Class Discretion and the Prosecution of Drug-Addicted Mothers." Buffalo Law Review 39,3 (Fall): 737–802.

Greider, Katherine 1995 "Crackpot Ideas." Mother Jones 20 (July/August): 52–56.

Griffith, Dan R. 1992 "Prenatal Exposure to Cocaine and Other Drugs: Developmental and Educational Prognoses." Phi Delta Kappan 74 (September): 30–34.

Hill, Robert B. 1977 Information Adoption Among Black Families. Washington, D.C.: National Urban League, Research Department.

Hoffman, Jan 1990 "Pregnant, Addicted—and Guilty?" The New York Times Magazine (August 19): 32–35.

Hopkins, Ellen 1990 "Childhood's End." Rolling Stone (October 18): 66–69; 71–72; 108–110.

Irwin, Katherine 1995 "Ideology, Pregnancy, and Drugs: Differences Between Crack-Cocaine, Heroin, and Methamphetamine Users." Contemporary Ding Problems 22 (Winter): 613–637.

Krauss, Deborah K. 1991 "Regulating Women's Bodies: The Adverse Effect of Fetal Rights Theory on Childbirth Decisions and Women of Color." Harvard Civil Rights Civil Liberties Law Review 26,4 (Summer): 523–548.

Langone, John 1988 "Crack Comes to the Nursery: More and More Cocaine-Using Mothers Are Bearing Afflicted Infants." Time 132 (September 19): 85.

Lieb, John J. and Claire Sterk-Elifson 1995 "Crack in the Cradle: Social Policy and Reproductive Rights Among Crack-Using Females." Contemporary Drug Problems 22 (Winter): 687–705.

Logli, Paul A. 1990 "Drugs in the Womb: The Newest Battlefield in the War on Drags." Criminal Justice Ethics (Winter/Spring): 23–29.

Mariner, Wendy K., Leonard H. Glantz, and George J. Annas 1990 "Pregnancy, Drugs, and the Perils of Prosecution." Criminal Justice Ethics (Winter/Spring): 30–41.

Moynihan, Daniel Patrick 1971 "The Tangle of Pathology." Robert Staples (ed.), The Black Family; Essays and Studies. Belmont, California: Wadsworth Publishing.

Murray, Charles 1984 Losing Ground—American Social Policy, 1950–1980. New York: Basic Books.

Musto, David F. 1973 American Disease: Origins of Narcotic Control. New Haven: Yale University Press.

Neil, Benjamin A. 1992 "Prenatal Drug Abuse: Is the Mother Criminally Liable?" Trial Diplomacy Journal 15: 129–135.

Neuspiel, Daniel R. 1996 "Racism and Perinatal Addiction." Ethnicity and Disease 6 (Winter/Spring): 47–55.

Neuspiel, Daniel R., Morri Markowitz, and Ernest Drucker 1994 "Intrauterine Cocaine, Lead, and Nicotine Exposure and Fetal Growth." American Journal of Public Health 84 (September): 1492–1495.

Paltrow, Lynn M. 1990 "When Becoming Pregnant Is a Crime." Criminal Justice Ethics (Winter/Spring): 42–47.

1986 "The Plague Among Us." Newsweek (June 16).

Plummer, William and S. Avery Brown 1990 "Children in Peril." People Weekly 33 (April 16): 82–91.

Pollitt, Katha 1990 "'Fetal Rights': A New Assault on Feminism." The Nation 250 (March 26): 409–411; 414–416.

Roberts, Dorothy E. 1991 "Punishing Ding Addicts Who Have Babies: Women of Color, Equality, and the Right of Privacy." Harvard Law Review 104,7 (May): 1419–1482.

Schroedel, Jean Reith and Paul Peretz 1995 "A Gender Analysis of Policy Formation: The Case of Fetal Abuse." Patricia Boling (ed.), Expecting Trouble: Surrogacy, Fetal Abuse, and New Reproductive Technologies. Boulder: Westview Press.

Sexton, Patricia A. 1993 "Imposing Criminal Sanctions on Pregnant Drug Users: Throwing the Baby out with the Bath Water." Washburn Law Journal 32 (Spring): 410–430. 1991 "Smoking Out Cocaine's in Utero Impact." Science News 140 (November 19): 302.

Sullum, Jacob 1992 "The Cocaine Kids." Reason 24 (August/September): 14.

Willwerth, James 1991 "Should We Take Away Their Kids?" Time 137 (May 13): 62–63.

Young, Iris Marion 1995 "Punishment, Treatment, Empowerment: Three Approaches to Policy for Pregnant Addicts." Patricia Boling (ed.), Expecting Trouble: Surrogacy, Fetal Abuse, and New Reproductive Technologies. Boulder: Westview Press.

Zitella, Julia J. 1996 "Protecting Our Children: A Call to Reform State Policies to Hold Pregnant Drug Addicts Accountable." John Marshall Law Review 29,3 (Spring): 768–798.

ENID LOGAN (3520 Pheasant Run Circle, #8, Ann Arbor, MI 48108, e-mail: elogan@umich.edu) is a fourth-year doctoral candidate in sociology at the University of Michigan in Ann Arbor. She obtained a bachelor of arts degree in 1994 from Yale University (where she majored in sociology and concentrated in African American Studies) and in 1997 received a Masters Degree in sociology from the University of Michigan. Her area of specialization is race and ethnicity, with a focus on the experience of blacks in the Americas. Her dissertation research will focus on constructs of race and nationhood in early 20th-century Cuba.

From *Social Justice*, Spring 1999, pp. 115–138. © 1999 by Social Justice. Reprinted by permission.

Drug Courts: Making Prison Sentences a Thing of the Past?

With America's prisons bulging at the seams with drug offenders, many states and localities are experimenting with new, cost-effective ways to cope with drug-related crime and punishment.

**by John J. Mountjoy, regional coordinator,
The Council of State Governments**

Ask any judge what sort of cases clog his docket. Ask any cop what causes the most problems on the street. The answer: drugs. Drug use and abuse has states searching for alternative methods of curbing this societal ill. Drug Strategies, a Washington, D.C.-based firm conducting research on drug-control issues, promotes the alternative sentencing/treatment of drug offenders with the use of drug courts in a recent study, *Cutting Crime: Drug Courts in Action.*

Two-thirds of men and women arrested test positive for illegal drug use at the time of arrest; in some cities, positive drug-test rates reach 84 percent.

Treatment or Jail

The report suggested that a large percentage of crime is or can be related to drug violations. "Two-thirds of men and women arrested test positive for illegal drug use at the time of arrest; in some cities, positive drug-test rates reach 84 percent," the report said. In addition, an already overworked probation system allows many of these drug abusers to slip through the cracks and does little to curtail further crime. "The drug problem creates a cycle of crime that goes beyond drug possession and sale. Drug abusers

are more likely than other criminals to become repeat offenders," the authors said.

Treatment is seen as the option that can help reduce this recidivism. The authors contended that drug offenders not only become repeat violators, they often continue their illegal behavior once in prison due to the large drug market within prison walls. Drug abusers not only continue their destructive habits in this environment, they lack access to educational opportunities or life skills development. Proper drug counseling and treatment are often ignored. Conversely, according to a 1995 survey by Peter Hart Research Associates cited by the report, "Fifty-three percent of Americans view drug abuse as a public-health problem, not a criminal justice problem, and 74 percent have confidence that it can be reduced through treatment."

Drug Court Development

Miami, Florida, became the first city to implement the alternative-sentencing method known as drug court. Targeting first-time felony drug offenders, the program allows criminals the choice of prosecution with the possibility of incarceration or participation in a one-year treatment program. The program makes good fiscal sense and is sound in that it promotes a better lifestyle for offenders while reducing crime. "When the Miami drug court opened, it cost about $30,000 to keep one offender in Dade County jail for a year, compared to $700 for each participant in the drug-court treatment program," the report said.

At the time of *Cutting Crime*'s printing, 48 states had or were planning drug courts. The report suggested that the program has brought a high level of overhaul and innovation in drug testing, courtroom procedures and information management. Innovations such as computerized information systems allow a judge to instantly reference an offender's criminal record as well as drug-testing reports. "If the judge suspects a participant is using drugs, a test can be done on the spot, with results in the judge's hand within the hour," the report said.

How'd They Do That?

Drug court design is in the hands of the particular jurisdiction and is largely determined by the kinds of cases moving their way through the local court system. Drug-court formats include both plea models and post-adjudication models. "In [the plea model] design, defendants must enter a guilty plea, which can be stricken upon successful completion of the program," the report said. Post-adjudication models allow offenders to participate in treatment prior to sentencing. After successful treatment, offenders may withdraw their guilty plea and possibly receive a lighter sentence or probation.

Drug courts, which operate "on a shoestring budget," obtain funding from various sources. "Parole, probation, pretrial services and other criminal justice agencies contribute funds from their budgets to support the drug courts," the authors said. In some jurisdictions, innovative administrators are diverting seized assets and funds from drug busts into drug-court programs. Still other programs are forming nonprofit corporations in order to facilitate both public and private contributions. The Federal government, through the Department of Justice's Drug Courts Program Office, awards planning, implementation and enhancement grants to various drug courts all over the country.

Teen Offenders

One aspect of drug courts that is rapidly evolving is their involvement with juvenile offenders. The authors reported that "Between 1991 to 1995, juvenile arrests overall rose some 20 percent. Drug arrests accounted for much of this increase, more than doubling from 65,800 to 147,107." In addition, 42 percent of violent juvenile offenders tested positive for illegal drugs at the time of arrest. Program design, although modeled after adult drug courts, requires special considerations such as:

- addressing the influence of peers, gangs and families
- completing thorough assessments while maintaining confidentiality
- motivating juveniles to change
- making programs developmentally appropriate for youth

These concerns have given rise to new strategies for juvenile drug courts. According to the report, they are:

- more comprehensive take-in assessments
- greater coordination among the courts, treatment providers, schools, and other agencies
- more active, continuous judicial supervision
- use of sanctions with both the juvenile and the family

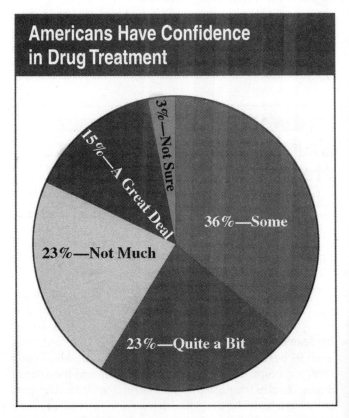

Americans Have Confidence in Drug Treatment

3%—Not Sure
15%—A Great Deal
36%—Some
23%—Not Much
23%—Quite a Bit

SOURCE: CUTTING CRIME: DRUG COURTS IN ACTION, 1997

Within some jurisdictions, not only are moderate-to-severe juvenile drug abusers able to participate in the program, but also those charged with theft, drunk driving, truancy and even assault. This step is taken to not only correct drug-abuse problems, but to also address other issues which can eventually lead to further criminal and/or drug-abuse behaviors.

Do They Work?

The report cautioned against measuring results by comparing different programs as each is uniquely shaped to address the problems of a particular community. However, when taken as a whole, the report suggested that, "… the overall impact is impressive." *Cutting Crime* stated that despite anticipated relapse in treatments, an impressive 50 to 65 percent of program participants remain drug-free after completing the program. Following completion of the course, drug abusers attend a graduation ceremony in which their efforts are recognized. For many, this recognition is the reinforcing factor in their remaining drug-free.

Another benefit of the program is that one year of treatment is generally 5 to 8 times cheaper than a year of incarceration. "It's cost-effective… But even if it doesn't work to the numbers that people would like, it works better than what the rest of the system is doing now," said Judge Stephen Marcus of the Los Angeles Drug Court. Reducing criminal recidivism is another major selling point of drug courts, says the report. Typically, this recidivism occurs in more than half of all drug cases. Those who participate in drug court, but do not graduate, have up to a 28 percent chance of repeat offenses, but of those who do graduate, only 4 percent exhibit this repeat behavior.

The Future of Drug Courts

Cutting Crime reported that in 1997 alone, "…the federal government [spent] $335 million on new prison construction, and new state prison construction topped out at $4 billion." These figures obviously provide a strong fiscal argument for supporting incarceration alternatives. But overall it is successful outcomes by offenders that will reinforce their effectiveness as a judicial tool. These outcomes are dependent on several factors including careful record keeping, extensive follow-up research, and availability of treatment, the report claimed. The downside of drug courts is that they cannot help everyone, even those who participate: 1 in 4 participants in a drug-court treatment program drop out, and a number of graduates relapse.

Current efforts are under way to strengthen and unify the structure of drug courts and form a common set of features and goals to aid in treatment, funding, and community relations. In cooperation with the Department of Justice's Drug Courts Program Office, the National Association of Drug Court Professionals developed a set of guidelines and key components for both establishing and maintaining successful drug-court programs. It is this attitude of cooperation combined with a caring, committed and creative attitude that is making a difference in the war on drugs, and giving citizens a chance to reclaim their lives.

For further information contact Drug Strategies at (202) 663-6090 or visit their Web site at *www.drugstrategies.org*.

From *Spectrum*, Winter 1999, pp. 16-18. ©2000 by Spectrum. Reprinted by permission.

Creating Visions and Achieving Goals:

The Women in Community Service's Lifeskills™ Program

By Tessa Hale

After 20 years of habitual heroin use leading to continual stints in prison, Melonee's family and friends had all but given up on her. Melonee could not stay clean despite participation in drug rehabilitation programs while serving her time. She smuggled drugs into prison and used there. She continued to use heroin when she returned to a drug-using culture each time she was released. It seemed Melonee would forever use drugs and spend the rest of her days in prison—if she survived.

Melonee's story is similar to those of the thousands of women who enter the correctional system each year. And the number of women in prison is increasing at a staggering rate—there has been a 500 percent increase since 1980, according to the U.S. General Accounting Office (GAO). Of all the women in prison, nearly two-thirds have minor children. Housing these female inmates without effective rehabilitation and transition programs will only contribute to a cycle of incarceration.

Once a woman is in prison, it is too late for the education and support necessary to prevent her from making poor choices. However, optimism and faith make the seemingly impossible happen for female offenders. With the right kind of support and programming, the time spent in prison can be an opportunity for women to confront issues that lead to criminal behavior, and to make attitudinal and lifestyle changes.

Today, for the first time since 1977, Melonee is off drugs and off parole. She proves that female offenders can successfully overcome barriers and attain new leases on life. Melonee attributes a large part of that success to Women in Community Service's (WICS') Lifeskills™ program.

"The confidence in myself and the support I got through the WICS Lifeskills program [at Columbia River Correctional Institution (CRCI) in Portland, Ore.] helped me with the determination to stay clean," says Melonee.

The Barriers Women in Prison Face

Statistics of female offenders demonstrate that the majority share similar histories, barriers and personal issues prior to their arrests and convictions. The most significant commonalities these women share are low self-esteem and a nearly nonexistent support system, says Michael McGee, superintendent of CRCI.

The GAO report on women in prison, published in December 1999, indicates that female offenders face a matrix of problems, including:

- Histories of sexual and/or physical abuse—57 percent of female inmates in state prisons.
- A lack of education or employable skills—only 36 percent of women in state prisons were high school graduates or had some college or more.
- Drug and/or alcohol dependencies—three-fourths of female inmates in state prisons said they had used drugs regularly at some time in the past.
- Involvement in a cycle of incarceration—50 percent of women in prison report that an immediate family member also served time.

Gender-Specific Programs

In 1980, the GAO reported to Congress that due to the relatively small numbers of women in U.S. correctional systems, programs and services for women were not viewed as a priority. It was generally believed that female inmates did not need the same type of training and vocational skills as male inmates nor programs designed for their rehabilitation.

Today, however, given the enormous increase of women in prison, programs designed specifically for female inmates are becoming recognized as a necessity. A 1998 National Institute of Justice report acknowledged that many needs of incarcerated women are different from those of men and require management approaches and programming tailored to their special characteristics and situations. It now is clear that effective rehabilitation for women in prison must be accomplished by different means than those currently used for men because of women's different issues and needs.

During his 10-year tenure as superintendent at CRCI, McGee observed the differing needs of male and female inmates as they prepared to return to the community. "Males form their identities primarily in relation to the greater world. Programs for males are more successful when they focus on rules and offer ways to advance within a structured environment," explains McGee. "Females, on the other hand, form their identities primarily in relation to other people. Programs for women are more successful when they focus on relationships with other people and offer ways to master their lives while keeping these relationships intact."

WICS Lifeskills Program

The WICS Lifeskills program uses a woman-centered learning model designed to both train and support female offenders by promoting self-sufficiency and economic independence. Program participants are provided with a comprehensive set of services incorporating job readiness, personal empowerment, support services and life management skills that effectively prepare them for their successful return to the community. WICS currently operates three programs for female offenders in Portland, Ore., Memphis, Tenn., and Dallas.

"WICS' prison programs empower participants by encouraging them to reassess their behavior, gain marketable skills and build self-esteem in addition to providing transitional support. These components of WICS programs are imperative because the majority of inmates will be returning to the environment they came from," says Jay Desiderio, deputy administrator of inmate services/programs at Shelby County Division of Corrections (SCDC) in Memphis, Tenn. "WICS' goal is to instill a strong sense of self and a reliable support network to prevent the women from reverting to the same harmful habits and groups of people with whom they associated before incarceration."

Delivered in a concentrated nine- to 12-week curriculum, the WICS Lifeskills program usually is completed within two months of female offenders' projected release dates. The class includes a comprehensive skills assessment and interactive life-management and job-readiness workshops. The class meets four days a week for approximately six hours per day. More than half the curriculum is presented by community agency representatives and volunteers. Many topics are covered, each with the objective of giving the participants a better understanding of themselves and the world in which they must function in order to avoid the former behaviors that resulted in their imprisonment.

Connie, a former drug addict and WICS Lifeskills graduate from SCDC, says the program provided her with the tools she needed to pro-actively construct a new way of living. "One of the most valuable lessons the WICS program teaches is that we have choices," explains Connie. "If you choose wisely, your life can turn around. I chose the roads I took and I don't blame anyone else for where I ended up. But I am grateful to WICS for showing me a greater variety of things to choose from."

The Role of Volunteers

"Female offenders need to be surrounded with healthy people to move into a new way of living their lives," says Desiderio. "WICS' program [at SCDC] provides that for them. They bring in mentors, volunteers and people who once were in their places who have succeeded. This shows the women how

to do it. They need this community support in and out of prison."

A core part of the WICS Lifeskills program, volunteers donate hundreds of hours serving as workshop facilitators, class presenters and mentors. All volunteers act as positive role models for the female inmates. McGee says it is crucial for women to see how and where they fit into society from people in the community who are not a part of the criminal subculture. Through example, WICS' program volunteers serve as teachers, reinforcing alternative lifestyle options and the available avenues to effectively alter detrimental habits of female inmates.

When Melonee was released from prison, a WICS volunteer took her to get a bed in a drug-free housing facility. Another volunteer helped her get a job. "One of the workshop presenters I met while I was in the program actually took me to the office to fill out the application for my first job," says Melonee. Now, Melonee returns as a volunteer for WICS, talking to the current participants about her own experience. She says when a WICS Lifeskills graduate talked to her class, it gave her hope and now she does her best to impart the same inspiration. "I knew if she could do it, I could do it," says Melonee.

Volunteer mentors are one of the most pivotal pieces of WICS' programs in prison. WICS mentors are individuals from the community who volunteer their time and energy to assist women in prison preparing to leave—and after their release—as they transition back into society. Mentors act as a window to a new lifestyle, both educating female offenders and lending the time and advice necessary to individuals in transition. Through this, female offenders develop caring, stable and continuous relationships, learning how to establish healthy support systems. Most WICS Lifeskills program participants have lacked this kind of relationship in their lives. "WICS mentors teach female offenders how to cope, survive and solve problems in a pro-social manner," says McGee. "They help [female offenders] find jobs, provide moral support and advice on both professional and personal levels." Connie says the unconditional support from volunteers and the WICS staff made it possible for her to kick her drug habit. While in the WICS program, she was off drugs, but after her release, she relapsed. She then entered a long-term drug rehabilitation program and has stayed clean ever since. "When I relapsed, the WICS staff and volunteers didn't turn their backs on me. My mentor was with me every step of the way helping me to get back on track," says Connie. "The mentor program was so important to me—and being surrounded by people who did not judge me."

Looking to the Future

The WICS Lifeskills program's primary purpose is to help women in prison create visions for their lives and gain the skills to achieve them. Women set goals and learn about who they are, what they need and what they want. With this purpose, skills are not just taught, but also are put into the meaningful context of how skills will help them achieve their visions. Through this approach, program participants gain a sense of self and the positive self-esteem they need to begin to believe that they all are people who can make it.

Melonee validates this approach in her experience of preparing for and encountering ultimate success in her return to society. "The most important thing I gained from the WICS program was an openness and a willingness to learn. I learned the skills to live—things I had never learned growing up. WICS opened me to new situations and helped me not to get stuck in my own rut. It helped me accumulate the tools to stay clean and sober and to live life on life's terms," says Melonee. "I never knew how to budget my paycheck. I just figured you got your paycheck, you paid your bills and that was that. Volunteers at WICS sat down with me and took the time to look at a paycheck and bills and, step-by-step, draw up a plan for me."

Proven Success

WICS has provided transitional and support services to low-income women for more than 36 years. For the last eight years, WICS has successfully established a niche in its work with female offenders. Independent research and evaluations indicate that the WICS Lifeskills program has a positive impact on helping participants obtain and retain employment, maintain sobriety and reduce recidivism. Three separate independent evaluations have been conducted on WICS' work with female offenders, including Portland State University (PSU), Brandeis University and independent evaluators, Thelma Crivens and Rita Dorsey, in Memphis, Tenn.

The most recent evaluation, based on data from the SCDC program, completed last September by Crivens and Dorsey, reveals that the WICS Lifeskills program reduces recidivism. The report states that the rearrest rate at SCDC for WICS Lifeskills graduates was significantly lower than the rate for females in other programs or those in a 1989 Department of Justice study by the Bureau of Justice Statistics, titled *Recidivism of Prisoners*. The report indicated a 40 percent rearrest rate; Crivens and Dorsey indicated a 48.32 percent rearrest rate for other SCDC inmates and a 34.85 percent rearrest rate for WICS Lifeskills graduates.

The 13 percent lower recidivism rate for WICS Lifeskills graduates compared to other female offenders can be attributed largely to the successful reintegration to the community that participants experience, including high rates of employment. According to the GAO, 49 percent of female inmates were unemployed prior to incarceration. The PSU results indicate that 84 percent of the 187 program participants interviewed received government assistance prior to their incarceration. Only 29 percent reverted to receiving aid after their graduation from WICS Lifeskills and their return to their communities. Eighty-three percent of the graduates found employment after their release and 67 percent were employed 40 or more hours per week.

Fifty-nine percent reported similar or higher income levels than before incarceration.

Today, with skills learned from WICS and the support and advice it provided, Melonee works as a housing coordinator for the Portland Alternative Health Center (PAHC). "I started out cleaning toilets and then moved up to a desk position," she says. Then they offered me my current position, in which I make $11 an hour. I also am enrolled at Lincoln City College in the entry-level counseling program."

WICS Lifeskills participants overwhelmingly believe the program successfully assists female offenders in their transitions to lives outside of prison. Ninety-seven percent of all women interviewed in the PSU study affirmed that WICS Lifeskills was a positive program, and virtually all the graduates said it was an effective tool for preparing them to re-enter the community.

Since exiting the WICS program and CRCI, Melonee has been able to stay clean and sober. She also has been able to reunite with her family, who she says she pushed away until, eventually, they lost faith in her.

"After I got out, [my family] watched to see what I was going to do. By that time, they had accepted that I was going to be a heroin addict forever. After a year went by and I was still clean, they started to have confidence in me again. And after two years went by, I think they were in shock," says Melonee. "Today, my mom has regained her trust in me. I even have the keys to her house now, something she never would have given me before, and with good reason. Before, I took advantage of them, but through the program, I gained the skills to be independent when I got out of prison. I remember I cried when my mom gave me those keys."

At a time when the number of women in prison is increasing at an alarming rate, WICS is successfully providing support and education that unquestionably improves the lives of female offenders. WICS teaches women in prison essential social, interpersonal and employability skills, and creates the support network necessary for them to maintain the positive changes they made in prison.

REFERENCES

Crivens, T. and R. Dorsey. 2000. *Final evaluation for WICS Lifeskills for women at the Shelby County Division of Corrections*. Sept. 21.

Jolin, Annette, Ph.D. 1997. *An evaluation of the WICS Lifeskills program for women at the Columbia River Correctional Institution*.

U.S. General Accounting Office. 1999. *A report to the Hon. Eleanor Holmes Norton, House of Representatives. Women in prison: Issues and challenges confronting U.S. correctional systems*. Washington, D.C.: Government Printing Office. (December).

Tessa Hale is manager of Community Outreach for Women in Community Service, and can be contacted at 1900 N. Beauregard St., Suite 103, Alexandria, VA 22311; (703) 671-0500, ext. 850; fax (703) 671-4489; e-mail: thale@ wics.org. Kate Boucek, associate specialist of communications for WICS, also contributed.

From *Corrections Today*, February 2001, pp. 33-34, 36-37. ©2001 by American Correctional Association.

Tougher Sentencing, Economic Hardships and Rising Violence

By Leonard Curry

Editor's Note: *Based on a previously published article in* Corrections Digest *on Sept. 29, 2000, this article has been expanded and updated by the author.*

There has been a shift in the gender composition of the nation's correctional population, for more than 950,000 females are under correctional supervision. This shift has been caused by tougher substance abuse sentencing guidelines, economic hardships and rising violence levels among women. Although the male inmate population remains significantly larger, the escalating numbers of women in prison are causing a tilt in the U. S. prison population.

An Increasing Trend

Within the past 20 years, statistics show that there has been an increasing trend in the amount of women being arrested, incarcerated and placed under supervision. These statistics indicate that the numbers are continuing to increase and also show that these women have come from similar backgrounds and have common characteristics.

In 1998, women accounted for 6.5 percent of state prison populations—an increase from the 1980 statistic of 4.1 percent, according to the Bureau of Justice Statistics (BJS). This trend is expected to continue because arrests of women have been rising at a faster rate than men—a 23 percent increase in the early 1990s, compared to a 13 percent increase for males. In 1998, women accounted for more than one out of five of the nation's 14.4 million arrests.

The average increase in female incarceration in the 1990s was 8.3 percent and the annual rate of women sentenced to jails and prisons exceeded 10 percent in 18 states, led by Tennessee at 15 percent, North Dakota at 14.9 percent, Montana at 14.7 and Idaho at 14.3 percent.

According to BJS, most incarcerated females have monthly incomes of less than $600 at the time of arrest, have suffered physical or sexual abuse, and have grown up in single-parent households.

Drug Offenses

The 1990s have shown a significant increase in the amount of women being charged for drug and alcohol use as well as an increase in incarcerated repeat drug offenders. Although most sentences can be traced to substance abuse, violent crime also is on the rise.

Of the women in all prisons and jails, 34 percent are serving time for drug offenses and 32 percent for property offenses often related to crimes committed to support drug habits. By self-admission, three of every four are substance abusers. At the federal level, 72 percent of female inmates were sentenced for drug offenses.

The population of females incarcerated for more than one year soared 79 percent in the 1990s, primarily due to new sentencing guidelines that required incarceration for repeat drug offenders, according to BJS. Prison sentences for most women can be traced to substance abuse, however, there has been a significant rise in both violent crime and recidivism.

BJS reported that the number of state and federal female inmates more than doubled from 44,065 in 1990 to 90,668 in 1999. "Women were being charged in the 1990s for offenses that they were not charged with in earlier years—drug and alcohol use," said a BJS statistician. "Most of the women are from lower socioeconomic backgrounds and they buy their drugs on the street, while women from middle- and upper-income brackets get prescriptions or buy from dealers who are not standing on street corners," the statistician said.

In addition, the General Accounting Office found that the number of women incarcerated for drug offenses nearly doubled from 1990 to 1997. Black women are more than twice as likely as Hispanic women and eight times as likely as white women to be incarcerated for drug offenses.

The largest increments of the female inmate population were in the South and the West, which doubled over the decade. According to BJS, the female population in Southern prisons soared 144 percent (37,525), while Western female prison populations grew 96 percent (19,333). California had the second largest number of women in prison—11,368. Of the 22,159

States With the 10 Largest Female Inmate Populations in 1999

State	1999	1990	Percent Change
Texas	12,502	2,196	469.3
California	11,368	6,502	74.8
Florida	3,820	2,664	43.4
New York	3,644	2,691	35.4
Ohio	2,841	1,947	45.9
Illinois	2,802	1,183	136.9
Georgia	2,607	1,243	109.7
Oklahoma	2,316	1,071	116.2
Louisiana	2,268	775	192.6
Virginia	2,119	927	128.6

Source: BJS

Women in the Correctional System, December 1998

Jails	63,800
Probation	721,400
Federal Prisons	9,200
State Prisons	75,200
Parole	82,300
Total	**951,900**

Source: BJS

Characteristics of Female Inmates, 1997

Characteristics	Percentage of Inmates
Drug use	84.0
Alcohol use	55.7
Under influence of drugs or alcohol at time of arrest	53.1
Physical or sexual abuse	57.2
Have minor children	64.3
Unemployed	49.3
Failed to complete high school	63.9

Source: BJS

Change in Female Incarceration, 1990-1999			
Jurisdiction	1999	1990	Average Percent Change
U. S. Total	90,668	44,065	8.3
Federal	9,913	5,011	7.9
All States	80,755	39,054	8.4

Source: BJS

States With 10 Fastest Annual Growth Rates of Female Incarceration, 1990-1999		
State	Annual Percentage Increase	Total Inmates in 1999
Tennessee	15.0	1,368
North Dakota	14.9	70
Montana	14.7	262
Idaho	14.3	399
Hawaii	13.9	553
West Virginia	13.6	239
Mississippi	13.5	1,405
Louisiana	12.7	368
Colorado	12.1	1,213

Source: BJS

rise in the South, Texas accounted for nearly half (10,306 inmates)—a more than 400 percent increase from 2,196 in 1990 to 12,502 in 1999. Female inmates jumped 88 percent (14,143) in Midwest states and increased 55 percent to 9,754 in the Northeast.

BJS statistics also show that among the large states, New York showed the smallest change, but still grew 35 percent. Vermont's female inmates declined from 24 in 1991 to 22 in 1998. The other states with fewer than 100 imprisoned females were Maine, North Dakota and Rhode Island.

Incarcerated Mothers

The number of children with incarcerated parents rose 60 percent in the 1990s and by 1999, affected one of every 50 children. The prison population grew at nearly that time pace—62 percent—during that period, reports BJS. Fewer than half the children were living with parents before incarceration and fewer than half visited

the incarcerated parents. However, about 60 percent of inmate mothers reported either getting telephone calls or mail from their children each week. *Incarcerated Parents and Their Children*, a BJS report, found that nearly 1.5 million minor children have mothers or fathers in prison, an increase of more than 500,000 since 1991.

Of the nation's 72 million minor children (up to age 17), an estimated 2 percent had imprisoned parents in 1999. In 1999, 721,500 federal and state inmates had minor children. More than half the children with incarcerated parents (58 percent) were younger than 20—the average age was 8.

Incarcerated parents were overwhelmingly male (93 percent) and predominantly held in state prisons, rather than federal facilities (89 percent compared to 11 percent). The number of incarcerated women with minor children rose 98 percent to 126,100 between 1991 and 1999.

Half the parents in state prisons were black, about one-quarter were white and one-fifth were Hispanic. In 1999, an esti-

mated 767,200 black children, 384,500 white children and 301,600 Hispanic children had parents in prison. The percentage of black children with incarcerated parents (7 percent) was nearly nine times higher than that of white children (.8 percent). Hispanic children were three times as likely as white children to have parents in prison (2.6 percent).

Although the male inmate population remains significantly larger, the escalating numbers of women in prison are causing a tilt in the U.S. prison population.

State inmate parents were less likely to be violent offenders (44 percent) than inmates without children (51 percent). Three-quarters of state inmates who were parents had prior convictions, and the majority (56 percent) had previously been incarcerated.

About 60 percent of parents in state prisons reported having used drugs in the month before their offenses and 25 percent reported histories of alcohol dependence. More than one-third of parents committed their offenses while under the influence of alcohol. About 14 percent of parents reported mental illnesses; 70 percent of parents did not have high school diplomas; and 27 percent of parents were unemployed at the time of their arrests.

Women's Health Care in Prison

Pregnancy, drug and alcohol addiction, HIV/AIDS and other sexually transmitted diseases (STDs) are just a few factors that make women's health care in prison a unique challenge. These problems are on the rise as the female prison population increases. Although data show that these women have a greater need for health care, health care distribution has been unbalanced, particularly in smaller states.

Even in the largest jurisdictions—California, Texas and the federal system—which house one-third of the female inmates, health care is disproportionate. Civil rights attorneys brought lawsuits against the Central California Women's Facility in Chowchilla and the California Institution for Women in Frontera to improve the delivery of health care, although the circumstances were extreme because a contract laboratory in 1997 falsified the results of Pap smears and hepatitis and HIV tests.

The incidence of HIV among women inmates is 50 percent higher than among males and the prevalence of mental illness is more than twice as high among women than men. One in every 20 female inmates is pregnant at admission.

Conclusion

Drug and alcohol use, unemployment, a history of sexual abuse and incomplete education are several factors that contribute to the increasing trend of women in prison. Although the male inmate population remains significantly larger, the female prison population has been escalating at a high rate during the past several years. The amount of women with HIV, AIDS and other STDs also has increased, causing unique challenges in the prison health care system. Pregnancy and incarcerated mothers also have caused a challenge for the prison system. The larger the increase, the larger these challenges will be in the coming years.

REFERENCES

Beck, Allen J. 1999. *Prisoners in 1999.* Washington, D. C.: U. S. Department of Justice.

Bureau of Justice Statistics. *Incarcerated parents.* Washington, D. C.: Department of Justice.

Bureau of Justice Statistics. *State and federal prisoners returning to the community.* Washington, D. C.: www.ojp.usdoj.gov/bjs/whtsnw2.htm

General Accounting Office. 1999. *Women in prison.* Washington, D. C.: General Accounting Office.

Leonard Curry is editor of Corrections Digest, *an independent news service for the corrections professional, printed 51 times a year.*

Article 38

___

Commentaries

Addressing the Threats of MDMA (Ecstasy): Implications for School Health Professionals, Parents, and Community Members

Ralph Wood, Linda B. Synovitz

Use of "club drugs" threatens the well-being of school-aged children, and therefore, school health professionals and parents need to address this issue. The National Institute on Drug Abuse (NIDA) has increased funding to study the effects of club drugs and initiated partnerships with several national organizations to launch a multimedia campaign to educate teens and parents about the dangers of club drugs.[1]

The term "club drugs" is a broad category that includes illicit drugs such as LSD, Ketamine, GHB, Rohypnol, and MDMA (Ecstasy). The physiological effects of these drugs range from sensory distortion (LSD) and sedation (GHB, Ketamine, Rohypnol) to stimulation/sensory distortion (MDMA). These drugs are labeled "club drugs" because of their use at dance clubs and all-night dance parties known as "raves."[2]

The designer drug, three, four methylenedioxmetharnphetamine (MDMA), better known among its users as "Ecstasy," is frequently the club drug choice among individuals (ravers) attending raves because it is believed to enhance empathy and closeness, to be relatively safe, and have a long-duration of effect.[2] Unfortunately, the safety of MDMA use has been overestimated. This article examines the prevalence of MDMA use by youth, the history and properties of MDMA, and the implications for school health educators and parents.

HISTORY

MDMA, first synthesized in the early 1900s by German chemists, was patented in 1914. The earliest use of MDMA was as an appetite suppressant for soldiers during World War 1.[3,4] Later, in the 1970s and early 1980s, MDMA was used therapeutically by psychotherapists to facilitate interpersonal relationships, increase self-esteem, and increase self-insight with patients.[3,4]

In the early 1980s, MDMA became popular among recreational drug users, leading to an evaluation of the potential harmful effects. In 1985, MDMA was reclassified by the Drug Enforcement Administration as a Schedule I controlled substance, banning all production and use of MDMA therapeutically or otherwise. This reclassification was met with some resistance among physicians and psychotherapists.[3,4] In the late 1990s, MDMA use became synonymous with the rave and dance scene club culture and glamorized in popular music and film.[2]

PROPERTIES AND EFFECTS

Properties

MDMA, most frequently referred to as Ecstasy, also may be known as Adam, XTC, Love Drug, and X.[2] Structurally, MDMA is similar to the naturally occurring hallucinogen, Mescaline, and synthetic methamphetamines, producing mild sensory distortion and central nervous stimulation, making this drug a more popular choice than traditional hallucinogens.[5] Other synthetic drugs similar to MDMA include di-methoxy-methamphetamine (DOM), methylene-dioxy-amphetamine (MDA), and methylene-dioxy-ethylamphetamine (MDE).[4,5]

The primary route of administration of MDMA is oral, typically in tablet or capsule form.[3] Other infrequent routes of administration include inhalation and injection. Typical doses of MDMA range from 110 to 150 milligrams.[3] The cost for a tablet ranges from $10 to $30. The purity and potency of street MDMA varies, leading to concerns about dose level and possible contaminants.[3,4]

Short-Term Psychological and Physiological Effects

The short-term effects of MDMA occur within 30 to 60 minutes of use, and the total effect time of the use of an average dose (120 mg) ranges from three to six hours. Frequently, users report feeling an initial "rush" of energy, which is common with stimulant use (eg, amphetamines).[3,4] After this immediate rush, users experience a plateau in the effects for approximately two to three hours and then a gradual decrease in the effects.[6] After the effect has worn off, as with use of most stimulants, users experience exaggerated feelings of fatigue[4] (Figure 1).

153

Figure 1
MDMA
3,4-Mentylenedioxymethamphetamine

Street Names: Ecstasy, XTC, Adam, X

Drug Classification: Hallucinogen/Stimulant—structurally similar to mescaline and methamphetamine.

Typical Use: Popular drug of use and abuse at dance clubs and raves, college campuses, and greater reported use in urban areas.

Route of Administration: Typically, oral in tablet or capsule form, infrequently inhaled or injected.

Typical Dose: 80 to 150 mgs.

Length of Effect: Immediate rush within first 60 minutes, 3 to 4 hour plateau period, followed by gradual decrease in effect, total time effect 3 to 6 hours.

Short-Term Effects:

Physiological	Psychological
1. Elevated heart rate	1. Increased sense of well-being
2. Insomnia	2. Increased empathy
3. Dehydration	3. Inability to focus
4. Dilated pupils	4. Visual hallucinations
5. Clenching of jaw	5. Paranoia
6. Grinding of teeth	6. Anxiety
7. Increase in body temperature	
8. Elevated blood pressure	

Long-Term Effects: Verbal and visual memory impairment, possible permanent damage to neurons. Prenatal exposure produces an increased risk of birth defects.

Toxicity:

Physiological	Psychological
1. Vomiting	1. Anxiety
2. Tachycardia	2. Panic reactions
3. Hyperthermia	3. Agitation
4. Seizure	4. Depression

If you suspect that somebody may be experiencing an overdose of MDMA, it is vital that you contact emergency medical services. The use of MDMA may cause an individual's body temperature to become dangerously high—possibly resulting in death.

MDMA users may experience several negative, short-term physiological and psychological effects. Physiological effects include elevated heart rate, insomnia, dehydration, dilated pupils, clenching of jaw, grinding of teeth, increase in body temperature, and elevated blood pressure.[3–5,7] Psychological effects include poor concentration, inability to focus, paranoia, visual hallucinations, and anxiety.[3,4,7] Frequently, these stimulant effects are overlooked by users because of the feelings of euphoria and energy associated with MDMA use.[3–5,7]

Perceived "positive" psychological effects have made MDMA a popular drug on the club scene and raves.[2] These effects include an increased sense of well-being, greater empathy, heightened sensuality, and increased social interaction.

Toxicity and Overdose

A growing body of research is indicating that MDMA use, even in small amounts, can result in severe acute toxic reactions.[2,3,8–11] Physiological symptoms of an MDMA overdose include vomiting, heart palpitations, tachycardia, and hyperthemia.[2,3] Psychological symptoms of MDMA overdose include panic reactions, anxiety, agitation, insomnia, and depression.[2,3] Management of overdose reactions includes treating the individual for symptoms of heat exhaustion, dehydration, muscle cramping, seizure, and anxiety.

Researchers have linked deaths due to MDMA overdose to the hyperthemic effect of the drug.[2,8] MDMA may cause a drastic increase in core body temperature, sometimes soaring close to 110° F which can contribute to renal failure.[4] In addition, others have linked MDMA use to intracerebral hemorrhage, water intoxication, and liver damage.[8–11]

Long-Term Physiological Effects

Few scientific studies have addressed the long-term physiological and psychological effects of MDMA use. Researchers at Johns Hopkins University conducted a series of studies exploring the long-term effects of MDMA on rats and nonprimates.[6,12] The results indicate that MDMA significantly damages the brain nerve cells (neurons) which produce serotonin, a neurotransmitter. Serotonin influences mood, appetite, sleep, and memory.[6,12] These studies also indicate that, in many cases, damaged neurons had regrown abnormally or failed to regrow at all. Based on these studies, MDMA was found to selectively damage serotonin receptors in all species.[6,12,13]

In addition, when comparing individuals who reported (MDMA) use to individuals who reported nonuse, those reporting MDMA use experienced verbal and visual memory impairment.[13] The higher the reported dose of MDMA, the greater the impairment.[13]

The MDMA user is not the only one who may be affected. A retrospective study exploring the relationship between prenatal MDMA use and birth defects indicated babies exposed to MDMA had a significantly increased risk of congenital birth defects, cardiovascular anomalies, and musculoskeletal anomalies.[14]

In addition, early reports indicate that prolonged use of MDMA also may affect dopamine, a neurotransmitter responsible for motor control or dopamine receptors. As a result of its affect on dopamine or dopamine receptors, one study linked MDMA use to Parkinson-like symptoms in at least one user.[15]

PREVALENCE OF MDMA USE BY YOUTH

National surveys note an increase in MDMA use over the past several years. The Monitoring the Future Survey (MTFS), conducted under a series of researcher-initiated grants from the National Institute on Drug Abuse,[16] examines the frequency of alcohol and drug use among US high school students. The 1999 MTFS revealed MDMA use among high school sophomores and seniors continued to rise in the past three years. For seniors, lifetime prevalence of MDMA use rose from 5.8% to 8.0%, a 2.3% increase.[16]

The Youth Risk Behavior Surveillance Survey (YRBSS), conducted by the Centers for Disease Control and Prevention, includes national, state, territorial, and local school-based surveys of high school students. The 1997 YRBSS was conducted from February 1997 to May 1997. At the national level, more than 16,200 students were surveyed with the national sample comprised of an approximate equal number of students in grades 9 (23.6%), 10 (23.9%), 11 (25.2%), and 12 (27.2%).[17] From 1991 to 1997, use of MDMA, heroin, stimulants, methamphetamine, and LSD increased 1.4%[18] (Table 1). In addition, Ecstasy was implicated in the death of several youth in the United Kingdom and United States.[8–10]

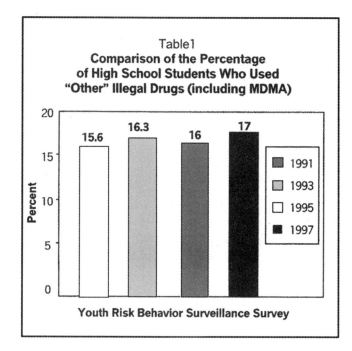

Table 1
Comparison of the Percentage of High School Students Who Used "Other" Illegal Drugs (including MDMA)

THE RAVE SCENE

MDMA use is closely tied to the rave scene.[2,3] The term rave is used to describe an all night dance party, typically held in large dance halls. This phenomenon began in England in the early 1990s and quickly became common in the United States.[2] Raves are associated with loud, repetitive, electronic music called "Techno" and commonly start late in the evening and last until dawn. The stimulant effects of MDMA allow the raver to dance most of the evening.[2,3]

The Community Epidemiological Work Group (CEWG), a research branch of the National Institute of Drug Abuse, reports that MDMA use is closely related to the rave scene in several large metropolitan areas including Boston, Chicago, Miami, Minneapolis/St. Paul, New Orleans, New York City, Phoenix,

Seattle, and Texas.[19] In addition, the CEWG reports MDMA use is increasing outside the rave, dance, and club scenes.[19]

IMPLICATIONS FOR SCHOOL HEALTH PROFESSIONALS AND PARENTS

Become Knowledgeable

Based on the most recent statistics from the Monitoring the Future Survey and the YRBSS, school health professionals and parents should expect MDMA use to increase among students. To address this problem, school health professionals and parents should listen for slang-terms and become familiar with their meaning. Students may refer to MDMA as Ecstasy, XTC, Rave, E, M, bean, roll, or X. These terms may be heard in student conversations or found on student notebooks and backpacks. In addition, several new "pop" films geared toward teen-agers have included scenes of MDMA use. Most recently, the motion picture "GO" centered on purchasing and using MDMA. Since use of MDMA and other dangerous designer drugs (GHB, rohypnol, ketamine, and LSD) frequently occur at raves, school health professionals and parents should become familiar with the latest trends in the adolescent substance use culture.

If school communities believe a drug problem may exist, a needs assessment should be conducted. Students should complete a drug use survey, and interviews with students, parents, teachers, psychological/counseling services, and law enforcement personnel via focus groups could result in obtaining more information about potential teen-age drug use and abuse problems. Not only is it important to ascertain if youth are using drugs such as MDMA, it is important to learn why.

Online Resources

Several online government and independent supported resource sites are available to school health professionals and parents desiring more information about MDMA or other designer drugs.

Government Supported Sites. Government sites provide considerable information about current patterns of drug use in the United States, as well as current drug and alcohol abuse prevention strategies. Of particular interest are the drug and alcohol fact sheets, which provide basic, essential information about substances of use and abuse. Contact: ***www.health.org; www.drugfreeamerica.org;*** or ***www.clubdrugs.org.***

Independent Sites. Independent sites provide a variety of information about MDMA and other recreational drugs. These sites, while geared toward the substance user, also may provide school health professionals with valuable information. The site, ***www.erowid.org/psychoactives/psychoactives.shtml,*** operated by a nonprofit organization, contains information about substances of use and abuse, including incidence and prevalence data and substance users' experiences. The site also includes links to scientific research on recreational drugs, including articles published in scholarly journals. The mission of the not-for-profit site ***www.ecstasy.org*** is to gather objective and up-to-date information about MDMA. The site contains various articles from scientific journals and the popular media. In addition, the site also includes Ecstasy users' experiences with the drug.

Dispel Myths

School health professionals and parents must dispel the myths associated with MDMA use. Talking points should emphasize the following:

- MDMA is not a harmless drug.
- Street MDMA is a man-made drug that is frequently impure.
- MDMA use can cause the user's body temperature to become dangerously high.
- Taking MDMA may prove fatal.

SUGGESTIONS FOR COORDINATED SCHOOL HEALTH PROGRAMS

Health Instruction

To address the MDMA threat, school health educators could include special units of instruction focusing on the risks associated with use of club drugs, particularly Ecstasy. Most importantly, psychosocial skills training, the most important component of any drug education program should be implemented. These skills should include: decision-making, problem solving, self-concept/self-esteem building, assertiveness, resistance, and stress management. To increase awareness of health risks from MDMA use, school health educators could plan and implement drug education seminars for parents, other school professionals, and community members.[20,21]

Physical Education

Physical educators can monitor student conversations in the locker room, as well as monitor student behavior during physical activity exercises, paying special attention to any student who seem to be exhibiting "more energy" than normal as this might be an indication of MDMA or other stimulant use.[22]

School Health Services

School nurses should become familiar with the short-term effects, particularly the signs and symptoms of an overdose, since they may serve as the first contact for a young person experiencing the negative effects of Ecstasy. In addition, school nurses can collaborate with school health educators and counselors to provide inservice programs for other faculty and staff.[23]

School Counseling Services

School counselors should monitor changes in student grades, behavior, and mood. Frequently, these are early indicators that youth may be using substances. In addition, the school counselor serves as a confidant to students. This position provides the counselor a unique opportunity to monitor changes in the adolescent subculture within the school.[24,25]

Healthy School Environment

A healthy school environment is an essential protective against the initiation and use of substances. All school health professionals can collaborate to initiate social marketing campaigns to educate students about the risks associated with sub-

stance use, as well as provide students opportunities to increase personal and social skills.[26]

Family and Community Involvement

Several avenues exist for collaboration between school health professionals, families, and community members to address the issues of Ecstasy use. The police department can monitor the frequencies of drug arrests related to Ecstasy use and raves. Collaboration with local substance abuse treatment professionals can provide useful information such as prevalence, age groups involved, and "best practice" intervention strategies. Substance abuse treatment professionals can also serve as guest speakers for health education classes or assemblies. Occasionally, treatment professionals could arrange to have youth who are participating in substance abuse treatment, come voluntarily to schools to relate their personal stories.

Families can become more informed and aware. A parent network can be established among parents to educate one another and share information about rave sites. In addition, parents can provide opportunities for their children, as well as their children's friends to participate in supervised, substance-free activities.[27]

Youth using MDMA place themselves at physical and psychological risk. With increased awareness, schools, parents, and community partners can do much to alleviate this growing health concern.

References

1. National Institute on Drug Abuse. Club drugs take center stage in new national education and prevention initiative by NIDA and national partners, December 2, 1999. *NIDA News Release.* 1999:1–2.
2. Schwartz RH, Miller NS. MDMA (Ecstasy) and the rave: a review. *Pediatrics.* 1997;100:705–708.
3. Randall T. Ecstasy-fueled 'rave' parties become dances of death for English youth. *JAMA.* 1992;268:1505–1507.
4. McEvoy AW, Kitchen ND, Thomas DGT. Intracerebral hemorrhage caused by drug abuse. *Lancet.* 1998;351:1029.
5. Henry JA, Jeffreys KJ, Dawling S. Toxicity and deaths from 3,4methylenedioxymethamphetamine (Ecstasy). *Lancet.* 1992;340:384–387.
6. Elk C. MDMA(Ecstasy): useful information for health professionals involved in drug education programs. *J Drug Educ.* 1996;26:349–356.
7. Kuhn C, Swartzwelder S, Wilson W. *Buzzed.* New York, NY: WW Norton and Co; 1998;70–76
8. Julien RM. *A Primer of Drug Action.* New York, NY: WH Freeman and Co; 1998;357–358.
9. Beck JE. *MDMA.* Drug Abuse Monograph Series: Health and Welfare Agency, CA; 1987:1–14.
10. McCann UD, Szabo Z, Scheffel U, Dannals RF, Ricaurte GA. Positron emission tomographic evidence of toxic effect of MDMA (Ecstasy) on brain serotonin neurons in human beings. *Lancet.* 1998;352(9138):1433–1437.
11. Green AR, Goodwin GM. Ecstasy and neurodegeneration: Ecstasy's long term effects are potentially more damaging

than its acute toxicity. *Br Med J.* 1996;312 (7045):1493–1494.

12. Bolla KI, McCann UD, Ricaurte G. A. Memory impairment in abstinent MDMA (Ecstasy) users. *Neurology.* 1998;51:1532–1537.

13. McElhatton PR, Bateman DN, Pughe CE, Thomas SHL. Congenital anomalies after prenatal ecstasy exposure. *Lancet.* 1999;354(9188):1441–1442.

14. Mintzer S, Hickenbottom, S, Gilman S. Parkinsonism after taking Ecstasy. *New Engl J Med.* 1999;340(18):1443.

15. Milroy CM, Clark JC, Forrest ARW. Pathology of deaths associated with Ecstasy and eve misuse. *J Clin Pathol.* 1996;9:149–153.

16. Johnston LD, O'Malley PM, Bachman JG. Drug trends 1999 are mixed *Dec. 17, 1999. University of Michigan News and Information Services: Ann Arbor, MI.* Available at: www.monitoringthefuture.org. Accessed January 21, 2000.

17. Kann L, Kinchen SA, Williams BI, et al. Youth risk behavior surveillance—United States, 1997. *MMWR.* 1998;47:1–4.

18. Centers for Disease Control and Prevention. Youth risk behavior survey-97. CD-ROM available from Centers for Disease Control and Prevention, Division of Adolescent and School Health; 1998.

19. National Institute of Drug Abuse. *Epidemiological Trends in Drug Abuse: Advance Report, December 1999.* Available at: 165.112.78.61/CEWG/AdvancedRep/1299ADV/1299adv.html. Accessed March 10, 2000.

20. Modzeleski W, Small ML, Kann L. Alcohol and other drug prevention policies and education in the United States. *J Health Educ.* 1999;30:S42–49.

21. Lohrmann DK, Wooley, SF. Comprehensive school health education. In: Marx E, Wooley SF, Northrop D, eds. *Health Is Academic.* New York, NY: Teachers College Press. 1998:43–66.

22. Seefeldt VD. Physical education. In: Marx E, Wooley SF, Northrop D, eds. *Health Is Academic.* New York, NY: Teachers College Press. 1998:116–141.

23. Duncan P, Igoe JB. School health services. In: Marx E, Wooley SF, Northrop D, eds. *Health Is Academic.* New York, NY: Teachers College Press. 1998:169–194.

24. Adleman H. School counseling, psychological, and social services. In: Marx E, Wooley SF, Northrop D, eds. *Health Is Academic.* New York, NY: Teachers College Press. 1998:142–168.

25. Lowry R, Cohen LR, Modezeleski W, Kann L, Collins JL, Kolbe LJ. School violence, substance use, and availability of illegal drugs on school property among US high school students. *J Sch Health.* 1999;69:347–354.

26. Henderson A, Rowe DE. A healthy school environment. In: Marx E, Wooley SF, Northrop D, eds. *Health Is Academic.* New York, NY: Teachers College Press; 1998:96–115.

27. Carlyon P, Carlyon W, McCarthy AR. Family and community involvement in school health. In: Marx E, Wooley SF, Northrop D, eds. *Health Is Academic.* New York, NY: Teachers College Press; 1998:67–95.

*Ralph Wood, PhD, CHES, Assistant Professor, (rwood@selu.edu); and **Linda B. Synovitz**, PhD, RN, CHES, FASHA, Assistant Professor, (lsynovitz@selu.edu); Dept. of Kinesiology and Health Studies, Southeastern Louisiana University, SLU 10845, Hammond, LA 70403. This article was submitted May 22, 2000, and accepted for publication September 18, 2000.*

UNIT 7

Creating & Sustaining Effective Drug Control Policy

Unit Selections

Key Points to Consider

- As you read the following articles, attempt to identify additional questions and issues that mold public opinion and shape public policy on drugs. Some examples worthy of discussion are: How serious is the drug problem perceived to be? Is it getting worse?

- What are the impacts of drugs on children and schools? How do drugs drive crime? What are the impacts of drugs on policing, the courts, and corrections?

- How are public opinion and public policy affected by public events, drug education campaigns, announced government policies, and media coverage?

 **Links: www.dushkin.com/online/**
These sites are annotated in the World Wide Web pages.

The Drug Reform Coordination Network (DRC)
http://www.drcnet.org

DrugWatch International
http://www.drugwatch.org

United Nations International Drug Control Program (UNDCP)
http://www.undcp.org

Marijuana Policy Project
http://www.mpp.org

Office of National Drug Control Policy (ONDCP)
http://www.whitehousedrugpolicy.gov

The drug problem consistently competes with all major public policy issues, including the economy, education, and foreign policy. Formulating and implementing effective drug control policy is a troublesome task. Some would argue that the consequences of policy failures have been worse than the problems they were attempting to address. Others would argue that although the world of shaping drug policy is an imperfect one, the process has worked generally as well as could be expected. Although the majority of Americans believe that failures and breakdowns in the fight against drug abuse have occurred in spite of various drug policies, not because of them, there is ever-increasing public pressure to rethink the get-tough, stay-tough enforcement-oriented ideas of the last two decades.

Policy formulation is not a process of aimless wandering. Various levels of government have responsibility for responding to problems of drug abuse. At the center of most policy debate is the premise that the manufacture, possession, use, and distribution of psychoactive drugs without government authorization are illegal. This premise is targeted frequently as misguided due to the consequences it is felt to perpetuate, such as syndicated crime and violent competition among criminal organizations and individuals alike. Media hype and the fervor it generates are powerful influences in the public's perception of any drug problem. The fact remains, however, that present-day drug control policy revolves around the majority consensus of prohibition.

One exception to prevailing public views that generally support drug prohibition may be the perceived softening of attitudes regarding the medical use of marijuana. Another surrounds the rising controversy of whether to release from prison those who are incarcerated for simple possession. There is much public consensus that criminalizing addiction that is not related to other criminal misconduct is unjustified. Prison is the nursery for human pathologies that simply wait to infect all who enter. Prison and punishment cause anger, concentration, and focus—something that is often returned to society in terms of tragedy. Society struggles at determining the levels at which drug users and addicts become criminals and felons.

Still, surveys typically report that the majority of Americans think that legalizing, and in some cases even decriminalizing, dangerous drugs is a bad idea. The fear of increased crime, increased drug use, and the potential threat to children are the most often stated reasons. Citing the devastating consequences of alcohol and tobacco use, most Americans question society's ability to use any addictive, mind-altering drug responsibly. Currently, the public favors both supply reduction and demand reduction as effective strategies in combating the drug problem. Concomitantly, policy analysts struggle with objectives. Shaping public policy is a critical function that greatly relies upon public input. Policy-making apparatus is influenced by public opinion, and public opinion is in turn influenced by public policy. When Presidents Bush and Clinton referred to crack and methamphetamine, respectively, as threats to national security, the impact on public opinion was tremendous.

The prevailing characteristic of today's drug policy still reflects a punitive, "get tough" approach to control. The leveling off of both adult as well as youth drug use over the past 2 years serves to sustain this policy and there are, in fact, about 10 million fewer drug users now than existed in 1985 during the height of the crack epidemic.

The prison experience is primarily one of retribution, not rehabilitation. There is typically little opportunity for treatment afforded to the vast majority of prisoners suffering from drug problems. A drug-abusing prisoner, initially committed to the prison system for drug offenses, who receives no drug treatment while in custody, is a virtual guarantee to re-offend. Correctional settings that are offering drug treatment to qualified offenders are reducing recidivism significantly. Court-directed coercion of drug offenders, as a mechanism to force offenders into treatment, is generally meeting with positive results. And in some cases, successful treatment and rehabilitation accompany the incentive to have arrests ultimately expunged and be rewarded with re-entering society as a citizen, not a felon. A state of California study found that every dollar spent on treatment saved $7 in hospital admissions and law-enforcement costs. Nevertheless, the degree to which Americans are willing to support and sustain a less enforcement-oriented response to drug policy questions remains to be seen. There is concern that even with a shift in policy toward education, prevention, and treatment, an intense, enforcement-oriented perspective will remain on the nation's poor, inner-urban, largely minority subpopulations.

Another complicated aspect of creating national as well as local drug policy is consideration of the growing body of research on the subject. The past 20 years have produced numerous public and private investigations, surveys, and conclusions relative to the dynamic of drug use in American society. Most literature reflects, however, an indirect influence of research on large-scale policy decisions. There is a saying that "policy makers use research like a drunk uses a lamppost—for support, rather than illumination."

Further complicating the research/policy-making relationship is that the policy-making community is largely composed of persons of diverse backgrounds, professional capacities, and political interests. Some are elected officials, others are civil servants, and many are private citizens from the medical and educational communities. In some cases, such as with alcohol and tobacco, powerful industry players assert a tremendous influence on policy. As you read on, consider the new research-related implications for drug policy, such as those addressing the incarceration of drug offenders.

Colombian Quagmire

War and Fear in Putumayo

Under the blazing sun, the crudely blacktopped road shimmers with oil, a black strip through the tropical green of banana trees and fields of coca plants. A family drenched in sweat pushes along the burned-out carcass of an automobile. The previous day, ignoring an order issued by the Revolutionary Armed Forces of Colombia (FARC) prohibiting vehicle traffic, the father had driven his 1972 Land Rover all the way to the border of Ecuador. Asked whether he resents the men of the country's main guerrilla movement for burning the tool he used to support his family and his brother's, the man casts his gaze downward. "No, I'm just grateful to them for sparing my life. About six feet away from me, they gunned down the guy driving the motorcycle behind us," he answers quietly.

When asked about the reasons for the "armed picket line" that has paralyzed highway traffic in Putumayo province in the far south of Colombia for the last several weeks, guerrilla commando Félix rattles off his answer: "The decision to interdict highway traffic is directed against the presence of paramilitary groups in Putumayo and against Plan Colombia, a plan by the government and the United States to wage war against the FARC and to displace the peasants."

This year, Washington has authorized an extraordinary aid package of $1.3 billion for Colombia as part of the war on drugs. This ambitious program to eradicate coca and poppy plots by aerial spraying is aimed mainly at Putumayo with its 138,000 acres of coca plots, representing half of all the illicit crops in the country. But this task will not be easy for the Colombian army. The FARC provides protection for the fields and the laboratories, crude facilities where the coca leaf is transformed into base paste and then into cocaine. The last major Marxist-Leninist guerrilla group in Latin America (15,000 armed men) today derives most of its resources from drugs.

Four units of the FARC, about a thousand guerrilla warriors, are currently operating in Putumayo, at the edge of the Amazon forest. The small U.S. prop planes assigned to spray the coca fields will thus be able to fly only with a military escort. At least this is the argument advanced by Washington to justify the size of the military component, which represents 80 percent of Plan Colombia, and the 60 military helicopters supplied by the Americans.

On the Drug War's Front Lines

The epicenter of the U.S. war on drugs is now Colombia's Putumayo province, where the Colombian army, backed by $1.3 billion in U.S. aid, has launched an offensive to eradicate coca fields in the stronghold of the Revolutionary Armed Forces of Colombia, the continent's largest insurgent movement. Critics of Plan Colombia, President Andrés Pastrana's antinarcotics and economic development strategy, charge that U.S. military involvement in the decades-long civil war raises the specter of escalation of the conflict and worsening human-rights abuses. Pastrana sought support in reducing drug trafficking, negotiating peace with the guerrillas, and investing in development programs to wean peasants away from coca-growing. What he got, instead, was a stepped-up counterinsurgency operation. Meanwhile, efforts to reduce demand for drugs in the United States, which consumes 75 percent of Colombian cocaine, are paltry. Less than a quarter of the annual $19-billion U.W. drug-control budget goes toward treatment.

The war against drugs is being waged against a constantly moving target—Pakistan, China, and Iran are now experiencing the most dramatic growth in drug abuse. The United Nations links declines in drug production with programs that foster alternative sources of income, and reduction of consumption with increased spending on prevention and treatment. For as long as there is demand, there will be a supply.

—Margaret Bald

A Globalized Solution

One of the great successes of this government [of President Andrés Pastrana] is having made the Colombian conflict the international community's problem. And it should be, because most of the fuel powering our irregular armies comes from the billions of dollars in drug traffic. This traffic is being generated thanks to unbridled demand from consumers, primarily in the United States and Europe.

Colombia's conflict is globalized. That is why we cannot lose sight of what is happening abroad, because, if we are ever going to emerge from this nightmare, it will be due not only to internal agreements on matters pertaining to the conflict, but also to external developments pertaining to the control of drug traffic. In other words: a globalized solution.

But what is happening abroad? First, let us observe what is not happening, beginning with the European Union, which, except for Spain, refuses to assume its responsibility, despite the fact that its citizens consume more than a third of the illegal drugs processed here.

The Europeans consider the aid they have offered, which certainly is slight, as a gesture of support rather than compensation for damages. As such, they impose the condition of its being invested only in social areas, and depending on progress in human rights. Noble objectives, to be sure, but the Europeans would do better to ask themselves whether the money received by [Colombia's] subversives, thanks to their millions of drug addicts, is being invested in weapons or in social projects.

With the United States, things are better, partly because the coordinated efforts of [Colombia's] president, the Foreign Ministry, and the embassy have been exemplary. Also, in part, because in Washington the Colombian guerrilla movement has never had the romantic image it has enjoyed until recently in European forums. But things could change, and drastically. The new Bush administration is in the process of formulating its foreign policy, and we could come out badly. Even the logical argument that the important thing is to reduce demand could redirect priorities.

The message will have to change. If we use only the argument of the battle against drug traffic, we vindicate those abroad who claim, with some reason, that the right policy is not to act on the source of supply (meaning Colombia), but rather on the reduction of demand.

Nothing would do Colombia more good than if the developed countries cured their voracious appetite for [drugs]. But when a driver unintentionally causes harm to third parties, he is obliged to assume responsibility. The same thing applies among nations.

—*Santiago Castro*, El País *(conservative), Cali, Colombia, Feb. 1, 2001.*

The American plan does not overly concern commander Félix and his comrades in arms. At the moment, their sworn enemies are the radical right-wing paramilitary militias, the United Self-Defense Forces of Colombia (Autodefensa Unida de Colombia-AUC) of Carlos Castaño. For local authorities, the decision of the guerrillas to interdict highway traffic is nothing more than a new phase in the war for control of the region and its accursed wealth, the coca crop.

The paramilitary forces have set an objective for themselves: to succeed where the army has failed, i.e., to finish off the guerrillas. In 1997, the AUC decided to "liberate the south," beginning with Puerto Asís, a major hub for drug trafficking. For the FARC, the paramilitary forces are merely an appendage of the regular army, "the new face of state terrorism directed against the peasant masses."

Small strips of Amazon forest and charred tree trunks stand as a reminder that Puerto Asís was only recently cleared for cultivation. In the 1960s, oil wells (now practically depleted) attracted the first settlers. The building of the pipeline opened the way for farming. Since the late 1980s, the successes in eradicating crops in Peru and Bolivia, the dismantling of the major Colombian drug cartels, and the guerrillas' weapons have contributed to rapid growth of coca cultivation. The large landowners have practically disappeared, replaced by small farmers

under guerrilla control. Enthroned on his plastic chair alongside a deserted road with his AK-47 on his knees, commander Félix is categorical: "The people under the FARC… know that everything that happens here is the fault of the government."

At Puerto Asís, food is in short supply. Under pressure from local officials, the government finally set up an airlift and organized the movement of trucks under military escort. Officials in Bogotá assert that 1,400 tons of food have been routed there. But this is a pittance. "The solution to the tragic situation we are experiencing in Putumayo does not depend on us," explains the mayor of Puerto Asís. "The guerrillas demand that measures be taken against the paramilitary groups. Therefore, it is up to the government and the guerrilla leaders to reach a settlement on this point."

After being engaged in a difficult peace process for nearly two years, the delegates of the government and FARC finally put Putumayo on the agenda for negotiations. On Nov. 14, 2000, the guerrillas' announcement of a unilateral suspension of negotiations had a chilling effect: The war in Putumayo is now set to last a long time. [In February 2001, peace talks resumed.—*WPR*]

It is an odd sort of war, where the combatants spend more time evading one another than fighting. If the army arrives in force (it is said to have 3,000 men in Putumayo), the guerrillas immediately move out, only to reoccupy the territory once the soldiers have their backs turned. The paramilitary militias hardly dare to venture into the countryside held by the guerrillas. While more intense than in the rest of the country, the confrontations between the FARC and the AUC remain sporadic. On the road, there are alternately soldiers, guerrillas, and paramilitary forces, sometimes one or two miles away from one another. It is indeed a strange sort of war, where the combatants resemble one another. Look beyond their military fatigues, and their faces all tell the same story of poverty. Only the boots allow an untrained eye to distinguish a government soldier, wearing laced leather boots, from a guerrilla, wearing rubber boots.

It is an ugly war, with civilians caught in the middle. The paramilitary's initial strategy was to exert pressure on the population by massacring people suspected of being in league with the guerrillas. "In 1997, there were 60 or 80 murders a month," confirmed the director of the hospital. Crimes of passion or killings to settle scores are commonplace. However, most of the murders are the doing of armed groups who, in an unending spiral, are attempting to eliminate the sympathizers of the enemy camp or drive them out of the region. People live in fear of summary executions and so-called reprisals.

One of the parishioners confirms that "the *paracos* (paramilitaries) would have never been able to clean La Hormiga without the complicity of the military; but it must be recognized that, despite the atrocities committed, they have managed to gain the population's esteem." An official from the mayor's office explains that "in Putumayo… the state is absent for all practical purposes. When the guerrillas had the monopoly over armed force, they were tolerated and even respected…. But the guerrillas have become arrogant and increasingly rapacious, so people got sick of them."

Now the paramilitaries, seeking to win people over, have opted for a policy of reducing taxes. While the guerrillas collect a tax of 300,000 pesos (US $134) per kilo of base paste (sold for about $1,070), the self-defense forces only ask for a third of that. Taxes on land and commercial activities are likewise intended to be competitive. Carlos Castaño, the head of the paramilitary militia, is said to have forbidden massacres from lists of targets. Instead there are selective executions and expulsions.

"El Galiván" (The Hawk), age 32, is now the urban commander of La Hormiga. He claims to have 600 men (official es-

timates cut that figure in half). The resources from taxes on coca make it possible to pay each member of the AUC a bonus of 700,001) pesos per month (US $313), almost three times the Colombian minimum wage. The majority of the AUC troops are small landowners, former mafia militiamen, retired soldiers, and former guerrillas. "After killing my father, the FARC told us to abandon our land. My brothers and I have joined the AUC to get rid of those vermin," Javier, 35, explains.

While "El Galiván" is holding a meeting in a cafeteria in the center of town, three soldiers pass by, but he hardly pays them notice. "Our relations with the army," he says, "pose no problem, as long as we let the military do their job, and they let us do ours. If the army moves in, we retreat." Colonel Díaz, commander of the 24th brigade of the Colombian army, categorically denies this. He takes out a large folder of documents intended to prove that members of paramilitary groups have actually been killed in the course of fighting or have been turned over to the justice system by the army.

On the ground, Plan Colombia has at least gotten everyone to agree on one point. While the environmental and health impact of the aerial spraying operations is still difficult to assess, nobody questions the social toll. Officially the AUC supports Plan Colombia but, in an aside, one commander in fatigues thunders: "If I were the boss, I can tell you that I would not tolerate it. How can we let the gringos spray the coca crops and reduce our peasants to misery?" On the ground, even the soldiers doubt the effectiveness of the plan. "It is useless to spray the crops; the peasants will just go somewhere else," muses Sergeant Vicente, who has served 11 years. He says he is sick of "this war in which my countrymen are killing one another."

The mayor of Puerto Asís does not share this assessment. "The peasants are sick and tired of growing coca, because it has brought only poverty and violence. They are ready to participate in a program to… eradicate the plants and to grow substitute crops. But this presupposes a… commitment by the state, which must build roads and ensure that the alternative crops can be sold," he asserts in a tone that is as categorical as it is disillusioned.

—*Marie Delcas*, Le Monde *(liberal), Paris, France,*
Jan. 11, 2001.

Symposium: Searching for Science Policy

SCIENCE AND DRUG ABUSE CONTROL POLICY

Mark A.R. Kleiman

"Science" has many meanings, and its ambiguity creates confusion about the proper role of science in policy-making. Few doubt, in principle, that the policy process ought to be informed by the scientific temperament, the attitude that gives to every proposition just the degree of assent warranted by evidence and argument. A good dose of "science," in that sense, is exactly what drug policy lacks, and needs.

But "science" also names a particular set of social enterprises, marked by the competitive pursuit of interesting new systematic knowledge of physical, biological, and social phenomena. No one doubts that science in this second sense has a great deal to contribute to policy-making, in the form of (1) predictive knowledge about what is likely to happen; (2) contingently predictive knowledge about the likely consequences of different actions; and (3) technological knowledge about the various means to accomplishing chosen ends. But that "science" so understood ought to dominate policy-making is much less clear.

First, some crucial bits of knowledge, as evaluated from the policy analyst's viewpoint, may not be interesting, new, or systematic as evaluated from the viewpoint of a working scientist. A prominent, though perhaps not important, example, is the question of the medical uses of cannabis. Delta-9. THC, the primary psychoactive agent in the cannabis plant, has already been approved for medical use. The remaining question from a drug-regulation standpoint is whether the inhaled vapors of the whole plant, containing a mix of psychoactive agents, might outperform the oral administration of the pure delta-9. Both anecdote and theory suggest that this might be true. Patients taking pure delta-9 tend to complain of unpleasant intoxication, and delta-9 has been shown to produce anxiety, while cannabidiol, one of the other active agents, has been shown to relieve it. Moreover, inhalation has advantages over pill-swallowing in both speed and the capacity for the patient to adjust the dose but the superiority of whole plant vapor over the THC pill has yet to be shown in controlled trials. Despite considerable huffing and puffing over the medical marijuana issue, including several state-level referenda, years of federal court litigation, and an Institute of Medicine report, no one has done the simple experiment of giving the two alternative drug/dosage forms to a group of patients and finding out what happens.

Part of the reason, to be sure, is deliberate obstructionism on the part of the National Institute on Drug Abuse, which has both a strong ideological position against the use of whole cannabis and a monopoly on research supplies of the drug. But there has been no flood of research applications, and NIDA has had no difficulty in finding a "lack of scientific merit" in those that have been submitted. The question of whether the vapors from a whole plant are better or worse medically than the oral administration of one of its components is simply not a scientifically interesting question. As a result, opponents of the medical use of the whole plant can continue to say, accurately though disingenuously, that its superiority to pure delta-9 "has not been scientifically established."

Second, part of the technique of science is manipulating phenomena so that only one independent variable changes at a time; that is what a controlled experiment is about. But the world that policymakers must live in is not so neat. The effect of maternal cocaine use on fetal development, controlling for maternal alcohol use, is no doubt an interesting topic in pharmacology, but since in fact cocaine consumption tends to increase alcohol consumption, the finding that cocaine itself is only modestly damaging to the fetus may be seriously misleading.

This situation is more typical than anomalous. Consider four fairly standard questions in drug policy—not in the debate over drug policy in the large that dominates media attention to this subject without having much impact on actual governmental behavior, but in day-to-day decision-making about drugs:

1. Should we raise the tax on a standard alcoholic drink, currently about a dime, to some substantially higher number, say twenty cents?

2. Should we reduce the number of cocaine dealers in prison by 20 percent, using some combination of reduced police activity, less vigorous prosecution, and changes in sentencing laws? (Or should we instead do nothing, or raise that number by 20 percent?)

3. Should we increase public funding for methadone maintenance therapy enough to raise the number of methadone clients at any one time by one-quarter?

4. Should schools devote an additional hour per week of class time to delivering anti-drug messages?

What kinds of scientific research would be helpful in making these decisions correctly? Put another way, what parameters about the world should be measured before choosing?

Decision #1: Alcohol Taxation

How does the policy work, for good and for ill? Higher taxes will raise prices; higher prices will lead to lower consumption of alcohol and its complements (very likely including cocaine and the amphetamines) and higher consumption of its substitutes (including cannabis possibly, alcohol treatment certainly). Reducing drinking will tend, other things remaining equal, to reduce drinking-related problems, both physical and behavioral, including the rate of addiction. Increasing the price of drinking will tend to impoverish those who remain heavy drinkers in the face of the tax increase. It will also cause some persons whose drinking was a harmless pleasure to cut back or even stop, reducing their well being and in some cases even damaging their health somewhat.

As policymakers, we should be interested in the absolute and relative magnitudes of these changes. If the gains from reduced problem drinking outweigh the losses from displaced harmless drinking plus the impoverishment effect on the skid-row wino class, the tax increase should be adopted; otherwise not. A partial list of (in principle) scientifically determinable facts relevant to this simple decision would therefore include:

- Price-elasticity of demand for alcohol, disaggregated by user characteristics (e.g., age, drinking intensity, preferred form of alcohol, behavior while drunk), and into effects on initiation, continuation, intensification, quit, and relapse rates for casual and problematic alcohol use.
- Cross-elasticity of demand (relationship of substitution or complementarity) between alcohol and other drugs.
- Impact on future drinking of price-induced changes in current drinking by minors.
- Dose-effect curves for physical toxicity (e.g., liver, heart, etc.).

- Dose-effect curves for behavioral toxicity (e.g., crime, accident, suicide, degradation of workplace and family performance).
- Estimates of the welfare losses to drinkers and their intimates from becoming addicted to alcohol (on some definition of "addicted") and of the gains from any given period of recovery.
- Impact on welfare and behavior of heavy drinkers who continue to drink heavily in the face of the tax-induced price increase.

Notice how the hot scientific topics (receptors, genetic predispositions, "rational addiction," etc.) have little or nothing to offer here. And yet the topic is arguably the most practically important in all of drug policy, since it concerns the drug that does the overwhelming bulk of the damage to users and others and a policy that is virtually self-implementing.

Decision #2, Cocaine Dealers in Prison

Changing the number of cocaine dealers in prison calls for much the same analysis as above, except that the effects on price (and non-price factors of availability), which we could assume as known in the alcohol-tax case, are in fact almost entirely speculative, and may depend a great deal on who goes to prison rather than the mere number of prisoners. But the basic logic of making a damaging drug more expensive or harder to get is the same: the key questions are how much a given change will reduce consumption, and how much that reduction in consumption will in turn reduce harms to users and others. By the same token, making cocaine more expensive can have bad impacts, especially since the revenues go to dealers rather than the public treasury.

In any case, knowing more about the neuroanatomical reward pathways in the nucleus accumbens is not likely to offer much in the way of social policy guidance. But again, the topic is of overwhelming importance; we have something like a third of a million cocaine dealers behind bars at any moment, costing a fortune (or, to think about it a different way, using up prison cells that could otherwise be holding muggers) and suffering greatly. If in fact, reducing that number substantially would not greatly increase cocaine consumption, there is an opportunity for huge gains in fiscal, crime-control, and humanitarian terms. But our scientists do not seem to be much help in making this choice wisely.

As Peter Reuter has eloquently pointed out, the drug research budget is very tightly concentrated on biomedicine, prevention, and treatment, while the drug abuse control budget is overwhelmingly devoted to enforcement. This means that even the most basic relationships between enforcement effort and drug-abuse (or even drug-market) outcomes remain almost entirely matters of speculation. This is not disadvantageous to the bureaucratic interests associated with law enforcement. But it does mean that we have neither any way of knowing whether enforcement does any good, and if so, what kind of enforcement does what kind of good, nor any way of optimizing the use of a given set of enforcement resources over a set of social objectives.

Decision #3, Methadone Maintenance Policy

We need to know how much damage is currently being done to and by those persons not now in methadone treatment who would be in such treatment if the supply were expanded, and how much less damage would occur if they were methadone clients instead of active heroin addicts. This is not a question that the standard "treatment effectiveness" studies are much use in answering. A substantial amount is known about the differences in behavior between methadone clients before and after their treatment entry, but using the difference as an estimate of the benefit of the treatment is highly problematic, since it requires that we ignore both self-selection and regression toward the mean. Nor would a random-assignment experiment tell us much about a world in which potential clients search for programs (and vice versa). Conceptually, the right experiment would involve the random assignment of some population (say, heroin abusers being released from prison), not to different treatments, but to different levels of treatment availability (e.g., by handing half the group coupons guaranteeing no-wait methadone treatment, the other half not).

Decision #4, Anti-Drug Education

Whether anti-drug education is effective surely depends both on the content of the classroom message and the competence with which it is delivered. The (rather depressing) prevention-evaluation literature has a great deal to say about the former, but tells us much less about the importance of the latter. Since an actual school district cannot count on having its actual teachers deliver anti-drug messages with the zeal or skill of those who run pilot programs, evaluation results are likely to be systematically over-optimistic.

But the deeper problem here involves time. What we really want to know is the effect of the program on the long-term risk of developing clinically significant substance abuse problems. But this outcome, viewed from the perspective of programs aimed at seventh-graders, is both long-deferred and rare. Even if someone were willing to fund the enormous sample sizes and long-term follow-ups required to learn about the efficacy of a program measured in these terms, the result would come so many years later than the intervention that its applicability to then-current conditions would be open to serious question. So instead we measure the impact of the programs on initiation rates to tobacco, alcohol, and cannabis, trusting that the correlation between early use and later problems is causal rather than reflecting unmeasured characteristics of the children involved. It is well known that "information only" prevention programs are counterproductive; they increase the rate of experimentation by making children feel that they are sophisticated drug consumers. That finding led to the development of newer prevention models, based on social influence. But note that an information-based program might increase the rate of initiation while reducing the risk of getting into trouble conditional on initiation. This is not a matter of going beyond range of what in principle is scientifically determinable. It is simply that the science involved would be too expensive and time-consuming to do.

The Limits of Science

In sum, then, doing more and better science of the kind we currently do will not give us much in the way of usable answers to these four rather typical drug-policy problems.

There are often unavoidable tensions between scientific interest and short-term practical utility. On this score, there is not much difference between drug abuse research and mental health research, where the families of those with severe Axis I disorders such as schizophrenia want work on treating those diagnoses, while the scientists want to learn how the brain works.

There are also unavoidable tensions between both the caution and the boldness of scientists (boldness in conjecture, caution about drawing firm conclusions) and the needs of legal and bureaucratic decision-makers for "hard evidence" or "scientific proof" to support decisions. Karl Popper's principle that scientific theories do not become "more probable" in the sense of the probability calculus as evidence mounts in their favor (because the truth is of measure zero in the mass of possible conjecture) means that the best-supported hypothesis, the one on the basis of which one can most productively conduct research, may not be the same as a reasonable Bayesian prior about some set of real-world relationships.

On top of these, there are avoidable problems, which resemble nothing so much as the "idols" Bacon saw as standing in the way of the proper scientific interpretation of nature. We can classify them roughly as idols of the newspaper, idols of the enterprise, and idols of the laboratory.

Idols of the Newspaper

The idols of the newspaper are the received "truths" about drugs and drug abuse, "known" to every reporter and newspaper-reader, but false-to-fact. To deny any of them is to discredit oneself. For example, any use of any illicit drug is officially believed to carry a high risk of developing into problem use. In fact, however, the most common pattern of the use of the most common psychoactive substances (except for nicotine in the form of cigarettes) is occasional and non-problematic. The lifetime probability of developing diagnosable substance abuse disorder, conditional on a non-trivial initiation to cannabis, powder cocaine, or alcohol, seems to run between 10 percent and 25 percent, with alcohol on the high end of that range, perhaps because of its ubiquity, and cannabis at the low end.

Moreover, substance abuse disorders are "known" to be chronic and relapsing and to rarely go into remission without professional help or participation in structured group self-help. In fact, the most common pattern of substance abuse disorder has a relatively rapid remission (several months to a few years) with no relapse, and the vast majority of those who have had, but no longer actively suffer from, diagnosable substance abuse disorder have had no formal treatment. They just quit when they got tired.

Those who cannot quit on their own and need formal treatment are indeed much more likely to have stubborn problems—use of tobacco cessation services is negatively correlated with the probability of successful quitting—but even among those who enter treatment, only a minority keeps cycling in and out. However, this group accounts for a large proportion of those in treatment at any given time, and is therefore taken by treatment professionals to represent the typical pattern.

The drug problem is "known" to consist primarily of illicit drug use; in fact, about 85 percent of all diagnosable substance abuse disorder involve alcohol as the primary or sole substance. Yet the newspapers routinely report that so-and-so drinks but does not use drugs. Similarly, everyone "knows" that babies exposed to cocaine *in utero* (the famous "crack babies") are irreparably damaged. In fact, the dimensions of such damage have not been established, and there is reason to think that bad parenting due to continued maternal substance abuse has more to do with bad outcomes than prenatal exposure.

It is certainly the case that total fetal damage from maternal use of alcohol, and total fetal damage from maternal use of tobacco (which is known to reduce measured IQ by about a third of a standard deviation) each dwarfs the damage from cocaine.

Anyone who pays scientific attention to the drug problem knows that these idols of the newspaper have feet of clay. But denying them is both dangerous in career terms and unlikely to make any headway against reporters' ignorance and editors' sense that they ought not to be interfering with the national anti-drug-abuse campaign by printing inconvenient facts, which most readers would not believe anyway.

Idols of the Enterprise

These are the organizational self-interests, whether embodied in public agencies or private industries, which would be damaged by the recognition of certain facts. Twice in the past fifteen years, agencies engaged in drug interdiction have hired tame research organizations to produce pseudo-scientific findings showing that the interdiction effort is highly valuable. Showing that this is false requires no analytic tools past first-year microeconomics. Yet, under congressional pressure the Office of National Drug Control Policy funded, and the National Academy of Sciences conducted, a solemn review in which one of these spoof documents was treated on an equal footing with a serious, though admittedly preliminary, piece of analysis, and both were even-handedly condemned.

The fact that the National Institute on Drug Abuse has a drug-abuse-prevention brief as well as a research brief imports idols of the agency into the process by which drug-related science is funded and its results disseminated. If there has ever been a NIDA press release about the finding that some illicit drug does not have some hypothesized danger, no one seems to have reported it. A recent study of dance-club drug-taking in Europe compared a group of extremely heavy Ecstasy users (Ecstasy is nominally MDMA, but there is evidence of substantial adulteration and mislabeling, in addition to substantial witting polydrug abuse in the sample) with two control groups: very heavy cannabis users, and those not using any drug heavily. It was not surprising that the official NIDA line was that the study showed MDMA to be a terribly dangerous drug, even though the actual measured impacts were rather slight given the truly heroic dosing patterns involved and despite the doubts about how much of the damage was actually from MDMA. It took more gall, though not more than the NIDA director proved to be master of, to simply ignore the finding that

the (extremely) heavy cannabis users were not measurably different from the other control group on any dimension of damage.

On the licit-drug side of the problem, both the alcohol and the tobacco industries have created pseudo-disputes over whether their products are "drugs." (One of the trade associations on the alcohol side offers the thought that because alcohol is used in grams-per-kilogram rather than milligrams-per-kilogram doses, it is not really a drug. I am not making this up.)

Idols of the Laboratory

These are principles for conducting and interpreting research that get in the way of the search for truth. Some are imposed from outside; others are intrinsic to the scientific enterprise. Start with the external problems. Whenever "science" is invested with legal or other political significance, interested parties will have reasons to try to cheat by influencing results, using some combination of funding, pressure, and outright lying. The result is often the creation of extra-scientific rules intended to make cheating harder. This leads to a process that might be called "forensic science" to distinguish it from the genuine article. Benefit/cost analysis, studies of environmental impacts and remediation, and the evaluation of proposed new pharmaceutical drugs all proceed under the rules of forensic science.

Perhaps the most sacred of such idols of the (forensic) laboratory is the double-blind placebo-controlled experiment. As a method, it builds in maximum protections against investigator deception and self-deception. But in the case of the psychoactive drugs, it can lead to either the impossibility of doing any experiment or to an experiment that misses the point. Keeping the subject "blind" to whether his or her neurons are being bombarded is often tricky, though the use of an "active placebo" can help. In cases where the intervention involves human interaction between therapist and patient rather than the mere administration of a chemical, it can be difficult or impossible to keep a competent clinician in the dark as to whether the patient has had an active dose or not. Even where possible, a double-blind study introduces an element of unrealism into the results, since in actual clinical practice patients and physicians do know what they are getting and giving. None of this is to say that double-blind trials are not worth doing. But to insist that only such trials are potential sources of scientific knowledge is surely idolatry.

Human-subjects protection rules can also function as extrinsic idols of the laboratory. Imposed on scientists after some fairly horrendous abuses, their implementation through Institutional Review Boards (IRB)—and in the special case of California, through something called, improbably, the California Review Advisory Panel—can serve as a convenient way of side-tracking research likely to lead to inconvenient results, especially when the potential benefits to subjects are ruled out of consideration because the subjects are not suffering from any disease. In particular, any attempt to give controlled drugs, and especially the hallucinogens, to drug-naive subjects is likely to be rejected out of hand, making it impossible to answer the rather important question, "What is the impact of a first dose?" The fact that some of the potential subjects will instead take the same drugs (or what they fondly imagine to be the same drugs) illicitly and therefore under uncontrolled conditions does not constitute a counter-argument as the IRB game is played.

A drug-specific idol of the laboratory is the convention, respected by funders and journals alike, that the sheerest anecdotal (i.e., case-series) or correlational data should be accepted as science if it seems to show that some drug does damage, but that only carefully controlled studies suffice to show benefit. This is related, but not identical, to the notion, enshrined in the practice of the Food and Drug Administration though not in statute, that the only legitimate use of a drug (psychoactive or not) is to treat some diagnosable pathology, and that improvements in normal functioning do not constitute "efficacy." The lack of restriction on off-level prescriptions allows many drugs approved for treatment of genuine disease to then be used widely for performance enhancement, as the case of Viagra graphically demonstrates. But without the existence of a clinical entity called erectile dysfunction, the mere desire of middle-aged men to perform better sexually would not have justified a drug approval.

Other idols of the laboratory have to do with the needs of normal science to produce papers and for funders to find projects to pay for. The theory of "rational addiction" is a case in point. It turns out that, with appropriate assumptions, some of the phenomena of addiction can be reproduced within the framework of the rational-actor model beloved of economists. The correspondence to real phenomena is not really very impressive; in particular, if addiction were truly a rational phe-

nomenon, it would not be much of a problem except for its external costs. But the theory allows the production of an almost unlimited number of well-crafted empirical papers testing the theory against various data sets. As a result, rational addiction has established itself as a major subfield within addiction studies, heavily funded by the National Institute on Alcohol Abuse and Alcoholism and done largely under the highly respectable auspices of the National Bureau of Economic Research.

There are thus both intrinsic and extrinsic reasons why science proper has less to contribute to making better drug abuse control policies than might be thought at first blush. The scientific temperament, however, remains our best hope for digging ourselves out of our current rut.

Mark A.R. Kleiman is professor of policy studies at the University of California-Los Angeles School of Public Policy and Social Research. He is the author of Against Excess: Drug Policy for Results *and of* Marijuana: Costs of Abuse, Costs of Control.

This symposium on Searching for Science Policy is based on a conference held on April 1 and 2, 2000 at Boston University under the auspices of the Institute for the Study of Economic Culture. Grateful acknowledgement is made to the Lynde and Harry Bradley Foundation for its generous support. [See Society, May/June 2001 for additional articles.]

The case for legalisation

Time for a puff of sanity

IT IS every parent's nightmare. A youngster slithers inexorably from a few puffs on a joint, to a snort of cocaine, to the needle and addiction. It was the flesh-creeping heart of "Traffic", a film about the descent into heroin hell of a pretty young middle-class girl, and it is the terror that keeps drug laws in place. It explains why even those politicians who puffed at a joint or two in their youth hesitate to put the case for legalising drugs.

The terror is not irrational. For the first thing that must be said about legalising drugs, a cause *The Economist* has long advocated and returns to this week, is that it would lead to a rise in their use, and therefore to a rise in the number of people dependent on them. Some argue that drug laws have no impact, because drugs are widely available. Untrue: drugs are expensive—a kilo of heroin sells in America for as much as a new Rolls-Royce—partly because their price reflects the dangers involved in distributing and buying them. It is much harder and riskier to pick up a dose of cocaine than it is to buy a bottle of whisky. Remove such constraints, make drugs accessible and very much cheaper, and more people will experiment with them.

A rise in drug-taking will inevitably mean that more people will become dependent—inevitably, because drugs offer a pleasurable experience that people seek to repeat. In the case of most drugs, that dependency may be no more than a psychological craving and affect fewer than one in five users; in the case of heroin, it is physical and affects maybe one in three. Even a psychological craving can be debilitating. Addicted gamblers and drinkers bring misery to themselves and their families. In addition, drugs have lasting physical effects and some, taken incompetently, can kill. This is true both for some "hard" drugs and for some that people think of as "soft": too much heroin can trigger a strong adverse reaction, but so can ecstasy. The same goes for gin or aspirin, of course: but many voters reasonably wonder whether it would be right to add to the list of harmful substances that are legally available.

Of Mill and morality

The case for doing so rests on two arguments: one of principle, one practical. The principles were set out, a century and a half ago, by John Stuart Mill, a British liberal philosopher, who urged that the state had no right to intervene to prevent individuals from doing something that harmed them, if no harm was thereby done to the rest of society. "Over himself, over his own body and mind, the individual is sovereign," Mill famously proclaimed. This is a view that *The Economist* has always espoused, and one to which most democratic governments adhere, up to a point. They allow the individual to undertake all manner of dangerous activities unchallenged, from mountaineering to smoking to riding bicycles through city streets. Such pursuits alarm insurance companies and mothers, but are rightly tolerated by the state.

True, Mill argued that some social groups, especially children, required extra protection. And some argue that drug-takers are also a special class: once addicted, they can no longer make rational choices about whether to continue to harm themselves. Yet not only are dependent users a minority of all users; in addition, society has rejected this argument in the case of alcohol—and of nicotine (whose addictive power is greater than that of heroin). The important thing here is for governments to spend adequately on health education.

The practical case for a liberal approach rests on the harms that spring from drug bans, and the benefits that would accompany legalisation. At present, the harms fall disproportionately on poor countries and on poor people in rich countries. In producer and entrepot countries, the drugs trade finances powerful gangs who threaten the state and corrupt political institutions. Colombia is the most egregious example, but Mexico too wrestles with the threat to the police and political honesty. The attempt to kill illicit crops poisons land and people. Drug money helps to prop up vile regimes in Myanmar and Afghanistan. And drug production encourages local drug-taking, which (in the case of heroin) gives a helping hand to the spread of HIV/AIDS.

In the rich world, it is the poor who are most likely to become involved in the drugs trade (the risks may be high, but drug-dealers tend to be equal-opportunity employers), and therefore end up in jail. Nowhere is this more shamefully true than in the United States, where roughly one in four prisoners is locked up for a (mainly non-violent) drugs offence. America's imprisonment rate for drugs offences now exceeds that for all crimes in most West European countries. Moreover, although whites take drugs almost as freely as blacks and Hispanics, a vastly disproportionate number of those arrested, sentenced and imprisoned are non-white. Drugs policy in the United States is thus breeding a generation of men and women from disadvantaged backgrounds whose main training for life has been in the violence of prison.

Legalise to regulate

Removing these harms would bring with it another benefit. Precisely because the drugs market is illegal, it cannot be regulated. Laws cannot discriminate between availability to children and adults. Governments cannot insist on minimum quality standards for cocaine; or warn asthma sufferers to avoid ecstasy; or demand that distributors take responsibility for the way their products are sold. With alcohol and tobacco, such restrictions are possible; with drugs, not. This increases the dangers to users, and especially to young or incompetent users. Illegality also puts a premium on selling strength: if each purchase is risky, then it makes sense to buy drugs in concentrated form. In the same way, Prohibition in the United States in the 1920s led to a fall in beer consumption but a rise in the drinking of hard liquor.

How, if governments accepted the case for legalisation, to get from here to there? When, in the 18th century, a powerful new intoxicant became available, the impact was disastrous: it took years of education for gin to cease to be a social threat. That is a strong reason to proceed gradually: it will take time for conventions governing sensible drug-taking to develop. Meanwhile, a century of illegality has deprived governments of much information that good policy requires. Impartial academic research is difficult. As a result, nobody knows how demand may respond to lower prices, and understanding of the physical effects of most drugs is hazy.

And how, if drugs were legal, might they be distributed? The thought of heroin on supermarket shelves understandably adds to the terror of the prospect. Just as legal drugs are available through different channels—caffeine from any cafe, alcohol only with proof of age, Prozac only on prescription—so the drugs that are now illegal might one day be distributed in different ways, based on knowledge about their potential for harm. Moreover, different countries should experiment with different solutions: at present, many are bound by a United Nations convention that hampers even the most modest moves towards liberalisation, and that clearly needs amendment.

To legalise will not be easy. Drug-taking entails risks, and societies are increasingly risk-averse. But the role of government should be to prevent the most chaotic drug-users from harming others—by robbing or by driving while drugged, for instance—and to regulate drug markets to ensure minimum quality and safe distribution. The first task is hard if law enforcers are preoccupied with stopping all drug use; the second, impossible as long as drugs are illegal. A legal market is the best guarantee that drug-taking will be no more dangerous than drinking alcohol or smoking tobacco. And, just as countries rightly tolerate those two vices, so they should tolerate those who sell and take drugs.

WHAT'S YOUR ANTI-DRUG?

Part One

NATIONAL DRUG POLICY
WILL BE MORE CONSERVATIVE
THAN COMPASSIONATE

BY STEVEN WISHNIA

In his first interviews as attorney general, John Ashcroft pledged to "reinvigorate," "renew," "refresh" and "re-launch" the war on drugs, arguing that the Clinton administration had been lax in fighting narcotics.

It's difficult to imagine how Bill Clinton could have been much harsher, short of public executions of drug dealers. Under his administration, federal prisons opened at a rate of almost one a month, confining a population that is now 58 percent drug offenders—almost three times the percentage in state prisons, according to figures from the Washington-based Sentencing Project. The Clinton administration also refused to fund needle-exchange programs, prosecuted medical-marijuana patients, and began to take sides in the Colombian civil war in the name of fighting cocaine.

A devout prohibitionist, Ashcroft is now the top-ranking federal official dealing with drugs. As of early March, President George W. Bush had not yet appointed anyone to head the White House drug-policy office. (Candidates mentioned include former Florida Rep. Bill McCollum, a militant prohibitionist, and Elizabeth Dole, who has backed both more drug treatment and more drug testing.) "Ashcroft is the only person in the country who thinks that drug treatment doesn't make sense," says Marc Mauer of the Sentencing Project.

Yet, facing a diverse and growing movement to ameliorate or end prohibition, Bush's drug policy may turn out to be less fanatically hardline than his father's. "He's made some good noises in some good directions," says Jerry Epstein, president of the Drug Policy Forum of Texas. Last year, Bush suggested that

medical marijuana was a states' rights issue. More recently, he has dropped hints about increasing spending for drug treatment and reducing the 100-to-1 disparity between federal sentences for crack and powder cocaine. (For his part, Ashcroft has advocated reducing the crack/coke sentencing disparity by increasing penalties for powder cocaine.)

Whether Bush means it is another story. After a Bush aide met with medical-marijuana patient Tiffany Landreth in Austin last September, his office issued a statement that "current federal law bans all marijuana use, and the governor does not support changing those laws." As governor, Bush signed a law in 1997 increasing the minimum for possession of less than a gram of cocaine—barely enough for one night of "youthful indiscretion"—from probation to six months in a state jail. About 3,000 people are now incarcerated under that law. And Bush also "adamantly supported" school districts that wanted to test all students for drugs, according to William Harrell, head of the Texas branch of the American Civil Liberties Union. "We should all collectively shiver," Harrell says. Bush's record, he adds, was one of "total militarized policing and total disregard for constitutional rights."

Harrell points out that in 1999 the Bush administration named undercover cop Tom Coleman "Lawman of the Year." Coleman's accomplishment was setting up the arrests of 43 people in the small Panhandle town of Tulia on cocaine charges. Forty of the people arrested were black, and the ACLU has filed a civil rights lawsuit charging that many of them were framed—in two separate trials, Coleman testified to being in different places at the same time (see box, "Easy Targets"). Harrell says the drug task force program that assigned Coleman to Tulia was "designed and directed" by Bush's office, and specifically targets users and small-time dealers in areas where convictions are easy to get.

Texas now has more people in prison than any state. According to state figures, its 107 prisons, 17 state jails and nine "substance abuse felony punishment" facilities hold 151,000 inmates. A 2000 study by the Washington-based Criminal Justice Institute found that Texas had 1 percent of its entire population (and 3.9 percent of its black population) in prisons or local jails, the second-highest rate in the nation after Louisiana. One-fifth of them were imprisoned on drug charges. Between 1988 and 1998, according to the Drug Policy Forum of Texas, the state opened 77 new prisons—but just one new state university campus. "Nothing that he did as governor indicated a willingness to move away from prohibition," Epstein says.

However, unlike his father, who reigned at the height of the '80s crack scare (and also looked the other way at the Nicaraguan contras' fundraising deliveries from Colombia to California), George W. Bush faces a growing anti-drug war movement that includes significant numbers of conservatives. The orthodoxy of prohibition—that illegal drugs breed violence and depravity and must be stamped out by any means necessary—is being challenged on numerous fronts. Nine states and the District of Columbia have passed laws legalizing medical marijuana, despite a 1970 federal law that declares marijuana to have "no accepted medical use."

One strain in what is awkwardly called the "drug-law-reform movement" focuses on "harm reduction" policies such as needle exchange. It is more realistic to expect addicts to take small steps toward self-preservation than one giant leap to abstinence, the argument goes, and it's better for them to shoot two bags of heroin with a clean needle than to shoot 10 bags with a virus-infested set of "gimmicks." Another strain, more libertarian and marijuana-oriented, asserts that the government has no right to jail people for private behavior comparable to drinking or home-brewing. Others question the length and inflexibility of drug sentences, the numbers of people in prison, and the racial disparities among those behind bars.

New Mexico Gov. Gary Johnson, a Republican with libertarian sensibilities, advocates legalizing marijuana. While he believes that employers have the right to drug-test workers, and personally opposes drug use, Johnson is one of the few politicians who doesn't say he "experimented" with marijuana. "I smoked it," he emphasizes. Another Republican, New York Gov. George Pataki, has proposed some easing of the state's draconian "Rockefeller laws," which mandate 15 years to life for possession of four ounces of heroin or cocaine, regardless of the defendant's role in the deal.

And with three-fourths of the nation's drug prisoners being black or Latino (that figure is more than 90 percent in New York, Maryland and Illinois), African-Americans, whose neighborhoods bore the worst of the crack-trade wars, are increasingly weary of seeing multitudes of their young men locked up. Black-community pressure got President Clinton to free Kemba Smith, who served six years of a 24-year sentence essentially for being a crack wholesaler's ex-girlfriend. "I don't think the law was intentionally designed to oppress one group of people over another. But in its implementation, it certainly has had a disproportionate effect on people of color," former Baltimore Mayor Kurt Schmoke told *High Times* last year.

Some of this dissent may reach into the Bush administration. Epstein speculates that policy ultimately will be determined by whoever wins the power struggle between committed drug warriors, advocates of more treatment and a handful of libertarians. One possibility that may emerge would be a "compassionate conservative" model: continued prohibition coupled with a few token statements and programs to give it a veneer of humanity. "Status quo with a little sugar on top," says Allen St. Pierre of the National Organization for the Reform of Marijuana Laws (NORML).

"I'm more hopeful than I expected to be," says Kevin Zeese of Common Sense for Drug Policy. He sees possible movement in five areas: increased treatment, easing mandatory minimum sentences, reducing racial profiling, eliminating the crack/cocaine sentencing disparity, and maybe legalizing needle exchanges. Ashcroft is an ardent foe of needle-exchange programs, Zeese notes, but Health and Human Services Secretary Tommy Thompson funded them while he was governor of Wisconsin.

Drug courts, in which defendants are sentenced to mandatory treatment instead of jail, would fit the "compassionate conservative" model perfectly. They are the centerpiece of Pataki's proposal in New York, which he released in January. It would allow judges to send some people charged with possession of cocaine or heroin to a court-run rehabilitation program, with probation if they complete it, and prison if they don't. However, most of the state's drug prisoners are low-level dealers with prior felony convictions and would not be eligible. (Democratic legislators have introduced a counterproposal that includes them.)

But compulsory treatment brings up several caveats. First, there's little funding for voluntary treatment, so focusing resources on compulsory treatment means that poorer addicts would have to to be arrested before they could get help. Second, if it is crossed with Bush's plans to turn social services over to "faith-based" groups, the result could be forcing drug users into programs telling them the only way to conquer their addiction is to accept Jesus Christ as their personal savior. Third, treatment costs money. Bush has promised to add $1 billion in federal funding, a small fraction of the amount spent on drug enforcement. It is generally estimated that about 30 percent of total government drug spending goes to treatment and education. President Clinton vowed to increase that proportion, St. Pierre recalls, but never did.

Whatever hopes people have about Bush, they do appear to contain at least some wishful thinking, largely stemming from the "Nixon going to China" theory: that it will take a Republican to end the war on drugs, someone free of any hippie-liberal "soft on crime" stigma. Gary Johnson might fit that bill, but it is extremely difficult to imagine George W. Bush legalizing marijuana.

For one, a significant part of his political base comes from the culture warriors of the Christian right, for whom marijuana and drugs are a central moral issue. The Family Research Council opposes legalizing industrial hemp, the minimal-THC strain of cannabis grown for fiber. FRC drug-policy specialist Robert Maginnis writes that "hemp is clearly identified with the counterculture" (not exactly untrue) and that legalizing it "sends the wrong message" about marijuana. The FRC also opposes medical marijuana. In a pending Supreme Court case, it filed one of only two amicus briefs supporting the government's appeal of a lower-court ruling that "medical necessity" may exempt an Oakland "cannabis buyers' club" from federal prosecution.

Bush also has to face a potential quagmire in Colombia. While U.S. intervention there clearly fails the "Powell Doctrine" tests of a clear objective and an easy victory, Bush seems unlikely to abandon a military mission in progress, especially one supposedly against the twin demons of drug cartels and leftist guerrillas. (Plan Colombia conveniently ignores the right-wing paramilitaries' involvement in the drug trade.)

Bush's delay in picking a drug czar could be a sign that he wants to avoid drug issues as much as possible. It is hard to argue that prohibition is not an awful flop. It can't stop what it's meant to stop: The nation's prison and jail population has quadrupled since Ronald Reagan took office 20 years ago, but cocaine and heroin prices have plummeted. Most Americans under 55 have either smoked marijuana themselves or know people who have, yet pot busts now average 700,000 a year, with 70,000 in New York City alone last year. And the excesses of the war on drugs, from search-and-seizure abuses to the racial disparities in who goes to prison, are increasingly obvious.

On issues such as racial profiling, Epstein says, "They have to do damage control. They can't avoid addressing it." But does Bush have the desire to make significant changes, or the courage to face the furious opposition that would come if he did? If you can't arrest your way out of the problem, but don't want to consider legalization, what do you do?

"He couldn't even tell his kids that he'd been arrested for drunk driving," notes NORML's St. Pierre. "Considering his inability to talk about drugs during the campaign, and his evasiveness about his own drug use, I hope lack of communication doesn't become national policy."

Steven Wishnia is a senior editor at *High Times* and the author of *Exit 25 Utopia* (The Imaginary Press).

Part Two

EASY TARGETS: THE DRUG WAR TEARS THROUGH A SMALL TEXAS TOWN

BY JASMINA KELEMEN TULIA, TEXAS

In the early morning hours of July 23, 1999, Swisher County police raided trailers and public housing units here, arresting residents accused of selling cocaine to an undercover mole. The culmination of an 18-month sting operation in conjunction with the Panhandle Narcotics Task Force, police arrested 43 people, 40 of whom were black—more than 10 percent of the town's black community.

Local newspapers quickly set about congratulating the operation. One editorial excoriated the "scumbag dealers" and likened them to a "cancer" deserving a "major dose of chemotherapy behind bars." The undercover police officer was later named "Lawman of the Year" by the Texas Department of Public Safety.

But the newspapers and accolades consistently failed to mention that no drugs, weapons nor assets were seized during the surprise morning raid. Indeed, residents insist they never saw evidence of the expensive type of drugs poor locals were accused and convicted of selling. In the nearly two years since the bust, the racial disparity of the arrests and the dubious testimony of the undercover agent has led to national press attention, lawsuits from the NAACP and ACLU and an investigation by the Justice Department.

Tulia is a scrappy town of 5,000 surrounded by fields of cotton, located between Lubbock and Amarillo. Faced with few opportunities besides manual labor jobs at the local livestock auctioning barn, the mostly black, idle and disillusioned kids who couldn't afford to escape after graduation became easy fodder for Texas police departments earning their bread and butter fighting the drug war.

"We're fighting the same battles as 10 years ago. You don't have to show impact, just numbers."

This type of operation is common throughout the state. Narcotics task forces depend on high body counts to keep the federal funds flowing. Devastated by a shrinking rural economy throughout this part of the country, blacks are those least able to seek their fortunes elsewhere. Hence, if a task force wants convictions, its best bet is to focus its investigations across the tracks. Statistics compiled by the Justice Policy Institute show that in Texas blacks are incarcerated at a rate seven times higher than whites. This is nearly 63 percent higher than the national average. Robertson County District Attorney John Paschall, former head of the South Central Texas Task Force, says the number of black men arrested is so high because "they're the easiest ones to get because they're selling on the street."

But Gary Buchanan, police chief of the east Texas town of Brenham and director of the Independence Narcotics Task Force, says task forces have lost sight of their goal and are more focused on catching easy targets rather than stemming the flow of drugs. "It's a numbers game," Buchanan says. "We're fighting the same battles as 10 years ago. Heroin is coming back. LSD is back. You don't have to show any impact, just numbers."

In Tulia, blacks experienced firsthand the dubious methods available to task forces that wish to artificially boost their statistics. The black community knew something had gone awry when they learned people were being indicted for selling powder cocaine. Police charged them with delivering "eight balls"—an eighth of an ounce of cocaine, which at $180 a pop is significantly more expensive than the small bags of marijuana and cheap rocks of crack cocaine usually found in this depressed rural community. "Ain't nobody got powder in this town," says Sam Barrow, a Tulia resident who had four relatives caught in the sting. "A $10 rock, OK. But they were accusing people of carrying an eight ball in their pockets, and you know just the other day he tried to get $5 off of you for gas."

Most of those arrested agreed to plea bargains with prosecutors. For those suspects whose cases went to trial, part-time cotton farmer and full-time civil libertarian Gary Gardner was skeptical they could receive a fair hearing in Tulia, because he felt the city had an interest in whipping up drug hysteria. He urged the defendants to request a change of venue. The requests were denied for all but two white defendants, and the court quickly began dispensing its own version of justice—multiple life sentences for several deliveries of cocaine and 20 years for a single delivery with no prior convictions. Additional felony charges were tacked onto the cases because the agent claimed the deals had occurred in a public park. In all, 22 of those arrested were sent to prison.

The stiff sentences were made possible by a series of laws then Gov. George W. Bush signed in 1997 as part of his "get tough on crime" platform. A first-offense cocaine charge, which had previously been a misdemeanor punished with mandatory probation, was upgraded to a felony. He also created "drug-free zones" around schools and parks, in which any drug activity was automatically a felony charge.

Even more disturbing was the incredibly low standard of evidence needed for a conviction. All of the indictments centered around the uncorroborated testimony of Tom Coleman, the undercover agent planted by the Panhandle Regional Task Force. The sole witness against the defendants, Coleman's police reports never amounted to more than a couple of paragraphs, and he frequently presented conflicting testimony while on the stand.

A probing defense attorney, Paul Holloway, discovered Coleman had been described as a "compulsive liar" in court documents and had been arrested during the sting operation for a string of unpaid debts in other counties. He also discovered that Coleman's former boss, Cochran County Sheriff Ken Burke, had filed a complaint with the Texas Commission of Law Enforcement (TCLE), the state agency that licenses police officers, in which he wrote: "Mr. Coleman should not be in law enforcement." The judge denied the defense motion to introduce any of the evidence about Coleman's past.

Further impugning Coleman's credibility was the case of Billy Wafer, who was arrested and charged with arranging the delivery of 2.3 grams of crack. Wafer was more than nine years into a 10-year probation, and faced life in prison once charges of breaking probation and delivering drugs near a "drug-free zone" were added. Yet timecards and his boss' testimony proved Wafer was at work when the alleged sale occurred, so the charges were dropped. But not before he spent two weeks in jail, lost his job and was turned down for a home loan.

Holloway charges that local law enforcement officials worked in concert to manufacture charges against Tulia's mostly indigent black community. Some defendants did admit selling crack to Coleman, but Holloway speculates that the cocaine found in the reported deliveries came from a single source that Coleman himself spliced and mixed with the crack to upgrade the charges. Holloway believes Coleman was charging the task force for purchases of cocaine but buying crack. A chemist found that the amount of cocaine in many of these baggies was not even enough to get high on and was of poor quality. Yet due to a quirk in Texas drug law, an eight ball has to contain only a trace of cocaine for the entire weight to be registered as a cocaine delivery. The judge refused to provide funds for an outside investigator and denied the request to run laboratory tests that could prove Holloway's theories.

What most upsets Holloway is that the judge's obstinacy and the jury's willingness to overlook Coleman's often conflicting testimony are perfectly legal according to Texas judicial procedure. "It's a joke to do criminal defense here," Holloway says. "If the jury wants to sit and watch a cop lie, they can. These were marginal people on the stand and [the jury] just decided to believe the cop."

William Harrell, head of the Texas ACLU, agrees and blames the Tulia debacle on Texas' poor record of indigent defense. Texas, he says, is at the "bottom of the barrel" when it comes to defending poor people. Although statewide statistics are not available, a 1999 Houston Chronicle study of 1,800 first-offense cocaine charges found that 21 percent of defendants who hired attorneys were sentenced to jail or prison time compared to 53 percent of defendants with court-appointed attorneys.

Judges in Texas are elected in a culture where "getting tough on crime" enjoys bipartisan support and constitutional niceties are often ignored, Harrell says. These same judges appoint defense attorneys and determine their salaries. Critics say the current method of appointing lawyers inherently discourages defense attorneys from mounting a zealous defense and pressures lawyers to seek plea bargains. "It's an unconstitutional system of criminal defense," Harrell says.

Holloway, who spent nearly 1,000 hours researching his defense, was authorized to receive payment for only the first 10 hours he spent on a case. "They didn't want me to defend this case," says Holloway, who ended up accepting a plea bargain for his clients. "It was like making a deal with the devil, I knew we couldn't win."

Yet as a result of the racial imbalance of the sting's victims and shoddy police work presented to the courts, the NAACP and the ACLU filed a lawsuit and a complaint with the Justice Department, claiming that Coleman conspired with the sheriff and the district attorney to deny local blacks their civil rights. Prisoners report that FBI agents have interviewed them about Coleman's behavior during the operation. County officials and Coleman's supervisors refused to comment on the charges.

Sadly, this small town is not alone. Harrell says the ACLU is currently investigating six "Tulias" around the state. "There's a pattern of narcotics task forces operating on DEA funding, hiring the most amazingly unscrupulous informants to hunt down suspects, 90 percent of whom end up being black or Latino."

To protect Texans against the drug war, the ACLU and the NAACP have proposed a series of laws they're calling the "Tulia Proposals," which would require corroboration for testimony of undercover officers, limit the authority of judges to exclude evidence pertaining to a person's innocence and provide public access to TCLE records.

"Our system rests on the premise that the gatekeeper of evidence will act justly," Holloway says. "Coleman could steamroll anyone because in a swearing match between a cop and a citizen, the cop wins. From my perspective it's a really scary world."

AMERICA'S SHADOW DRUG WAR

THE WAR AGAINST THE WAR ON DRUGS

As Bush proposes a hard-line drug czar, many states are retreating from the "lock-'em-up" approach

By Margot Roosevelt

HOW DO YOU FEEL ABOUT THE WAR ON drugs? That may depend a bit on how you feel about the never-ending drama of Robert Downey Jr. Already facing a court date this week for a drug-related arrest in November, Downey was busted again last week when police found him lurking after midnight in an alleyway behind a motel in Culver City, Calif. He was cited for suspicion of being under the influence of a controlled substance. More serious charges, if any, will await the results of a urine test administered that night. Downey, who was immediately fired from *Ally McBeal*, quickly checked himself into a rehab clinic, a step that may or may not help him much when he stands before a judge yet again.

So let's agree that the drug-infatuated actor is a loser. But is he a loser who needs medical help to break out of his addiction? Or is he one who ought to get more hard time—he has already done a year behind bars—because that's the only way to get some users to take rehab seriously? Is he a threat only to himself? Or is he the carrier of an infection that could spread if we don't lock him away? In short, should we treat him or trash him?

Twenty years after the war on drugs got under way in earnest, the U.S. remains far from a consensus on that question. Even now, no one knows quite where George W. Bush stands on it. Signs are growing, how-

ever, that he sides more with the hardliners, even as states are backing away from the "lock-'em-up" policies they adopted in the past. Just last week the President told TIME that addiction "does require treatment, and I think we ought to look at all sentencing laws." But one day earlier, word leaked that Bush plans to nominate as his "drug czar" a man who has emphasized what he calls the "moral lesson" of law enforcement. John Walters, 49, who was chief deputy to former czar William Bennett in the first Bush Administration, believes nonviolent drug offenders should be diverted to treatment on first and second offenses. But he thinks only fear of jail time, be it weeks or months, will get some hard-core addicts (Robert Downey Jr.) into treatment and keep them there.

Bennett describes Walters as "a hardliner on all fronts" but says he is "not somebody who's ignorant of the effectiveness of good treatment and education." Walters already served briefly as drug czar after Bennett departed but quit in 1993, sharply criticizing then President Bill Clinton for offering "no moral leadership or encouragement" in the fight against drugs.

Some 460,000 Americans are behind bars for drug offenses—a tenfold increase over 1980. (In 1996, referring to violent offenders, Walters said, "I am against the discussion... that there are too many people in jail.") Two weeks ago, in another

sign that his heart is with the hard-liners, President Bush asked Congress to allocate $4.7 billion to the federal-prison system, projecting a 32% increase in inmates over the next five years, a jump largely fueled by mandatory drug sentences. Some $40 billion a year is already being spent by federal and state governments to prosecute and imprison drug offenders and to try to stem the flow of narcotics across the border. Drug use is down during the past 20 years, which is one important marker of success. But drugs are cheaper, purer and more plentiful than ever. More than three-quarters of Americans tell pollsters that the war on drugs is failing.

Even before the film *Traffic* broadcast its bleak evaluation of the war, things had begun to change at the state level, where overburdened criminal-justice systems handle most drug offenses. In the past four years, states have passed 17 of 19 proposed ballot initiatives that loosened tough drug laws. While Congress shows little interest in repealing stiff federal "mandatory minimum" drug sentences, some 700 drug courts have been created or are being planned by various states to shepherd narcotics abusers through treatment rather than prison. Utah and Oregon curtailed police powers to forfeit the assets of suspected drug users. Nine states have legalized medical marijuana, including Oregon, Maine and Nevada.

ONE STATE'S APPROACH

Patients, Not Prisoners

At first glance, the stuffy basement room in the Maricopa County courthouse seems unremarkable: a black-robed figure looming over the dais; lawyers and sheriff's deputies at the ready; a line of 72 convicted felons up for sentencing. First comes the lanky forklift driver caught with crystal meth. Then the surly mechanic, father of three, busted for cocaine. And the pale 19-year-old with shorn red hair, on probation for using marijuana, who has failed his latest drug test. He shuffles his feet as his mother looks on, wipes away a tear and mumbles, "I messed up."

Yet however familiar the scene, the criminals in Judge Colleen McNally's courtroom have little to fear. They are first offenders, convicted of possessing drugs for personal use—not of dealing—and, as such, benefit from a groundbreaking Arizona statute barring their imprisonment. McNally's sentences are about rehabilitation, even repentance. Part shrink, part scold, McNally rules with revivalist fervor. "You're going to get a lot out of this journey," she tells a woman sentenced to counseling and urine testing. The audience is invited to clap—and they do so, loudly—as she praises a man who has stayed clean for six weeks and hands him free tickets to the local science museum. The young redhead gets community service: washing windows in his church.

Arizona's Proposition 200, which passed four years ago, was a radical departure for a conservative Republican state. Before the vote, former Presidents Ford, Carter and Bush released a letter attacking it. Drug czar Barry McCaffrey flew to Phoenix and warned that it amounted to "the legalization of all drugs." But the politicians may have been out of touch with popular sentiment. Recalls political consultant Sam Vagenas, who steered the Arizona initiative: "When we asked focus groups if we were winning the war on drugs, people just laughed."

Today the law excites little debate in Arizona as it funnels 6,000 new drug felons a year into treatment rather than jail. To be sure, Maricopa County district attorney Richard Romley complains about offenders who are "refusing treatment and thumbing their nose at the court." But a 1999 report by the Arizona supreme court—now being updated—found that 77% of offenders stayed off drugs during the year following their arrest and that the state had saved $2.5 million in prison costs. Probation officer Jim Frost, a 30-year veteran, didn't think treatment would work "without jail hanging over someone's head." Now he says, "Boy, was I wrong. Drug users are not apathetic people with glazed eyes. They care about succeeding—pretty much like everyone else."

On that day in her courtroom, McNally sent the sometime meth user back to his forklift and the mechanic and recovering cocaine addict back to his three kids. The pot-smoking teenager trailed behind his mother. Says the judge: "When somebody's threatening to throw you in jail it doesn't feel like they care about you. Now there's a different attitude." And it is showing results.

—By M.R./Phoenix, Ariz.

Much of the effort is being bankrolled by three prominent philanthropists: New York City financier George Soros; Cleveland, Ohio, insurance magnate Peter Lewis; and Phoenix, Ariz., entrepreneur John Sperling. Working together they have spent more than $15 million to promote the voter initiatives. Their consultants are scoping out Florida, Maine, Michigan, Missouri and Ohio for 2002 ballot propositions. "States are going to be the engines of reform," predicts New Mexico Governor Gary Johnson, a Republican who has pushed through two addiction-assistance bills this year. "It's still too hot to touch from a national political standpoint," he says.

In the largest experiment of all, California voters last November passed Proposition 36. Modeled after a vanguard policy in Arizona (see box), it is expected to divert some 100,000 first- and second-time drug offenders from prisons into rehab over the next three years. "California's Proposition 36 highlights the disgust many feel for our current system," says Rocky Anderson, the Democratic mayor of Salt Lake City, Utah, which has been dealing with a spate of heroin overdose deaths. "Punitive policies, at tremendous taxpayer expense, are an unmitigated failure." Anderson and like-minded officials are sending a message to the White House that if the Bush war on drugs means warehousing users, many states will be conscientious objectors.

—**With reporting by Jess Cagle/ Los Angeles and Elaine Shannon/ Washington**

PUBLIC NUISANCES

Drug Crazy Feds

by R. Emmett Tyrrell, Jr.

Capitol Hill politics is actually even more interesting than the Sunday morning talk shows would have you believe. One popinjay shrieking from the left and another from the right about last week's headlines is not the whole of Washington's political dramas. Occasionally, American politics is more complicated and more momentous.

The scheming and orating in Washington now going on over a little-known legislative monstrosity called the Methamphetamine Anti-Proliferation Act (MAPA) would go down as an enormous bore on any Sunday morning talk show. Yet its outcome is of vital importance to our freedoms as citizens and its opponents demonstrate that sometimes our elected officials do more than feel our pain and kiss babies. MAPA, if passed by Congress, would empower federal agents to search your home and take your property without immediately informing you—possibly without ever informing you. Naturally it gives unscrupulous law enforcement officials opportunities to plant evidence or to spice it up pursuant to getting an easy conviction.

The diversity of the political forces that have come together to oppose MAPA constitute politics at its most interesting and most serious—even more serious that the soap opera between Bill Clinton and his fabled "Clinton-haters." The American Civil Liberties Union's stalwart campaign against MAPA is being aided and abetted by the liberal Democratic Congresswoman Sheila Jackson-Lee and the conservative Republican Congressman Bob Barr.

According to the Justice Department, methamphetamine is a brain buzzer increasingly popular with young people. It is concocted in "meth labs" throughout the country, and Justice hopes its agents will suppress the production and trafficking in "meth" with MAPA. The bill increases criminal penalties selling meth and appropriates funds for hunting down and closing "meth labs." It also would appropriate funds for treatment of the meth monsters. Slipped into this pot-pourri of good deeds unfortunately are amendments that would allow agents to search homes, workplaces, and vehicles without informing their owners. The agents would also be able to remove property without fully inventorying it. It could be months before the inventories were submitted to property owners.

Former federal prosecutor Barr argues that these provisions "change present laws regarding search warrants, loosening up the need to provide notice and the requirement for inventories of property seized." He claims that these insidious provisions would then be used by other law enforcement agents for a wider array of searches. "Agents without search warrants could enter unoccupied houses and offices and search, copy, or seize information, even on computer hard drives."

Whether the liberal Democrat Jackson-Lee and the conservative Republican Barr succeed in thwarting MAPA, this particular struggle on behalf of civil liberties highlights a particularly menacing threat to

ANNUAL EDITIONS

civil liberties, Barr says, given the present balance of power in Washington between Republicans and Democrats.

Republicans are always strong law and order advocates. Despite the wide streak of libertarianism in their ranks, they are suckers for FBI claims that such instrumentalities as MAPA are necessary in the war against drugs and terrorism. Democrats, whether soft on law and order or libertarian regarding law enforcement, are easily manipulated by their guy in the White House.

The consequence is that Justice Department officials intent on making their job of apprehending criminals easier, are having an easier time passing laws that may make ordinary Americans' lives less easy. Your security from a rashly executed search warrant will be weakened by MAPA. If the feds secretly enter your home rather than the home of the guy next door, who will find out? If the guy next door is their target, lucky him. And whatever is taken from which home, only the feds will know.

Yet an alliance of Republicans and Democrats may make all this happen. The price of liberty is vigilance, as the Founding Fathers knew back in the good old days.

Adapted from RET's weekly *Washington Times* column syndicated by Creators Syndicate.

From *The American Spectator*, July/August 2000, p. 16. © 2000 by The American Spectator. Reprinted by permission.

A Setback for Medipot

After a Supreme Court decision, distributors of medical marijuana fear a federal shutdown

BY MARGOT ROOSEVELT

LOS ANGELES

Sales were strong at 7494 Santa Monica Boulevard last week. Prices were neatly posted; customers paid by credit card; computers tracked inventory; a Better Business Bureau plaque gleamed behind the counter. On the lounge TV, a video showed Los Angeles County Sheriff Leroy Baca praising the place: "A great success... things are done properly and people who need services are getting those services."

But the success and services of the Los Angeles Cannabis Resource Center and similar medical-marijuana distributors across the country could soon be history. Last week the U.S. Supreme Court in a unanimous decision declared that illness is no excuse for legalizing marijuana—not even to ease the suffering of patients with cancer, AIDS or other life-threatening diseases. The folks on Santa Monica Boulevard, however respectable, are committing a federal crime as they collect baggies of Maude's Mighty Moss ("large and luscious reddish green buds, easy to break and roll," $18 a gram) and Adobe ("compressed green bud, fresh and tasty, with seeds and stems," $4 a gram).

The court's foray into the medipot conflict did little to resolve the highly politicized issue. Justice Clarence Thomas' opinion was narrow. It affirmed the government's power to shut down a cannabis cooperative in Oakland, Calif., but stopped short of invalidating laws passed by nine states allowing marijuana for medical use. Thomas' opinion skirted the states'-rights issue at the heart of the case—does California have the right to legalize medipot?—and a concurring opinion from three liberal Justices, led by John Paul Stevens, chided the conservative majority for

"overbroad language... given the importance of showing respect for sovereign states." Stevens also suggested that while medical necessity can't be invoked by a mass distributor, it might still be a defense against prosecution of an individual—"a seriously ill patient for whom there is no other means of avoiding starvation or extraordinary suffering."

THE STATE OF MEDIPOT

- States that allow use of medical marijuana
- Legislation pending
- Ballot initiatives circulating for voter signatures
- Legislation failed

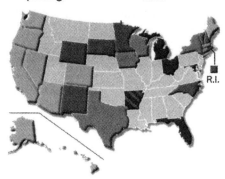

R.I.

Sources: Americans for Medical Rights; Marijuana Policy Project

That's a good description of the 880 members of the Los Angeles cooperative, three-quarters of whom have AIDS. The rest suffer from cancer, multiple sclerosis or other diseases, and all have marijuana prescriptions from licensed physicians. Leanne Orgen, 46, an insurance broker with liver cancer, buys pot-laced chocolate-chunk brownies—a "miracle drug" for chemotherapy-induced nausea, she says.

Jeffrey Farrington, 32, who has glaucoma, explains that if he stops smoking marijuana, which relieves ocular pressure, he loses more than 7 ft. of vision daily. "If they shut us down," he says, "I'll go blind and I'll watch my friends die of AIDS."

Two years ago, the Institute of Medicine concluded that marijuana has potential therapeutic value. Polls show nearly three-quarters of Americans favor medical-marijuana use, and juries are increasingly reluctant to convict sick people for possession. Oregon, Alaska and Hawaii have set up state registries for medipot users; Colorado, California, Nevada and Maine are debating similar moves. Such grassroots enthusiasm carries little weight with drug warriors, who dispute the scientific data and argue that marijuana leads to hard narcotics. In an interview with Time last week, Attorney General John Ashcroft praised the Supreme Court decision. "We can't function well as a country if each state makes its own rules about what's available health-care-wise," he argued. "If Congress wants to exempt various people from the laws of this country, it's their duty."

That's unlikely. But neither the Justice Department nor the DEA has said whether the court ruling will cause them to mount a new offensive against medical-marijuana clinics. And as a practical matter, most individual pot infractions fall under state and local jurisdiction, and an increasing number of local law-enforcement officers are refusing to prosecute medipot cases.

Still, Scott Imler, president of the L.A. center and an epileptic who smokes weed to control his seizures, fears the worst. "If they march in here with storm troopers and seize the building, I can't imagine it would be politically popular," he says. "But maybe they don't care."

—With reporting by Elaine Shannon/ Washington

UNIT 8
Prevention and Treatment

Unit Selections

Key Points to Consider

- How effective are drug education and prevention programs? Are they too generic? How are they assessed and evaluated?

- Does the responsibility for drug education and prevention programs lie with the family, the schools, the police, or the federal government? Explain. Who is willing or unwilling to get involved?

- How effective is drug treatment? Do you agree or disagree that providing free, publicly sponsored drug programs would be one way to greatly reduce America's drug problem?

- What must treatment programs and treatment philosophy consider when providing services to a diverse population of clients? If an addicted friend or loved one asked your advice on finding treatment, how would you respond? What are your options?

- How does the prevailing American attitude toward drug addiction reflect an uncomfortable resistance toward becoming involved?

 **Links: www.dushkin.com/online/**
These sites are annotated in the World Wide Web pages.

Creative Partnerships for Prevention
http://arts.endow.gov/partner/Creative.html
D.A.R.E.
http://www.dare-america.com
Hazelden
http://www.hazelden.org
Indiana Prevention Resource Center
http://www.drugs.indiana.edu/home.html

There are no magic bullets for preventing drug abuse and treating drug-dependent persons. As one commentator stated, "Drug addicts can be cured, but we're not very good at it!" History is replete with accounts of the diverse attempts of frustrated societies to reclaim or reject their fallen members. Addicts have been executed, imprisoned, and treated with ambivalent indifference. In some circles, the debate still rages as to whether addicts suffer from a pernicious disease or simply a weak character. The evolution of processes used to rehabilitate addicted persons and prevent future abuse has been slow and filled with paradox. Yet the case is not lost. On the contrary, great new strides have been made in not only understanding the various genetic, physiological, psychological, and environmental frameworks that combine to serve as a basis for addiction but in using these frameworks successfully to treat and prevent dependency. Research continues to establish and strengthen the role of treatment as a critical component in the fight against drug abuse. Some drug treatment programs have been shown to reduce dramatically the costs associated with high-risk populations of users. For example, recidivism associated with drug abuse has been shown to decrease 50 percent after treatment. Treatment is a critical component in the fight against drug abuse but it is not a panacea. Society cannot "treat" drug abuse away just as it cannot "arrest" it away.

Drug prevention and treatment philosophies subscribe to a multitude of modalities. Everything seems to work a little and nothing seems to work completely. The articles in this unit illustrate the diversity of methods utilized in prevention and treatment programs. Also illustrated is the struggle in which prevention and treatment programs compete for local, state, and federal resources.

Prevention: A primary strategy of drug prevention programs is to prevent and/or delay initial drug use. A secondary strategy is to discourage use by persons minimally involved with drugs. Both strategies include: (1) educating users and potential users, (2) teaching adolescents how to resist peer pressure, (3) addressing problems associated with drug abuse such as teen pregnancy, failure in school, and lawbreaking, and (4) creating community support and involvement for prevention activities.

Prevention programs are administered through a variety of mechanisms. Schools are an important delivery apparatus, as are local law enforcement agencies. Over 10 thousand police officers are involved in the Drug Abuse Resistance Education program (D.A.R.E.), provided to over 5 million students each year. Other prevention programs are community-based and sponsored by civic organizations, church groups, and private corporations. All programs pursue funding through public grants and private endowments. Federal grants to local, state, and private programs are critical components to program solvency.

The multifaceted nature of prevention programs makes them difficult to assess categorically. School programs that empha-size the development of skills to resist social and peer pressure produce generally varying degrees of positive results. Research continues to make more evident the need to focus prevention programs with specific populations in mind.

Treatment: Like prevention programs, drug treatment programs enlist a variety of methods to treat persons dependent upon legal and illegal drugs. There is no single-pronged approach to treatment for drug abuse. Treatment modality may differ radically from one user to the next. The user's background, physical and mental health, personal motivation, and support structure all have serious implications for treatment type. Lumping together the diverse needs of chemically dependent persons for purposes of applying a generic treatment process provides confounding results at best. In addition, most persons needing and seeking treatment have problems with more than one drug—polydrug use. Studies have shown that 54 percent of drug abusers and 37 percent of alcohol abusers have, in addition to their drug problem, at least one serious mental illness. Identifying a user's drug and associated mental health problem is referred to as dual diagnosis. The implications of such a diagnosis are serious, as it is estimated that there are 30 to 40 million chemically dependent persons in this country. The popularity of cocaine and methamphetamine use is felt to have increased the percentage of dually diagnosed persons because of the potential of these drugs to negatively alter neurochemical balances, pushing already troubled persons into the realm of mental illness. Providing treatment services to dually diagnosed persons is one of the most difficult and troubling aspects of the treatment equation. Historically, drug treatment programs have avoided or denied services to addicts suffering from psychological disorders such as schizophrenia. Mental health service providers have responded similarly due to their inability to treat drug addiction.

Although treatment programs differ in methods, most provide a combination of key services. These include drug counseling, drug education, pharmacological therapy, psychotherapy, relapse prevention, and assistance with support structures. Treatment programs may be outpatient-oriented or residential in nature. Residential programs require patients to live at the facility for a prescribed period of time. These residential programs, often described as therapeutic communities, emphasize the development of social, vocational, and educational skills.

The number of available treatment programs is a continual political controversy with respect to federal and state drug budget expenditures. The current trend is toward increasing the availability of treatment programs. This year's federal drug budget includes a $111 million increase in funding for treatment programs and $105 million increase for scientific research on drug abuse. The best evidence suggests that while providing drug treatment is costly, not providing it is more costly.

Talk to kids about drugs? Parents just don't do it

"Like a fool, I thought my kid was becoming more interested in personal hygiene."

By Stacey Schultz

When Laura Langanki found extra towels in the laundry smelling lemony fresh, she never dreamed that meant her 13-year-old son was on drugs. "We were going through three to four bottles of air freshener a week," says the 42-year-old nurse from Plymouth, Minn. "Like a fool, I thought my kid was becoming more interested in personal hygiene." Instead, Jake was "huffing"—spraying the contents into towels and inhaling the fumes for a short-lived buzz. By the time she caught on two years later, he was smoking pot, using acid and crystal methamphetamine, drinking alcohol, and snorting cocaine.

WHAT TO LOOK FOR

Troubles in school or changes in sleeping habits might indicate drug use. So can these signs:

- **Clothes** or jewelry depicting a marijuana leaf or mushrooms
- **"Bowls,"** or smoking devices made by denting and poking holes in soda cans
- **Baggies** in the bedroom. That's how drugs typically are stored.
- **Eye drops** get the pot-induced red out.

Laura had warned Jake not to try illegal drugs when he was younger and felt sure he got the message. But according to a new

U.S. News poll, even parents who believe they talk often with their kids about drugs can be mistaken. Of 700 parents and 700 teens surveyed, 1 in 3 parents claimed to talk about drugs "a lot" with his or her teen, while only 14 percent of teenagers felt they had frequent conversations on the subject with Mom or Dad.

That failure to communicate can have dire consequences. In a 1999 survey of nearly 10,000 parents and teens by the Partnership for a Drug-Free America, teens who received antidrug messages at home were 42 percent less likely to use drugs. "This may sound like soft advice," says Steve Dnistrian, executive vice president of the group. "But hard numbers quantify that parental communication is the single most important thing we can do to prevent children from using drugs." Indeed, parents received the highest vote of confidence from 63 percent of the teens polled by *U.S. News*, outranking siblings, teachers, and friends.

Most teens act as if they would rather clean their room than talk to their parents about touchy subjects like drugs or sex. Don't be deterred, says Rhonda Sykes, associate clinical director for Hazelden Chicago, a drug treatment center for adolescents. "Teens don't say, 'Thanks for the great advice.' But they do hear what their parents are saying."

No butts. Brandi Domiano, a 16-year-old from Old Forge, Pa., who has never tried cigarettes or alcohol, credits her mother for the choices she makes now.

"When I was in sixth grade, my mother would talk to me about how bad drinking and smoking are for you," Domiano says. Her mother also gave her books to read about the harmful effects of drugs.

Experts agree conversations about drugs should begin early and continue throughout adolescence. "Start talking about it when the child is around age 8," says Richard Gallagher, director of the Parenting Institute at New York University Child Study Center. Explain the difference between legal drugs prescribed by doctors and illegal drugs used for fun. Let your children know that other kids may offer these substances to them and that you want them to stay away from drugs because of the harmful effects on health and well-being, Gallagher says.

Many parents will have to do homework on the dangers of drugs. "The only thing worse than no information is bad information," says Paul Ciborowski, professor of counseling at Long Island University's C. W. Post campus. Ask youth counselors and teachers which drugs are common at your child's school so you can emphasize the right ones. The Internet can provide research on the ill effects of certain drugs.

Resist the temptation to lecture. Ask lots of questions, and listen to your child's opinions and feelings. And make sure your kids get the message that you're talking about the topic because you're concerned and you want them to be safe.

Polling parents and teens

Guess what: Parents and their teenage children do agree about something. In a U.S. News-Family Circle-YM *poll, 3 out of 4 say illegal drugs are easy to obtain. But when it comes to communication, there can be quite a gap.*

CRIME AND PUNISHMENT

68%	of parents would just talk to a teen if a bag of pot was found in a jacket pocket.
12%	would ground or punish the teen.
28%	of teens think they'd be grounded or punished.

TALKING ABOUT DRUGS

39%	of teens say their parents rarely or never talk to them about drugs.
13%	of parents say they rarely or never talk to their teens about drugs.
14%	of teens say their parents talk to them "a lot" about drugs.
35%	of parents say they talk to their teens "a lot" about drugs.

DECEIVING PARENTS

24%	of teens say they've lied to their parents about drug or alcohol use.
16%	of parents think their teens have lied to them about drug or alcohol use.

U.S. News-Family Circle-YM poll of 700 parents of teens and 700 teens ages 14 to 17 conducted by Celinda Lake of Lake Snell Perry & Associates and Ed Goeas of the Tarrance Group Sept. 8–15, 1999. Margin of error: plus or minus 3.8 percent

Kids may fire back with the dreaded question: "Did you do drugs when you were young?" "No need to let it all hang out," Ciborowski says. Be honest, but don't spell out everything. Stress lessons you learned, and talk about people you knew who had a hard time because they used drugs. "Real stories of people who were separated from their families or had to do jail time are what keep me off drugs," says Thomas Brennan, 16, of New York City.

If there is alcoholism in the family, you need to explain to your children that they are at higher risk, says Sandra Bernabei, a substance abuse specialist at Barnard College. That's what Alex Benson's parents did. "I definitely think about it and it scares me," says the 15-year-old from Springfield, Vt. "My uncle is an alcoholic and I know that one day it could be me."

Bernabei also warns parents not to assume that all kids use drugs. According to the latest findings from the University of Michigan Institute for Social Research, 55 percent of high school seniors say they have tried illicit drugs. In the past year, close to 40 percent smoked marijuana, almost 6 percent used inhalants, 8 percent took LSD, 6 percent used cocaine, 1 percent took heroin, and close to 6 percent say they used MDMA, also known as Ecstasy. "The truth is, a minority of kids use drugs or binge drink regularly," Bernabei says.

Conveying the idea that all kids use drugs may make your child feel pressure to join in. And parents aren't the only ones guilty of exaggerating; 25 percent of the teenagers in our poll said most teens use drugs on a regular basis. But only 8 percent said close friends are frequent users.

At the same time, don't assume that your child is not being exposed. According to a new study from researchers at Columbia University, teens in small towns and rural areas are far more likely to use drugs than urban kids. "It's not about boredom, it's about monitoring," says NYU's Gal-

lagher, who explains that rural and small-town kids can find lots of secluded hangouts.

It's also about consequences. When kids say, "My parents will kill me if I use drugs," they really don't know what will happen. Experts advise parents to make it clear that even one infraction will bring a punishment—something with teeth, but still reasonable, like a temporary grounding. If parents learn that a child is using drugs habitually, they need to seek treatment.

Ultimately, your child will decide whether to try drugs, and even the best parents cannot always prevent it. But don't give up. Once Laura Langanki became aware of Jake's drug use she battled back, spending her savings to get him into a residential rehabilitation program. At 18, he just celebrated his 18th month of sobriety. When asked to complete an essay assignment on a significant person in his life, he chose to write about his mom.

Deep Cravings

New research on the brain and behavior clarifies the mysteries of addiction.

by Craig Lambert

THE BOMBSHELL DROPPED in 1976, when "The Natural History of Chipping" appeared in the *American Journal of Psychiatry*. In their article, Norman Zinberg, then clinical professor of psychiatry at Harvard, and his research assistant R.C. Jacobson described five case studies, representative of 54 identified long-term heroin users who had regularly injected the drug for from two to 23 years, yet had never become addicts. These "chippers," whose existence Zinberg had noted as early as 1964, actively developed social rituals and usage strategies that permitted stable, controlled use of heroin.

"The idea of addictive drugs makes no sense. It's magical thinking to imagine that drugs have this power."

That article demolished the received wisdom of decades. Ever since 1898, when Bayer & Co. of Germany, makers of another painkiller, Bayer aspirin, introduced heroin to the pharmaceutical market, popular and scientific mythology had enshrined it as the most addictive of drugs. (The word *heroin*, allegedly referring to heroic feelings stimulated by the drug, was originally a Bayer trademark.) The finding that people could take heroin without forming habits challenged the whole idea that drugs themselves were addictive.

Since then, the ethos has shifted markedly. "The idea of addictive drugs makes no sense," says Howard Shaffer. "It's magical thinking to imagine that drugs have this power." Shaffer, associate professor of psychology in the department of psychi-

atry and director of the division on Addictions at Harvard Medical School, has studied both drug addicts and compulsive gamblers and notes, "We don't talk about addictive dice."

"If you look at all drug addictions, one clear statement applies to all of them: uncontrolled use despite negative consequences."

The old-fashioned concept of "addictive personality" has also collapsed. Today, the word *addiction* does not appear in standard psychiatric nomenclature. Rather, addiction seems to characterize neither a substance nor a personality type, but a *form of relationship*. Clinicians now speak of addiction to gambling, sex, aerobic exercise, work, day-trading, eating carrots, shopping, even excessive drinking of water. The term is vastly popular: people laughingly refer to themselves as "TV addicts" or "chocoholics." But Bertha Madras, professor of psychobiology in the department of psychiatry, objects: "The word is grossly overused. Addiction is a neurobiological disorder. Clinically, it's a very clear syndrome. If you look at all drug addictions from tobacco to heroin, there's only one clear statement that applies to all of them: uncontrolled use despite negative consequences."

Classically, drug addiction means tolerance (the need for increasing doses to obtain the same effect) and withdrawal (psychic and/or bodily ailments, sometimes lethal, that accompany sudden cessation of use). Both signs indicate *neuroadaptation*: repeated intake of a drug alters the brain in profound ways that both stimulate more drug use and render choice more difficult. Yet "pathological gamblers show physiological signs of tolerance and withdrawal, just like narcotic addicts," says Shaffer. "And hospital patients medicated for pain can develop tolerance and withdrawal, but don't show signs of addiction, such as drug-seeking behavior. We can't be sure if it's the drugs or the behaviors that are changing the brain chemistry." The emerging consensus, he says, is that both factors are at work.

Such riddles suggest why addiction research spans many disciplines, from neurobiology to social policy. The Division on Addictions, founded in 1993, is one of nine such divisions focusing on areas that do not fit well into the Medical School's regular academic departments. Addiction is as old as human history, and remains one of the costliest and most intractable of all social problems. It confounds rationality: millions of addicts persist in their blatantly self-destructive behavior despite the loss of family, friends, jobs, money, and health. (Some studies have shown the death rate for untreated heroin addicts to be as high as 7 percent annually.) To use the analogy of professor of psychiatry George Vaillant '55, M.D. '59, the addict can resemble a cigar smoker in an elevator, oblivious to something that is obvious to everyone else. Research is now beginning to show what makes addicted brains, bodies, minds, and spirits so different.

The Addicted Brain

MOST ANIMALS WILL GLADLY TAKE any drug that humans use, excepting marijuana and certain psychedelics like LSD. "The addictive potential of drugs appears to be reflected in many mammalian species," says Madras, who studies the effects of cocaine on macaque monkey brains at the Harvard-affiliated New England Regional Primate Research Center. Pigeons, rats, and monkeys will all press levers to access cocaine or opiates, suggesting that addiction taps into widely shared neural pathways. This makes sense because psychoactive drugs generally exert their most important effects on older brain structures, those areas sometimes called the "reptile brain." In fact, some current research suggests that these pathways may have evolved even before reptiles appeared.

Biologist Tristan Darland, a postdoctoral fellow in the laboratory of Cabot professor of the natural sciences John Dowling, is currently running experiments on zebra fish—common residents of home aquariums whose brains have enough cortex to let them learn some behaviors, though far less effectively than mammals. Darland begins by having the fish swim for 30 minutes in a tank that has a wick saturated with cocaine at one end. The next day, he returns the zebra fish to the same tank for two minutes, but with no cocaine on the wick. Nonetheless, the fish usually prefer the end of the tank where they encountered the cocaine—and spend 70 to 80 percent of their time there. Even during their initial "conditioning" swim, the fish gravitate toward the cocaine end, but "prior exposure to cocaine evokes a stronger response. Evidently, they see it as pleasurable," Dar-

land explains. Results from more than 100 fish show that at least 85 percent prefer the side they associate with cocaine.

The zebra fish may be undergoing some systematic changes in brain chemistry. Psychoactive drugs alter patterns of communication within the brain, via neurotransmitters (molecules that convey messages in the nervous system). "The chemical structure of drugs happens to resemble the chemical structure of the brain's own neurotransmitters," Madras explains. "I call them 'the great brain impostors.' They target the same communication systems as the brain's natural messages. But the complex communication and control systems in the brain are geared for the natural message, not the impostor. As a result, the brain adapts to, and compensates for, the abnormal signals generated by the drug. Here is where the addictive process begins. Brain adaptation is central to addiction. In the case of drugs that produce physical or psychological withdrawal, there is a compulsion to restore the brain to the status it had when it was awash with drugs."

A central enzymatic pathway in the midbrains of vertebrates produces an important neurotransmitter called dopamine, which occurs at high concentrations in a part of the brain called the nucleus accumbens. "All addictive drugs seem to increase dopamine release in the nucleus accumbens," says Darland. "It's been hypothesized that the dopamine system in potential addicts is somehow different. Addictive drugs cause a big increase in dopamine release, with different mechanisms involved, depending on the drug. Cocaine seems to block dopamine uptake, keeping it in circulation. Morphine apparently shuts off inhibitory neurons in the ventral tegmental area of the brain, where the dopamine pathway begins.

"Dopamine release is associated with eating, with sex—with many pleasurable states. It's a 'feel-good' molecule," Darland continues. "These pathways didn't evolve for the sake of doing drugs. They are there to keep humans procreating and eating."

"In a sense, these drugs are stressors. They shock the system when taken in these amounts."

Draper professor of psychiatry Joseph Coyle says, "It looks like there are some final common pathways through which addictive drugs work, in the nucleus accumbens and the amygdala, and which involve the neurotransmitters dopamine and enkephalin. This leads to some interesting things. It's rare to see an individual who uses only cocaine or heroin; these brain systems are involved in other addictive behaviors. Howard Shaffer, for example, has studied gamblers and finds that you rarely see a person who is *just* a pathological gambler—usually it's a gambler who also smokes and drinks too much, or may have a drug habit. Regarding treatment, it also might explain why Naltrexone, an opiate receptor antagonist, has been shown to be effective in reducing relapse among alcoholics."

To better define the sites in the brain where these molecular firestorms occur, instructor in psychiatry Hans Breiter is using

A Taboo Passion

ADDICTION IS THE NAME we give to a taboo passion," says Ann Marlowe '79, G '80, author of *how to stop time: heroin from A to Z* (Basic Books, 1999), a rare literary treatment of heroin that neither defends nor demonizes the drug. Marlowe is an intense woman of strong views who used heroin both occasionally and regularly between 1988 and 1995, when she quit. She only sniffed, never injected, was never arrested, and did not ruin her life. On the contrary, she has an M.B.A. from Columbia and for 13 years has been a prosperous headhunter for tax and pension attorneys.

"You see a lot of people who are truly youthful looking. But their insides are also frozen in time."

"I never felt it was a big deal. I could quit anytime, and I did," she says. "Heroin is not magical, not irresistible. Withdrawal is like having a cold or the flu for a few days. A lot of what we perceive as classic withdrawal symptoms are there from the start. As your body becomes more skilled at processing heroin, it goes through you more quickly. At first you don't feel so great the morning after taking it, then only six hours after, then an hour or two. Following this path leads to a narrowing focus and a demeaning obsession with your immediate physical state, which is one reason heroin addicts can be so tiresome to be around. It's not a fit focus for an intelligent person."

Marlowe's core thesis, summarized in her title, is that heroin use functions as a way of stopping time, or postponing life. Taking opiates, she says, forestalls both aging and maturation: "You see a lot of people who are truly youthful looking—they are truly pickled by the drug. It's like a Dorian Gray effect. But their insides are also frozen in time. You don't age, and you don't grow either.

"Nothing about doing heroin interferes with functionality," Marlowe continues. "A lot of the pathology of heroin is really the pathology of poverty. What's the point in getting straight, if it's to work at Kinko's the rest of your life? Heroin does have ill effects. It's not harmless. It can be bad for your cardiovascular and pulmonary systems. If drug education told the real truth, instead of focusing on half-truths, taboos, and scare stories, fewer people would do it."

Marlowe has some unconventional theories about the drug, drawn from her years of experience in Manhattan's East Village heroin-chic world, where her fellow users tended to have trust funds and prep-school educations. Experienced street junkies might laugh their way through some of her aperçus, such as "Organic foods are popular with dope users." (As Marlowe notes, "Everyone who writes about the stuff is an exception and generalizes from their experience.") Other ideas could bear research. She believes "heroin cures the effects of jet lag, and jet lag cures heroin addiction." Marlowe tells of a friend who quit a sizable five to 10-bag-per day habit, suddenly and without withdrawal symptoms, by flying from New York to Australia. She also thinks there is a connection between heroin, jet lag, and seasonal affective disorder (SAD), the syndrome of depression that affects some people in the winter, when days are short: "People who are very susceptible to SAD, those who have trouble resetting their biological clocks, are also susceptible to heroin. Before Prozac, opiates were the best-known cure for depression."

Marlowe places heroin in a mainstream socioeconomic context. "We only see heroin as a medical condition, a psychiatric problem, or an example of the awesome power of drugs. But why not look at escalating consumption as exactly that—why don't we see it as a subspecies of greed, of overindulgence, in a consumer society?" she asks. "I could have chosen to do $300 worth of heroin a day, or to buy $300 worth of shoes per day—and I'd feel ridiculous and contemptible making either choice." Yet she thinks individuals ought to be able to make this choice if they want to. "I think all drugs should be legal," she says. "I'm a libertarian, a free-market capitalist."

---

magnetic resonance imaging (MRI) to view patterns of neuronal activity in the brains of cocaine addicts. He has begun to identify the brain centers that become active during *euphoria* (when addicts are high on the drug) and to distinguish them from those that fire when the user experiences *craving* (strong desire for cocaine). Some preliminary data suggest that the same brain centers may show parallel activity in compulsive gamblers, possibly indicating—as Shaffer has suggested—that addictive pathways in the brain can exist independent of drug input.

But the neuroscience of addiction is far from settled. Madras, for example, dissents from the current model that sees drug ef-

fects converging on the dopamine system. She cites the different effects of drugs, their different targets in the brain, the inability of one drug to substitute for another (cocaine will not relieve morphine withdrawal, nor is methadone an effective treatment for cocaine addiction), and the fact that adverse circumstances such as fear or electric shock also prompt the release of dopamine. "Dopamine may not be the brain's euphoriant," she says, "but the brain's adrenaline."

"In a sense, these drugs are stressors," explains Gene Heyman, Ph.D. '77, lecturer on psychology in the department of psychiatry. "Besides their hedonic properties, they shock the system when taken in these amounts. Rats on opiates, stimulants, or alcohol reliably show increases in corticosterone, a stress-related hormone. Clinical evidence shows parallel findings with heroin addicts. This suggests that opiates and perhaps other addictive drugs have a short-term effect of easing stress, but a long-term effect of increasing susceptibility to stress." Jack Mendelson, professor of psychiatry, draws a parallel between the hormonal responses caused by cocaine and those associated with thrilling or frightening pursuits like hang-gliding and bungee-cord jumping: "Cocaine triggers major stress hormones like epinephrine [adrenaline], norepinephrine, adrenocorticotropic hormone [ACTH], and serotonin. These are the same ones that surge up during bungee jumping."

"These pathways didn't evolve for the sake of doing drugs. They are there to keep humans procreating and eating."

TRISTAN DARLAND

Even if these chemical responses are common to all drugs of abuse, they are not uniform in degree among all individuals. Darland and Dowling are now attempting to breed zebra fish with increased cocaine sensitivity, which may help identify genetic predispositions to drug addiction. In humans, several lines of research suggest such genetic sensitivities. In the 1960s and 1970s, Scandinavian researchers followed up families of alcoholics to find that the prevalence of alcoholism was four times greater in individuals from alcoholic backgrounds. The researchers clearly demonstrated that genetic variables, rather than family behavior, were at work. More recent research has indicated that hospital patients of Asian background need relatively higher doses of opiates to relieve pain, suggesting that they may metabolize opioids more rapidly, and hence are perhaps at greater risk for opiate addiction. Differences in gene pools may influence cultural practices. "In France and Italy, children drink wine with meals at early ages, whereas in Ireland they are discouraged from drinking before age 21," says Barry Kosofsky, associate professor of neurology. "Some cultures may fear alcohol more, perhaps due to genetic predispositions for alcoholism."

Not only genes but prenatal environments may incline an organism toward drug sensitivity. Neurotransmitters "sculpt" the brain by controlling its early development. Kosofsky investigates the effect of drugs on the developing brain by studying children born to women addicted to crack cocaine. "The intrauterine environment is critical in terms of brain development," he says. "Alcohol, nicotine, or cocaine in a pregnant woman can all have great impact on the fetal brain." Kosofsky hopes to learn whether exposure to cocaine in the womb will increase the likelihood of someone becoming addicted to cocaine as an adult. "This," he says, "would raise the possibility that infants exposed to drugs before birth are more likely to beget others who are also exposed to drugs in the womb"—creating a kind of nongenetic "inheritance" of drug abuse.

Early experiences with drugs, whether in the womb or as an adult, have ineradicable effects. Drug users often describe a wish to recapture the bliss of their first high. But this goal proves elusive because once the brain has neuroadapted to drugs, it is physiologically and structurally changed. The director of the National Institute on Drug Abuse and many others argue that *voluntary* drug consumption alters the brain in ways that lead to *involuntary* drug consumption. The question of whether drug habits are voluntary or not leads us to ask how people get over their addictions, and raises some of the moral issues surrounding compulsive behavior.

The Ambivalent Addict

Even if we all have the neural wiring to become addicts, only a few of us actually do so. Bertha Madras estimates that 5 to 10 percent of those who experiment with a drug become compulsive users or abusers. (Cigarettes are the exception: data show habituation rates ranging from 10 to 70 percent.) What distinguishes that 5 or 10 percent who get hooked? Some studies indicate that children who have "personality disorders," earn poor grades, or have been sexually abused are at higher risk for drug abuse. Yet Howard Shaffer says, "I don't think there is an addictive personality, nor does the scientific literature support the concept." George Vaillant states flatly, "The 'addictive personality' probably doesn't exist," noting that "addictions tend to distort personality. You can't predict this—alcoholics look like everyone else until they become alcoholics, much as cigarette smokers do." Some theorists postulate that "novelty-seeking" or "sensation-seeking" personalities are prone to drug abuse, but Vaillant observes, "They are seeking the high, not addiction." Similarly, he adds, "People with miserable childhoods may look like addictive personalities, but they are seeking pain relief, not addiction."

Clinical professor of psychiatry Edward Khantzian has written extensively about addiction as a form of self-medication. "The nature of suffering is at times overwhelmingly intense—or elusive, vague, and beyond people's control," he says. "The drug user suddenly feels some control over what had felt uncontrollable. I do think there's a specificity involved. People with a lot of rage and irritability find the opiates very soothing. Stimulants may appeal to those individuals who are dysphoric, de-energized, or depressed. Some say that drugs hijack the reward centers of the brain, but I believe that what is hijacked is the *emotional* brain."

According to clinical instructor in psychiatry Stephen Bergman '66, M.D. '73, "All addictions feed the ego, the self. The ego is insatiable. If you are into your ego, you can never get enough—not enough drugs, sex, money, alcohol, relationships, not enough anything. Enough, that is, to feel 'not bad.' Many of these people don't like it if they have to be in a room by themselves for a while. In 12-step programs, those who recover do it by asking for *help*. The connection has to change, from the self to a *we*. The only thing that helps is getting beyond yourself."

The Poet of Needle Park

HE IS SURELY the most famous Harvard-educated heroin addict, and one of the most famous addicts anywhere: William Seward Burroughs '36 (1914–97) was a kind of *über*-junkie, a writer whose heavy drug use was the foreground of his literary persona. His poetic evocations of opiated states and the nightmares of withdrawal—the desire for heroin coming on him "like a cold black wind through the bones," for example—brought a deeply foreign experience to readers worldwide.

His Harvard classmates, almost to a man, became businessmen, bankers, or lawyers; Burroughs instead mounted a frontal assault on every mainstream American value. The titles of the first two books he wrote, the autobiographical *Junky* and *Queer*, could hardly have flouted conventional proprieties more completely. Yet he went much further in his masterpiece, *Naked Lunch*, which brought him both renown and notoriety. Despite its vivid, farcical, terrifying portrayals of both drug addiction and sexual perversities—all dragged out for inspection in Boston in 1965–66 at what proved to be the last major censorship trials of printed matter in the United States—Burroughs asserted, "From the beginning I have been far more concerned, as a writer, with addiction itself (whether to drugs, or sex, or money, or power) as a model of control and with the ultimate decadence of humanity's biological potentials, perverted by stupidity and inhumane malice."

The grandson of the founder of the Burroughs Adding Machine company, he was born in St. Louis and attended private schools there and in Los Alamos, New Mexico, before matriculating at Harvard. Between 1938 and 1940 he pursued graduate work at Harvard in anthropology, living in "a small frame house on a quiet tree lined street beyond the Commodore Hotel." Then he moved to New York and, beginning around 1944, quite deliberately became a heroin addict. He befriended future Beat writers Jack Kerouac and Allen Ginsberg; Kerouac described him as "Tall, 6 foot 1, strange, inscrutable because ordinary looking (scrutable), like a shy bank clerk with a patrician thinlipped cold blue-lipped face." The only Beat writer not influenced by Buddhism, Burroughs was, as one of many websites now calls him, "the hard man of hip."

Later, in Mexico, he killed his common-law wife, Joan Vollmer Adams, in a drunken attempt to shoot a highball glass off her head with a pistol. He traveled to South America looking for a psychedelic drug, yage, and sent Ginsberg a hilarious epistolary travelogue later published as *The Yage Letters*. He reached Tangier, Morocco, in 1954 and stayed for years, experiencing "the depression and hopelessness of heavy addiction... the numb, despairing feeling of being buried alive." He said he could sit in his room in Tangier after shooting heroin and look at the tip of his boot for hours without moving.

"I live with the constant threat of possession, and a constant need to escape ... from Control."

But in 1957 Burroughs kicked his heroin habit, in London, with the help of a drug called apomorphine. "It was as though an inner dam had broken," he wrote, "I felt reborn and was content to spend long hours at the typewriter, transcribing the images and characters of the novel [*Naked Lunch*], which took shape as though of its own volition. It was assembled in two weeks from a mass of pages, the balance of which were to form the basis for [later novels] *The Soft Machine, The Ticket That Exploded,* and *Nova Express*." Burroughs dramatized the ways in which addiction enables the exercise of power, whether it be the drug dealer's power over the user or a political establishment's power over the citizens. "I live with the constant threat of possession, and a constant need to escape from possession, from Control," he wrote.

He continued to publish during his later years and became something of a pop-culture icon. Rock bands (The Soft Machine and Steely Dan) took their names from his works and director David Cronenberg made a feature film of *Naked Lunch* in 1991. Burroughs spent the last 17 years of his life in the quiet college town of Lawrence, Kansas. Having surprised everyone by living into his eighties, he sustained his heavy use of intoxicants to the end. A visitor in 1995 recalled the author's "jerky, relentless vigor... pulling revolvers out of his pocket and demonstrating the workings of the safety mechanisms, steadily chugging on a beaker of vodka and Coke that is regularly replenished."

Shaffer's studies of compulsive gamblers may support Bergman's notion. "Gambling at slot machines seems to have more addictive potential than table games like cards, dice, or roulette," he says. "There's a lot of social ritual at the gaming tables, but fewer social controls available at the slot machines. Similarly with compulsive shopping: if you don't shop with other people, there are fewer social controls. The excessive shopper shops alone." Other isolated addicts come readily to mind—the solitary drinker, the solo food binges of the bulimic, the workaholic executive alone in the penthouse office at midnight. Connections with other people interrupt the addictive cycle; they redirect attention away from the self-reinforcing feedback of the addictive activity that can quickly escalate to excessive levels.

Addiction is not all pharmacology, neurotransmitters, and intrapsychic states; the social settings of drug consumption have powerful effects. They can influence basic brain chemistry—which is one reason Gene Heyman rejects the notion that "addictive behavior is insensitive to persuasion, that there's an irresistible urge to take the drug." Heyman agrees that drugs alter the brain, but disputes the idea that they change the brain in ways that make choice impossible—he does not believe, in other words, that neuroadaptation makes drug use involuntary. Exhibit A, he says, is 50 million ex-smokers who have voluntarily ended their intake of nicotine.

Many external factors can influence the choice to use drugs. Culture matters: drug intake is far less prevalent in places where religion plays a major role—Israel, Islamic nations, Mormon communities. Laws, too, have an effect: during Prohibition, the incidence of cirrhosis of the liver, probably the best epidemiological index of alcoholism, plummeted. Social class predicts some use patterns: differential quitting rates for tobacco use have strengthened the correlation between smoking and lower levels of education. Then there are social norms: the precipitous drop in the social desirability of smoking has supported quitters. And money talks: in experimental situations, social psychologists have offered addicts cash rewards—say, $50—for not smoking, drinking, or doing cocaine. "There are powerful positive results—addiction will stop in the short run," Heyman says. "If drug use really is involuntary, it doesn't matter whether it's short- or long-term. You can't pay someone not to have dandruff, not to be depressed, not to hallucinate."

One reason people believe drug use is involuntary is that recovery rates for addicts treated at clinics are quite bad. Within one year of treatment, relapse rates of 67 to 90 percent are common for alcohol, opiate, cocaine, and tobacco users. "But most of the people who become addicted to drugs don't go to clinics," says Heyman. "Actually, only 30 to 40 percent go to clinics. Yet this clinic population has greatly influenced our vision and concept of addiction."

It turns out that addicts who *don't* go to clinics have much *higher* recovery rates. Heyman cites two large community surveys, one from 1980 to 1984 and another from 1990 to 1992, that interviewed a cross-section of the general population and reliably identified individuals who met recognized criteria for drug dependence. "Most of those who had been addicts were no longer addicted," says Heyman. "Fifty-nine to 76 percent had been in remission for the previous year or longer. Smaller scale ethnographic studies of general populations also report high remission rates for addicts, and these results strongly suggest that for most, remission is permanent."

Another fascinating finding is the well-known 1975 study, conducted by Lee Robins of Washington University Medical School in St. Louis, of U.S. servicemen who became heroin addicts in Vietnam. Thousands of men got hooked, and 80 percent of those who initially took heroin more than three times became regular users, taking the drug at least once per week. Those who stayed in Vietnam longer often moved on from sniffing to injection. Yet three years after these veterans returned to the States,

more than 90 percent had quit. (This contrasts sharply with relapse rates that often exceed 90 percent for heroin addicts in treatment.) The veterans' success in kicking their habits wasn't simply due to decreased drug availability: half of the Vietnam addicts used heroin at least once after they returned home. But "what's really interesting is what happened to the 6 percent of the Vietnam addicts who went into treatment," Heyman says. "For this group, the relapse rate was about 70 percent! In other words, Vietnam vets who go into treatment look pretty much like other Americans who go into treatment."

The question of how addicts who present themselves for treatment differ from other addicts is not well studied, Heyman says. "What has emerged is that treatment seekers are much more likely to have other psychiatric disorders—depression, schizophrenia, affective disorders, or conduct disorders like sociopathy. These psychiatric syndromes may undermine the mechanisms and processes that assist in recovery." Consider that 30 years ago, there was no apparent correlation between smoking and depression. Today, there is one, Heyman explains—"linked to a selective quit rate as a function of psychiatric disorders."

He suggests we "think of addiction not as compulsion, but ambivalence. Alcoholics often recognize that the alcohol is doing them in, yet they keep right on drinking. These data lead people to conclude that the drinking is involuntary, out of control, since continuing to drink doesn't make sense. Another view is that people are inconsistent and contradictory, and predictably so—it's a slightly starker view of human nature. When talking to his therapist, the guy says he wants to stop. But that's looking at his life as a whole—after all, it's hard to be a heavy drinker, or a heroin or cocaine user, without having tons of problems. Yet at a given instant, when the alcoholic is looking at a glass of wine, the frame of reference is, 'What do I want to do right now?' The situations in which they say they want to stop are different from those in which the drug or substance is presented.

"When drinking, people are much more likely to engage in all kinds of dangerous behavior—wife beating, child abuse, unprotected sex with strangers, smoking ..."

GEORGE VAILLANT

"Humans are inconsistent. Their preferences change with the setting," Heyman continues. "To end an addiction, people need an alternative to drug use, something better to do. The clinic population, people with other psychiatric disorders, have a much harder time changing their situations to ones where drug use is less preferred. If you see it as preference rather than compulsion, you can account for all the data."

Lethal Liquids, and Some Ways Out

ONE OF THE FOREMOST SCHOLARS doing longitudinal research (studies that follow up subjects over many years) in psychiatry is George Vaillant, who directs the Study of Adult Development, based at Harvard Medical School. Vaillant's 1983 book *The Natural History of Alcoholism*, a milestone in the field, analyzes drinking patterns in two populations of World War II era men: a group from Harvard and another group from working-class, inner-city Boston. Generations of researchers have followed these men as they have aged. "Alcohol is more often the horse and less often the cart than any other social ill I can think of," Vaillant says. "I find it terribly interesting that people are much more concerned with every other form of addiction than they are with alcoholism, which—as a problem to humanity—is as big as all other addictions combined. It costs as much as all infectious and pulmonary disease. And it has more impact on others. Drug addicts harm themselves, but that's small beer compared with 25,000 alcohol-related traffic fatalities per year."

Even though cigarette smoking is the direct cause of 400,000 American deaths annually, while alcohol directly causes only 100,000 deaths, "alcoholism is a major reason that people don't stop smoking," says Vaillant. "Those who keep on smoking after age 50 tend to be alcoholics." In hospitals, alcoholics cost six times as much as other patients. Half of all people who show up in emergency rooms with severe multiple fractures are alcoholics. "But the emergency rooms treating multiple fractures ignore blood alcohol levels," Vaillant says. "The causal link isn't made."

"No other drug of addiction impairs one's aversion to punishment the way alcohol does," he continues. "Yes, compulsive gambling impairs your aversion to being poor, and heroin use impairs your aversion to being arrested. But alcoholism goes across the board. When drinking, people are much more likely to engage in all kinds of dangerous, life-threatening behavior—wife beating, child abuse, unprotected sex with strangers, smoking, drunk driving. You can be five foot two and willing to take on anyone in the bar."

Such imperviousness to punishment also tends to forestall recovery. In any case, "the best intentions in the world don't help you with addiction," says Vaillant. "Will power is not a prognostic factor in recovery. Addiction resides in what is often referred to as our reptilian brain, and—well, alligators don't come when they're called. What *does* matter, over the short term, is hitting bottom and having something to lose—the employed, married, upper-middle-class drinker does better at the Betty Ford Center than the homeless alcoholic. But over the long term, inner-city men recovered twice as often from alcoholism as the Harvard men did. The difference has nothing to do with treatment, intelligence, self-care, or having something to lose. It *does* have to do with hitting bottom. Someone sleeping under the elevated train tracks can at some point recognize that he's an alcoholic, but the guy getting stewed every night at a private club may not."

How, then, to change addictive behavior? We may start with the new understanding of the problem—that the roots of addiction lie in both brain chemistry *and* behavior. "It's a wrongheaded bias to think that these are *either* psychological or biological problems," says Gene Heyman. Both voluntary and involuntary behaviors have biological bases. Successful treatments for addiction need to address both realms at once—say, combining a drug like Naltrexone, which influences neurotransmitters, with a healthier alternative to the drinking, drugging, or gambling life.

Vaillant's studies have convinced him that there are four factors, common to all addictions, that predict success in breaking a habit.

Find a competing behavior that is less disruptive. "Say a drinker goes to Alcoholics Anonymous, sobers up, and starts drinking a lot of coffee and smoking cigarettes," he says. "Then he quits smoking, by chewing the erasers off pencils and overeating, so he gains weight. Now his problem is obesity, so he winds up hanging around Overeaters Anonymous and drinking a gallon of water a day. It's what teachers call 'redirecting.' You may not be able to stop two four-year-olds from fighting, but you can say, 'Let's go get ice cream cones.'"

An external superego. "If I tell you you'll get liver disease if you keep on drinking, you could care less," Vaillant says. "But if I say that as an M.D. I'm going to do random checks on your urine, you may pay attention. Or if, when you drink Jack Daniels, it burns your stomach. Methadone is an external superego, since it blocks the effect of heroin. Someone who engaged in compulsive sex might not care if it hurt their spouse's feelings, but if there were an electric bracelet that could transmit a shock at crucial moments, that might make a difference."

"I get no kick from cocaine." "It's fascinating that heroin addicts get better when they fall in love with someone new," Vaillant says. "Our brains are wired for falling in love, because that's good for nature—but you can short-circuit that pathway with morphine, nicotine, caffeine. Love gets the whole brain involved. Romantic attachment not only competes with the addiction, but takes place in a nonaddictive way."

Spiritus contra spiritum. "Charismatic religions offer a conversion experience, as described by William James and C.G. Jung. Suddenly you find your higher power, and booze is no longer important," Vaillant explains. "There is also the protective wall of a human community—something that AA, for example, provides. It's important to find a new social group, since you owe money to all your old ones. Religion offers an oceanic high—the sense that a higher power loves you. To the addict, heroin, cocaine, and booze are like mother's milk. Religion is, too."

Craig A. Lambert '69, Ph.D. '78, is deputy editor of this magazine.

From *Harvard Magazine*, March/April 2000, pp. 60-68. © 2000 by Harvard Magazine and Craig Lambert.

DRUG EDUCATION: THE TRIUMPH OF BAD SCIENCE

DARE AND PROGRAMS LIKE IT DON'T STOP KIDS FROM USING DRUGS. BUT THERE'S TOO MUCH AT STAKE TO REPLACE THEM

by JASON COHN

IN FEBRUARY, THE HEAD OF DRUG ABUSE Resistance Education—used in seventy-five percent of U.S. school districts and fifty-five countries worldwide—made the extraordinary admission that the program has not been effective. Nonetheless, the Robert Wood Johnson Foundation gave DARE a $13.7 million grant to bring the curriculum up to date and to scientifically evaluate its usefulness. The foundation reasoned that it would be easier to change DARE than to bring another program to its level of penetration. And so, in September, DARE will launch its new and improved program with great fanfare in six cities, including New York and Los Angeles. In March 2002, administrators will implement it worldwide.

The DARE-makeover announcement is being interpreted by some as a signal that science is coming to the rescue at last in the politically sensitive field of drug education. Zili Sloboda, the former director of the Division of Epidemiology and Prevention Research at the National Institute on Drug Abuse, was chosen to oversee the evaluation of the renovated program. She says that DARE "will do everything it can to update its programs and to make them evidence-based."

But many social scientists are unimpressed: They argue that drug-prevention education must be the only category in their field where failure—such as DARE's—is used as an occasion to continue and even expand a program.

IN FACT, THE PROBLEM GOES WAY BEYOND DARE. In interviews with more than a dozen experts, a picture emerges of a dysfunctional and highly politicized drug-education environment in which even the "research-based programs" now favored by the federal government don't stand up to scientific scrutiny. In fact, many say, despite all the "scientific" claims to the contrary, drug-prevention education—at least the abstinence-based model that reigns in America's schools—is just as likely to have no effect or to make kids curious as it is to persuade them not to use drugs.

Here's why the current models are flawed: Drug-education researchers generally evaluate their own programs, and, with few exceptions, they tend to parse out their data so programs seem more successful than they actually are. Scientists call it "over-advocating." Positive results in limited situations are exaggerated, and instances of increased drug use are obscured or suppressed. Such practices should never survive the process of peer review, critics say, but they do.

The federal government plays a major role. Key agencies set unrealistic guidelines that ensure failure, and they continue to nurture programs despite bountiful evidence that they don't work. What's worse, drug education is big business. Fueled by a perpetual sense of crisis, schools and communities pour scarce resources into prevention programs. Each year, the federal government spends upward of $2 billion on drug-prevention education, and states

and localities contribute more, according to data extrapolated by Joel Brown, director of the Center for Educational Research and Development, in Berkeley, California. Estimates on total expenditures range as high as $5 billion annually. Researchers who evaluate their own programs stand to profit only when they can report success. And these same researchers are often asked to sit on exclusive government panels, deciding which programs will be recommended for sale to the nation's schools.

DARE MAY BE "THE ONLY GAME IN town," as Sloboda puts it, but that hasn't kept other researchers from developing programs to fight for a share of the market. These competitors have been buoyed by DARE's public-relations woes and by a 1998 law limiting Department of Education drug-prevention funds to programs that at least minimally demonstrate "the promise of success" in reducing teen drug use.

Only one of the programs deemed exemplary by all three major agencies—the Department of Education, NIDA and the Center for Substance Abuse Prevention—is commercially available nationwide. That program is called Life Skills Training. While LST is not nearly as big as DARE, the program is currently in about 3,000 schools, and an estimated 800,000 students have gone through it to date, according to a spokesman.

LST has never been evaluated independently; two studies are going on now, with the results expected this summer. But the program's creator, Gilbert Botvin, a professor of psychology and public health at Cornell University, claims that the program reduces tobacco, alcohol and marijuana use in young people by up to an incredible seventy-five percent. He has published more than a dozen articles in leading journals, including the *Journal of the American Medical Association*, saying as much. These would be remarkable outcomes indeed, enough to warrant implementing LST in every school in the country, if it weren't for one thing: They are probably not true.

As LST has risen in prominence, other researchers have begun analyzing Botvin's published articles, and many have discerned a common pattern. "Botvin gets positive effects but only in a very small subsample," says Dennis Gorman, an expert in prevention and evaluation methodology at the Texas A&M University System Health Center.

As an example, Gorman showed in the 1998 article "The Irrelevance of Evidence in the Development of School-based Drug-Prevention Policy, 1986–1996," in *Evaluation Review*, that Botvin emphasizes specific data from students who were exposed to at least sixty percent of the program's curriculum. Gorman states that the students Botvin ends up focusing on are likely to be those who were most motivated and least inclined to be involved with drugs in the first place. Botvin responds that breaking down the data from only the high-implementation group tells you most about the usefulness of a program. (This is a practice that the National Academy of Sciences called "misleading" in a report that condemned the quality of current prevention research.)

Others have gone beyond Gorman in criticizing Botvin's methods. In an article in the April issue of *Journal of Drug Education*, Joel Brown found that when students received fifty-nine percent or less of Life Skills Training, their drug use was actually higher than that of students who didn't go through LST at all. Botvin categorically denies any negative results: "The fact of the matter is, we present more data than any of these other researchers."

Another person who takes issue with Botvin's claims is Stephanie Tortu, an associate professor of public health at Tulane University in New Orleans. In 1984, she was project manager on one of LST's first major studies—an investigation of the ef-

fectiveness of the program in fifty-six schools across New York state.

She says that when Botvin presented her with the draft of the study's results, she was shocked to discover that crucial data on the students' alcohol use had been left out. Tortu and the other researchers had found that students who went through LST were more likely to drink alcohol than students who weren't exposed to the program, but this information was nowhere to be found in the report.

She and several colleagues on the project, including Barbara Bettes, a data analyst, sent Botvin a memo documenting their concern and asking that an investigation of the alcohol findings be made their highest priority.

"He was the principal investigator," Tortu says. "When he saw that alcohol use was up in his prevention group, he should have been trying to figure out why. I felt he was required ethically to call attention to it and investigate it." Shortly afterward, Tortu says, Botvin denied her a standard raise, a message she interpreted as punishment for sticking her neck out. Soon after that, Botvin informed her that there was no longer enough money to keep her on the project.

"To be straightforward and candid," says Botvin, "we've produced the strongest effects for tobacco, and also strong effects for marijuana, but the alcohol effects in some studies have been inconsistent." And he maintains that the data at issue in the staff memo was just preliminary. Bettes counters that Botvin felt comfortable using the same set of data to announce positive effects on tobacco and marijuana.

In the end, the report delivered to New York state did not indicate that alcohol use had increased among students who went through the program. Joel Moskowitz, director of the Center for Family and Community Health at UC-Berkeley, notes that "unfortunately, Botvin is not the only researcher to engage in such practices of overstating positive program effects or neglecting to report negative program effects and limitations of the research."

Tortu maintains that, ultimately, Botvin has a conflict of interest in both evaluating and profiting from LST, but Botvin says that he has fully disclosed the fact that he receives royalties from sales of the program. Furthermore, he says, the evidence confirming LST's success is superior. "In my view, the quality of the science in the Life Skills Training research is higher than for any other prevention program that I'm aware of in America," he says.

That may not be far from true, but it's also not saying a whole lot. Botvin has been careful to distance LST from DARE and other programs that have been found to be ineffective. He calls LST a "comprehensive" approach to drug education.

"Life Skills Training deals with a broad array of skills that we think kids need to navigate their way through the dangerous minefield of adolescence," Botvin says. "Skills that will help them be more successful as adolescents and help them to avoid high-risk behaviors, including pressures to drink, smoke or use drugs." These skills include how to make conversation with strangers and politely end a conversation when it could lead to offers of drugs. "It goes beyond 'Just Say No' to identifying unreasonable requests and reacting to those requests in an appropriate way," Botvin says.

But critics of LST, who include top DARE officials, say the difference is not so great as Botvin likes to make out. "DARE has 'Eight Ways to Say No,' LST has 'Nine Ways to Say No,'" says DARE spokesman Ralph Lochridge. "A lot of these programs look, talk and walk like DARE."

DESPITE RECENT CRITICAL ATTENTION, LST has emerged as the leading contender to DARE. Major news organizations have hyped it, and Botvin even seems to see DARE's ongoing troubles as an opportunity. After the recent DARE announcement, he wrote a letter to the *New York Times* and also encouraged me to paint LST as a David to DARE's Goliath. "Why wait two, three or five years to find out whether or not [the new DARE] works," Botvin asks, "when we already have prevention programs available today that have been extensively researched and for which there is strong scientific evidence of effectiveness?" Even Sloboda, now in DARE's camp, is quick to list LST as an exemplar of "highly effective prevention programs in use today."

LST may be ready for its close-up, but has the program gotten an easy ride from scholarly journals and the government agencies that endorse it? Some researchers think so.

"If I had been asked to review these studies, I would not have recommended publication," says Richard Clayton, director of the Center for Prevention Research at the University of Kentucky. "Some people have a vested interest in saying that our current drug prevention strategies work. They're looking for a poster child for prevention to take attention away from DARE, and they've chosen LST. But that doesn't mean it works."

Lst AND DARE ARE ONLY TWO OF THE many programs drawing criticism from those in the prevention-research community who have grown disgusted with the field.

Prevention science, they say, is a niche that tends to attract those more concerned with waging the War on Drugs in America's classrooms than with performing careful science. Evidence is ignored or used so selectively that it becomes irrelevant. When studies turn up negative or neutral results, prevention boosters employ a variety of deceptions, according to critics.

One tactic is to continually change the measurements for success. Rather than looking for changes in drug behavior, researchers might look for changes in reported attitudes toward drugs. If attitudes haven't changed much, they can always test how much kids know about the dangers of drugs. DARE, for example, has continued to claim success because kids who go through the program tend to have a better attitude toward the police—as if the goal of the program was to raise awareness for law enforcement rather than to keep kids off drugs.

Another common trick is to revise the program. Since any longitudinal evaluation requires, by definition, years to compile, researchers can always deflect criticism by saying the program has evolved since the evaluation began.

As with other aspects of the War on Drugs, hawkish prevention makes for good politics, and the truth be damned. The Center for Substance Abuse Prevention has developed a set of talking points for advocates to present. The title? "Winning the Numbers Game: How to Keep Saying 'Prevention Works' When the Numbers Say Something Else."

This dissing of science is part of what makes independent researchers conclude that the whole enterprise of drug prevention is run through with politics and ideological arthritis. Since it's a small area of study, they say, the same group of scientists is continually chosen to sit on the panels that recommend programs to schools and to review articles for publication, a practice that encourages mutual back-scratching rather than critical investigation. (One prominent figure calls it a "research mafia.") It's a closed feedback loop that works in favor of those researchers whose programs fit the narrow guidelines defined by the federal government. They get the big grants, so they publish the most research and are consequently chosen to peer-review the research of others.

The federal guidelines in question are found in the 1994 Safe and Drug Free Schools and Communities Act, which codified zero-tolerance drug policy as a "no-use" education strategy. The philosophy of no-use is similar to abstinence-based sex education: Kids learn that they have a choice between keeping their bodies pure or… not. This is a "choice" that few kids will fail to see as rigged.

While it may seem appropriate that schools play that role, no-use programs, from DARE on down, have never been shown to help keep kids off drugs. Even the General Accounting Office, which evaluates how effectively federal money is being spent, reported, "There is no evidence that the no use approach is more successful than alternative approaches, or even successful in its own right."

Federal policymakers have chosen to ignore the GAO's recommendation that they broaden the search for effective prevention strategies. So today, schools and researchers who want federal funding must demonstrate that their programs teach abstinence as the only option.

NOT ALL RESEARCHERS HAVE GONE ALONG with the policy. Joel Brown, for one, wants to study an alternative program based on "resilience education," the subject and title of his recent book. Brown says resiliency is a general scientific concept that focuses on young people's ability to adapt and thrive in the face of educational challenges. Applying the idea to drug education is natural, he says.

"Over the course of their lives, kids will inevitably face a variety of decisions about drugs, including legal drugs and alcohol when they are of the right age," Brown says. Rather than starting with the idea that kids don't have the capacity to make wise decisions if they're dealt with honestly, a resiliency approach would allow educators to deal credibly with students on the issue of drugs. In this way, Brown says, teachers can help kids become skilled decision makers rather than merely telling them which decision is the right one.

Brown says a resilience-based program would not condone youth drug use. However, he says, it's critical to provide honest, accurate and complete drug information while focusing on health and safety. Marsha Rosenbaum, director of the San Francisco office of the Lindesmith Center-Drug Policy Foundation, says that this approach is exactly what America's schools need.

"What's missing from 'drug education' is education," says Rosenbaum. "For the kids who don't say no, where can they go for honest, realistic information about drugs in a life-or-death situation?" she asks. "They sure can't go to the so-called educator in a no-use prevention program."

Realistically, educators must recognize that some kids will do drugs no matter what they're told, Rosenbaum says. And that means adults have the responsibility to provide information that can help save lives. She offers the example of Ecstasy, whose most common health risk comes from dehydration when people take it and go dancing. Some deaths have occurred when kids either fail to drink water or drink so much that they literally drown.

But such useful information is rarely taught in America's schools. Federal policy and the overall zeitgeist of the War on Drugs make it too difficult to implement and study programs based on resiliency or its less comprehensive cousin, harm reduction, Rosenbaum says.

If education is missing from drug education, then reality is what's missing from federal policy. In addition to prescribing no-use messages, the Safe and Drug Free Schools Act also set as a goal "that by the year 2000, all schools in America will be free of drugs and violence." It was unsuccessful in more ways than one. By chasing unrealistic goals, the policy has endangered the most at risk students and failed to properly educate anyone.

JASON COHN *is a freelance journalist based in San Francisco.*

From *Rolling Stone,* May 24, 2001, pp. 41, 42 & 96. © 2001 by Wennner Media LLC. Reprinted by permission.

HOLLYWOOD HIGH

Whether they are recovering or relapsing, substance-abusing celebs have never had more support—maybe that's the problem. Just ask Robert Downey Jr.

BY BENJAMIN SVETKEY

ONCE AGAIN, ROBERT DOWNEY JR. FOUND HIMSELF BEING LED away in handcuffs. This time—just past midnight last Tuesday morning—police spotted him lurking in a deserted alley on Washington Boulevard, a semi-industrial section of Los Angeles, and busted him on suspicion of being under the influence of a controlled substance (possibly methamphetamine or cocaine). It was, of course, Downey's second arrest since emerging from a 12-month prison stretch last August as an allegedly changed man (or, at least, changed enough to be hired for a costarring gig on *Ally McBeal*). Clearly, though, some things never change. And not just for Downey.

Less than three months ago, Aaron Sorkin was accepting a crystal bowl—the Phoenix Rising Award—in recognition of his hard fought victory over substance abuse. In front of 300 guests at the Regent Beverly Wilshire, where the Phoenix House drug prevention organization was holding a Hollywood fundraiser, the Emmy winning *West Wing* creator recalled how, five years earlier, he'd pulled himself from the coils of cocaine addiction.

The 39-year-old executive producer choked back tears as he described how the drug could have robbed him of his first experience of fatherhood with his new baby daughter. He railed like Josiah Bartlet against insurance companies that refuse to pay for rehabilitation treatments. "All I could think was 'They must be doing an awful lot of blow at Blue Cross/Blue Shield if they think my condition isn't serious,'" Sorkin joked about his own rejected $15,000 rehab claim. Then he got serious again. "My point is," he said, "I had $15,000. Most people don't. And those are the people who usually end up in jail."

Usually. Earlier this month, Sorkin spent a little time inside a jail cell himself—about three hours—when he was arrested at the Burbank Airport, en route to Las Vegas, after security agents opened his carry-on to find a bag of psychedelic mushrooms, a small stash of marijuana, and a suspicious-looking pipe (currently being tested at a police lab). Given his recent high profile remarks regarding recovery (ironically, he and the show were scheduled to win an award from the National Council on Alcoholism and Drug Dependence on April 26), it is perhaps not surprising that Sorkin fainted as airport police were called in. He's out on $10,000 bail, due to be arraigned on charges of possession of a controlled substance April 30.

As it happens, April 30 will be a big day for Downey, too. He'll be spending it in a different California courtroom for his Nov. 25 arrest in Palm Springs for possession of cocaine, and he'll be back in court again May 4 for this latest arrest. In the meantime, he was released to his parole officer and, according to his publicist, "voluntarily checked himself into an undisclosed rehabilitation facility." Matthew Perry, 31, meanwhile, recently faced another type of trial: After a second stab at rehab (he spent a month in 1997 at Hazelden in Minnesota for Vicodin addiction), he returned to the set of *Friends* to tape the sitcom's season finale. (His May 2000 car accident had nothing to do with drugs, according to police.)

There is an obvious pattern in all this—but maybe a not-so-obvious one as well. The news here, after all, isn't that celebs sometimes develop drug and alcohol problems. Andy Dick (who crashed *his* car two years ago, in an admitted substance related accident), Kelsey Grammer (who, while under the influence in 1996, flipped the Viper that NBC had given him), Melanie Griffith, Tim Allen, Brett Butler, Kurt Cobain, Courtney Love, Scott Weiland, John Belushi, Elvis Presley, Marilyn Monroe, practically the entire Barrymore gene pool at one time or another—there's no shortage of drug- and alcohol-abuse drama in Hollywood. Nor is it any longer possible to make the case that the entertainment industry actively encourages drug use among its stars; the days when Louis B. Mayer was supposedly shaking bottles of pills down Judy Garland's throat are a thing of the past.

What is news, or at least what's starting to get noticed, is how some stars just can't seem to get it together no matter how hard Hollywood tries to help. In recent years, recovery has practically become L.A.'s second biggest industry (and maybe its biggest social scene, with celeb AA meetings turning into A list events). On set drug counseling is offered on some lots (like David E. Kelley's)—probably because former substance abusers are now being hired by the bushel (*The West Wing* alone has two outspoken recovering alcoholics in its cast: John Spencer and Rob Lowe). And yet, despite all those efforts—the 12-step programs, the 28-day treatment centers, the endless interventions, and countless second chances—despite it all, this town is still murder on stars trying to go straight.

IN RETROSPECT, THERE MAY HAVE BEEN WARNING SIGNS THAT Sorkin was slipping into old habits. According to a source close to the set of Sorkin's erstwhile ABC series *Sports Night*, he had taken previous trips to Las Vegas (not in itself terribly incriminating, but it is a city where partying isn't exactly unheard of). Sometimes these trips seemed curiously timed, like the April 15 jaunt the police ended up canceling. Why was Sorkin shuttling drugs to Vegas on such a—excuse the pun—high note, the day after *The West Wing*'s celebratory annual wrap party and just prior to shooting the season finale? If you go by awards, he's at the top of his game. And the same could be said for Downey and Perry, both of whom should be relishing the most rewarding years of their careers right now.

Having people watch you as you attempt recovery is "like using a Band-Aid when you've been gored by a rhinoceros."

—RECOVERING SCREENWRITER

If there's a common thread among the entertainment industry's chronic backsliders, it's that success seems to equal relapse. Such a contradiction naturally confounds many both in the industry and outside of it. Yet in that one rock-bottom respect, being a star with a drug problem is no different from being a gardener with one. "I've known hundreds of people who have been addicts—some famous, some not," says one screenwriter who's both famous and (now) sober. "They all share one

thing: They feel a huge emptiness they thought could be filled with some finite substance—drugs, booze, women."

Fame, however, is a distinct disadvantage when it comes to recovery. "People want to be your friend, they're interested in giving you what you want," says the screenwriter (who, like a lot of former addicts interviewed for this story, did not want his name published). "They're invested in flattering you, telling you you're a genius and special and that everything you do is right. But if you want to get off drugs, the enemy of recovery is [the belief] that you are right and special."

Buddy Arnold, a professional saxophonist and ex-junkie who created the Musicians' Assistance Program (MAP), an organization that helps musicians get into recovery treatments, says, "The mind-set of many musicians we see is that they really believe they're legends—legends in their own mind."

There's even a catchy new psychiatric-sounding term for this sort of celebrity dysfunction circulating around the recovery movement: acquired situational narcissism (coined by Dr. Robert Millman, who as medical consultant to Major League Baseball has also encountered plenty of legends in their own minds). Such stars "feel they are different, that they're not like the rest of us, that they're invulnerable," explains Mark Greenberg of the Betty Ford Center (the mother of all celebrity treatment clinics). "These individuals with recognizable names and faces are harder to treat. There is always somebody to pick up the pieces for them because of who they are. Even with multiple relapses, somebody will be there to pick them up."

That cycle of relapse and recovery can form a vicious circle all its own, especially for the famous. In fact, the notoriety of failed recovery—with the intense media scrutiny and constant surveillance during work hours (often by bodyguards paid by the studios to keep stars clean)—can accelerate self-destructive tendencies. Having people watch you as you attempt recovery is "like using a Band-Aid when you've been gored by a rhinoceros," says the screenwriter. "Who gives a f— who's watching you when you're in a hotel room with an eight-ball, and you've chosen Palm Springs, of all godforsaken places? You're not really thinking about what so-and-so thinks of you. You're thinking about how [you] can die."

DAVID E. KELLEY NO DOUBT HAD THE BEST OF INTENTIONS when he brought Robert Downey Jr. aboard *Ally McBeal* last August, just one week after the actor's release from prison. "Robert's really a sweet man," Kelley told EW at the time. "When you meet him you want to cheer for him." And by all accounts, Kelley bent over backward to make Downey's life on set as low-pressure as possible. "Their interest seems to be Downey the person, not Downey the actor," says a source inside Downey's circle. "They've taken an interest in him like I've never seen." (Those days may be over; Kelley issued a statement after Downey's most recent arrest saying, "We are wrapping up the stories on the final few episodes of *Ally McBeal* for the season without him.")

Others, though, have less pure intentions. "That's the problem with being surrounded by yes-men all the time," says the screenwriter. "They don't understand your creative spark.

They're afraid it'll be extinguished if you go into rehab. They're afraid you're going to start talking about spirituality and 12-step programs and then they're going to lose their 10 percent. They don't want you going to Betty Ford because what if you come out all earnest and talking about a higher power? What happens to their houses then?"

"People are like, 'You're screwing up my paycheck,'" says Marc Flanagan, who lived through Brett Butler's erratic flame-outs when he exec-produced *Grace Under Fire* in the mid-1990s. "Because of what happened to Brett, people lost their jobs. People never really think about that."

Actually, a lot of people are paid to think about that—like the studio lawyers who try to write ironclad contractual codicils designed to keep stars sober (Charlie Sheen, for instance, has had financial incentives built into his contracts; if he relapsed he supposedly lost additional bonuses). Such legal safety nets don't always succeed in catching a star before he falls, though—and they don't make stalled productions any less frustrating. Paramount can't be smiling over its potential losses on *Servicing Sarah*, the half-finished movie which Perry left in limbo in February and to which he now likely won't be able to return until after the actors' strike. ("We just hope Matthew's okay" is what a spokesperson for the film has been telling the press.) Warner Bros. Television, which produces *Friends*, probably isn't thrilled with Perry either. This latest time-out for rehab meant the show had to awkwardly shoot around the star for at least two episodes, nearly ruining Monica's season-long wedding plans.

"Stars want people to feel sorry for them. The big excuse of pressure is nonsense. What pressure does Matt Perry have?"

—TELEVISION PRODUCER

And that's precisely the sort of behavior that makes so many inside the industry—and outside—unsympathetic. "The worst misconception is that stars are driven by such hard work," says a former *Home Improvement* producer who survived Tim Allen's alcohol problems in the '90s. "A sitcom star works 25 weeks a year. The last time I counted, I think there were 52 weeks in a year.... Stars want people to feel sorry for them. The big excuse of pressure is nonsense. What pressure does Matt Perry have?" (How about not nodding off between takes on the set of *Servicing Sarah*, as one witness says Perry periodically did?) "A star who has a substance-abuse problem is a terrorist to all of the people he or she works with," the producer goes on. "They are held hostage because the star ultimately determines the course of every day." Hostages who are sometimes treated to bizarrely entertaining behavior—Butler, for instance, reportedly flashed her breasts to an underage costar and once climbed a tree and wouldn't come down—but hostages nevertheless.

Not surprisingly, the music industry hasn't embraced the recovery movement as enthusiastically as the rest of the entertainment industry—without drugs, after all, it's merely sex and rock & roll. "I know people in personal management who cover for addicts for years, make it completely easy for them to continue to do what they're doing," says a former major-label recording artist with his own drug past. "'Why did he miss the performance?' 'Uh, fatigue.' 'Why is he canceling the rest of the tour?' 'Oh, he's totally tired.' I mean, he's tired from getting *loaded* every night."

But even the labels are often forced to intervene on occasion—especially when big money is involved. "I'm sure you know situations where people aren't touring or the record is delayed," says the artist. "They're trying to get their s— together. The industry has to allow it, because if your artist is strung out he can't produce. They'll hire people to guard him on tour. They'll put him through rehab. They'll put him in a distant sleep-away camp somewhere. They'll do all these things to try to make it so this guy can continue to produce."

And if he still can't produce, schedules are sometimes readjusted to accommodate the star's cascading brain chemistry. Hollywood tends to be forgiving that way, mostly because it has no choice. "Once you hire [a star] for your show, they have a huge financial impact on you," says a former high-level exec at DreamWorks, which produces *Spin City*, home to rehab rebounder Sheen. "It's hard to do *Frasier* without Frasier."

It is, of course, a terrible double standard. In most businesses, an unshakable drug problem will get you fired. In Hollywood, it gets you a costarring gig with Calista Flockhart and a Golden Globe award (just five and a half months after leaving prison). Indeed, like everything else in entertainment, a juicy recovery story can be turned into a publicity gold mine. It's not accidental, for instance, that *Ally McBeal*'s buzz perked up when Downey started to appear; watch *The West Wing*'s ratings in the next couple of weeks to see how Sorkin's sorrows sweeten the show's Nielsens.

Such bonuses make it virtually impossible for a drug-addled star to ever hit rock bottom—which many addiction experts insist is crucial to recovery. Neither Downey nor Perry, for instance, will ever have to pawn his VCR for a hit. It almost seems as if they're allowing themselves a tumble into the abyss, knowing the industry's safety net will catch them. "Hollywood lets these people off the hook," says Betty Ford's Greenberg. "What ends up happening is the stars develop more arrogance. The denial becomes more entrenched than in a normal person."

"[Hollywood] means well, they think they're protecting a star from himself, but it's not making it any easier for him to see what's really going on," says celebrity drug counselor Harry Shannon, who's beginning to believe that in some cases, jail time isn't the worst option. "It may be the first time in an addict's adult life that he ever faces a logical consequence for an outrageous action."

Maybe, but try convincing a celeb who's actually lived through a public addiction that there are not consequences. "There's humiliation. There's people staring at you in the street. There's losing your family," offers Mark Hudson, the '70s star-turned-producer who's worked on albums for Aerosmith, Bon Jovi, and Celine Dion (and who's been alcohol-free for more than eight years). "I differ with those who say there are not consequences. There are *huge* consequences. I guarantee you there's not a day that goes by that Robert Downey Jr. does not think about his kid."

"Last time Robert Downey Jr. got arrested, I almost cried," says Bob Forrest, former frontman for the L.A. alternative group Thelonious Monster (and a former heroin addict). "It's unbelievable that he has to do it in public. Everywhere these people go, they're different to begin with. They go to a rehab center and they're treated differently. Everybody's making money off of them. They are the product. Robert Downey Jr. *is* the product. So when that person has the illness, what to do about it seems to be measured by economics."

THE CONSEQUENCES FOR SORKIN PROBABLY WON'T BE ALL THAT severe—assuming the pipe police are looking into doesn't contain anything more serious than pot. Downey, on the other hand, faces stiffer possible penalties. If convicted of the Nov. 25 charges, he could be looking at almost five years in prison. His recent run-in with the law, which violated his parole, could add even more time.

At least Sorkin has the solace of his craft; he can turn his experience into *West Wing* episodes. President Bartlet announces he's suffering from a Vicodin addiction and inspires the nation with his valiant fight back to sobriety. Or Sam gets arrested at the airport when police mistake the corncob pipe in his bag for a semiautomatic weapon. Something like that—Sorkin can work out the details.

With time and hard work, the day may even come when Sorkin will be presented with another crystal-bowl award to celebrate his sobriety. In fact, at this rate, he'll probably collect enough to open a bridal registry. As for Downey, he could conceivably be accepting an Emmy from his jail cell come September. And that, of course, is precisely the problem.

(Additional reporting by Rob Brunner, Tricia Johnson, Lynette Rice, Jessica Shaw, Dan Snierson, and Allison Hope Weiner)

FROM THE SOURCE

Principles of Drug Addiction Treatment: *A Research-Based Guide*

The following excerpts from a report by the National Institute of Health's National Institute on Drug Abuse offers policy-makers numerous suggestions to help fight drug addiction.

Drug addiction is a complex illness, characterized by compulsive at times uncontrollable drug craving, seeking, and use that will persist even in the face of extremely negative consequences. For many people, drug addiction becomes chronic, with relapses possible even after long periods of abstinence.

The path to drug addiction begins with the act of taking drugs. Over time, a person's ability to choose not to take can be compromised. Drug seeking becomes compulsive, in large part as a result of the effects of prolonged drug use on brain functioning and, thus, on behavior.

The compulsion to use drugs can take over the individual's life. Addiction often involves not only compulsive drug taking but also a wide range of dysfunctional behaviors that can interfere with normal functioning in the family, the workplace, and the broader community. Addition also can place people at increased risk for a wide variety of other illnesses. These illnesses can be brought on by behaviors, such as poor living and health habits, that often accompany life as an addict, or because of toxic effects of the drugs themselves.

Because addiction has so many dimensions and disrupts so many aspects of an individual's life, treatment for this illness is never simple. Drug treatment must help the individual stop using drugs and maintain a drug-free lifestyle, while achieving productive functioning in the family, at work, and in society. Effective drug abuse and addiction treatment programs typically incorporate many components, each directed to a particular aspect of the illness and its consequences.

Three decades of scientific research and clinical practice have yielded a variety of effective approaches to drug addiction treatment. Extensive data document that such addiction treatment is as effective as are treatments for most other similarly chronic medical conditions.

In spite of scientific evidence that establishes the effectiveness of drug abuse treatment, many people believe that treatment is ineffective. In part, this is because of unrealistic expectations.

Many people equate addiction with simply using drugs and therefore expect that addiction should be cured quickly, and if it is not, treatment is a failure. In reality, because addiction is a chronic disorder, the ultimate goal of long-term abstinence often requires sustained and repeated treatment episodes.

Of course, not all drug treatment is equally effective. Research also has revealed a set of overarching principles that characterize the most effective drug abuse and addiction treatments and their implementation.

- No single treatment is appropriate for all individuals.
- Treatment needs to be readily available.
- Effective treatment attends to multiple needs of the individual, not just his or her drug use.

- An individual's treatment and services plan must be assessed continually and modified as necessary to ensure that the plan meets the person's changing needs.
- Remaining in treatment for an adequate period of time is critical for treatment effectiveness.

FAST FACTS ...

- Remaining in treatment for an adequate period of time is critical for treatment effectiveness.

- Prisoners who participated in a treatment program in the Delaware State Prison and continued to receive treatment in a work-release program after prison were 70 percent less likely than nonparticipants to return to drug use and incur arrest.

- According to several studies, drug treatment reduces drug use by 40 percent to 60 percent and signficantly decreases criminal activity during and after treatment.

- Treatment can improve the prospects for employment, with gains of up to 40 percent after treatment.

- Medical detoxification is only the first stage of addiction treatment and by itself does little to change long-term drug use.

- Treatment does not need to be voluntary to be effective.

- Counseling (individual and/or group) and other behavior therapies are critical components of effective treatment for addiction.
- Medications are an important element of treatment for many patients, especially when combined with counseling and other behavioral therapies.
- Addiction or drug-abusing individuals with coexisting mental disorders should have both disorders treated in an integrated way.
- Medical detoxification is only the first stage of addiction treatment and by itself does little to change long-term drug use.
- Treatment does not need to be voluntary to be effective.
- Possible drug use during treatment must be monitored continuously.
- Treatment programs should provide assessment for HIV/ AIDS, hepatitis B and C, tuberculosis and other infectious dis-

eases, and counseling to help patients modify or change behaviors that placed themselves or others at risk of infection.
- Recovery from drug addiction can be a long-term process and frequently requires multiple episodes of treatment.

Frequently asked questions

How effective is drug treatment? In addition to stopping drug use, the goal of treatment is to return the individual to productive functioning in the family, workplace and community. Measures of effectiveness typically include levels of criminal behavior, family functioning, employability and medical condition. Overall, treatment of addiction is as successful as treatment for other chronic diseases such as diabetes, hypertension and asthma.

According to several studies, drug treatment reduces drug use by 40 percent to 60 percent and significantly decreases criminal activity during and after treatment. For example, a study of therapeutic community treatment for drug offenders demonstrated that arrests for violent and nonviolent criminal acts were reduced by 40 percent or more.... Treatment can improve the prospects for employment, with gains of up to 40 percent after treatment.

What helps people stay in treatment? Since successful outcomes often depend upon retaining the person long enough to gain the full benefits of treatment, strategies for keeping an individual in the program are critical.... Individual factors related to engagement and retention include motivation to change drug-using behavior, degree of support from family and friends, and whether there is pressure to stay in treatment from the criminal justice system, child protection services, employers or the family.

Within the program, successful counselors are able to establish a positive, therapeutic relationship with the patient. The counselor should ensure that a treatment plan is established and followed so that the individual knows what to expect during treatment. Medical, psychiatric and social services should be available.

According to several conservative estimates, every \$1 invested in addiction treatment programs yields a return of between \$4 and \$7 in reduced drug-related crime, criminal costs and theft alone.

What role can the criminal justice system play in the treatment of drug addiction? Increasingly, research is demonstrating that treatment for drug-addicted offenders during and after incarceration can have a significant beneficial effect upon future drug use, criminal behavior and social functioning. The case for integrating drug addiction treatment approaches with the criminal justice system is compelling. Combining prison- and community-based treatment for drug-addicted offenders reduces the risk of both recidivism to drug-related criminal behavior and relapse to drug use.

For example, a recent study found that prisoners who participated in a therapeutic treatment program in the Delaware State Prison and continued to receive treatment in a work-release program after prison were 70 percent less likely than nonparticipants to return to drug use and incur arrest....

Research has demonstrated that individuals who enter treatment under legal pressure have outcomes as favorable as those who enter treatment voluntarily....

The most effective models integrate criminal justice and drug treatment systems and services. Treatment and criminal justice personnel work together on plans and implementation of screening, placement, testing, monitoring and supervision, as well as on the systematic use of sanctions and rewards for drug abusers in the criminal justice system. Treatment for incarcerated drug abusers must include continuing care, monitoring and supervision after release and during parole.

Is drug addiction treatment worth its cost? Drug addiction treatment is cost-effective in reducing drug use and its associated health and social costs. Treatment is less expensive than alternatives, such as not treating addicts or simply incarcerating addicts. For example, the average cost for one full year of methadone maintenance treatment is approximately $4,700 per patient, whereas one full year of imprisonment costs approximately $18,400 per person.

According to several conservative estimates, every $1 invested in addiction treatment programs yields a return of between $4 and $7 in reduced drug-related crime, criminal costs and theft alone. When savings related to health care are included, total savings can exceed costs by a ratio of 12-to-1. Major savings to the individual and society also come from significant drops in interpersonal conflicts, improvements in workplace productivity and reductions in drug-related accidents.

For information on this report, contact the National Institute on Drug Abuse, 6001 Executive Blvd., Bethesda, MD 20892-9561, or call (301) 443-1124.

Prevention: still a young field

Psychologists are helping to shape a new—and smarter— generation of prevention programs.

BY DEBORAH SMITH

Monitor staff

Since the Drug Free Schools and Communities Act of 1986, virtually all elementary and secondary schools provide some classroom programming on alcohol, tobacco and illicit drugs.

But do they work? The results so far have been mixed.

Use among adolescents

By the 8th grade, **52** percent of adolescents have consumed alcohol, **41** percent have smoked cigarettes and **20** percent have used marijuana.

SOURCE: Robert Wood Johnson Foundation

For example, a major longitudinal study in the *Journal of the National Cancer Institute (JNCI)* (Vol. 92, No. 24) last year confirmed researchers' doubts about social influences programs, which teach children to resist peer pressure and other influences and try to change their perceptions that many teens use drugs and smoke. In that study, researchers compared the social influences approach with control schools that conducted whatever drug and alcohol education was already occurring in the school. They found no differences between the two.

Prevention efforts shouldn't stop at high school graduation. Instead, substance abuse education should be considered across the life span. "We should be looking at all the different intervention points in a person's life. From birth to death."

Ruth Sanchez-Way
Center for Substance Abuse Prevention

"This doesn't mean that everything is settled," explains University of Washington psychologist Irwin Sarason, PhD, one of the researchers, "But what it *does* provide is a wake up call

to rethink the whole question of what we should be doing."

Research results like this do not signal failure, says psychologist Meyer Glantz, PhD, of the Division of Epidemiology Services and Prevention research at the National Institute on Drug Abuse (NIDA). "People forget that prevention is a young field," he explains.

Sure, there's a lot of room for the further development of prevention, say psychologists. But based on disappointments like those identified in the *JNCI* study and program successes, researchers have a clearer idea of the program elements that can successfully prevent drug and alcohol abuse—among them a combination of social influence, instructional and other treatments, such as teaching life skills and changing community norms about whether underage drinking and smoking are acceptable. They also know that curricula should be age-specific, span several years and include booster programs in high school.

"Now," says Glantz, "we're moving on the development of programs for specific problems or groups."

Daring to be different

Among the most visible prevention programs is the Drug Abuse Resistance Education (DARE) program. The elementary version, which is taught in roughly 75 percent of all U.S. schools, uses police officers to teach students about the physical and social effects of drug abuse. The goal was to build decision-making skills to help them resist drug abuse. But for all its good intentions, several studies found the elementary program alone had no effect on youth drug use. And while DARE offers programs for junior high and high school students, most schools do not offer these versions, despite growing evidence that elementary programs alone cannot impact use.

Building on lessons learned, DARE announced in February that it will study a new middle school and high school curriculum designed by sociologists Zili Sloboda, ScD, and Richard C. Stephens, PhD, at the University of Akron. The Robert Wood Johnson Foundation is funding the revamped program with a $13.7 million grant.

Drawing on the literature of effective substance abuse programs and from discussions with DARE police officers, Sloboda and curriculum specialists determined that DARE's initial program was undermined by too much information.

"There wasn't sufficient time allowed for the critical elements, therefore compelling the DARE officers to lecture and for the students to be more passive," explains Sloboda, former director of the Division of Epidemiology and Prevention Research at NIDA.

In response, the new program streamlines content, with emphasis on three areas: the normative beliefs of adolescents regarding substance abuse; perceptions of the social, psychological and health risks when using drugs and alcohol; and problem-solving, communication and assertiveness skills. With the content changes, DARE officers will now facilitate students' discussions rather than only instruct.

Teaching life skills and changing community norms

Researchers have also found that prevention programs are more effective when they blend social influence approaches with methods that teach self-management and social skills.

A prominent example of this approach is Life Skills Training, developed by psychologist Gilbert Botvin, PhD. Targeted toward middle school or junior high adolescents, the program focuses on enhancing teens' general social competence, such as coping with stress and conversation skills. It also teaches students how to resist pressures from peers to smoke, drink and use drugs.

Children at risk

The latest data from the National Household Survey on Drug Abuse (1996) finds that among children:

- **6** percent (4 million) had at least one parent in need of treatment for illicit drug abuse.
- **4** percent (3 million) lived with at least one parent who was dependent on illicit drugs.
- **8** percent (6 million) lived with at least one parent who was dependent on alcohol.
- **14** percent (11 million) lived with one or more parents who reported past-year use of illegal drugs, while 11 percent (8 million) lived with at least one parent who reported past-month use.
- **50** percent (38 million) lived in a household where at least one parent reported cigarette use in the past month.

SOURCE: National Institute on Drug Abuse.

"Social influences assumes that kids engage in behaviors because

they don't have the refusal skills and that they naturally want to say 'no,' but all kids don't want to say that," explains Botvin. "You have to go beyond that to a broader focus that targets a larger array of factors."

The program has been found to cut tobacco, alcohol and marijuana use roughly in half and pack-a-day smoking by 25 percent in suburban schools.

Other researchers are exploring approaches that seek to change community norms to combat drug and alcohol use. Researchers at the Pacific Institute for Research and Evaluation's Prevention Research Center, for example, have shown that a five-year, multifaceted community intervention reduced the harmful effects of high-risk alcohol consumption in three communities. Rather than targeting drinking per se, the interventions addressed environmental conditions and drinking patterns that are likely antecedents to trauma, such as responsible beverage service and sales, increasing law enforcement and media advocacy.

Five years later, the communities experienced substantial reductions in the quantity of alcohol consumed per occasion, and reports of "having too much to drink" declined by 49 percent.

"The effects on drinking seemed to be rising from general community efforts and a substantial change in community norms," notes researcher Peter Gruenwald, PhD. "The attitudes toward drinking shifted rather substantially." The study, funded by the National Institute on Alcohol Abuse and Alcoholism (NIAAA), was published in *Journal of the American Medical Association* (Vol. 284, No. 18).

Other National Institute on Alcohol Abuse and Alcoholism-funded community prevention programs, such as Project Northland, developed by Cheryl L. Perry, PhD, Carolyn Williams, PhD, and colleagues, and Communities Mobilizing for Change on Alcohol, by Alexander C. Wagenaar, PhD, and David Murray, PhD, have also found that when communities mobilize, they can make a difference.

Northland, launched in 1991, was a 22-community randomized drinking prevention trial in Minnesota. It targeted young adolescents through a social and behavioral curriculum, peer leadership, parental involvement and education, and community-wide task force activities, such as passing ordinances for responsible alcohol sales or increasing law enforcement. After three years, students in the intervention schools reported less initiation of drinking, and drinking prevalence was lower in the intervention communities than comparison sites—especially among those who were nonusers at baseline.

Communities Mobilizing for Change on Alcohol targeted 18-to 20-year-olds by reducing alcohol availability to minors and changing adults and teen's social norms about underage drinking with the help of local government, law enforcement and media. Alcohol merchants increased age-ID checking and reduced selling to minors, particularly in bars and restaurants. The results? The target group reduced its propensity to provide alcohol to other teens, was less likely to try to buy alcohol, reported more difficulty getting alcohol and was less likely to drink within the past 30 days than those in the control communities.

The future of prevention

A variety of other research directions are topping psychologists' prevention study wish-list. They include:

• **Taking an ecological approach**. Many psychologists believe it's essential to probe the idea that a person's choice to try drugs and to progress in substance use is the result of many interrelated factors.

"Until we begin to nest individuals in environmental contexts and look for how they interact to predict substance use we are probably not working with the entire set of causal factors," explains Richard Clayton, PhD, a sociology professor in the Kentucky School of Public Health.

He suggests that psychologists, anthropologists, neurobiologists, economists, communication specialists and other professionals collaborate to design, test and disseminate prevention programs that take into account the many influences in children's and adolescents' lives.

• **Layering programs**. Broad prevention programs aren't always

strong enough for children with multiple risk factors, such as children who exhibit problem behaviors and have alcoholic parents.

"We need to get some more research going on how to deal with high-risk youth because they're definitely a special population and we really do not have adequate preventions for them," says psychologist Gayle Boyd, PhD, program director for research on youth at NIAAA's Division of Clinical and Prevention Research.

Prevention saves money

For every **$1** spent on comprehensive drug abuse prevention, communities can save **$4** to **$5** in costs for drug abuse treatment and counseling.

SOURCE: National Institute on Drug Abuse.

Combining targeted interventions with broad prevention programs may be a more efficient way to reach at-risk children.

• **Including the family**. Psychologists' research has repeatedly shown that families make a big impact in children's lives, and researchers are looking into how to harness that power in prevention efforts.

"To date, we have the indication that trying to do something with families is helpful, but there hasn't been any research that shows beneficial effects on drug abuse in family-based interventions," says NIDA's Glantz.

"This doesn't mean that everything is settled. But what it *does* provide is a wake up call to rethink the whole question of what we should be doing."

Irwin Sarason
University of Washington

One promising program is Strengthening Families, developed by psychologist Karol Kumpfer, PhD,

a former Center for Substance Abuse Prevention director and now a researcher at the University of Utah. The first version of Strengthening Families targeted children of substance users, but the program has now expanded its reach to an array of families. The program has been found to decrease children's impulsivity and intent to use substances and improve their behavior at home and in sibling relationships. In parents, the program has decreased drug use, stress, depression and use of corporal punishment, and increased parental efficacy.

• **Making new partners**. While most prevention programs are based in schools, that may not be the best place to reach all teens, some researchers suggest. For example, Strengthening Families is run in churches, community centers, businesses and prisons as well as schools.

Another potential partner in prevention is the medical community. Family physicians can identify adolescents who are at-risk or using substances, and can help parents identify precursors and early signs of substance abuse.

"There are data that suggest that nurses and physicians acting as an adjunct to a school program can be useful," says sociologist Jan Howard, PhD, chief of the Prevention Research Branch at NIAAA's Division of Clinical Prevention and Research. "But what we don't really know is whether we can impact in a preventative way by somehow capturing HMOs and individual practitioners to do preventative work using their authority."

And since the health-care system has a limited involvement, Glantz also points to better interaction with the criminal justice system, which often serves as society's second line of institutional defense for drug abuse prevention and early intervention.

• **Improving dissemination, implementation and evaluation**. Several government agencies are working to make science-based programs more readily available. CSAP is developing a national registry of science-based programs that are suitable for replication, including programs like Life Skills and Project Northland. NIDA and the U.S. Department of Education also cite model programs. Many also publish free in-depth materials for schools and parents, such as NIDA's "Preventing Drug Use among Children and Adolescents" and CSAP's "Keeping Youth Drug Free."

However, choosing a good program doesn't mean it will be effective.

"We need to look at what happens when you take programs out of the context of well-controlled studies and put them in the hands of local practitioners," says Botvin. And that includes not only helping schools overcome barriers to implementation, but also how the community evaluates the effectiveness of a program.

• **Expanding prevention's definition**. No program or array of programs can stop everyone from initiating drug or alcohol use, explains Boyd. To help those who do progress, researchers should work to expand what's meant by prevention. For example, few programs are designed to help teens who are already experimenting with drugs and alcohol. Prevention programs and early treatment programs targeting escalation or progression could prevent early abusers from developing a drug abuse disorder or addiction, says Glantz.

And prevention efforts shouldn't stop at high school graduation. Instead, substance abuse education should be considered across the life span, says CSAP Director Ruth Sanchez-Way, PhD.

"We should be looking at all the different intervention points in a person's life," she explains. "From birth to death."

From *Monitor on Psychology*, June 2001, pp. 70-72. © 2001 by the American Psychological Association. Reprinted with permission.

Issues in the Treatment of Native Americans With Alcohol Problems

The author reviews the literature on the treatment of Native Americans who have alcohol abuse or dependence disorders and provides an interpretation of the research on this topic. The most common alcohol treatment modalities used with Native Americans are described and critiqued, including adapted versions of standard treatments. Several practical recommendations are made regarding revising standard treatments to make them more culturally appropriate for Native Americans.

Timothy C. Thomason

This article focuses on the most significant reports regarding treatment modalities and their efficacy for Native Americans with alcohol problems. The literature on alcoholism in Native Americans is comprehensive and includes information on the social and psychological aspects of alcoholism among this population (Beauvais, 1992; May, 1994) and information on incorporating traditional healing methods into standard treatment methods (Edwards & Edwards, 1988; Hall 1986; Parker, 1990). See May for an excellent summary of general information about alcohol abuse among Native Americans.

NATIVE AMERICANS AND ALCOHOL

According to leading researchers, "there is no universal and all encompassing explanation for drug and alcohol abuse among American Indians" (Trimble, Padilla, & Bell, 1987, p. 5). Factors that seem to be related to alcohol abuse in this population include cultural dislocation (the feeling of not fitting into either traditional Native American culture or the general U.S. culture), the lack of clear sanctions or punishments for alcohol abuse, and strong peer pressure and support for alcohol abuse (Bell, 1988; Edwards & Edwards, 1984). Many researchers in this area speculate that alcohol abuse is related to poverty, school failure, unemployment, poor health, feelings of hopelessness, and the breakdown of the Native American family (Duran & Duran, 1995; Edwards & Edwards, 1984; Trimble, 1984). Griffith (1996) pointed out that compared with the majority population, Native Americans experience four times as much alcohol-related mortality, three times as much alcohol-related illness,

and increased rates of alcohol-related accidental deaths, suicides, and homicides. Royce and Scratchley (1996) emphasized that there is no single reason for the prevalence of alcoholism among Native Americans and state that 42 different theories have been proposed. It is important to know the causes of alcohol problems in Native Americans because prevention and treatment efforts could be more focused if specific causes were known. It is clear that there is not consensus on this issue.

RESEARCH ON ALCOHOL TREATMENT FOR NATIVE AMERICANS

Many different alcohol treatment programs and modalities have been used with Native Americans. Weibel-Orlando (1989) described five common treatment models: the Medical Model, the Psychosocial Model, the Assimilative Model, the Culture-Sensitive Model, and the Syncretic Model. The Medical Model is based on the Disease Model of alcoholism, which is also a basic assumption of Alcoholics Anonymous (AA) and of U.S. society. At the other extreme is the Syncretic Model, which has primarily a Native American orientation, including the use of techniques such as the medicine wheel, talking circles, the sweat lodge, and tribal healers. The Red Road is one example of a specifically Native American treatment approach (Arbogast, 1995; Books & Berryhill, 1991). Nativized treatments are standard treatment modalities that have been adapted to be more culturally appropriate for Native Americans, usually by including discussion of traditional Native American concepts and the use of Native American healing techniques.

The Medical Model of alcoholism is often criticized as being culturally inappropriate when applied to Native Americans. Many Native Americans do not accept the Disease Model, although most would readily admit that alcohol abuse results in dysfunction and various problems in living. "This model [AA] has proven a poor fit for clients who see themselves as neither sick nor diseased" (Kinney & Copans, 1989, p. 12). Other models are likely to be more acceptable to Native Americans, such as Weibel-Orlando's (1989) Psychosocial Model, the Culture-Sensitive Model, or the Syncretic Model.

It is reasonable to think that certain findings from the general literature on the efficacy of alcohol treatment probably apply to the treatment of alcohol abuse in Native Americans. For example, there is no reason to think that there is one treatment modality that is effective with all Native Americans; different treatments probably have various degrees of effectiveness with Native Americans, treatment should be tailored to each individual Native American client, and Native American clients should be matched to optimal treatments, based on the results of controlled research.

All of this is, of course, easier said than done. Given the relatively small number of Native Americans (less than 1% of the U.S. population), treatment programs specifically for Native Americans usually only exist in areas where there are concentrated numbers of Native Americans, such as on reservations and tribal homelands and in some urban areas. Such small programs are rarely able to offer a wide choice of treatment modalities because of practical constraints. There are many alcoholism treatment programs that have special programs for Native Americans (Vanderbilt & Schacht, 1998), but it is difficult to get information on the specific treatments used or their success rates.

There are no empirical, research-based findings on the relative efficacy of various treatments for alcohol problems in Native Americans. According to Kinney and Copans (1989), "studies of Native American alcohol treatment program results have described the outcomes as ranging from mixed to disappointing" (p. 12). Given the lack of controlled studies specifically on Native Americans with alcohol problems, treatment recommendations are usually based on clinical experience. Many researchers call for studies and treatment programs that are sensitive to tribal, cultural, age, and sex differences. They also often state the importance of involving the Native American client's extended family in the treatment, instead of just the nuclear family.

Gordon (1994) stated that treatment programs have been largely unsuccessful in dealing with Native Americans, probably because standard treatments are geared to the culture of the general, middle-class U.S. population. He agrees with other researchers that the Disease Model of alcoholism is not relevant to Native Americans because the development of alcoholism in this population does not fit the pattern defined in the Disease Model, which does not consider social and cultural factors. Gordon described several specifically Native American treatment-related organizations, including the Native American Church, the Indian Shaker Church, the Poundmaker's Lodge, the Red Road, and the Alkali Lake community. Gordon recommended that standard programs incorporate traditional Native American healing practices, although he provided no data to es-

tablish that such programs are more effective than programs that do not include them.

According to Duran and Duran (1995), "alcoholism treatment outcome evaluations for Native American patients, although contradictory, indicate a very low level of success" (p. 97). They report that studies on Indian Health Service alcoholism treatment programs rarely have well-defined criteria for success and seldom assess long-term success. They also speculate that AA may not be effective for Native Americans because of its emphasis on alcoholism as a disease, its middle-class orientation, and its lack of cultural relevance.

An example of a tribe that addressed its alcoholism problem successfully with a variety of approaches is the Alkali Lake Band of the Shuswap tribe, which is reported to have reduced its alcoholism rate from 95% to 5% in 10 years (Guillory, Willie, & Duran, 1988). Part of the approach, which was used in a small, isolated community in British Columbia, Canada, was "creating a community culture which no longer tolerated alcoholism as individual behavior, while concurrently revitalizing traditional culture" (p. 30). Members of the Alkali Lake Band got rid of bootleggers, revived traditional ceremonies, joined mutual support groups, and instituted many other changes. The entire effort started with one person who decided to quit drinking. This case study is certainly interesting, but unfortunately it is impossible to determine which specific changes made the crucial difference or whether the effort succeeded only because of the synergy of all the changes made together. It is difficult to generalize from the Alkali Lake experience to other tribal communities, but the methods used are suggestive, especially the emphasis on family and peer pressure to stop drinking. This approach is probably much more applicable to small, isolated communities than large or urban communities or Native Americans who are geographically dispersed. A set of three videotapes dramatize and describe the Alkali Lake experience (Lucas, 1987).

In their treatment of Native American clients with alcoholism, Duran and Duran (1995) seem to use a unique combination of Freudian psychology and Jungian mystical techniques mixed with traditional Native American purification methods, such as smudging therapy rooms with burning sage. Clients are sometimes taught how to work with their subconscious thoughts and feelings, using dream and fantasy interpretation, making drawings, or writing poetry. Alcoholism is seen as a spiritual problem. They also endorse the use of peyote for the treatment of alcoholism, a practice of the members of the Native American Church. Unfortunately, the authors provide no data regarding the effectiveness of any of these treatment methods, and a review of the research literature does not provide support for their use.

Community ties tend to be much stronger in collective societies such as those of Native Americans than in individualistic societies such as the general U.S. society. This suggests that Native Americans may be more successful in stopping or controlling their alcohol use if the treatment approach includes a family, group, or community component. However, this may be true only for traditionally oriented Native Americans who are not highly acculturated to the general U.S. culture. Although acculturation stress, poverty, racism, and many other social factors may influence drinking behavior, and may be correlated to it, there is no evidence that they cause it. As mentioned earlier, the cause of alcoholism is multifactorial, and there are likely to be different causes of alcoholism is multifactorial, and there are likely to be different causes for different people.

Kinney and Copans (1989) stated that AA has been widely used as part of alcohol treatment programs for Native Americans, but that it is the most controversial treatment modality because it is often seen as incongruent with Native Americans' cultural orientation. "A major problem is the 'confessional' public style of AA that is counter to the private family-centered setting traditionally viewed as the site of handling problems" (p. 11). The authors recommended a comprehensive treatment program, including medical care, rehabilitation, follow-up, family counseling, self-help groups, and traditional healing and purification ceremonies for Native American clients.

Young (1992) reviewed the literature on the treatment of Native Americans with alcoholism and concluded that "very little data assessing the efficacy of the various intervention strategies…has been published" a "very little information is available about what constitutes a successful treatment strategy" (p. 13). The author speculates that effective programs would include a spiritual component and a concern for Native American culture and values. He states that although AA is a frequently used modality with Native Americans, using it is difficult because many Native American clients are reluctant to express their feelings or confess their problems in counseling sessions or public group meetings. Young suggests that most Native American clients prefer a combination of traditional healing practices and standard U.S. treatment strategies. However, the traditional Native American healing strategies would preferably be tribe-specific rather than pan–Native American. According to Young (1992), at the time his paper was published no such programs existed.

Watts and Gutierres (1997) interviewed 58 Native American clients at three residential treatment facilities in the Phoenix area to get their ideas about what kinds of treatment modalities were most helpful. Most of the clients were in a treatment program that integrated AA meetings with counseling and traditional Native American practices, such as the sweat lodge and talking circles. The participants described both the traditional practices and the AA-related practices as helpful. The researchers provided no data on the actual success rates of the treatment centers or the relative effectiveness of traditional and standard treatment modalities.

Schacht and Baldwin (1997) reported on their research regarding alcohol treatment programs for Native Americans, which included both surveys and qualitative research, including interviews with clients. Programs surveyed were chosen based on the recommendations of rehabilitation counselors who were asked to identify exemplary alcohol treatment centers for Native Americans. The 1993 survey of 31 centers revealed that 90% of the centers that responded to the survey could be categorized as using either a Culture-Sensitive or a Syncretic approach (the most Native American types of treatment). Almost all of the centers used an AA or related twelve step orientation, with adaptations to make them more culturally appropriate for Native Americans. When centers were asked what percentage of their Native American clients were successfully rehabilitated, responses ranged from 1% to 95%. These were simply the claimed success rates of the centers; the actual success rates are unknown. No single treatment approach had a success rate that was statistically superior to the other approaches.

A follow-up survey by Schacht and Baldwin (1997) in 1996 showed that half of the 14 responding treatment centers "Nativized" their program by using traditional Native American methods such as sweat lodges, meditation, and the medicine wheel as a part of treatment. Nine of the centers reported using all of the twelve steps in the AA approach; the other centers used only the first steps. Even among these supposedly exemplary centers, reported success rates over 50% were rare, and centers that used traditional Native American healing methods did not claim to have success rates significantly higher than those of other centers. One of Schacht and Baldwin's conclusions was that "Alcoholics Anonymous is a support group, and should not be used as a substitute for a treatment program" (p. 21).

McCrady and Delancy (1995) reviewed many issues involved in providing or promoting self-help groups for clients with alcohol problems. They pointed out that the current practice of many treatment professionals is to refer most or all alcoholic clients to AA, but that "it is not clear that this is optimal practice, since no evidence suggests that all problem drinkers benefit from what AA has to offer" (p. 161). They add that AA's own surveys show that the vast majority of people who begin attending AA meetings discontinue their involvement in less than a year.

Rather than review in detail the hundreds of treatment suggestions found in the literature relevant to Native American with alcohol problems, I refer the reader to a recent annotated bibliography that summarizes 135 articles, book chapters, and program descriptions (Thurber & Thomason, 1998). A review of this literature reinforces the idea that there are very few empirical studies on the effectiveness of alcohol treatment programs for Native Americans. Of course, the suggestions and speculations of treatment program staff and researchers about "what works" are better than nothing.

DISCUSSION

Very few research studies have been conducted to study the efficacy of using various alcohol treatment modalities when working with Native Americans. Overall, there is no evidence that any single treatment modality works especially well with Native Americans. However, certain suggestions and recommendations are repeated many times in the literature on Native Americans and alcohol treatment. Although these recommendations are rarely based on empirical research, they may at least, represent the consensus of many clinicians who work with Native American clients.

Before beginning treatment, it is crucial for treatment providers to assess the identity and acculturation level of Native American clients. Clients who are nominally Native American but who are highly acculturated to the mainstream culture and have little emotional investment in Native American culture can probably be treated similarly to individuals who are not Native

Americans. This means they should be treated with modalities such as brief interventions, social skills training, motivational enhancement, community reinforcement, and other approaches with well-documented efficacy for members of the general population (Miller et al., 1995).

Although there is little evidence addressing many of the relevant issues, it is possible to make some limited recommendations, based on the research reviewed above. Just as is done with any other clientele, Native Americans should be offered a variety of treatment modalities, and treatments should be specifically tailored for each client whenever possible. Native American clients who do not respond to one treatment approach within a few weeks should be offered a different treatment approach. Among the first treatments to be offered should be brief interventions, social skills training, motivational enhancement, and community reinforcement. Brief interventions are most appropriate for alcohol abusers rather than alcoholics. Behavioral, marital, or family therapy and cognitive-behavioral approaches should also be considered.

AA and many other approaches that have not been validated cannot be considered treatments of choice unless and until unbiased researchers are able to demonstrate their efficacy in controlled studies. AA support groups may help some clients maintain sobriety but are most likely to be helpful for Native Americans who are highly acculturated to the general U.S. society, because most AA groups are not culturally appropriate for Native Americans.

Native Americans who have a strong Native American identity and are greatly involved in their traditional culture may respond better to a treatment program that takes their culture into account, although there is no empirical data to suggest that this will result in improved outcomes. However, such "Nativized" programs would at least have more "face validity" for traditional clients and might encourage participation. For example, having the client participate in tribal purification and healing ceremonies might be helpful. Some treatment programs report that clients find the use of sweat lodges, talking circles, or medicine wheels, and other traditional Native American rituals and ceremonies helpful. For very traditional clients, especially those from rural and reservation areas, referral to tribal healers where the client lives might also be helpful. Clients who are interested in trying this should be encouraged to do so, with the understanding that if it is not effective, other treatment modalities should be used.

There are some difficulties with the idea of Nativizing standard alcohol treatment models. One problem is that they could only be used with groups of purely Native Americans. Even then, some Native Americans do not have traditional values and might not be interested in Nativized treatment. According to Guyette (1982), only 10% of surveyed Native Americans with substance abuse problems said they preferred an exclusively Native American treatment approach, and 76% said they preferred a combination of Native American healing practices and European American treatment practices.

In many locations, it would be difficult to have an ongoing Nativized treatment group simply because there might not be enough Native Americans in the area to attend it. For example,

Young (1992) reported that only 4 of the 21 reservations in Arizona had an alcohol treatment program. It would be even more difficult to form Native American treatment groups in nonreservation rural areas and urban areas. Another problem is that there is a severe shortage of Native American treatment providers, so that even if Nativized treatment groups specifically for Native American clients existed, it would be very difficult to find Native Americans to operate them.

Another problem with Nativizing standard alcohol treatment programs is that there is no standard way to Nativize the treatments. Traditional Native American healing strategies are not written down or systematized, and traditionally the healing methods are meant to be practiced by only trained Native American healers. Not all Native American counselors or therapists are knowledgeable about traditional healing methods or empowered by their tribes to practice them. In addition, given the diversity of Native American tribes, ideally Nativized treatment programs would be tribe-specific rather than pan-Indian although some techniques, such as the sweat lodge ceremony, are used by members of many tribes. See Jilek (1994) for a description of several "Nativized" approaches to alcohol treatment.

More attention should be paid to the importance of teaching Native Americans with alcohol abuse problems (and all people with alcohol abuse problems) skills to manage negative emotions that lead to drinking. Although poverty, racism, and acculturation stress may lead some Native Americans to drink as an escape, treatment programs would probably be better advised to focus on teaching clients the skills needed to stop drinking and resist the recurring urge to drink. Of course, treatment providers should work for social justice for Native Americans (and all other Americans), but this work is likely to be separate from their alcohol treatment programs.

Given the many gaps in the research on the efficacy of alcohol treatment for Native Americans, much work remains to be done. Given the magnitude of this problem, it is very important that researchers address this issue, preferably with controlled studies that have the most likelihood of resulting in useful information.

REFERENCES

Arbogast, D. (1995). *Wounded warriors: A time for healing*. Omaha, NE: Little Turtle.

Beauvais, F. (1992). An integrated model for prevention and treatment of drug abuse among American Indian youth. *Journal of Addictive Diseases*, 11(3), 63–79.

Bell, R. (1988). Using the concept of risk to plan drug use intervention programs. *Journal of Drug Education*, 18, 135–142.

Books, D., & Berryhill, P. (1991) *The red road* (Cassette Recording No. 5634). Center City, MN: Hazelden.

Duran, E., & Duran, B. (1995). *Native American postcolonial psychology*. Albany, NY: State University of New York Press.

Edwards, E., & Edwards, M. (1984). Group work practice with Native Americans. *Social Work with Groups*, 7(30), 7–21.

Edwards, E., & Edwards, M. (1988)). Alcoholism prevention/treatment and Native American youth. *Journal of Drug Issues*, 18, 103–114.

Gordon, J. U. (1994). *Managing multiculturalism in substance abuse services*. Thousand Oaks, CA: Sage.

Griffith, E. H. (1996). *Alcoholism in the United States: Racial and ethnic considerations,* Washington, DC: American Psychiatric Press.

Guillory, B. M., Willie, E., & Duran, E. F. (1988). Analysis of a community organizing case study: Alkali Lake. *Journal of Rural Community psychology, 9*(1), 27–36.

Guyette, S. (1982). Selected characteristics of American Indian substance abusers. *The International Journal of the Addictions, 17,* 1001–1014.

Hall, R. A. (1986). Alcohol treatment in American Indian populations. *Annuals of the New York Academy of Sciences, 472,* 168–178.

Jilek, W. G. (1994). Traditional healing in the prevention and treatment of alcohol and drug abuse. *Transcultural Psychiatric Research Review, 31,* 219–258.

Kinney, J., & Copans, S. (1989). Native American alcohol and substance use. In J. Kinney & S. Copans (Eds.), *Alcohol use and its medical consequences* (pp. 141–165). Hanover, NH: Project Cork Institute, Dartmouth Medical School. (Available from Milner-Fenwick, Inc., 2125 Greenspring Drive, Timonium, MD 21093)

Lucas, P. (Producer). (1987). The honour of all [Videotape]. (Available from Native American Public Broadcasting Consortium, 1800 North 33rd Street, P.O. Box 83111, Lincoln, NE 68501)

May, P. (1994). Epidemiology of alcohol abuse among American Indians: The mythical and real properties. *American Indian Culture and Research Journal, 18,* 121–143.

McCrady, B. S., & Delaney, S. I. (1995). Self-help groups. In R. K. Hester & W. R. Miller (Eds.), *Handbook of alcoholism treatment approaches* (2nd ed., pp. 160–175). Boston: Allyn & Bacon.

Miller, W. R., Brown, J. M., Simpson, T. L., Handmaker, N. S., Bien, T. H., Luckie, L. F., Montgomery, H. A., Hester, R. K., & Tonigan, J. S. (1995). What works? A methodological analysis of the alcohol treatment outcome literature. In R. K. Hester & W. R. Miller (Eds.), *Handbook of alcoholism treatment approaches* (2nd ed., pp.12–43). Boston: Allyn & Bacon.

Parker, L. (1990). The missing component in substance abuse prevention efforts: A Native American example. *Contemporary Drug Problems, 17*(2), 251–270.

Royce, J. E., & Scratchley, D. (1996). *Alcoholism and other drug problems.* New York: The Free Press.

Schacht, R.M., & Baldwin, J. (1997). *The vocational rehabilitation of American Indians who have alcohol or drug abuse disorders.* (Available from American Indian Rehabilitation Research and Training Center, PO Box 5630, Flagstaff, AZ 86011)

Thurber, H. J., & Thomason. T. C. (1998). *Treatment of American Indians with alcohol problems: Literature review summaries.* (Available from American Indian Rehabilitation Research and Training Center, PO Box 5630, Flagstaff, AZ 86011)

Trimble, J. (1984). Drug abuse prevention research needs among Native Americans and Alaska Natives. *White Cloud Journal, 3*(3), 22–34.

Trimble, J., Padilla, J.A., & Bell, C. (1987) *Drug abuse among ethnic minorities* (DHHS Publication No. ADM 87–1474). Washington, DC: National Institute on Drug Abuse Office of Science.

Vanderbilt, R., & Schacht, R. M. (1998). *NCADI's 1995 national directory of drug abuse and alcoholism treatment and prevention programs that have a special program for American Indians/Alaska Natives.* (Available from the American Indian Rehabilitation Research and Training Center, PO Box 5630, Flagstaff, AZ 86011)

Watts, L. K., & Gutierres, S. A. (1997). A Native American-based cultural model of substance dependency and recovery. *Human Organization, 56,* 9–18.

Weibel-Orlando, J. (1989). Treatment and prevention of Native American alcoholism. In T. D. Watts & J. Wright (Eds.), *Alcoholism in minority populations* (pp. 121–139). Springfield, IL: Thomas.

Young, R. S. (1992). *Review of treatment strategies for Native American alcoholics: The need for a cultural perspective.* (Available from Native American Research and Training Center, 1642 E. Helen St., University of Arizona, Tucson, AZ 85719)

Timothy C. Thomason is an associate professor of educational psychology at Northern Arizona University, Flagstaff. Correspondence regarding this article should be sent to Timothy C. Thomason, PO Box 5774, Northern Arizona University, Flagstaff, AZ 86011 (e-mail: timothy.thomason@nau.edu).

From *Journal of Multicultural Counseling and Development,* October 2000, pp. 243-252. © 2000 by American Counseling Association. All rights reserved. Reprinted by permission.

Substance Abuse
Treatment for
WOMEN
WITH CHILDREN

By Arthur F. Miller

There is a nationwide shortage of substance abuse treatment facilities for women with young children. According to the *Addiction Resource Guide*, there are only four accredited facilities in the entire country. As a result, the implementation of local outpatient programs, such as those listed in the sidebar, may be the only realistic option for meeting the specific needs of these clients.

A Critical Need

The physical and mental health consequences of alcohol and other drug use for women often are different from those of men. In addition, women usually arrive at substance abuse treatment later than men do. One reason for this is the notion that the majority of crimes women commit are less violent than those committed by men. Therefore, women are less likely to be incarcerated/placed in a controlled environment in which substance abuse treatment is coerced. In the case of single mothers, substance abuse treatment is given a lower priority than the adequate provision for the immediate safety and physical needs of their children. These factors require different approaches to the treatment of drug use itself and to the lifelong task of relapse prevention.

Women who are substance-dependent are more likely to have coexisting mental illnesses. According to the Department of Health and Human Services (DHHS), more than one-third of females with drug use problems have experienced major depressive episodes during the past year and 45 percent have experienced at least one of several mental health problems. These rates are more than double those found in men with similar levels of substance abuse.

Substance-abusing women are more likely to be victims of domestic violence. The relationship between domestic violence and substance abuse is well-documented and recent consensus panels of the Substance Abuse and Mental Health Services Administration (SAMHSA) conclude that "failure to address domestic violence issues interferes with treatment effectiveness and contributes to relapse." SAMHSA also stated that women in substance abuse treatment had much higher rates of partner violence than non-substance-abusing women in comparative community studies—often two, three or four times higher, depending on the specific type of violence.

Substance dependency also is related to increased involvement of women in the criminal justice system. According to U.S. Department of Justice statistics, sales of illicit drugs and drug use have contributed to the enormous 386 percent rise in the female prison population between 1980 and 1994.

According to DHHS/SAMHSA, women are more likely than men to be heads of households, and substance-abusing women often lack parenting skills. Following the same dysfunctional family patterns many of them experienced in their own childhoods, they can overreact with harsh discipline or neglect their children out of physical/mental incapacity or apathy. Substance-dependent parents often are oblivious to the effects their compulsive-addictive behavior has on their children, and essentially are unaware of what they are inadvertently teaching them about the use of alcohol and drugs, effective conflict resolution and family management/socialization skills. For those who do realize that their children are being hurt, they may be too enmeshed in their addictions to do little more than wish for things to get better.

What Would Increase the Likelihood for Program Success?

Assist women in meeting their basic needs. Addressing families' multiple needs is critical for successful participation in substance abuse treatment and related services. Often, a family's basic needs (such as food, shelter and safety) are so pressing that they must be addressed before a substance-dependent mother has the ability to focus on her addiction. Further, a crisis in any single area of family life may cause women to relapse or drop out of treatment. If a treatment program does not or cannot help clients address what they believe to be a family's most significant problem(s), they are likely to view the program as useless.

Help women build confidence as parents. Many mothers who enter substance abuse treatment are motivated to do so out of concern about their parenting skills and how their addictions are affecting their children. As detailed in the DHHS/SAMHSA 1999 report, *Blending Perspectives and Building Common Ground: A Report to Congress on Substance Abuse and Child Protection*, at least three separate studies have been conducted on parental attitudes, skills and the behaviors of drug-dependent mothers. M. Kearney, S. Murphy and M. Rosenbaum found that these women felt a strong responsibility toward their children and were quite proud of them. While studying how these mothers were unsuccessful at balancing their addictions with their parenting responsibilities, researchers found that "the basic problem crack cocaine presented to mothers was its drain on their attentiveness, their financial resources and their efforts to be appropriate role models for their children." T. Hawley, T. Halle, R. Drasin and N. Thomas found that motherhood often was the only legitimate social role valued by drug-dependent women and that most women in treatment were very concerned about how their substance abuse had affected their children—indeed, such concern was a powerful treatment motivator. R. F. Catalano, R. Ashery, E. Robertson and K. L. Kumfer have found that providing a parenting program to clients in drug treatment, in fact, also reduces relapse after treatment. Because of the importance that being a good parent holds for many of these clients, it makes sense that offering effective parenting programs during outpatient or inpatient residential treatment improves retention and outcomes for parents and children, in addition to reducing relapse. These types of programs have shown particular success if they have:

- Removed barriers to attendance by allowing the women to come into treatment with their children;
- Provided child care, children's skills training and substance abuse education for the children to simultaneously address their emotional and behavioral problems; and
- Provided parent training and support services to improve the women's confidence about being more effective mothers.

Increase interagency cooperation. Federal legislation (42 CFR Part II) has made it legal for agencies that have an existing agreement of consent from the client—a formalized agreement between specific agencies and a system of transferring and handling sensitive personal information—to share confidential substance abuse client information in the performance of their duties. For example, provided the above criteria are met, it is legal for a relapse prevention facilitator to report specifically identified information on client attendance, progress, urine screen results, etc., to the client's probation officer or child protective services caseworker. Regardless, agencies have a long way to go toward improving how they work together to serve their mutual clients. In fact, SAMHSA states that obstacles such as different client definitions, existing legal and policy constraints, what outcomes are expected on what time lines, and conflicting responses to setbacks/relapses often impact the ability and willingness of these agencies to cooperate with one another. As a result, no community has yet put in place an entirely satisfactory response network to balance the concerns of child welfare, the requirements imposed by adult supervision and the issues surrounding the treatment of mothers' substance dependency.

Select a sustainable program. A number of parenting interventions have been tested in federally funded research projects involving substance-dependent parents. The Department of Health Promotion and Education maintains performance statistics on several available outpatient programs. Some of these programs have specifically been found to significantly improve parenting skills and the ability to maintain sobriety, and many have been culturally adapted for different ethnic populations. The sidebar contains a synopsis of three of these off-the-shelf training programs.

Obtain adequate program funding. There are several important funding sources for states and local communities to expand substance abuse treatment for child welfare clients. In addition to funding from traditional sources, such as Medicaid, the new Substance Abuse Prevention and Treatment (SAPT) block grant and the Safe and Stable Families Program can promote the building of new state and local programs to foster the safety and permanency for children and sobriety for families. According to DHHS, the experience of substance abuse treatment programs, particularly those geared toward parents and their children, demonstrates that many clients can and do improve their lives and many are able to resume their parenting roles. This proves that the potential exists to develop an outpatient approach to substance abuse treatment that helps the mother deal with her addiction while simultaneously ensuring that she learns the skills and receives the support necessary to take care of her children.

It's a Matter of Supply and Demand

Although suitable residential treatment is scarce, the demand is great and the adult supervision and substance abuse treatment professional's caseload is increasingly comprised of drug-dependent single mothers. Until more residential treatment is available, proactive communities will need to promote an environment that encourages interagency cooperation and they will need to provide adequate support, both government-sponsored and from the community-at-large, for pragmatic outpatient substance abuse treatment programs.

Outpatient "Off-the-Shelf" Training Programs

Source: Department of Health Promotion and Education: www.strengtheningfamilies.org.

Nurturing Program for Families in Substance Abuse Treatment and Recovery

The Nurturing Program for Families in Substance Abuse Treatment and Recovery (NPFSATR) is a family skills training program designed to strengthen relationships in families affected by parental substance abuse when a parent is in treatment or recovery. The program is intended to be provided as a component of substance abuse treatment or through family and community service agencies. Parents need not be participating in a formal treatment program in order to participate in or benefit from the program. However, parents should have at least three months of abstinence. The program was modified during implementation at two women's residential substance abuse treatment programs. The goals of the program include: reducing risk factors contributing to substance use/abuse by both parents and children in families affected by parental substance abuse, enhancing relationships between parents and children (i.e., strengthening family protective factors) and strengthening parents' sobriety.

The NPFSATR consists of 18 sessions, each 90 minutes in length, but it can be adapted to fewer sessions of one hour each. The program is designed to be used in a variety of settings: residential or outpatient treatment programs, community and family service agencies and early intervention programs. While the parenting curriculum is for parents only, a companion volume, *Family Activities to Nurture Parents and Children*, has been developed to provide guidelines for family activities when the program is implemented with parents and children together. There are restrictions regarding ages of children or special characteristics of families or of family members.

For more information contact, Norma Finkelstein, Ph.D., Executive Director, Institute for Health and Recovery, 349 Broadway, Cambridge, MA 02139; (617) 661-3991; fax (617) 661-7277.

Strengthening Families Program

The Strengthening Families Program (SFP) is a family skills training program designed to reduce risk factors for substance use and other problem behaviors (including behavioral, emotional, academic and social problems) in high-risk children of substance abusers. The SFP builds on protective factors by improving family relationships, parenting skills and improving the youths' social and life skills. It is designed for families with children ages 6 to 10 and has been modified for African-American families, Asian/Pacific islanders in Hawaii and Utah, rural families and young teens in the Midwest and in Hispanic families.

The SFP provides 14 weekly, two-hour meetings. It includes three separate courses: parent training, children's and family-life skills training. Parents learn to increase desired

behaviors in children by using attention and reinforcements, communication, substance use prevention, problem-solving, limit-setting and maintenance. Children learn communication, how to understand feelings, social skills, problem-solving, how to resist peer pressure and are able to ask questions and participate in discussions about substance use and compliance with parental rules. Families practice therapeutic child play and conduct weekly family meetings to address issues, reinforce positive behavior and plan activities together. The SFP uses creative retention strategies such as transportation, child care and family meals.

For more information, contact Dr. Karol L. Kumpfer, University of Utah, 250 South, 1850 E., Room 215, Salt Lake City, UT 84112; (801) 581-8498; fax (801) 581-5872; e-mail: karol.kumpfer@health.utah.edu.

Strengthening Families Program: For Parents and Youths 10 through 14

The Strengthening Families Program: For Parents and Youths (SFPY) ages 10 through 14 resulted from an adaptation of SFP, originally developed at the University of Utah. The long-range goal for the curriculum is reduced substance use and behavior problems during adolescence. Intermediate objectives include improved skills in nurturing and child management by parents and improved interpersonal and personal competencies among youths. Parents of all education levels are targeted and printed materials for parents are written at an 8th-grade reading level. All parent sessions, two youth and two family sessions use videotapes portraying prosocial behaviors and are appropriate for multiethnic families.

The SFPY is comprised of seven, two-hour sessions for parents and youths who attend separate skill-building groups for the first hour and spend the second hour together in supervised family activities. Four booster sessions are designed to be used six months to one year after the end of the first seven sessions to reinforce the skills gained in the original sessions. Youth sessions focus on strengthening goal-setting, dealing with stress and strong emotions, communication skills, increasing responsible behavior and improving skills to deal with peer pressure. Youth booster sessions focus on making good friends, handling conflict and reinforcing skills learned in the first seven sessions. Parents discuss the importance of both nurturing their youths while, at the same time, setting rules, monitoring compliance and applying appropriate discipline. Topics include making house rules, encouraging good behavior, using consequences, building bridges and protecting against substance abuse. Parent booster sessions focus on handling parents' stress, communicating when partners do not agree and reinforcing earlier skills training.

Continued on following page

Outpatient "Off-the-Shelf" Training Programs

continued from previous page

For more information, contact Drs. Virginia Molgaard and Richard Spoth, Iowa State University, Institute for Social and Behavioral Research, 2625 N. Loop Drive, Suite 500, Ames, IA 50010; (515) 294-8762; fax (515) 294-3613; Web site: www.exnet.iastate.edu/Pages/families/strength.html.

Currently Available Treatment Facilities for Women and Children

Source: Addiction Resource Guide: www.addictionresourceguide.com.

Although information on the access to treatment and treatment availability was not readily available from the *Addiction Resource Guide*, based on the author's knowledge, the demand is countrywide and supply is geographically limited. Many single-parent clients are in financial extremes, and many already qualify for some type of public assistance. The replacement program for Aid to Families with Dependent Children usually are amenable to paying for shelter/facility stays that provide the essential housing and food needs of the clients while they are engaged in life skills training and substance abuse recovery/treatment.

Women's and Children's Center

This facility is a 12-step individualized treatment program for women, including women with children under 10, with chemical dependency problems. Client Capacity, Average Length of Stay and Cost: 32 beds; 50 days average; $130/day (self-pay); however, public assistance also is accepted for clients who qualify. Contact Information: 3333 36th St., Kentwood, MI 49512; (616) 242-6400.

Crossroads for Women

This facility provides intensive, individualized treatment for women and women with children with alcohol and other drug dependencies. Client Capacity, Average Length of Stay and Cost: 14 women's and eight children's beds; 41 days average; $1,498/week (self-pay); however, public assistance also is accepted for clients who qualify. Contact Information: 114 Main St., Windham, ME 04062; (207) 892-2192.

Avery House/Halfway House for Women and Children

Avery House has been designed to meet the needs of recovering women and their children in a safe, structured, supportive and sober environment. Client Capacity, Average Length of Stay and Cost: 20 women's and children's beds; 225 days average; first month free (federally funded); $150/month thereafter (self-pay). Contact Information: 14705 Avery Road, Rockville, MD 20853; (301) 762-4651.

Awakenings

This facility provides quality and affordable treatment for chemically dependent women and their family units to foster and promote independent living. Client Capacity, Average Length of Stay and Cost: Eight women's and four children's beds; 180 days average; cost varies depending on family size (self-pay); however, public assistance and Medicare coverage also are accepted for clients who qualify. Contact Information: P. O. Box 368, Belmont, OH 43718; (740) 484-4141.

References

Addiction Resource Guide. www.addictionresourceguide.com

Catalano, R. F. 1999. In Ashery, R. E. Robertson and K. L. Kumfer. 1999. *Drug abuse prevention through family interventions*. Rockville, Md.: DHSS, National Institute on Drug Abuse.

Department of Health and Human Services and Substance Abuse and Mental Health Services Administration. *Substance abuse treatment locator*: www.samhsa.gov.

DHHS/SAMHSA. 1999. *Blending perspectives and building common ground: A report to Congress on substance abuse and child protection*. (April).

Hawley, T., T. Halle, R. Drasin and N. Thomas. 1995. *Children of addicted mothers*: Effects of the "crack epidemic" on the caregiving environment and the development of preschoolers. *American Journal of Orthopsychiatry*, 65: 364–379.

Kearney, M., S. Murphy and M. Rosenbaum. 1994. Mothering on crack: A grounded theory analysis. *Social Science and Medicine*, 38: 351–361.

Knitzer, Jane. 1999. *Helping young children and parents affected by substance abuse, domestic violence and depression in the context of welfare reform*. New York: National Center for Children in Poverty.

Strengthening families program. Department of Health Promotion and Education. Salt Lake City: University of Utah. www.strengtheningfamilies.org.

Arthur "Butch" F. Miller, is a substance abuse counselor intern and community corrections volunteer for the Virginia Beach 23rd District, Virginia Department of Corrections. He also is a U. S. Naval intelligence officer who currently is assigned as an instructor at the Naval and Marine Corps Intelligence Training Center in Virginia Beach, Va.

From *Corrections Today*, February 2001, pp. 88-91. © 2001 by Corrections Today.

Glossary

Absorption The passage of chemical compounds, such as drugs or nutrients, into the bloodstream through the skin, intestinal lining, or other bodily membranes.

Abstinence The total avoidance of a specific substance, such as alcohol, tobacco, and/or drugs.

Abstinence violation effect The tendency of a person who has been abstaining and slips to go on and indulge fully, because the rule of abstinence has been broken.

Acetylcholine A cholinergic transmitter thought to be involved in the inhibition of behavior.

Acetylsalicylic acid (aspirin)A generic over-the-counter analgesic drug (painkiller).

Acid LSD.

Acupuncture A traditional Chinese health care technique for treating illness or administering anesthesia by inserting needles into specific points of the body in order to stimulate the production of natural endorphins.

Acute Referring to drugs, the short-term effect or effects of a single administration, as opposed to *chronic*, or long-term, effects of administration.

Addiction Use of a substance in a chronic, compulsive, or uncontrollable way.

Additive effects When two different drugs add up to produce a greater effect than either drug alone.

Adrenergic system The group of transmitters, including epinephrine, norepinephrine, and dopamine, that activates the sympathetic nervous system.

Affective educatio n Education that focuses on emotional content or emotional reactions, in contrast to *cognitive* content. In drug education an example would be learning how to achieve wanted "feelings" (for example, of excitement) without the use of drugs.

Aftercare In drug or alcohol treatment programs, the long-term maintenance support or follow-up that comes after a more intense period of treatment.

AIDS Acquired immunodeficiency syndrome is a disease in which the body's immune system breaks down, leading eventually to death. The disease is more prevalent in intravenous drug users who share needles because it is spread through the mixing of body fluids. HIV (human immunodeficiency virus) is the infectious agent.

Alcohol abuse A pattern of pathological alcohol use that causes impairment of social or occupational functioning. *See also* Alcohol dependence.

Alcohol dependence Considered a more serious disorder than alcohol abuse, dependence includes either tolerance or withdrawal systems.

Alcoholic personality Personality traits such as immaturity and dependency are frequently found in alcoholics in treatment. Many of these consistent traits might be the result of years of heavy drinking rather than a *cause* of alcoholism.

Alcoholics Anonymous (AA) A voluntary organization founded in 1935, consisting of individuals seeking help for a drinking problem. The AA program is based on total abstinence, achieved by following a 12-step process.

Alcoholism Any use of alcoholic beverages that causes damage to the individual or to society. *See also* Disease model.

Amotivational syndrome Apathy and loss of motivation that is believed to occur in long-term marijuana users.

Amphetamine psychosis A psychotic disorder characterized by loss of contact with reality and hallucinations brought on by the stopping or cutting back of doses of amphetamines by an amphetamine-dependent person.

Amphetamines A class of drugs, similar in some ways to the body's own adrenaline (epinephrine), that act as stimulants to the central nervous system.

Anabolic steroids Synthetic derivatives of the male hormone testosterone. Use results in increased muscle mass.

Analgesics Drugs that relieve pain selectively.

Anesthetic A medication that produces an artificial loss of sensation in order to relieve pain.

Angel dust Slang term for phencyclidine (PCP), a synthetic depressant drug.

Anorectic A drug that decreases appetite.

Antabuse Brand name of dusulfiram, a drug that interferes with the normal metabolism of alcohol by causing a person who drinks alcohol after taking disulfiram to become quite ill.

Antianxiety tranquilizers Tranquilizers, like Valium and Librium, used to relieve anxiety and tension, sometimes called minor tranquilizers.

Anticholinergics Drugs that block the transmission of impulses in the parasympathetic nerves.

Antidepressants Synthetic drugs used to relieve or prevent psychological depression by increasing the activity of the-neurotransmitter norepinephrine in the brain. *See also* Depression.

Antihistamines Drugs that relieve allergy or cold symptoms by blocking the effects of histamine production.

Antipsychotics This group of drugs is used to treat psychotic disorders such as schizophrenia. Also called neuroleptics or major tranquilizers.

Ataxia Loss of coordinated movement; for example, the staggering gait of someone who has consumed a large amount of alcohol.

Atropine An alkaloid derivative of belladonna and related plants that blocks responses to parasympathetic stimulation.

Aversion therapy A form of treatment that attempts to suppress an undesirable behavior by punishing instances of the behavior. The drinking of alcohol, for instance, might be punished by electric shocks or by a drug that causes nausea.

Axon The core of the nerve fiber that conducts impulses away from the nerve cell to the neurons and other tissue.

Barbiturates Drugs used for sedation and to relieve tension and anxiety.

Benzodiazepine A minor tranquilizer; the best-known brand name for benzodiazepine is Valium.

Benzoylecgonine A metabolite of cocaine that can be detected in urine samples.

Bioavailability The availability of molecules of a drug at the site of the drug's action in the body. One preparation of a generic drug might dissolve better or be absorbed more readily than another.

Bipolar disorder A mental illness characterized by intense mood swings of extreme elation and severe depression. Also known as manic depression.

Black tar A type of illicit heroin usually imported from Mexico.

Blackout The period of time during which a person was behaving but of which the person has no memory. Excessive alcohol consumption is the most common cause of this phenomenon. Blackouts are indications of pathological drinking.

Blood alcohol level (BAC) The concentration of alcohol in the blood, usually expressed in percent by weight.

Brain stem The region of the brain that links the cerebrum to the spinal cord.

Caffeine An alkaloid found in coffee, tea, and kola nuts that acts as a stimulant.

Cannabis *See* Marijuana.

Central nervous system (CNS) The brain and spinal cord.

China White A synthetic reproduction of fentanyl, a widely used anesthetic and depressant. China White is very similar to heroin in its duration, blockage of pain, and euphoric effect.

Chipping Using narcotics occasionally without developing an addiction.

Chlorpromazine An antianxiety tranquilizer, manufactured under the name of Thorazine, used for treating severe psychoses. Also used as an antagonist to LSD panic reactions.

Choline A transmitter, part of the cholinergic system.

Chronic Occurring over time. Chronic drug use is long-term use; chronic drug effects are persistent effects produced by long-term use.

Cirrhosis A serious, largely irreversible, and frequently deadly disease of the liver, usually the result of long-term heavy alcohol use.

Cocaethylene A potent stimulant formed when cocaine and alcohol are used together.

Cocaine A white, crystalline narcotic alkaloid derived from the coca plant and used as a surface anesthetic and a stimulant.

Codeine A narcotic alkaloid found in opium, most often used as an analgesic or cough suppressant.

Coke Slang term for cocaine.

Cold turkey Slang expression for abrupt and complete withdrawal from drugs or alcohol without medication.

Contraindications A condition that makes it inadvisable or hazardous to use a particular drug or medicine.

Controlled drinkin g The concept that individuals who have been drinking pathologically can be taught to drink in a controlled, nonpathological manner.

Controlled substances All psychoactive substances covered by laws regulating their sale and possession.

Controlled Substances Act of 1970 Federal act that classifies controlled substances into five categories and regulates their use. Schedule I drugs are those most strictly controlled; they include heroin, marijuana, LSD, and other drugs believed to have high abuse potential. Schedule II drugs are also strictly controlled but have some medicinal uses; these drugs include morphine, methadone, and amphetamines. Schedule III, IV, and V substances include drugs that have increasingly less abuse potential; over-the-counter medicines not subject to any refill regulations fall into Schedule V.

Crack A drug made by mixing cocaine, baking soda, other chemicals, and water, heating the mixture, and letting it solidify into "rocks" that are smoked.

Crank The street name for illicitly manufactured methamphetamine.

Crash At first referred to the rapid emotional descent after a binge of amphetamine use. One symptom, prolonged, led to the use of the word for sleeping in general.

Crystal meth Street term for a form of methamphetamine crystals, also called *ice.*

Crisis intervention The process of diagnosing a drug crisis situation and acting immediately to arrest the condition.

Cumulative effects Drug effects that increase with repeat administration, usually due to drug buildup in the body.

DARE Drug Abuse Resistance Education, the most popular prevention program in schools.

Date-rape drug A substance given to someone without her knowledge to cause unconsciousness in order to have nonconsensual sex. Rohypnol and GHB have become known for such use. A 1996 law provides serious penalties for using drugs in this manner.

DAWN Drug Abuse Warning Network, a federal government system for reporting drug-related medical emergencies and deaths.

DEA United States Drug Enforcement Administration.

Decriminalization The legal process by which the possession of a certain drug would become a civil penalty instead of a criminal penalty. *See also* Legalization.

Deliriants Substances, like some inhalants, that produce delirium.

Delirium State of temporary mental confusion and diminished consciousness, characterized by anxiety, hallucinations, delusions, and tremors.

Delta-9 tetrahydrocannabinol (THC) A psychoactive derivative of the cannabis plant.

Demand reduction Efforts to control drug use by reducing the demand for drugs, as opposed to efforts aimed at reducing the supply of drugs. Demand reduction efforts include education and prevention programs, as well as increased punishments for drug users.

Dependence A state in which one cannot readily give up or stop the use of a drug; there are two types of dependence—physical and psychological.

Dependence, physical The physical need of the body for a particular substance such that abstinence from the substance leads to physical withdrawal symptoms. *See also* Addiction; Withdrawal symptoms.

Dependence, psychological A psychological or emotional reliance on a particular substance; a strong and continued craving.

Depressants Also known as sedative-hypnotics, depressants produce a state of behavioral depression while also depressing chemical transmission between nerve cells in the brain. Effects of depressants include drowsiness, some behavioral excitation, and loss of inhibition. Alcohol, barbiturates, and antianxiety drugs are depressants.

Depression A mental state characterized by extreme sadness or dejection far out of proportion to the reality of the situation over which the sufferer is depressed. Depression can be a neurosis or psychosis, depending on its severity or duration.

Designer drug Any drug that is designed to match a client's desired effect and manufactured by chemists in illicit laboratories. Ecstasy and China White are examples of designer drugs.

Detoxification Removal of a poisonous substance, such as a drug or alcohol, from the body. Often the first step in a treatment program.

Deviance Behavior that is different from established social norms and that social groups take steps to change.

Disease model A theory of alcoholism, endorsed by AA, in which alcoholism is seen as a disease rather than a psychological or social problem.

DMT Dimethyltryptamine, a psychedelic drug.

DNA Deoxyribonucleic acid, the carrier of chromosomes in the cell.

Dopamine A neurotransmitter that helps control and coordinate movement.

Downers A slang term for drugs that act to depress the central nervous system.

Drug Any substance that alters the structure or function of a living organism.

Drug abuse The taking of a drug in a manner that causes bodily or mental harm.

Drug misuse Use of prescribed drugs in greater amounts than, or for purposes other than those prescribed by a physician or dentist.

Drug paraphernalia Materials, like hypodermic syringes, that are used for the preparation or administration of illicit drugs.

Glossary

DSM-IV, Diagnostic and Statistical Manual of Mental Disorders, fourth edition Published by the American Psychiatric Association, this manual has become the standard for naming and distinguishing among mental disorders.

Duster A PCP-laced joint.

DWI Driving while intoxicated.

Dysphoria Emotional state characterized by anxiety, depression, and restlessness, as opposed to euphoria.

Ecstasy A derivative of nutmeg or sassafras, causing euphoria and sometimes hallucinations; also known as XTC, Adam, or MDMA.

EMIT Enzyme multiplied immunoassay test. Most commonly used urine-screening technique for detecting the presence of various drugs.

Employee assistance program (EAP) A program offered as a workplace benefit by an employer, providing counselling and referral services to employees with personal problems, including substance abuse.

Endogenous drugs Drugs that are produced inside the body.

Endorphins Any group of hormones released by the brain that have painkilling and tranquilizing abilities.

Enkephalins Opiate-like chemicals that occur naturally in the brains of humans and other animals. The enkephalins are smaller molecules than the endorphins.

Epinephrine An adrenal hormone that acts as a transmitter and stimulates autonomic nerve action.

Ethical drugs Drugs dispensed by prescription only.

Euphoria Exaggerated sense of happiness or well-being.

Experimental drug use According to the U.S. National Commission on Marijuana and Drug Abuse, the short-term non-patterned trial of one or more drugs, either concurrently or consecutively, with variable intensity but maximum frequency of ten times per drug.

Fetal alcohol syndrome (FAS) A pattern of birth defects, cardiac abnormalities, and developmental retardation seen in babies of alcoholic mothers.

Fix Slang for a mood-altering drug dosage; an intravenous dose of an opiate.

Flashbacks Spontaneous and involuntary recurrences of psychedelic drug effects after the initial drug experience.

Food and Drug Administration (FDA) Agency of the U.S. Department of Health and Human Services that administers federal laws regarding the purity of food, the safety and effectiveness of drugs, and the safety of cosmetics.

Freebase A prepared form of cocaine that can be smoked.

Gas Slang term for nitrate oxide.

Gateway substances Alcohol, tobacco, and sometimes marijuana are substances that most users of illicit substances have tried before their first use of hard drugs.

Generic drugs Prescription drugs manufactured to match the chemical composition of brand name drugs after their copyrights have expired.

Glass See Ice.

Grain neutral spirits Ethyl alcohol distilled to a purity of 190 proof (95 percent).

Habituation Chronic or continuous use of a drug, with an attachment less severe than addiction.

Hallucination A sensory perception without external stimuli.

Hallucinogenic drugs Drugs that cause hallucinations. Also known as psychedelic drugs.

Harrison Narcotics Act Federal act passed in 1914 that controlled the sale and possession of prescription drugs, heroin, opium, and cocaine.

Hashish The dried resin of the marijuana plant; often smoked in water pipes.

Head shops Stores that sell drug-related products.

Henbane A poisonous plant containing anticholinergic chemicals and sometimes used for its hallucinogenic properties.

Herb Commonly, any one of various aromatic plants used for medical or other purposes.

Heroin An opiate derivative of morphine.

High Intoxicated by a drug or alcohol; the state of being high.

HIV Human immunodeficiency virus is the infectious agent responsible for AIDS.

Hog Slang for PCP (pencyclidine).

Hypnotic Sleep-inducing. With drugs, refers to sleeping preparations.

Ibogaine Hallucinogen that has been shown to reduce self-administration of cocaine and morphine in rats and is proposed to reduce craving in drug addicts.

Ibuprofen An over-the-counter pain reliever that is an alternative to aspirin and acetaminophen; the active ingredient in Motrin, Advil, and Nuprin.

Ice A smokable form of methamphetamine.

Illicit drug An illegal drug; any drug or substance whose distribution to the general public is prohibited by the federal Controlled Substances Act of 1970.

Illy Marijuana and mint leaves soaked in a deadly combination of embalming fluid and PCP.

Inhalants Substances that emit fumes or gases that are inhaled and have the effect of psychoactive drugs. Also known as deliriants.

Insomnia Inability to sleep. The most common complaint is difficulty falling asleep. Often treated with a hypnotic drug.

Interferon A group of protein factors produced by certain cells in response to the presence of viruses.

Interleukin 2 A group of protein factors that acts as a messenger between white blood cells (leukocytes) involved in immune responses.

Intoxication Medically, the state of being poisoned. Usually refers to the state of being drunk, falling between drunkenness and a mild high.

Intravenous (IV) drug user s Drug users who use hypodermic needles as a means of administering drugs; among the drugs normally administered in this manner is heroin, which may be injected either directly into a vein ("mainlining") or just under the surface of the skin ("skin popping").

Joint A marijuana cigarette.

Junkie A heroin addict.

Ketamine A close relative of PCP, it is a legally prescribed drug for use as an anesthetic.

Legalization The movement to have the sale or possession of certain illicit drugs made legal.

Limbic system A set of structures in the brain that influences motivation and emotional behavior.

LSD Lysergic acid diethlamide-25, a hallucinogen.

Ludes Tablets of methaqualone (Quaalude).

Mainline To inject a drug intravenously.

Marijuana A preparation of the leaves and flowering tops of the cannabis plant, the smoke of which is inhaled for its euphoric effects. Also spelled: marihuana.

MDMA See Ecstasy.

Medical model A theory of drug abuse or addiction in which the addiction is seen as a medical, rather than a social, problem.

Mescaline A hallucinogenic alkaloid drug, either derived from the peyote plant or made synthetically.

Methadone A synthetic opiate sometimes used to treat heroin or morphine addiction.

Methamphetamines Stimulant drugs derived from and more potent than amphetamines. Also known as speed.

Methaqualone A nonbarbiturate sedative/hypnotic drug, used to bring on feelings of muscular relaxation, contentment, and passivity. Also known as quaaludes.

Methylphenidate Also known as Ritalin, its most popular brand name, methylphenidate is a stimulant used in treating hyperkinetic children (children who are hyperactive but have no academic difficulties).

Morphine An organic compound extracted from opium; a light anesthetic or sedative.

Motivational interviewing A technique for encouraging alcoholics or addicts to seek treatment by first assessing their degree of dependence and then discussing the assessment results. Direct confrontation is avoided.

Multimodality programs Programs for the treatment of drug abuse or alcoholism involving several simultaneous treatment methods.

Narcotic A drug that has both a sedative and a pain-relieving effect. Opiate drugs are narcotics.

Narcotics Anonymous (NA) An organization modeled after Alcoholics Anonymous to assist recovering drug dependents.

Neuroleptic Any major, or antipsychotic, tranquilizer.

Neuron The basic element responsible for the reception, transmission, and processing of sensory, motor, and other information of physiological or psychological importance to the individual.

Neurotransmitters The chemicals that transmit messages from one neuron to another.

Nicotine The main active ingredient of tobacco, extremely toxic and causing irritation of lung tissue, constriction of blood vessels, increased blood pressure and heart rate, and, in general, central nervous system stimulation.

Norepinephrine Hormone found in the sympathetic nerve endings that acts as an adrenergic transmitter and is a vasoconstrictor.

NORML The National Organization for the Reform of Marijuana Laws.

Opiate antagonist Any of several drugs that are capable of blocking the effects of drugs. Used in emergency medicine to treat overdose, and in some addiction treatment programs to block the effect of any illicit opiate that might be taken. Nalorphine and naltrexone are examples.

Opiate narcotics A major subclass of drugs that act as pain relievers as well as central nervous system depressants; includes opium, morphine, codeine, and methadone.

Opiates The class of drugs that include opium, codeine, morphine, heroin, methadone, and other drugs derived from or chemically similar to opium; opiates are primarily used for pain relief.

Opium A bitter brown narcotic drug that comes from the dried juice of the opium poppy, and from which such narcotics as heroin and morphine are derived.

Opoids The group of synthetic drugs, including Demerol and Darvon, that resemble the opiates in action and effect.

Overmedication The prescription and use of more medication than necessary to treat a specific illness or condition.

Over-the-counter drugs Drugs legally sold without a prescription.

Papaver somniferum The opium poppy.

Paraphernalia The equipment used in an activity; specifically, drug paraphernalia might include such items as syringes, pipes, scales, or mirrors.

Parasympathetic nervous system The part of the autonomic nervous system that inhibits or opposes the actions of the sympathetic nerves.

Parasympathomimetics Drugs that produce effects similar to those of the parasympathetic nervous system.

Parkinson's disease A progressive disease of the nervous system characterized by muscular tremor, slowing of movement, partial facial paralysis, and general weakness.

Passive smoking Inhalation of tobacco smoke from the air on nonsmokers.

Peyote A drug derived from either the peyote or the mescal cactus, possessing hallucinogenic properties.

Phantastica Hallucinogens that reproduce altered perceptions but do not generally impair communication with the real world.

Phencyclidine (PCP) A synthetic depressant drug used as a veterinary anesthetic and illegally as a hallucinogen. Popularly called "angel dust."

Phenylpropanolamine (PPA) A medication used to prevent or relieve nasal and upper respiratory congestion. PPA is also used as an appetite suppressant.

Phobias Persistent, intense fears of specific persons, objects, or situations, accompanied by a wish to flee or avoid the fear-provoking stimulus.

Physical dependence A form of dependence in which the body's physical need for a particular substance is such that stopping use leads to physical withdrawal symptoms.

Placebo An inactive substance used as a control in an experiment.

Polyabuse Abuse of various drugs simultaneously.

Pop To swallow a drug in pill form.

Poppers Slang for amyl nitrate.

Pot Slang term for marijuana.

Potency Term used to compare the relative strength of two or more drugs used to produce a given effect.

Potentiate To augment a depressant's effect by taking a combination of two or more depressants.

Prescription drugs Drugs dispensed only by a physician's prescription.

Primary prevention Efforts designed to prevent a person from starting to use drugs.

Proof A measure of a beverage's alcohol content; twice the alcohol percentage.

Proprietary drugs Medicines that are marketed directly to the public. Also called OTC, patent, or nonprescription medicines.

Psilocybin A naturally occurring psychedelic agent derived from the *Psilocybe Mexicana* mushroom.

Psychedelic drug A drug that causes hallucinations; a hallucinogen.

Psychoactive Affecting the mind or behavior.

Psychological dependence A form of dependence in which the user's attachment to the emotional or psychological effects of a drug is such that he or she finds it difficult or impossible to stop use voluntarily; may or may not be accompanied by physical dependence.

Psychopharmacology The study of the effects of drugs on mood, sensation, or consciousness, or other psychological or behavioral functions.

Psychosis Severe mental disorder, characterized by withdrawal from reality and deterioration of normal intellectual and social functioning.

Psychosomatic Describing a variety of physical reactions that are assumed to be closely related to psychological phenomena.

Psychotherapeutic drugs Drugs that are used as medicines to alleviate psychological disorders.

Psychotomimetics Drugs that produce psychosis-like effects.

Recidivism Return to former behavior.

Recombinant DNA DNA prepared in the laboratory by the transfer or exchange of individual genes from one organism to another.

Recreational drug use Drug use that takes place in social settings among friends who want to share a pleasant experience; characterized by less frequency and intensity than addictive drug use. Also called social-recreational drug use.

Rehabilitation Restoration of a person's ability to function normally.

Reinforcement A stimulus that increases the probability that a desired response will occur.

Glossary

Reticular activating system A cluster of cell groups located in the upper part of the brain stem that controls the flow of information from the sensory organs to the cerebral cortex.

Reyes syndrome An often fatal childhood disorder whose cause is unknown, but has been associated with the use of aspirin as a treatment for chicken pox.

Risk factors Attitudes, behaviors, or situations that correlate with a later deviance-prone lifestyle that includes drugs or alcohol abuse.

Rock Another name for crack, the smokable form of cocaine.

Rush Slang term for an immediate feeling of physical well-being and euphoria after the administration of a drug.

Schedules Categories of drugs as defined in the Controlled Substance Act of 1970.

Scopolamine Poisonous alkaloid found in the roots of various plants, used as a truth serum or with morphine as a sedative.

Score To obtain a supply of drugs.

Secondary prevention Early treatment of drug abuse to prevent it from becoming more severe.

Sedative A drug that depresses the central nervous system. Also known as sedative-hypnotics, sedatives include barbiturates, antianxiety drugs, and alcohol.

Sedative/hypnotics A more technical term for depressants, drugs that are used for general anesthesia, induction of sleep, relief from anxiety, and recreational disinhibition (alcohol).

Serotonin A neurotransmitter that is produced in the brain stem and is involved in sleep and sensory experiences.

Set The combination of physical, mental, and emotional characteristics of an individual at the time a drug is administered.

Setting The external environment of an individual at the time a drug is administered.

Side effects Secondary effects, usually undesirable, of a drug or therapy.

Sinsemilla High-grade, flowering, seedless tops of marijuana.

Snort To inhale a powdered drug.

Snuff A preparation of pulverized tobacco that is inhaled into the nostrils.

Sobriety The quality of being free from alcohol intoxication.

Social-recreational drug us e*See* Recreational drug use.

Socioeconomic Both social and economic.

Somatic nervous system That part of the nervous system that deals with the senses and voluntary muscles.

Speed Slang term for methamphetamine, a central nervous system stimulant.

Stages of change Theoretical description of the cognitive stages through which an addict would go on moving from active use to treatment and abstinence: precontemplation, contemplation, preparation, action, and maintenance.

Stereospecificity The matching of both electrical and chemical characteristics of the transmitter and receptor site so that binding can take place.

Stimulants Chemical compounds that elevate mood, induce euphoria, increase alertness, reduce fatigue, and, in high doses, produce irritability, anxiety, and a pattern of psychotic behavior. Stimulants include amphetamines, nicotine, caffeine, and cocaine.

STP Early slang term for phencyclidine.

Street value The theoretical value of an amount of drugs if sold in small quantities on the street.

Subcutaneous Beneath the skin.

Substance abuse Refers to cigarette smoking, alcohol abuse, or drug abuse.

Super K Slang term for ketamine.

Sympathetic nervous system The part of the nervous system that carries neural signals that stimulate the body and prepare it for action.

Sympathomimetic Any drug that produces effects like those resulting from stimulation of the sympathetic nervous system.

Synapse The space, or gap, between two neurons.

Synesthesia The blending of the senses so that two or more are perceived in combination in reaction to one stimulus.

Tars The dark, oily, viscid substances created by burning tobacco, known to contain carcinogenic agents.

Temperance The practice of moderation, especially with regard to alcohol consumption. The Temperance Movement was a popular movement in the nineteenth and twentieth centuries to restrict or prohibit the use of alcoholic beverages.

Tertiary prevention Treatment to prevent the permanent disability or death of a drug abuser.

THC Tetrahydrocannabinol, a psychoactive derivative of the cannabis plant.

Therapeutic community Setting in which persons with similar problems meet and provide mutual support to help overcome those problems.

Titration The ability to determine desired drug dosage.

Toke An inhalation from a pipe or cigarette.

Tolerance The capacity to absorb a drug continuously or in large doses with no adverse effect.

Trance Dazed or hypnotic state.

Tranquilizers Drugs that depress the central nervous system, thus relieving anxiety and tension and sometimes relaxing the muscles, divided into the major tranquilizers, or antipsychotics, and minor tranquilizers, or antianxiety tranquilizers.

Treatment Drug treatment programs can be drug-free or maintenance, residential or ambulatory, medical or nonmedical, voluntary or involuntary, or some combination of these.

Uncontrolled substance Any chemical or drug whose distribution to the general public is unrestricted by governmental regulations (controls) other than those rules that apply to any similar consumer item.

Uppers Slang term for amphetamines, and, sometimes, cocaine.

Valium A brand name for benzodiazepine, a minor tranquilizer.

Wernicke-Korsakoff syndrome Chronic mental impairments produced by heavy alcohol use over a long period of time.

Withdrawal symptoms The (usually unpleasant) set of physical symptoms experienced by the user as a result of stopping use of a drug upon which he or she has become dependent; these may include anxiety, insomnia, perspiration, hot flashes, nausea, dehydration, tremors, weakness, dizziness,convulsions, or psychotic behavior.

SOURCE

Drugs, Society, and Human Behavior, Oakley Ray and Charles Ksir, 1999, WCB/McGraw-Hill, New York, NY.

Drugs, Society, and Behavior (Wellness), 1992. Dushkin/McGraw-Hill, Guilford, CT 06437.

Index

Index

We Want Your Advice

ANNUAL EDITIONS revisions depend on two major opinion sources: one is our Advisory Board, listed in the front of this volume, which works with us in scanning the thousands of articles published in the public press each year; the other is you—the person actually using the book. Please help us and the users of the next edition by completing the prepaid article rating form on this page and returning it to us. Thank you for your help!

ANNUAL EDITIONS: Drugs, Society, and Behavior 02/03

ARTICLE RATING FORM

Here is an opportunity for you to have direct input into the next revision of this volume.
We would like you to rate each of the articles listed below, using the following scale:

1. **Excellent: should definitely be retained**
2. **Above average: should probably be retained**
3. **Below average: should probably be deleted**
4. **Poor: should definitely be deleted**

Your ratings will play a vital part in the next revision.
Please mail this prepaid form to us as soon as possible.
Thanks for your help!

RATING	ARTICLE	RATING	ARTICLE
	1. The Perils of Pills		34. The Wrong Race, Committing Crime, Doing Drugs, and Maladjusted for Motherhood: The Nation's Fury Over "Crack Babies"
	2. E-commerce		
	3. American Banks and the War on Drugs		35. Drug Courts: Making Prison Sentences a Thing of the Past?
	4. America's War on Drugs		
	5. Stumbling in the Dark		36. Creating Visions and Achieving Goals: The Women in Community Service's Lifeskills Program
	6. Drugs That Flip Your Switches: Top to Toe		
	7. Learning About Addiction From the Genome		37. Tougher Sentencing, Economic Hardships and Rising Violence
	8. Addiction and the Brain—Part II		
	9. Cognition Is Central to Drug Addiction		38. Addressing the Threats of MDMA (Ecstasy): Implications for School Health Professionals, Parents, and Community Members
	10. How It All Starts Inside Your Brain		
	11. How Addictive Is Cigarette Smoking?		
	12. Alcohol, the Brain, and Behavior: Mechanisms of Addiction		39. War and Fear in Putumayo
	13. Medical Consequences of Alcohol Abuse		40. Science and Drug Abuse Control Policy
	14. The Andean Coca Wars: A Crop That Refuses to Die		41. The Case for Legalisation
	15. Drinking to Get Drunk		42. What's Your Anti-Drug?
	16. The Drug That Pretends It Isn't		43. The War Against the War On Drugs
	17. Speed Demons		44. Drug Crazy Feds
	18. Cocaine Colonialism		45. A Setback for Medipot
	19. Drug War Aids Heroin Trade		46. Talk to Kids About Drugs? Parents Just Don't Do It
	20. The Changing Face of Marijuana Research		47. Deep Cravings
	21. Welcome to Meth Country		48. Drug Education: The Triumph of Bad Science
	22. Playing With Pain Killers		49. Hollywood High
	23. Are You Man Enough?		50. Principles of Drug Addiction Treatment: A Research-Based Guide
	24. Recreational Pharmaceuticals		
	25. Scouting a Dry Campus		51. Prevention: Still a Young Field
	26. Convenience-Store High: How Ordinary Cough Medicine Is Being Abused for Its Mind-Altering Effects		52. Issues in the Treatment of Native Americans With Alcohol Problems
	27. Natural Hazards		53. Substance Abuse Treatment for Women With Children
	28. Recognizing the Dangers of GHB		
	29. Heroin Trade Helped Fuel Bin Laden's Rise		
	30. Organized Crime in Narcotics Trafficking		
	31. Drugs, Crime, Prison, and Treatment		
	32. Women in Jail: Is Substance Abuse Treatment Enough?		
	33. Cracking Down on Ecstasy		

(Continued on next page)

BUSINESS REPLY MAIL
FIRST-CLASS MAIL PERMIT NO. 84 GUILFORD CT

POSTAGE WILL BE PAID BY ADDRESSEE

McGraw-Hill/Dushkin
530 Old Whitfield Street
Guilford, Ct 06437-9989

ABOUT YOU

Name   Date

_____

Are you a teacher? ❑   A student? ❑
Your school's name

_____

Department

_____

Address   City   State   Zip

_____

School telephone #

_____

YOUR COMMENTS ARE IMPORTANT TO US!

Please fill in the following information:
For which course did you use this book?

_____

Did you use a text with this ANNUAL EDITION? ❑ yes ❑ no
What was the title of the text?

_____

What are your general reactions to the *Annual Editions* concept?

_____

Have you read any pertinent articles recently that you think should be included in the next edition? Explain.

_____

Are there any articles that you feel should be replaced in the next edition? Why?

_____

Are there any World Wide Web sites that you feel should be included in the next edition? Please annotate.

_____

May we contact you for editorial input? ❑ yes ❑ no
May we quote your comments? ❑ yes ❑ no